MOON

P9-CKH-492

COASTAL OREGON

JUDY JEWELL & W. C. McRAE

Contents

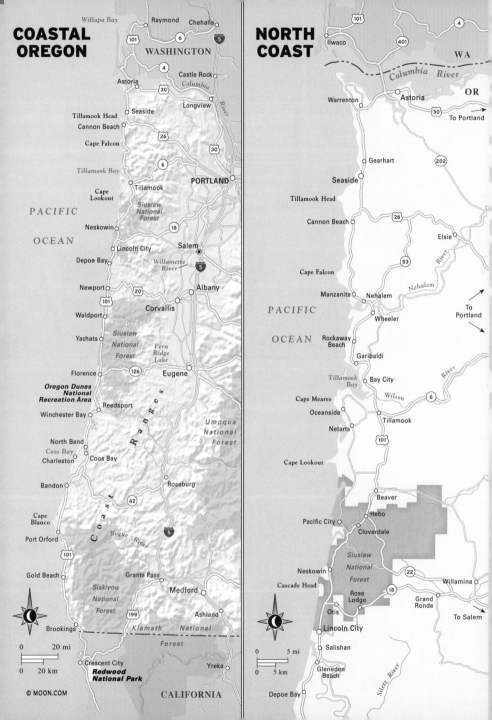

COASTAL OREGON

NORTH COAST

Coastal Oregon map labels

Willapa Bay
Raymond
Chehalis
101
6
5
WASHINGTON
4
Castle Rock
Astoria
30
Columbia
Longview
Tillamook Head
Seaside
Cannon Beach
26
Cape Falcon
30
6
Tillamook Bay
PORTLAND
Cape Lookout
Tillamook
Siuslaw National Forest
PACIFIC
Neskowin
18
OCEAN
Lincoln City
Salem
Depoe Bay
5
Willamette River
Newport
20
Albany
101
Corvallis
Waldport
Yachats
Siuslaw National Forest
Fern Ridge Lake
Florence
126
Eugene
Oregon Dunes National Recreation Area
Reedsport
Winchester Bay
Umpqua National Forest
North Bend
Coos Bay
Charleston
Coos Bay
Bandon
Roseburg
42
Coast Ranges
Cape Blanco
Rogue River
5
Port Orford
101
Gold Beach
Grants Pass
Siskiyou National Forest
Medford
199
Ashland
Klamath National Forest
Brookings
0   20 mi
0   20 km
Crescent City
Redwood National Park
Yreka
CALIFORNIA
© MOON.COM

North Coast map labels

101
4
Ilwaco
401
WA
Columbia River
OR
Warrenton
Astoria
30
To Portland
Gearhart
202
Seaside
Tillamook Head
Cannon Beach
26
Elsie
53
River
Cape Falcon
Nehalem
Manzanita
Nehalem
To Portland
Wheeler
PACIFIC
Rockaway Beach
OCEAN
Garibaldi
River
Tillamook Bay
Bay City
6
Wilson
Cape Meares
Oceanside
Tillamook
Netarts
101
Cape Lookout
Beaver
Hebo
Pacific City
Cloverdale
Siuslaw National Forest
Neskowin
22
Cascade Head
Willamina
Rose Lodge
18
Grand Ronde
Otis
To Salem
Lincoln City
0   5 mi
0   5 km
Salishan
Siletz River
Gleneden Beach
Depoe Bay

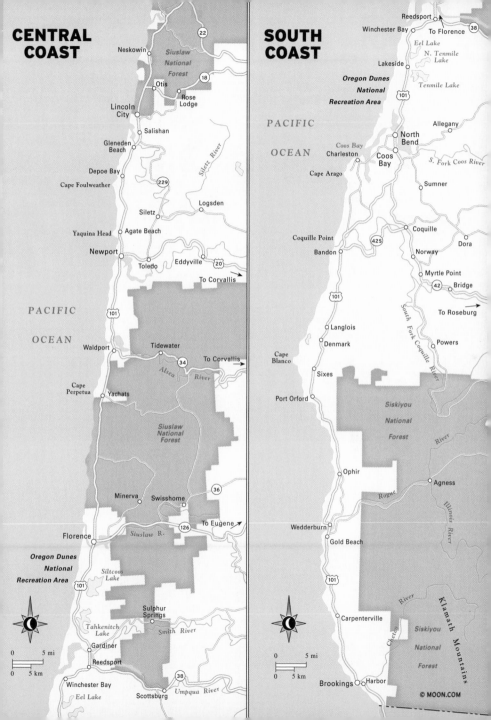

DISCOVER

Coastal Oregon

In few other places on earth is the meeting of land and sea as dramatic and beautiful as along Oregon's 360 miles of Pacific coastline, from the mouth of the Columbia River to the redwood forests at the California border. Here, at the far western skirt of the continent, nature has found an expansive stage on which to act out the full range of its varied and ceaseless dramas, from the microcosm of a tide pool to the ferocious storms that make first landfall here. Rocky headlands rise high above the ocean, dropping away to the pounding waves in cliffs hundreds of feet high. Lone fingers of rock poke through sandy beaches and march out far into the surging waves. Seals, sea lions, puffins, and innumerable shorebirds make their home in this marine wilderness.

Here you can find intense solitude, in the company of only the calling seabirds, and experience firsthand why residents refer to this coast as "The Edge"— yet the comforts of civilization and human company are always close by in an inviting string of towns and villages, each with its own character and charm.

Don't neglect the opportunity to get outdoors and experience the full range of recreation available here. Cycling the Oregon Coast Bike Route is a rite of passage for many bicyclists from around the world. The Oregon Coast Trail

Clockwise from top left: yurt at coastal Oregon campground; seafood restaurant in Newport; horseback riding on the beach; view off the southern Oregon coast; old cannery in Astoria; Cannon Beach.

provides hikers many opportunities to explore the coastline. The bays and estuaries are tempting destinations for kayakers, as they provide a watery backdrop
for excellent marine bird and wildlife viewing. Diminished wild salmon runs have
limited some coastal sportfishing expeditions, but the catch is still good for halibut, tuna, and bottom fish. And when fishing boats from Newport, Depoe Bay,
Garibaldi, and Astoria aren't seeking the catch of the day, many offer whale-
watching trips. Surfing the chill waters of the north Pacific demands a particular brand of hardiness, but many find that, with the right wetsuit, they're able to
catch some waves.

Considering the scenic splendor of the Oregon coast, it may seem odd that
it remains largely unblemished by upscale tourism infrastructure. In part, this is
due to a farsighted state government, which in the 1910s set aside as public land
the entire length of Oregon's Pacific coastline. The Oregon coast belongs to the
people. It's a place where human visitors can encounter the creatures of the sea
and forest, and observe the mighty forces of nature.

Clockwise from top left: tidal fountain at Cape Perpetua; Astoria Brewing Company; intertidal rock
in Tillamook Bay; Garibaldi seafood spot.

10 TOP
EXPERIENCES

1 **Embark on an Epic Road Trip:** Oregon's 360 miles of coastline make for the scenic drive of a lifetime (page 20).

ᐯ
ᐯ
ᐯ

2 **Climb to the Top of a Lighthouse:** From the lighthouses at **Heceta Head** (page 137) and **Cape Blanco** (page 177), the views go on forever.

3 **Explore Tide Pools at Haystack Rock:** At low tide, **Cannon Beach**'s iconic sea stack is a fine place to see starfish, anemones, and other marinelife (page 68).

4 **Take a Hike:** For epic views at continent's edge, head to the trails at spots like **Cape Lookout** (page 92) and **Cape Perpetua** (page 131).

13

5 **Go Whale-Watching at Depoe Bay:** At the state's whale-watching capital, you can spot these magnificent creatures from land or sea (pages 112 and 114).

6 **Walk through an Underwater Tunnel:** It's the highlight of the **Oregon Coast Aquarium,** one of the state's most popular attractions (page 116).

>>>

7 **Wander the Oregon Dunes:** Hiking on the ever-shifting piles of sand is exhausting but exhilarating (page 148).

8 **Snap a Pic along the "Fabulous 50 Miles":** The Samuel H. Boardman State Scenic Corridor is considered one of the most dramatic meetings of rock and tide in the world (page 191).

9 **Feast on Fresh Fish:** Hit some of the best seafood restaurants along the coast—or catch your own (page 26)!

10 **Jet up the Rogue River:** This trip from Gold Beach promises spectacular views of landscape and wildlife (page 183).

Planning Your Trip

Where to Go

Although part of a seamless whole, sharing a common shoreline and linked by an unbroken scenic highway, each part of the coast possesses a distinct regional flavor.

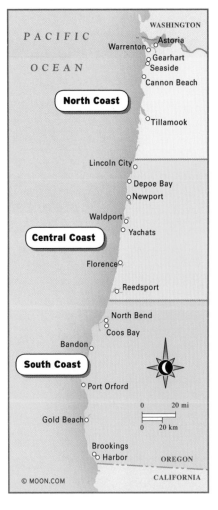

North Coast

In the north—journey's end for Lewis and Clark—steep headlands break up wide sandy beaches. The northern Oregon coast, just 1.5 hours from Portland, is the most developed and heavily populated part of the coast. Historic **Astoria,** fun-loving **Seaside,** and artsy **Cannon Beach** are all within a short drive of one another, but are remarkably different in character. But don't think it's just one town after another—huge areas of the coast are set aside as **state parks,** and there are ample opportunities to hike, camp, and explore tide pools.

Central Coast

The central coast is anchored at its northern end by sprawling **Lincoln City** and its family-friendly wide beaches, and is centered around **Newport,** the largest city in the area, with charming older neighborhoods, good restaurants, an active fishing port, and the **Oregon Coast Aquarium.** Farther south, Florence and Reedsport border the astounding **Oregon Dunes,** an otherworldly sand-scape with massive sand dunes, lakes, and broad lazy estuaries.

South Coast

The south coast feels far from everything: a landscape of ocean-fronting mountains cloaked by dense evergreen forest, wild rivers, and black-sand beaches punctuated with dramatic rock formations. Postindustrial Coos Bay needn't delay you, but just to the west are wild and beautiful natural areas, including **Cape Arago** and the fascinating estuarine area at **South Slough.** Bandon is small, cozy, and full of tourists, many here for the world-class golf courses at **Bandon Dunes.** The southernmost part of Oregon's coastline may well be its most scenic, especially the stretch between **Port Orford** and **Brookings.**

If You Have . . .

- **A WEEKEND:** Visit Astoria, Seaside, and Cannon Beach on the north coast.

- **ONE WEEK:** Explore the central coast and add Lincoln City, Newport, and an excursion to the Oregon Dunes.

- **TWO WEEKS:** Explore the south coast and add Bandon, Port Orford, and Gold Beach. If you have any extra time, the coastal estuaries south of Coos Bay are worth the trip.

When to Go

Unless you're a dyed-in-the-wool rain-loving Pacific Northwesterner, you'll most likely want to visit the Oregon coast during the **summer and early fall** (July-September), when there's a far better chance of sunshine. Even then, coastal fogs can put a chill on things, so it's nearly essential to bring a fleece jacket, as well as a windbreaker for the gale-force gusts that locals call "the breeze." It's also best to bring rain gear—we somewhat superstitiously consider it to be insurance against a summertime storm. But it's not always cold here: Don't be surprised if a mid- to late-summer trip sees you wearing little more than shorts, a T-shirt, flip-flops, and sunscreen.

From **late fall through spring,** storm watchers come to the coast to feel the blustery bite of rain pelting their faces as they walk the beaches. It can be really thrilling to stay in a beachfront motel or cottage (paying a fraction of the summertime rates) and watch the storm clouds roll in. The big secret is that there can be absolutely beautiful weather in between storms when the sun breaks through, and temperatures are generally much milder than in other parts of the state.

Another reason to visit in **December** or **late March** (roughly Christmastime or spring break) is to see whales migrating between their winter homes off Baja California and their summertime grounds near Alaska. Look for "Whale Watching Spoken Here" signs to find good vantage points.

beach trail

Coastal Road Trip

For many travelers, following the coastal highway U.S. 101 along the rugged Oregon coast is the trip of a lifetime. Although the coast route counts just 360 miles, don't try to rush this trip or squeeze it into anything less than three days. Twisting roads, slow-moving traffic, and jaw-dropping vistas are sure to slow you down, so start out by planning flexibility into your schedule.

If you're not lucky enough to have time for a trip spanning the entire coast and need to sample just a section, it's easy to use the I-5 freeway corridor (roughly 60-80 miles inland) as a quick north or south arterial, cutting over to the coast near your destination.

So feel free to tinker with this strict north-south itinerary. If you are flying into and out of Portland, it may make sense to leapfrog your way down the coast, catching the intervening towns on your way back north.

Day 1

From Portland, drive 95 miles northwest to **Astoria,** a city full of history and spunky do-it-yourself charm. Visit the **Columbia River Maritime Museum** to learn about the area's maritime past (and present), and check out the city's vibrant art and dining scene. Walk the hilly streets behind downtown to view resplendent Victorian homes. Spend the night at the Cannery Pier Hotel beneath the more than four-mile-long **Astoria-Megler Bridge,** which spans the mighty Columbia.

Day 2

Drive south about 8 miles to **Fort Clatsop National Memorial,** which features a replica of the winter home Lewis and Clark used in 1805-1806. If the day is fair, drive another 7 miles to **Fort Stevens State Park** to stroll along the shore and watch the Columbia River roll into the Pacific, or simply continue 22 miles to **Cannon**

hiking path at Cape Perpetua

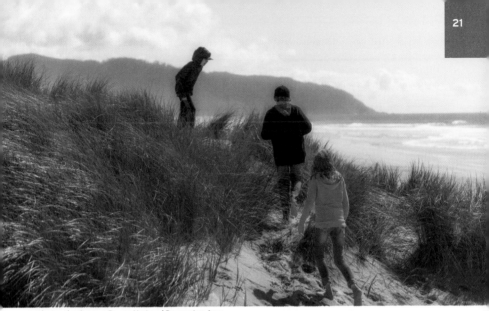

exploring the Oregon Dunes National Recreation Area

Beach, with its dramatic shoreline dominated by sea stacks. Stroll through the town's attractive and mazelike downtown shopping district, and spend the night at the Stephanie Inn.

Day 3

From Cannon Beach, drive about 10 miles south to drop through the lush temperate rainforest in **Oswald West State Park,** stopping for a hike to the beach or a stunning view of the ocean from 700-foot-high cliffs on the flanks of Neahkahnie Mountain. Stop for lunch in the commercial fishing village of **Garibaldi,** 21 miles to the south, with some of the freshest and tastiest fish-and-chips you're likely to eat. In Tillamook (10 miles), it's almost mandatory for visitors to stop at the **Tillamook Creamery,** both for the cheese (now made off-site) and the tasty ice cream cones. Continue another 44 miles south to **Lincoln City** via U.S. 101, staying at the Starfish Manor Hotel.

Day 4

From Lincoln City continue 12 miles south to **Depoe Bay,** worth a stop to admire the pocket harbor and scan for spouting whales, then take the Otter Crest scenic loop, cresting at the Cape Foulweather vista. It's only another 12 miles to **Newport,** so you'll get there before lunch—which is lucky, because you'll want to have two meals' worth of eating to explore the good food here. Spend the afternoon at the **Oregon Coast Aquarium** and the night at the Inn at Nye Beach.

Day 5

This is another short day of driving, because you'll want to save time to hike. Proceed 24 miles south to **Yachats,** one of the coast's most charming towns and gateway to **Cape Perpetua,** a wonderful natural area where mountains meet the sea and acres of tide pools rise above the surf. Check in at the comfortable Overleaf Lodge, and reward yourself for hiking along Cape Perpetua with dinner at one of Yachats's excellent restaurants.

Day 6

Florence is set alongside the Siuslaw River 25 miles south of Yachats, and its riverside Old Town will briefly steal your attention away from the ocean. It's a good base for exploring the **Oregon Dunes,** which start just south of town and rise up to 500 feet high. Hike through this striking habitat, or go for the thrills of sandboarding or a dune buggy ride. Spend the night in Florence.

Day 7

Although **Coos Bay** doesn't beckon the average traveler, this city 50 miles south of Florence is the gateway to some astoundingly beautiful headlands and beaches just west. Don't miss blustery **Cape Arago** and the gardens of **Shore Acres State Park.** Head south about 25 miles along Seven Devils Road and spend the night in **Bandon.** With its Old Town, beaches, and golfing at the internationally acclaimed **Bandon Dunes Golf Resort,** this town demands attention. Bandon is laid-back and easy to explore on foot, with more good restaurants than you'd expect.

Day 8

It's tempting to shrug off **Gold Beach**'s jet-boat tours up the mighty **Rogue River** as hokey tourist schlock, but these rides are actually pretty great, with good commentary and the chance to see bald eagles and other wildlife. It's 55 miles from Bandon to Gold Beach; be sure to get there in time to meet your boat.

Day 9

Between Gold Beach and Brookings (28 miles), the coastline is at its finest, with many pullouts offering paths down to secluded rocky beaches. Come prepared with a sweatshirt and a windbreaker and spend an afternoon exploring this stretch. In **Brookings,** it's important to stop for a walk and some bird-watching at **Harris Beach State Park,** but it's also worthwhile to get off the coastal strip and explore the Chetco River. **Alfred A. Loeb State Park** has good river access and a path through myrtle and redwood trees.

Day 10

If you're heading back to the I-5 corridor after your tour of the coast, consider dropping down to Crescent City in California, then heading inland on U.S. 199. This highway, which you pick up 22 miles south of the state border, passes through the northern edge of the California redwoods on its way to I-5 at Grants Pass, Oregon (83 miles).

Coastal Camping

NORTH COAST

- **Fort Stevens State Park:** Bike trails, a shipwreck, an old military fort, and a long beach where the Columbia River crashes into the Pacific make this a family-friendly campground. It's big too, with over 500 sites, including yurts and cabins, so it's usually possible to find accommodations.

- **Nehalem Bay State Park:** This campground has beach access to the Pacific on one side and sandy Nehalem Bay on the other; bike and hiking trails make it easy to get around.

- **Cape Lookout State Park:** At the base of a secluded sand spit, with easy access to hiking on Cape Lookout—one of the coast's top hiking trails—this campground has popular yurts and cabins in addition to traditional tenting sites.

CENTRAL COAST

- **South Beach State Park:** Just south of Newport, this large campground has easy access to the beach. It's a great base camp for a guided paddle trip up the nearby Beaver Creek estuary.

- **Carl G. Washburne State Park:** On the central coast between Florence and Yachats, camp on the inland side of the highway in a thicket of huge salal bushes. Pile your gear into a wheelbarrow (provided) and trundle it to one of the great walk-in campsites, then hike along the Hobbit Trail. There are also plenty of standard spots for car and RV camping.

- **Jessie M. Honeyman Memorial State Park:** A few miles south of Florence, this large campground is a playground for sandboarders and dune riders. Two miles of sand dunes separate the park from the ocean. The two freshwater lakes within the park's boundaries are popular places to boat and swim.

SOUTH COAST

- **Sunset Bay State Park:** Not only is this bay-fronting campground lovely, it's home to the Oregon coast's only real swimming beach

Most state park campsites also rent yurts.

and adjacent to several of the southern Oregon coast's top sights: Shore Acres State Park, Cape Arago, and South Slough National Estuarine Research Reserve.

- **Cape Blanco State Park:** A beautiful and often blustery campground at the state's westernmost point, just north of Port Orford and Humbug Mountain. Campground trails lead down to the beach and to the nearby lighthouse.

- **Harris Beach State Park:** Just north of Brookings, this magical campground sits in a grove of spruce and firs, and just off the beach are menhir-like sea stacks busy with seabirds.

- **Alfred A. Loeb State Park:** On the north bank of the Chetco River, find aromatic old-growth myrtlewood and the nation's northernmost naturally occurring redwood trees at Loeb State Park. The 1.2-mile nature trail winds through the redwoods, passing one tree with a 33-foot girth. When the south coast is foggy and cold on summer mornings, it's often warm and dry here.

Trails and Tide Pools

Coastal Oregon has a large number of high-quality state parks. There are nearly 80 state parks—19 with campgrounds—easily accessible from U.S. 101 in Oregon. Parks are located at all of the coast's most beautiful places, making access easy and affordable. Each of these itineraries makes for a great weekend trip, or you could combine them for a weeklong adventure.

North Coast

DAY 1

A dramatic start to a tour of the coast's parks begins at the point where the Columbia River enters the Pacific, at the northern edge of the huge **Fort Stevens State Park.** Miles of bike and hiking trails lead past abandoned gunneries (this was originally a Civil War military fortification); along the beach, the skeletal remains of the *Peter Iredale* shipwreck are a focal point. The campground here is the state's largest—stay here if you want showers and a kid-friendly atmosphere; for

more solitude and almost no amenities except for those provided by nature, head south and inland a bit to camp at **Saddle Mountain State Natural Area,** at the base of a fantastic hiking trail.

DAY 2

Get up early and drive south past Cannon Beach to **Oswald West State Park,** where trails through an old-growth forest lead to Short Sands Beach, Cape Falcon, and Neahkahnie Mountain. Plan to spend the night a few miles south by the dunes at **Nehalem Bay State Park,** just a beach walk south of the lovely town of Manzanita.

DAY 3

Head south to Tillamook and pick up the **Three Capes Scenic Loop.** Take time to explore the parks at Cape Meares (bring binoculars and look for puffins on the rocks here) and Oceanside. The 2.5-mile Cape Lookout Trail takes you out onto a narrow, steep-sided finger of land jutting into

---

Oswald West State Park

colorful tide pool life

the sea. It's one of the coast's most dramatic hikes, and particularly popular during the late-March whale-watching season. South of Cape Lookout, visit **Cape Kiwanda** to climb up on the bluff and run down the sand dunes.

Central Coast
DAY 4
As you pass through the more developed areas of Lincoln City, Depoe Bay, and Newport, stop at some of the day-use parks along the way. **Boiler Bay,** a mile north of Depoe Bay, is a great place to ponder the power of the surf; at **Yaquina Head,** at the north end of Newport, spend a couple of hours visiting the lighthouse and exploring tide pools. **Beachside State Park** has a campground between the towns of Waldport and Yachats.

DAY 5
Hike the trails and explore the dramatic rocky beach at Cape Perpetua, then continue south to the **Oregon Dunes.** Hikes in the dunes can be either random (even disorienting) explorations or can follow more defined routes. The blue-topped posts marking the John Dellenback Trail, about 10 miles south of Reedsport, guide you through a narrow band of coastal evergreen forest and 2.5 miles of 300- to 400-foot-high dunes to the beach.

Here you'll have your choice between a number of U.S. Forest Service campgrounds between Florence and Reedsport, including those near the Waxmyrtle, Carter Dunes, and Taylor Dunes Trails, and a couple of state park spots (Tugman and Umpqua Lighthouse) south of Reedsport.

South Coast
DAY 6
Head to the western edge of the continental United States and pitch your tent at **Cape Blanco State Park.** Along with the trails around the cape and down to the beach, visit the historic lighthouse.

Take your time on the trip south from Cape Blanco. The 1,756-foot-high **Humbug Mountain,** six miles south of Port Orford, is the highest mountain rising directly off the Oregon shoreline. A three-mile trail to its top yields both great views of the coastline and a chance to see wild rhododendrons 20-25 feet high. Rising above the rhodies and giant ferns are bigleaf maple, Port Orford cedar, and Douglas and grand firs.

DAY 7

In the far-south stretch between Gold Beach and Brookings are the many roadside pullouts along the 12-mile **Samuel H. Boardman State Scenic Corridor.** Drop in for a walk along the beach, or hike the Oregon Coast Trail between a couple of coves. At the north end of Brookings, **Harris Beach State Park** is a bustling campground near another lovely beach.

Catch of the Day

TOP EXPERIENCE

Fishing, crabbing, clamming, and mussel-gathering isn't just fun—it will fill your dinner plate too. There's plenty for foragers to eat along the Oregon coast, if you know where to look for it. If apprehending your own dinner from the sea isn't your style, then rest assured that almost every port town on the Oregon coast will have a crab shack or fish-and-chips shop where you can find exceedingly fresh and tasty seafood. Often these venues are right in the harbor or on the piers. What they may lack in upscale ambience is made up for with authenticity.

All crabbers and clam diggers need a **shellfish license,** available at pretty much anyplace that rents crab traps ($10 Oregon residents, $28 nonresidents).

Clamming is best during a minus tide, when more beach is exposed. Equipment consists of a shovel, a bucket, and—ideally—rubber boots. It's also helpful to have a dowel or stick to use as a probe and clam marker. Look for the clam holes, then dig toward the ocean side.

Pay attention to the signs at the entrance to the beach—they may be telling you about health precautions. Occasionally shellfish toxins mandate the closure of certain areas. These higher levels of bacteria and toxins are most likely to occur during the summer, and they are carefully monitored by the Oregon Department of Agriculture (check www.oregon.gov for details).

Astoria

The mother of all salmon rivers is the Columbia. While Astoria was once one of the world's top fishing ports, precipitous declines in salmon runs have spelled doom for its abundant salmon-packaging plants. However, there is **seasonal sportfishing** for most salmon runs, and tuna, halibut, and bottom-fish harvesting is strong.

Catch Your Own: Plenty of **charter fishing** operations are ready to take you out to where the big ones are biting.

Best Restaurant: Join the lines at popular **Bowpicker Fish and Chips,** a food cart-style operation in a boat.

Garibaldi

Garibaldi is a scrappy little fishing village on Tillamook Bay. **Crabbing** is also a high point, as are **local oysters.**

Catch Your Own: You'll have no trouble joining a **charter boat** heading out for whatever's in season.

Best Restaurant: Head to the **Pacific Oyster** processing plant at nearby Bay City, where you can forgo foraging and just buy and eat your seafood while watching shuckers tackle a mountain of bivalves.

Newport

Oregon's second-largest **fishing fleet** departs from Newport, and the bayfront here is a wonderful spot to plan a fishing or **whale-watching** trip.

Catch Your Own: Newport offers abundant **ocean fishing** options from the busy Bayfront area, but you can also rent **crab** traps and try your luck for a mess of crabs from public piers at the base of Abbey Street and Bay Street, in the heart of the harbor.

Best Restaurant: Both a market and a

restaurant, **Local Ocean Seafoods** serves up Newport's freshest fish and seafood from its perch right above the fishing piers.

Cape Perpetua

The black-shelled bivalves that coat the rocks and tide pools here are particularly good eating.

Catch Your Own: Harvesting **wild mussels** along the rugged Cape Perpetua shores is easy. Bring a pot, a bottle of white wine, and some garlic. Light a campfire, and you've got a meal. Before you harvest, look for signs warning of toxic algal blooms and dangerous levels of bacteria, particularly in hot summer weather.

Best Restaurant: Just north of Cape Perpetua is Yachats, where the owner of tiny **Luna Sea Fish House** serves absolutely fresh salmon, tuna, halibut, and crab caught from his own commercial fishing boat.

Winchester Bay

Just south of Reedsport, the tiny town of Winchester Bay is almost entirely given over to fishing.

Catch Your Own: Along with a busy commercial fishing port, there are many charter operators here who will take you out to the ocean for **salmon, halibut, tuna,** or **bottom fish.**

Best Restaurant: If you aren't fishing, stop for a meal at one of the dockside restaurants like funky **Crabby's Bar & Grill** to find excellent local oysters, crab, and whatever's fresh from the fishing fleet, or pick up some excellent canned tuna at the dockside cannery.

Charleston

Seafood so thoroughly pervades Charleston that even an angler's grudging spouse will get caught up in the excitement.

Catch Your Own: Don't like fishing charters, or want to forage on the cheap? No problem: Get to **crabbing** and **clamming** instead. Local shops here rent gear; you can crab right off the pier and clam on the beaches at Charleston or on Coos Bay's North Spit.

Best Restaurant: There are plenty of excellent seafood shacks and restaurants on the Charleston docks,

Newport fishing vessel

fish cannery near Astoria

but if you like oysters, stop by **Qualman's** for incredibly fresh oysters plucked from its nearby beds.

Bandon

Bandon isn't your typical fishing village—it's also an artsy, New-Agey hangout and an international golf destination—but you'll find excellent casual seafood munching options.

Catch Your Own: Stop at the bait store at the Old Town docks to pick up some **crab** traps, then go toss them over the side of the dock. Hang around and check the traps every so often—if you bring in a haul and don't want to fuss with the cooking and cleaning, ask the bait store to prepare them.

Best Restaurant: Order your crab sandwiches, rockfish tacos, or grilled salmon and then take a seat at picnic tables at **Tony's Crab Shack,** a bustling harbor-front landmark.

Rogue River

Anglers will want to stay a couple of days in Gold Beach, either in town or up the Rogue River. **Spring chinook salmon, fall king salmon, silver salmon, summer and winter steelhead**—all these runs are of legendary proportion.

Catch Your Own: It's best to go with a guide in a boat, and just about every local you'll meet is a guide. **Best Restaurant:** At **Spinner's Seafood, Steak and Chophouse,** check out the daily specials that feature Rogue River salmon in season, or the recommended cioppino seafood stew.

Chetco River

Although it's not as well-known as the Rogue, the Chetco River upstream from Brookings is also good for late fall and winter salmon and steelhead fishing.

Catch Your Own: Brookings is a good place to take a charter out into the ocean to fish for **salmon** and **bottom fish.**

Best Restaurant: Head to Brookings's harbor area to find **Catalyst Seafood,** a bar and grill whose owner operates a fishing boat and offers some of the freshest fish and seafood for miles around.

Top 10 Photo Ops

The Oregon coast is so photogenic that both professional and amateur photographers vie for the best shots, which, given coastal conditions, can be challenging. Greg Vaughn, professional landscape photographer and author of the helpful guide *Photographing Oregon,* notes that during the long light-drenched summer days, photographers must get up really early and stay out late to capture the "golden hours." He also notes that cloudy or foggy days are ideal for photographing the forests and waterfalls in the Coast Range mountains, and winter storms make for the most dramatic seascapes.

While there are stunning vistas around nearly every corner along the Oregon coast, here are some don't-miss photo opportunities.

Sunset: Astoria-Megler Bridge

This soaring, four-plus-mile bridge across the vast **Columbia River** is photographic eye candy. Directly south of the bridge, **Alameda Avenue** is carved into Astoria's steep hillsides, making it an excellent perch for snapping photos of the oceangoing vessels on the water and the distant hills of Washington State.

Sunrise: Ecola State Park and Haystack Rock

Cannon Beach offers postcard-perfect views of sea stacks and craggy offshore islands. Haystack Rock serves as a looming backdrop to nearly every beach photo taken here, while the scattered rocks of Ecola State Park are more like chess pieces tossed out to sea—perfect as a foreground for sunrise photos.

Midday: Oswald West State Park

It's not always easy to get up close and personal with giant trees in coastal old-growth forests, but at Oswald West, it's as easy as a stroll to **Short Sands Beach:** The trail winds through a grove of centuries-old Sitka spruce whose massive size will clog your viewfinder. In winter, shoot (but don't eat) colorful mushrooms.

Late Afternoon: Kites at Lincoln City

Nothing says fun at the beach like colorful kites diving and dancing in the air, and the long breezy expanses of sand at Lincoln City make it a center for kite-flying. Even when there's not a kite festival on, this is one kite-loving town. Climb the **steep bluffs behind the beach** for a rare bird's-eye view of kiting activity.

Sunset: Yaquina Bay Bridge

Of the many handsome bridges designed by 1930s bridge-design master Conde McCullough, this high-flying structure, which spans Newport's harbor, is the most striking. With the busy boat basin in the foreground, it's one of the top photo subjects in the state, particularly from viewpoints east along **Bay Boulevard,** which runs along the waterfront.

Morning: Cape Perpetua

Drive up to the top of the cape and take the short **Whispering Spruce Trail** to a fabulous overlook. Then head back down to the beach and explore this area's **tide pools** during low tide.

Sunset: Heceta Head Lighthouse

Rumored to be the most photographed vista in Oregon, this **stark white lighthouse** wedged into the flanks of a 1,000-foot rocky outcrop is impossible to miss. You'll run through millions of megapixels trying to capture the crashing waves, deep forests, and offshore crags from a cannily placed highway turnout just west of the Cape Creek Bridge.

Morning Low Tide: Tide Pools at Cape Arago State Park

Rocky tide pools filled with neon-hued starfish, spiky sea urchins, and shell-appropriating hermit

Sometimes the coastal weather is a little daunting. And although we strongly encourage you to layer up, get out there, and enjoy yourself in the pelting rain, we know that these wet outings need to be brief and interspersed with some inside time. Fortunately, there are plenty of indoor places to enjoy along Oregon's coast without feeling like you could be just anywhere.

ASTORIA

- **Columbia River Maritime Museum:** We'll gladly visit this museum in any kind of weather, but when storms rage outside, it gives visitors special insight into the dangerous jobs of those who guide ships across the Columbia River's bar and up its braided channel.

- **Fort Clatsop:** Lewis and Clark wrote of being "cold, wet, and miserable" here, but remember, they were here all winter. This is your chance to relive history.

SEASIDE

- **Arcades:** It's the tackiest sort of beach fun, but sometimes the whole family needs to pile into bumper cars.

LINCOLN CITY

- **Lincoln City Glass Center:** Blow your own glass float or paperweight at this Taft-neighborhood studio. Other galleries in the area feature glass and other art.

NEWPORT

- **Oregon Coast Aquarium:** Trance out watching jellyfish or walk through the Passages of the Deep, a 200-foot-long acrylic tunnel offering 360-degree underwater views in three diverse habitats, from Orford Reef to Halibut Flats to Open Sea, where you're surrounded by free-swimming sharks. It's easy to spend several hours here.

Columbia River Maritime Museum

FLORENCE

- **Sea Lion Caves:** Join about 200 Steller sea lions in this cliffside cave north of Florence. These sea lions occupy the cave during the fall and winter; in spring and summer, they breed and raise their young on the rock ledges just outside the cave.

BANDON

- **Face Rock Creamery:** After several cheeseless years, Bandon once again is home to a cheese factory. Stop in to sample some aged cheddar or Black Jack; Umpqua ice cream is another extremely popular option.

BROOKINGS

- **Brewpubs:** Hunker down and while away the day in a brewpub. *The Lord of the Rings*-themed **Misty Mountains Brewing,** where you can enjoy a Grey Pilgrim Pale Ale and fantasize about sunny days in the Shire, is particularly atmospheric.

crabs make fascinating photo subjects: Some of the **best tide-pooling** along the coast is at this state park. From the parking area, the north cove trail also offers views of **seals and sea lions** basking on offshore rock ledges, although this trail is closed in summer when these sea mammals are rearing their young (the south cove trail remains open year-round).

Mid-Morning: Bandon

Bandon's beautiful beach is studded with rocky fingers and promontories, but the most arresting vista is of **Face Rock,** a basalt monolith pounded by waves that from certain angles takes on a human profile. Native American legend claims it's the visage of a young woman frozen into rock. It's a postcard-ready image that bespeaks the beauty and mystery of the Oregon coast.

Sunset: Samuel H. Boardman State Scenic Corridor

It's often referred to as the most scenic 12 miles along the Oregon coast, but photographers don't find it easy to capture the drama of this stunning seascape: It's hard to encapsulate the vastness of the scene. Of the 11 named stops along this stretch of U.S. 101, **Whaleshead Island** is perhaps the most photogenic viewpoint, with tripod-ready vistas of a tiny beach flanked by rocky crags and wave-pounded islands.

suspension bridge at Oswald West State Park

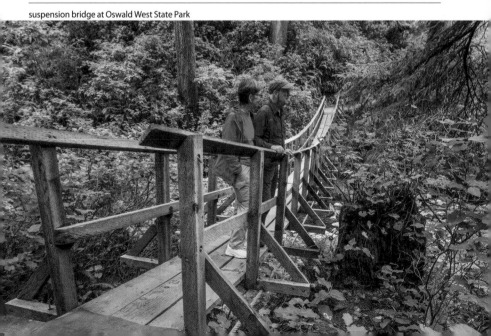

Undiscovered Beaches

With 360 miles of coastline, Oregon has lots of sandy waterfront. However, not all beaches are created equal. Here are some of our favorite, lesser-known beaches.

Hug Point State Recreation Site

When nearby Cannon Beach is just too busy, head a few miles south to Hug Point. You can see **Haystack Rock** in the distance, but not the crowds. Check out the two **caves** in the headlands and the old wagon trails carved into the stone—stagecoaches used to travel along the beach before roads were cut into the forests.

Short Sands Beach

This small beach, part of **Oswald West State Park,** is wedged between the rocky cliffs of Neahkahnie Mountain and Cape Falcon, making it feel cut off from the rest of the world. You'll need to follow a 0.5-mile trail through old-growth rainforest to reach the beach, which is nearly always active with surfers.

Rockaway Beach

Sure, the town of Rockaway may lack upscale charm, but the seven-mile-long beach itself is lovely. Just offshore are the **Twin Rocks,** two massive promontories, one carved through with an arch. This is a magical spot to watch the sunset.

Seal Rock State Recreation Site

Stop at this quiet beach about halfway between Newport and Waldport to find a bit of the best of everything: broad sandy strands, **tide pools,** curious rock formations in the surf, and shady picnic tables. The park is named for a large seal-like rock, and in fact you can often spot real **seals** on the islands. **Whales** pass by here on their twice-yearly migration.

Twin Rocks at Rockaway Beach

Cozy Seaside Inns

Smaller inns and bed-and-breakfasts are top spots for a comfortable and intimate stay.

ASTORIA

Astoria's **Hotel Elliott** isn't really an inn—in fact, when it was built in the 1920s, it was the classiest place to stay in Astoria. And with its lovingly restored rooms and rooftop sitting area, it still is. This historic hotel, situated in Astoria's vibrant downtown, will get a coast trip off to a great start.

MANZANITA

The six-block walk to the beach down Manzanita's charming main drag is easy, but if you're bunking at one of the perfectly fitted-out **Coast Cabins,** you may be content to just settle in and relax.

DEPOE BAY

The **Channel House** in Depoe Bay offers that perfect contrast of luxury and rustic charm. Watch the surging tides collide with the rocky shore and fishing boats negotiate the narrow harbor from the comfort of your outdoor whirlpool tub.

NEWPORT

History and literature intersect at the **Sylvia Beach Hotel** in Newport, a one-of-a-kind historic hotel-turned-B&B where all the rooms are decorated in literary themes. The Edgar Allan Poe room, anyone?

PORT ORFORD

Drop into a meditative calm at **Wildspring Guest Habitat,** perched above the Pacific Ocean in Port Orford. Everything here is designed to lead you to a state of serenity, whether it's the labyrinth

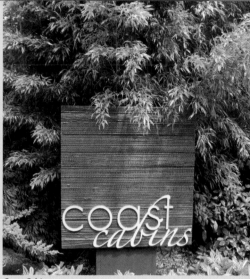

Coast Cabins

walk, the exquisite hot tub, the meditation alcoves, or the hammock outside your cabin.

GOLD BEACH

Upriver from Gold Beach, **Tu Tu Tun Resort** is the only full-on resort on the south coast, and it's a wonderful place to feel pampered in a thoroughly Oregonian kind of way.

BROOKINGS

Down in Brookings, stay at the **South Coast Inn B&B,** an elegant Bernard Maybeck-designed house.

Neptune State Park

At this magical spot south of Yachats, tongues of lava form mazelike walls in the sand, to the delight of children of all ages. It's a great place to play hide-and-seek or to spread a blanket and picnic. Immediately to the south (and also part of the state park) is **Strawberry Hill,** a wayside that gives access to acres of tide pools, where a broad expanse of ancient lava meets the Pacific.

Scenic Beach Loop

South of Bandon, drive the Scenic Beach Loop and witness some of the most evocative offshore rock formations in the state. With names like Cat

Elephant Rock on the Scenic Beach Loop

and Kittens Rocks, Face Rock, and the Garden of the Gods, you'll likely search for something magical in the various monoliths and islands. As you walk along the beach, watch for seabirds—**Elephant Rock** is a rookery for puffins, murres, and auklets.

Battle Rock Park

Just below the town of Port Orford, a craggy, steep-sided headland rises from the sands. In 1851, this promontory was the site of conflict between local Native Americans and would-be settlers, earning it the name Battle Rock. You can climb the trail to the rock's crest, where the settlers took shelter during a 14-day siege. Scattered along the beach are other dramatic sea stacks; this is also a good spot to **beachcomb** for agates.

Myers Creek Beach

The southern Oregon coastline is chock-a-block with dramatic vistas. Out of the many choices, a personal favorite is the sea-stack-studded beach at Myers Creek, part of **Pistol River State Park** south of Gold Beach. The cove is brimming with wave-battered monoliths, and the mile-long beach is just big enough for a good saunter but small enough to feel private.

North Coast

The enchanting north coast—from the mouth of the Columbia River south to Lincoln City—is little more than an hour's drive from the Portland metro area. It's the most popular part of Oregon's Pacific shoreline. Still, apart from the weekend crush at Cannon Beach and Seaside, there's more than enough elbow room for everyone.

Overlooking the Columbia River as it flows into the Pacific, the formerly shabby shipping and fishing center of Astoria has rediscovered its own potential, with a lively arts scene, adventurous cuisine, and fine hotels and B&Bs hosting overnighters. Its long-idle waterfront is busy again with tourist attractions—most notably the Columbia River Maritime Museum, one of the best museums in Oregon.

Highlights

Look for ★ to find recommended sights, activities, dining, and lodging.

★ **Columbia River Maritime Museum:** One of Oregon's top museums tells the story of seafaring on the Columbia River (page 44).

★ **Fort Clatsop National Memorial:** This replica of Lewis and Clark's 1805-1806 winter camp offers a fascinating glimpse into frontier life (page 46).

★ **Haystack Rock:** This soaring sea stack on Cannon Beach is home to thousands of seabirds (page 68).

★ **Oswald West State Park:** Walk an easy trail through an old-growth forest to the cove-like Short Sands Beach, or embark on a longer hike to Cape Falcon (page 78).

★ **Hiking at Cape Lookout:** Go for the great views of rocks and surf, the chance to see a whale, or to immerse yourself in the foggy coastal atmosphere (page 92).

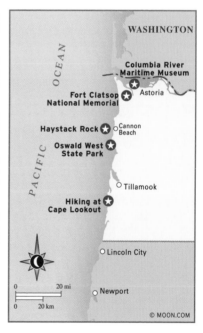

West of Astoria, at Oregon's far northwestern tip, where the mighty Columbia River meets the Pacific, visitors to Fort Stevens State Park can inspect the skeleton of a century-old shipwreck and a military fort active from the Civil War to World War II, as well as revel in miles of sandy beaches. Fort Clatsop National Memorial, part of Lewis and Clark National Historical Park, includes a re-creation of the Corps of Discovery's winter 1805-1806 quarters—a must-stop for Lewis and Clark buffs.

Cannon Beach and Seaside are two extremely popular resort towns that are polar opposites of one another. Cannon Beach, an enclave of tastefully weathered cedar-shingled architecture, is chockablock with art galleries, boutiques, and upscale lodgings and restaurants. A few miles north, Seaside is Oregon's quintessential family-friendly beach resort, with a long boardwalk, candy and gift shops, and noisy game arcades.

Just south of Cannon Beach, Oswald West State Park is a gem protecting old-growth forest and handsome little pocket beaches—as well as, some believe, a Spanish pirate treasure buried on Neahkahnie Mountain. Beyond Neahkahnie's cliff-top viewpoints along U.S. 101, the Nehalem Bay area attracts anglers, crabbers, and kayakers, as well as discriminating diners who come from far and wide to enjoy surprisingly sophisticated cuisine.

Tillamook County, home to more cows than people, is synonymous with delicious dairy products—cheese and ice cream in particular. It's no surprise that Tillamook's biggest visitor attraction is cheese-related. More than a million people a year come to the Tillamook Creamery to view the cheese-making operations and sample the excellent results. The Tillamook Air Museum is another popular diversion, housing an outstanding collection of vintage and modern aircraft in gargantuan Hangar B, the largest wooden structure in the world. Tillamook Bay, fed by five rivers, yields oysters and crabs, while the active Garibaldi charter fleet targets salmon, halibut, and tuna in the offshore waters.

South of Tillamook, the Coast Highway

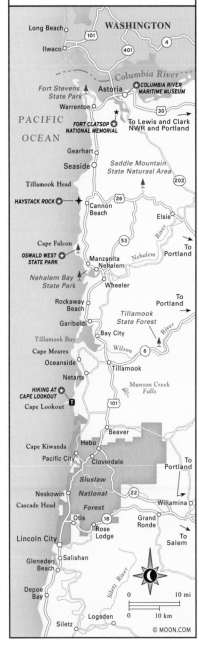

North Coast

wends inland through lush pastureland to Neskowin. It's a pleasant enough stretch, but the Three Capes Scenic Loop, a 35-mile scenic coastal detour, is a more attractive, if time-consuming, option. The spectacular views and bird-watching from Capes Meares and Lookout are the highlights of this beautiful drive. At Pacific City, at the southern end of the Three Capes Loop, commercial anglers launch their dories right off the sandy beach and through the surf in the lee of Cape Kiwanda and mammoth Haystack Rock—a sight not seen anywhere else on the West Coast. Just north of Lincoln City, Cascade Head beckons hikers to explore its rare prairie headlands ecosystem.

PLANNING YOUR TIME

Although most Oregonians have a favorite beach town that they'll visit for weekends and summer vacations, if this is your grand tour of the Oregon coast, plan to spend a few days exploring the northern coast's beaches and towns. If you're interested in history, architecture, or ship-watching, spend a night in **Astoria**—it's one of our favorite coastal cities, even though it's several miles from the Pacific Ocean. If you can't wait to walk on Pacific beaches, head to **Cannon Beach** (for a more upscale stay) or **Seaside** (which the kids will love) and begin your trip there. By driving north-south, you'll be able to pull off the highway more easily into beach access areas. Campers might want to reserve a space at Nehalem Bay State Park, near the small laid-back town of **Manzanita,** a few miles south of Cannon Beach; Manzanita is also a good place to rent a beach house for a weekend. Aside from the near-mandatory stop at the Tillamook Creamery, you'll probably want to skip the town of Tillamook and head to the **Three Capes Loop,** where a night in Pacific City offers easy access to Cape Kiwanda as well as comfy lodgings and a good brewpub. On your way south to the central coast, or to the Highway 18 route back through the Willamette Valley wine country to Portland, do stop for a hike at **Cascade Head.**

Astoria and Vicinity

The mouth of the mighty Columbia River, with its abundance of natural resources, was long a home for Native Americans; artifacts found in the area suggest that people have been living along the river for at least 8,000 years. Early European explorers and settlers also found the river and its bays to be propitious as a trading and fishing center. Astoria's dramatic location and deep history continue to attract new settlers and travelers drawn to the area's potent allure.

Astoria (pop. about 10,000) is the oldest permanent U.S. settlement west of the Rockies, and its glory days are preserved by museums, historical exhibits, and pastel-colored Victorian homes weathered by the sea air. Hollywood has chosen Astoria's picturesque neighborhoods to simulate an idealized all-American town, most notably in the cult classic *The Goonies.*

What sets Astoria apart from other destinations on the northern Oregon coast is that it's a real city, not a waterfront town made over into a resort. While the decline in the logging and fishing industries dealt the city many economic blows in the late 20th century, there's plenty of pluck left in this old dowager, and her best years may be yet to come as a thriving haven for artists and free spirits.

Astoria has many charms: Colorful Victorian mansions and historic buildings downtown are undergoing restoration, cruise

Previous: Haystack Rock; Cannon Beach; the Seaside Brewing Company.

Astoria and Vicinity

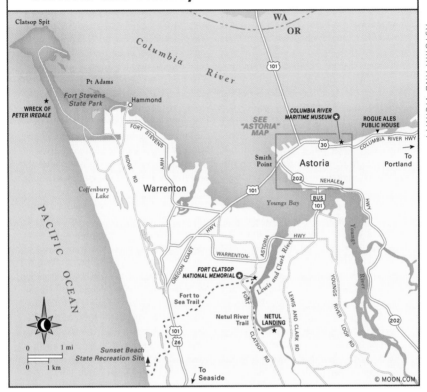

ships are calling, fine restaurants are multi-plying, a lively arts scene is booming, and there's new life along the waterfront, anchored by the excellent Columbia River Maritime Museum.

History

The Clatsop people, a Chinook-speaking group, lived in this area for thousands of years before Astoria's written history began. When Lewis and Clark arrived in 1805, the Clatsops numbered about 400 people, living in three villages on the south side of the Columbia River, but their steady decline began soon after contact with whites.

The region was first chronicled by Don Bruno de Heceta, a Spanish explorer who sailed near the Columbia's mouth in August 1775. He named it the Bay of the Assumption of Our Lady, but the strong current prevented his ship from entering. U.S. presence on the Columbia began with Captain Robert Gray's discovery of the river in May 1792, which he named after his fur-trading ship, *Columbia Rediviva*.

Thereafter, Lewis and Clark's famous expedition of 1804-1806, with its winter encampment at Fort Clatsop, south of present-day Astoria, helped incorporate the Pacific Northwest as part of a new nation. In 1811, John Jacob Astor's agents built Fort Astoria on a hillside in what would eventually grow into Astoria—the first U.S. settlement west of the Rockies. The trading post was occupied by the British between 1813 and 1818, and the settlement was renamed

Fort George. Real development began in the 1840s as settlers begin pouring in from the Oregon Trail. During the Civil War, Fort Stevens was built at the mouth of the Columbia to guard against a Confederate naval incursion.

Commerce grew with the export of lumber and foodstuffs to gold rush-era San Francisco and Asia. Salmon canneries became the mainstay of Astoria's economy during the 1870s, helping it grow into Oregon's second-largest city—and a notorious shanghaiing port, where young men, often drunk, were kidnapped from bars to serve as unwilling sailors on commercial and military ships. From that time through the early 1900s, the dominant immigrants to the Astoria area were Scandinavian, and with the addition of these seafaring folk, logging, fishing, and shipbuilding coaxed the population up to 20,000 by World War II.

Some believe that the port city at the mouth of the Columbia might have grown to rival San Francisco or Seattle had it not been for the setback of a devastating fire in 1922. In the early morning hours of December 8, a pool hall on Commercial Street caught fire; the flames spread rapidly among the wooden buildings, many supported on wooden pilings, in Astoria's business district. By daybreak, more than 200 businesses in a 32-block area had been reduced to ashes. The downtown was rebuilt in the ensuing years, largely in brick and stone, but the devastation changed the fate of Astoria.

Near the end of World War II, a Japanese submarine's shelling of Fort Stevens made it the only fortification on U.S. soil to have sustained an attack in a world war. After the war, the region's fortunes ebbed and flowed with its resource-based economy. In an attempt to supplement that economy with tourism, the State Highway Division began constructing the Astoria-Megler Bridge in 1962 to connect Oregon and Washington.

Orientation

The waters surrounding Astoria define the town as much as the steep hills it's built on. Along its northern side, the mighty Columbia, four miles wide, is an aquatic highway carrying a steady flow of traffic, from small pleasure boats to massive cargo ships a quarter mile long. Soaring high over the river is an engineering marvel that's impossible to miss from most locations in town. At just over four miles long, the Astoria-Megler Bridge is the longest bridge in Oregon and the longest bridge of its type (cantilever through-truss) in the nation. When it opened in 1966, the bridge provided the final link in the 1,625-mile-long U.S. 101 along the Pacific coast.

On Astoria's south side, Young's River, flowing down from the Coast Range, broadens into Young's Bay, separating Astoria from its neighbor Warrenton to the southwest. A few miles to the west, the Columbia River finally meets the Pacific, 1,243 miles from its headwaters in British Columbia. Where the tremendous outflow (averaging 118 million gallons per minute) of the River of the West encounters the ocean tides, conditions can be treacherous, and the sometimes-monstrous waves around the bar have claimed more than 2,000 vessels over the years. This river's mouth could well be the biggest widow-maker on the high seas, earning it the title "Graveyard of the Pacific." Lewis and Clark referred to it as "that seven-shouldered horror" in a journal entry from the winter of 1805-1806.

Any visitor to Astoria should consider crossing the Astoria-Megler Bridge to visit the extreme southwest corner of Washington State. Here the sands and soil carried by the Columbia create a 20-mile-long sand spit called the Long Beach Peninsula. Some of the West Coast's most succulent oysters grow in Willapa Bay, the body of water created by this finger of sand. Historic beach communities plus numerous Lewis and Clark sites also reward visitors to this charming enclave.

1: Astoria-Megler Bridge **2:** Blue Scorcher Bakery Cafe **3:** the Astoria waterfront

SIGHTS

After getting a bird's-eye view from the Astoria Column, you might want to take a closer look at Astoria on foot. The town is home to dozens of beautifully restored 19th-century and early 20th-century houses.

Here's a suggested route: From the Flavel House Museum at 8th and Duane Streets, start walking south on 8th Street and turn left on Franklin Avenue. Continue east to 11th Street, then detour south one block on 11th Street to Grand Avenue; head east on Grand, north on 12th Street, and back to Franklin, continuing your eastward trek. Walk to 17th Street, then south again to Grand, double back on Grand two blocks to 15th Street, then walk north on 15th to Exchange Street and east on Exchange to 17th, where you'll be just two blocks from the Columbia River Maritime Museum. This route takes you past 74 historic buildings and sites.

One of Astoria's most impressive sights is the commanding vista of the **Astoria-Megler Bridge.** To get there from the Flavel House Museum, head south (uphill) on 8th Street and turn right (west) on Franklin Avenue. Follow Franklin six blocks until it turns into Skyline Avenue. After one block, turn onto West Grand Avenue, which hugs the ridge. For the ultimate perch directly over the bridge, turn off West Grand to follow Lincoln Street north (downhill) to Alameda Avenue where you're eye-to-eye with the bridge's soaring span.

Astoria Column

The best introduction to Astoria and environs is undoubtedly the 360-degree panorama from atop the 125-foot-tall **Astoria Column** (2199 Coxcomb Dr., 503/325-2963, www.astoriacolumn.org, dawn-dusk daily, $5 parking) on Coxcomb Hill, the highest point in town. Patterned after Trajan's Column in Rome, the reinforced-concrete tower was built in 1926 as a joint project of the Great Northern Railway and the descendants of John Jacob Astor to commemorate the westward sweep of discovery and migration. The graffito frieze spiraling up the exterior illustrates Robert Gray's 1792 discovery of the Columbia River, the establishment of U.S. claims to the Northwest Territory, the arrival of the Great Northern Railway, and other scenes of the history of the Pacific Northwest. The vista from the surrounding hilltop park is impressive enough, but for the ultimate experience, the climb up 164 steps to the tower's top is worth the effort.

If you have kids in tow, stop by the tiny gift shop to buy a balsa-wood glider. Lofting a wooden airplane from the top of the tower is an Astoria tradition.

Get to the Astoria Column from downtown by following 16th Street south (uphill) to Jerome Avenue. Turn right (west) one block and continue up 15th Street to the park entrance on Coxcomb Drive. Avoid the parking fee by parking on the road leading up the hill and hiking the final stretch.

The Waterfront

While most of Astoria's waterfront is lined with warehouses and docks, the **River Walk** will get you front-row views of the river. The River Walk provides paved riverside passage for pedestrians and cyclists along a five-mile stretch between the Port of Astoria and the community of Alderbrook, at the eastern fringe of Astoria.

An excellent way to cover some of the same ground, accompanied by commentary on sights and local history, is by taking a 50-minute ride on Old 300, the **Astoria Riverfront Trolley** (503/325-6311, www.old300.org, weather permitting noon-6pm daily Memorial Day-Labor Day, see trolley shelters for fall-spring schedules, $1/ ride or $2 all day), which runs on Astoria's original train tracks alongside the River Walk as far east as the East Mooring Basin. Trolley shelters are at nine stops along the route; you can also flag it down anywhere along the way by waving a dollar bill. The lovingly restored 1913 trolley originally served San Antonio and later ran between Portland and Lake Oswego in the 1980s.

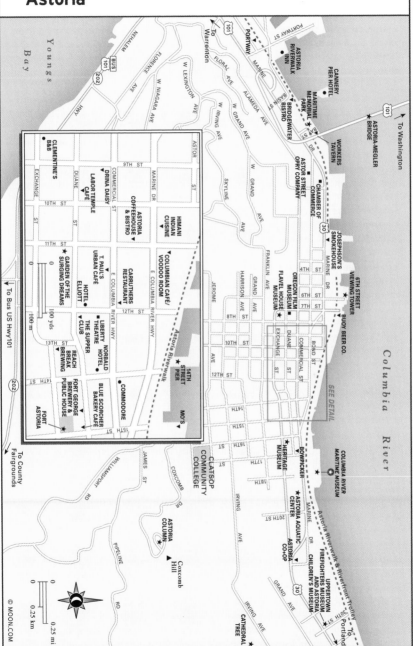

© MOON.COM

Toward the eastern end of the River Walk, at Pier 39, the **Hanthorn Cannery** (100 39th St., 503/325-2502, 9am-6pm daily, free) is a rather informal but fascinating museum housed in an old Bumble Bee tuna cannery. Exhibits include some lovely old wooden boats, eye-catching photos, and canning equipment. There's also a coffee shop and a brewpub at this location, so it's a good place to take a break.

★ Columbia River Maritime Museum

On the waterfront a few blocks east of downtown Astoria, the **Columbia River Maritime Museum** (1792 Marine Dr., 503/325-2323, www.crmm.org, 9:30am-5pm daily, closed Thanksgiving and Christmas, $14 adults, $12 seniors, $5 ages 6-17, free under age 6) is hard to miss. The roof of the 44,000-square-foot museum simulates the curvature of cresting waves, and the gigantic 25,000-pound anchor out front is also impossible to ignore. What's inside surpasses this eye-catching facade. The introductory film is excellent and intense, giving a good glimpse of the jobs of bar pilots, who climb aboard huge ships to navigate them across the Columbia Bar and up the river. Floor-to-ceiling windows in the Great Hall allow visitors to watch the river traffic in comfort.

Historic boats, scale models, exquisitely detailed miniatures of ships, paintings, and artifacts recount times when Native American canoes plied the Columbia, Lewis and Clark camped on the Columbia's shores, and dramatic shipwrecks occurred on its bar. Local lighthouses, the evolution of boat design, scrimshaw, and harpoons are the focus of other exhibits here.

The museum also now houses two of three cannons that gave nearby Cannon Beach its name. These early 19th-century cannons, from the USS *Shark*, which met its end on the Columbia River Bar in 1846, were set adrift and washed up some 30 miles south of the Columbia's mouth, near Cannon Beach. The first of the cannons was discovered in 1894,

and the last two were found in 2008. All were studied at Texas A&M University for a number of years, and two are now on display in the museum, along with an officer's sword from the *Shark* found in the 1970s, and the Shark Rock, a large boulder into which survivors of the shipwreck carved their names.

Museum admission lets you board the 128-foot lightship *Columbia*, now permanently berthed alongside the museum building. This vessel served as a floating lighthouse, marking the entrance to the mouth of the river and helping many ships navigate the dangerous waters. The gift shop has a great collection of books on Astoria's history and other maritime topics.

Heritage Museum and Research Library

The **Heritage Museum** (1618 Exchange St., 503/325-2203, www.cumtux.org, 10am-5pm daily May-Sept., 11am-4pm Tues.-Sat. Oct.-Apr., $4 adults, $2 ages 6-17) is housed in a handsome neoclassical building that was originally Astoria's city hall. It has several galleries filled with antiques, tools, vintage photographs, and archives chronicling various aspects of life in Clatsop County. The museum's centerpiece exhibit concentrates on the culture of the local Clatsop and Chinook peoples, from before European contact up to the present day. Other exhibits highlight natural history, geology, early immigrants and settlers in the region, and the development of commerce in such fields as fishing, fish packing, logging, and lumber. The **research library** is open to the public.

Flavel House Museum

Captain George Flavel, Astoria's first millionaire, amassed a fortune in the mid-19th century through his Columbia River Bar piloting monopoly, and later expanded his empire through shipping, banking, and real estate. Between 1884 and 1886 he had a home built in the center of Astoria overlooking the Columbia River, now the **Flavel House Museum** (441 8th St., 503/325-2203,

The *Peter Iredale*

the remains of the 1906 wreck *Peter Iredale* at Fort Stevens State Park

One of the best known of the hundreds of ships wrecked on the Oregon coast over the centuries is the British schooner *Peter Iredale*. This 278-foot four-master, fashioned of steel plates on an iron frame, was built in Liverpool in 1890 and came to its untimely end on the beach south of Clatsop Spit on October 25, 1906. En route from Mexico to pick up a load of wheat on the Columbia River, the vessel ran aground during high seas and a northwesterly squall. All hands were rescued, and with little damage to the hull, hopes initially ran high that the ship could be towed back to sea and salvaged. That effort proved fruitless, and eventually the ship was written off as a total loss. Today, over a century later, the remains of her rusting skeleton protrude from the sands of **Fort Stevens State Park** as a familiar sight to most who have traveled the north coast. Signs within Fort Stevens State Park lead the way to a parking area close to the wreck.

10am-5pm daily May-Sept., 11am-4pm daily Oct.-Apr., $6 adults, $5 seniors and students, $2 ages 6-17, free under age 6), where he retired with his wife and two daughters. From its 4th-story cupola, Flavel could watch the comings and goings of his sailing fleet.

When the Clatsop County Historical Society assumed stewardship in 1951, the mansion was slated for demolition, to be paved over as a parking lot for the adjacent courthouse. Fortunately, thanks to the efforts of the historical society and many volunteers, the house still stands today at the corner of 8th and Duane Streets. The splendidly extravagant Queen Anne mansion reflects the rich style and elegance of the late Victorian era and the lives of Astoria's most prominent family.

The property encompasses a full city block. With its intricate woodwork inside and out, period furnishings, and art, along with its extravagantly rendered gables, cornices, and porches, the Flavel House ranks with the Carson Mansion in Eureka, California, as a Victorian showplace. The Carriage House, on the southwest corner of the property, serves as an orientation center for visitors with exhibits, an interpretive video, and a museum store.

Garden of the Surging Waves

A small garden and outdoor art display, **Garden of the Surging Waves** (11th St. and Duane St.) commemorates Astoria's Chinese heritage. At the center is a pavilion with nine stone columns ornately carved with dragons.

The garden's east facade is a finely worked metal screen with quotations from Chinese pioneers. This park is the first feature in the repurposing of an underutilized downtown parking lot into the Astoria Heritage Square, which in time will also feature an amphitheater and an open-air market.

Fort Astoria

In a tiny park at the corner of 15th and Exchange Streets, a reproduction of a rough-hewn log blockhouse and a mural commemorate the spot where Astoria began, when John Jacob Astor's fur traders originally constructed a small fort in 1811. It's worth a quick stop for buffs of early Pacific Northwest history.

Lewis and Clark National Wildlife Refuge

Six miles east of Astoria in the Burnside area is the **Twilight Creek Eagle Sanctuary.** To get there, drive seven miles east of town on U.S. 30 and turn left at Burnside. A viewing platform on the left, 0.5 mile later, overlooks the 35,000 acres of mudflats, tidal marshes, and islands (which Lewis and Clark called "Seal Islands") of the **Lewis and Clark National Wildlife Refuge.** Bald eagles live here year-round, and the area provides wintering and resting habitat for waterfowl, shorebirds, and songbirds. Beavers, raccoons, weasels, mink, muskrats, and river otters live on the islands; harbor seals and California sea lions feed in the rich estuary waters and use the sandbars and mudflats as haul-out sites at low tide.

★ Fort Clatsop National Memorial

In November 1805, after a journey of nearly 19 months and 4,000 miles, the Lewis and Clark expedition reached the mouth of the Columbia River, where they decided to winter. They chose a thickly forested rise alongside the Netul River (now the Lewis and Clark River), a few miles south of present-day Astoria, for their campsite. There, the Corps of Discovery quickly set about felling

trees and building two parallel rows of cabins, joined by a gated palisade. The finished compound measured about 50 feet on each side. The party of 33 people, including an enslaved African American man and a Native American woman and her baby, moved into the seven small rooms on Christmas Eve and named their stockade Fort Clatsop, for the nearby Native American people.

The winter of 1805-1806 was cold, wet, rainy, and generally miserable. Of the 106 days spent at the site, it rained on all but 12. The January 18, 1806, journal entry of expedition member Private Joseph Whitehouse was typical of the comments recorded during the stay: "It rained hard all last night, & still continued the same this morning. It continued Raining during the whole of this day."

While at Fort Clatsop, the men stored up meat and other supplies, sewed moccasins and new garments, and traded with local indigenous people, all the while coping with the constant damp conditions, illness and injuries, and merciless plagues of fleas. As soon as the weather permitted, on March 23, 1806, they finally departed on their homeward journey to St. Louis.

Within a few years the elements had erased all traces of Fort Clatsop, and its exact location was lost. In 1955, local history buffs took their best guess and built a replica of the fort based on the notes and sketches of Captain Clark. In 1999, an anthropologist discovered a 148-year-old map identifying the location of Lewis and Clark's winter encampment, and as it turns out, the reproduction is sited close to the original. In 2005 this replica of Fort Clatsop burned, and a new replica, built mostly by volunteers using period tools, was reopened in 2006. Compared to the previous one, this new Fort Clatsop is a more authentic replica of the actual fort that housed the intrepid Corps of Discovery.

Today, in addition to the log replica of the fort, a well-equipped visitors center, museum, and other attractions make **Fort Clatsop Visitor Center and Fort Clatsop Replica** (92343 Fort Clatsop Rd., 503/861-2471, www.

Lewis and Clark National Historical Park

In 2004, President George W. Bush signed a bill into law to create the 59th national park in the United States. The Lewis and Clark National and State Historical Parks honor explorers Meriwether Lewis and William Clark, whose journey in 1804-1806 paved the way for the U.S. settlement of the West. The park focuses on the sites at the mouth of the Columbia River, where the Corps of Discovery spent the famously wet winter of 1805.

The park is somewhat unusual in that it is essentially a rebranding of current national park facilities and a federalization of current state parks. It includes a dozen sites linked to Lewis and Clark exploration, campsites, and lore. One of these, **Fort Clatsop National Memorial,** south of Astoria and where the Corps actually spent the winter, was already operated by the National Park Service, while **Cape Disappointment State Park** (formerly Fort Canby State Park), on the Washington side of the Columbia, remains a Washington state park but is managed by the national park entity.

Besides these two existing facilities, units of the new national park include the **Fort to Sea Trail,** a path linking Fort Clatsop to the Pacific; **Clarks Dismal Nitch,** a notoriously wet campsite near the Washington base of the Astoria-Megler Bridge; **Station Camp,** another improvident campsite for the Corps; the **Salt Works** in Seaside, where the Corps boiled seawater to make salt; **Netul Landing,** the canoe launch area used by Lewis and Clark near Fort Clatsop; and a **memorial to Thomas Jefferson** yet to be constructed on the grounds of Cape Disappointment State Park.

The new national park also encompasses the existing **Fort Columbia State Park** in Washington, which preserves a turn-of-the-20th-century military encampment, and **Fort Stevens** and **Ecola State Parks** as well as **Sunset Beach State Recreation Site** in Oregon.

The national park designation changes little for these once-disparate sites, at least for the moment. Fort Clatsop has been expanded to 1,500 acres, and the **Lewis and Clark Interpretive Center** at Fort Disappointment State Park was revamped. Visitors will mostly notice new and consistent signage throughout the park units. Ranger-guided hikes and living-history reenactors promise to bring to life the famous, often very wet, events that took place here over 200 years ago.

nps.gov/lewi, 9am-6pm daily mid-June-Labor Day, 9am-5pm daily Labor Day-mid-June, $7 adults, free under age 16) a must-stop for anyone interested in this pivotal chapter of American history. The expedition's story is nicely narrated here with displays, artifacts, slides, and films, but the summertime "living-history" reenactments are the main reason to come. Paths lead through the grove of old-growth Sitka spruce, with interpretive placards identifying native plants. A short walk from the fort leads to the riverside, where dugout canoes are modeled on those used by the Corps while in this area. In addition, the 6.5-mile **Fort to Sea Trail** follows the general route blazed by Captain Clark from the fort through dunes and forests to the Pacific at Sunset Beach.

The winter of 1805-1806 put a premium on wilderness survival skills, some of which are exhibited here by rangers in costume. You may see the demonstrations of flintlock rifles, tanning of hides, making of buckskin clothing and moccasins, and the molding of tallow candles and lead bullets. In addition, rangers also lead guided hikes along the river.

This 1,500-acre park sits six miles southwest of Astoria and three miles east of U.S. 101 on the Lewis and Clark River. To get there from Astoria, take Marine Drive and head west across Young's Bay to Warrenton. On the south side of the bay, look for signs for the Fort Clatsop turnoff; turn left off the Coast Highway about a mile after the bridge and follow the signs to Fort Clatsop.

Fort Stevens State Park

Ten miles west of Astoria, in the far northwest corner of the state, the Civil War-era outpost of **Fort Stevens** (100 Peter Iredale Rd.,

Hammond, 503/861-3170, ext. 21, or 800/551-6949, www.oregonstateparks.org, $5 day-use for historic military area and Coffenbury Lake, $22 tent camping, $32-34 RV camping, $48-58 yurts, $93-103 cabins) was one of three military installations (the others were Forts Canby and Columbia in Washington) built to safeguard the mouth of the Columbia River. Established shortly before the Confederates surrendered on April 9, 1865, Fort Stevens served for 84 years, until just after the end of World War II. Today, the remaining fortifications and other buildings are preserved along with 3,700 acres of woodland, lakes, wetlands, miles of sand beaches, and three miles of Columbia River frontage.

Although Fort Stevens did not see action in the Civil War, it sustained an attack in a later conflict. On June 21, 1942, a Japanese submarine fired 17 shells on the gun emplacements at Battery Russell, making it the only U.S. fortification in the 48 states to be bombed by a foreign power since the War of 1812. No damage was incurred, and the U.S. Army didn't return fire. Shortly after World War II, the fort was deactivated and the armaments removed.

Today, the site features a **Military Museum** (503/861-2000, http://visitftstevens.com, 10am-6pm daily June-Sept., 10am-4pm daily Oct.-May) with old photos, weapons exhibits, and maps, as well as seven different batteries (fortifications) and other structures left over from almost a century of service. Climbing to the commander's station for a scenic view of the Columbia River and South Jetty are popular visitor activities. The massive gun batteries, built of weathered gray concrete and rusting iron, eerily silent amid the thick woodlands, also invite exploration; small children should be closely supervised, as there are steep stairways, high ledges, and other hazards.

During the summer months, guided tours of the underground **Battery Mishler** (call for schedule, $6 adults, $4 ages 6-12) and the fort's 37 acres on a two-ton U.S. Army truck are also available. Summer programs include Civil War reenactments and archaeological digs.

Nine miles of bike trails and five miles of hiking trails link the historic area to the rest of the park and provide access to Battery Russell and the 1906 wreck of the British schooner *Peter Iredale.* You can also bike to the campground one mile south of the Military Museum.

Parking is available at four lots about a mile from one another at the foot of the dunes. The beach runs north to the Columbia River, where excellent surf fishing, bird-watching, and a view of the mouth of the river await. South of the campground (east of the *Peter Iredale*) is a self-guided nature trail around part of the two-mile shoreline of **Coffenbury Lake.** The lake also has two swimming beaches with bathhouses and fishing for trout and perch. Other activities include disc golf and mushrooming (pick up a park brochure to help with identification, keep track of where you wander, and eat only if you are an experienced mushroom gatherer).

To get to Fort Stevens State Park from U.S. 101, drive west on Harbor Street through Warrenton on Highway 104 (Ft. Stevens Hwy.) to the suburb of Hammond and follow the signs to Fort Stevens Historic Area and Military Museum.

RECREATION
Hiking

An in-town hike that's not too strenuous begins at 28th and Irving Streets, meandering up the hill to the Astoria Column. If you drive to the trailhead, park along 28th Street. It's about a one-mile walk to the top. En route is the **Cathedral Tree,** an old-growth fir with a sort of Gothic arch formed at its roots.

The **Oregon Coast Trail** starts (or ends) at Clatsop Spit, at the north end of **Fort Stevens State Park** (100 Peter Iredale Rd., Hammond, 503/861-1671 or 800/551-6949, www.oregonstateparks.org, $5 day-use). The most northerly stretch extends south along

---

1: coastal wetlands along the Columbia River near Astoria **2:** food cart pod **3:** Bowpicker Fish and Chips **4:** Fort Clatsop National Memorial

Biking the Oregon Coast

Biking all or part of the Oregon coast is the surest way to get on intimate terms with this spectacular region. Because the prevailing winds in summer are from the northwest, most people cycle south on U.S. 101 to take advantage of a tailwind. You'll also be riding on the ocean side of the road with better views and easier access to turnouts, and generally wider bike lanes and shoulders. The entire 370-mile trip (380 miles if you include the Three Capes Scenic Loop) involves nearly 16,000 feet of elevation change. Most cyclists cover the distance in 6-8 days, pedaling an average of 50-65 miles daily.

If you want to cycle the full length of the coast, fly into Portland and ride to Astoria. (Unpack your bike and take it on the MAX train, which can take you through town to the western suburbs to start your trip.) It's a little harder to figure out how to end your trip, as public transportation is rather limited on the southern Oregon coast. Consider riding about 25 miles into California, where you'll find Greyhound service in Crescent City.

Before going, get a free copy of the **Oregon Coast Bike Route** map from the **Oregon Department of Transportation** (503/986-3555, www.oregon.gov/ODOT) or from coastal information centers. This brochure features strip maps of the route, noting services from Astoria to the California border. With information on campsites, hostels, bike repair facilities, elevation change, temperatures, and winds, this pamphlet does everything but map the ruts in the road.

the beach for 14 miles to Gearhart. It's a flat, easy walk, and your journey could well be highlighted by a sighting of the endangered silverspot butterfly, a small orange butterfly with silvery spots on the undersides of its wings.

You might also encounter cars on the beach. This section of shoreline, inexplicably, is the longest stretch of coastline open to motor vehicles in Oregon. Call the **State Parks and Recreation Division** (800/551-6949) for an up-to-date report on trail conditions before starting out.

Fort Stevens State Park has nine miles of hiking trails through woods, wetlands, and dunes. One popular hike here is the two-mile loop around **Coffenbury Lake.**

In 2005, as part of the expansion of Lewis and Clark National Historical Park, the **Fort to Sea Trail** was created to link Fort Clatsop to the Pacific. The 6.5-mile trail follows the route through forest, fields, and dunes that the Corps traveled as they explored and traded along the Pacific coast.

The Fort to Sea Trail starts from the visitors center at Fort Clatsop. The first 1.5 miles involve a gentle climb past many trees blown down in a big 2007 storm to the Clatsop Ridge,

where on a clear day you can see through the trees to the Pacific Ocean. The ridge makes a fine destination for a short hike, but the really beautiful part of the trail is the hikers-only (no dogs) stretch from the overlook to the beach, where you'll pass through deep woods and forested pastures dotted with small lakes. The trail goes through a tunnel underneath U.S. 101 and continues through dunes to the Sunset Beach-Fort to Sea Trail parking lot. From there, a one-mile path leads to the beach.

Unless you plan to return along the trail—which makes for a long day's hike—you'll need to arrange a pickup.

Bicycling

You don't need a fancy bike to pedal the River Walk; rent a hefty cruiser from **Bikes and Beyond** (1089 Marine Dr., 503/325-2961, www.bikesandbeyond.com, 10am-6pm Mon.-Sat., 11am-5pm Sun., $5/hour, $20/day). This friendly little shop also caters to bicycle travelers.

Fishing Charters

More than any other industry, commercial fishing has dominated Astoria throughout its history. Salmon canneries lined the waterfront at the turn of the 20th century. In the modern era, commercial fishing has turned to tuna, sole, lingcod, rockfish, flounder, and other bottom fish. If it's not enough to watch these commercial operations from the dock, try joining a charter. Expect to pay $150-200 per person for a day of fishing, depending on what you're fishing for; given the retail price of fresh salmon, you could theoretically pay for a charter trip by landing a single fish. If you're after a big Chinook salmon, book your trip for August-September.

Astoria Fishing Charters (503/436-2845, www.astoriafishing.com, $120-250 pp/day) will take you out for salmon, steelhead, bottom fish, and sturgeon, depending on the season. Trips depart from the dock just off Industry Drive near the West Mooring Basin. **Gale Force Guides** (trips depart from Warrenton, 503/861-1494, www.galeforceguides.com, $225 pp) takes sport anglers fishing for salmon in either salt- or freshwater, depending on the season. Sturgeon and crabbing trips are also offered.

On your own, go after trout, bass, catfish, steelhead, and sturgeon in freshwater lakes, streams, and rivers. Lingcod, rockfish, surfperch, and other bottom fish can be pursued off jetties or along ocean beaches.

Diving and Kayaking
Astoria Scuba (on Pier 39, 503/325-2502, www.astoriascuba.com, 9am-6pm daily) offers diving supplies and kayak rentals ($25 half-day).

Zip-Lining
Explore the Northwest forests and lakes on the eight zip-line tours at **High Life Adventures** (92111 High Life Rd., Warrenton, 503/861-9875, http://highlife-adventures.com, 11am-4pm Sun.-Thurs., 11am-6pm Fri.-Sat., $99 over age 15, $69 under age 16), five miles south of Astoria off U.S. 101. The tours soar above a 30-acre preserve of freshwater dune-trapped lakes and coastal forests. The Maple zip line

even offers participants a chance to take a dunk in the lake.

ENTERTAINMENT
For the lowdown on all the happenings in and around Astoria, get your hands on a copy of *Hipfish,* Astoria's spirited monthly tabloid, distributed free all over town.

Nightlife
BREWPUBS
In an old fish-processing warehouse right on the edge of the river, **Buoy Beer Company** (1 8th St., 503/325-4540, www.buoybeer.com, 11am-10pm Sun.-Thurs., 11am-11pm Fri.-Sat., $10-26) has good beer and a seafood-centered menu; dine on excellent fried oysters as you watch freighters go upriver and sea lions swim under a swatch of glassed-in floor. (Kids love the sea lions at this family-friendly pub.)

For beer snobs, the place to go is **Fort George Brewery and Public House** (1483 Duane St., 503/325-7468, www.fortgeorgebrewery.com, 11am-11pm Sun.-Thurs., 11am-midnight Fri.-Sat., $8-12), whose powerful ales have won it a reputation as one of Oregon's top breweries. The regular pub grub is basic, but the pizzas served on the 2nd floor are excellent. There's free live music every Sunday evening.

Astoria's oldest brewpub, the **Astoria Brewing Company** (144 11th St., 503/325-6975, www.astoriabrewingcompany.com, 11am-8pm Sun.-Thurs., 11am-9pm Fri.-Sat., $9-15) is home to the Astoria Brewing Company, maker of excellent handcrafted microbrews, with a full bar available. The café is housed in a cavernous remodeled former waterfront warehouse, with good views of the river. The food is good basic pub grub: fish-and-chips, burgers (including seafood burgers), sandwiches, and salads.

The **Rogue Ales Public House** (100 39th St., 503/325-5964, 11am-8pm Sun.-Thurs., 11am-9pm Fri.-Sat., $9-18) is set inside a rather dark wood-plank structure atop a former cannery pier east of downtown in the Hanthorn Pier development, and offers

Astoria Goes to the Movies

In recent decades, the Victorian homes and ocean view in Astoria's hillside neighborhoods and the surrounding maritime settings have provided the backdrop for such fanciful modern sagas as *Free Willy I* and *II, Kindergarten Cop, Teenage Mutant Ninja Turtles III, Short Circuit, Come See the Paradise,* and *The Goonies.* The last movie, a cult favorite shot in 1985, concerns a gang of local kids hunting for pirate's treasure; happy memories of the movie continue to attract a steady stream of visitors looking for the locations used in the film. More recently, films shot in Astoria have gravitated toward horror, including *The Ring Two* and *Cthulhu,* a film based on the horror novels of H. P. Lovecraft. A guide to movie locations is available at the Oregon Welcome Center in Astoria, the Heritage Museum, Flavel House Museum, and the Warrenton Visitors Center. Stop by the **Oregon Film Museum** (732 Duane St., 503/325-2203, www.oregonfilmmuseum.org, 10am-5pm daily May-Sept., 11am-4pm daily Oct.-Apr., $6 adults, $2 ages 6-17), which ostensibly celebrates the various films shot in Oregon, but is mostly a paean to all things Goonie. The museum is housed in the old Clatsop County Jail (from 1914), which famously starred in *The Goonies* jailbreak scene.

excellent ales, plus burgers, pizza, and sandwiches. It's hard to get more Astorian than this, especially if you paddle up to the pier.

Reach Break Brewing (1343 Duane St., 503/468-0743, noon-8pm Sun.-Thurs., noon-9pm Fri., 11am-9pm Sat., 11am-8pm Sun.) has developed a delicious selection of wild yeast-powered sour beers as well as light *saisons* and more traditional Northwest IPAs. Reach Break doesn't have its own kitchen; instead it relies on a clutch of food carts ($8-13) parked outside to feed the hungry crowds, with both outdoor and indoor seating.

BARS

Befitting of a vintage fishing port, Astoria has lots of old bars and watering holes. As a tribute to Astoria's scrappy spirit, explore some of the city's classic bars. The **Portway** (422 W. Marine Dr., 503/325-2651) is the oldest bar in the oldest American settlement west of the Rockies. The present building dates from 1923, and it's loaded with character and characters. Directly under the bridge, the **Workers Tavern** (281 W. Marine Dr., 503/338-7291) is a classic old bar with a notable drink special: the Yucca. Also try the marvelously crispy onion rings. The **Labor Temple Café & Bar** (939 Duane St., 503/325-0801) is the oldest communal union hall in the Pacific Northwest and not to be missed.

The clientele is a mix of longtime union activists, 20-something artists, and rowdy young sailors, making for some interesting dynamics. The **Voodoo Room** (1114 Marine Dr., 503/325-2233, www.columbianvoodoo.com) is a dark and cluttered bar with hipsters, cocktails, and occasional live music.

The Arts

The handsome **Liberty Theatre** (1203 Commercial St., 503/325-5922, http://libertyastoria.org), whose colonnaded facades along Commercial and 12th Streets converge at the corner box office, is a vibrant symbol of Astoria's ongoing rejuvenation. The ornate Mediterranean-style building in the heart of downtown began its life in 1925 as a venue for silent films, vaudeville acts, and lectures. The theater continued as a first-run movie house, but after decades of neglect this grande dame was badly showing her age, and it looked as though the Liberty would eventually meet the sad wrecking-ball fate of so many fine old movie palaces. Fortunately, though, a nonprofit organization undertook efforts to restore the theater to its original elegance and equip it as a state-of-the-art performing arts center. The Liberty currently hosts concerts, recitals, theater, and other events, including the Astoria Music Festival.

Astoria's long-running *Shanghaied in*

Astoria (122 W. Bond St., 503/325-6104, www.shanghaiedinastoria.com, evening Thurs.-Sat. mid-July-mid-Sept., $10-20), based on the town's dubious distinction as a notorious shanghai port during the late 1800s, is a good old-fashioned melodrama. Chase scenes, bar fights, and a liberal sprinkling of Scandinavian jokes will have you laughing in between applauding the hero and booing the villain. Performed with gusto by the Astor Street Opry Company, the show has been running since 1985, and has spawned a number of related shows including a "junior" *Shanghaied in Astoria* for kids and the holiday season *Scrooged in Astoria.* Check the website for a growing roster of entertainment, including children's theater productions in March and April and other off-season productions from this lively troupe of thespians.

Cinema

The **Columbian Theater** (1102 Marine Dr., 503/325-3516, www.columbianvoodoo.com, usually 7pm, $4, $2 under age 13) sits adjacent to the Columbian Cafe and screens the big movies you may have missed a month earlier in their first run. Enjoy beer, wine, cocktails, pizza, and other munchies while you watch. **Astoria Gateway Cinema** (1875 Marine Dr., 503/338-6575) is a modern movie multiplex, showing the usual stuff, where you can pass an afternoon trying to forget the often dismal weather.

Festivals and Events

FISHER POETS GATHERING

Modeled after Elko, Nevada's popular Cowboy Poets Gathering, the **Fisher Poets Gathering** (www.fisherpoets.org) provides a forum in which men and women involved in the fishing and other maritime industries share their poems, stories, songs, and artwork in a convivial seaport setting. The annual late-February event, which dates back to 1998, draws writers and artists from up and down the Pacific coast and farther afield for readings, art shows, concerts, book signings, workshops, films, a silent auction, and other activities at pubs, galleries, theaters, and other venues around town.

Participation isn't limited to fisherfolk but extends to anyone with a connection to maritime activity. Themes range from the rigors (and humor) of life on the water to environmental issues. Admission ($15) covers all events for the weekend. For more details and a full schedule, check the website.

ASTORIA WARRENTON CRAB, SEAFOOD AND WINE FESTIVAL

The **Astoria Warrenton Crab, Seafood and Wine Festival** (Clatsop County Fairgrounds, 92937 Walluski Loop, 503/325-6311 or 800/875-6807, http://astoriacrabfest.com, 4pm-9pm Fri., 10am-8pm Sat., 11am-4pm Sun., $5-10 adults, free ages 12 and under), held the last weekend in April, is a hugely popular event that brings in crowds from miles around. Scores of booths feature a cornucopia of seafood and other eats, regional beers and Oregon wines, and arts and crafts. Activities include continuous entertainment, crab races, a petting zoo, and activities for kids. A traditional crab dinner caps off the evening. To get to the fairgrounds from Astoria, take Highway 202 for 4.5 miles to Walluski Loop and watch for signs. Parking is limited at the fairgrounds. It's smart to take the frequent shuttle that transports folks between the fairgrounds and park-and-ride lots, downtown, the Port of Astoria, and local hotels and campgrounds.

ASTORIA MUSIC FESTIVAL

A three-week classical music showcase in June, the **Astoria Music Festival** (1271 Commercial St., 503/325-9896, http://astoriamusicfestival.org) brings top-ranked classical musicians to the northern Oregon coast. Since its beginning in 2002, the festival has quickly grown in stature and now features three different operatic performances (usually in concert) and numerous symphonic and chamber performances each year. Most events are in the small, acoustically splendid Liberty Theater or the Clatsop Community College Performing Arts Center (Franklin Ave. and 16th St.).

The Long Beach Peninsula

If you've come as far as Astoria, at the edge of the continent and at the mouth of the Columbia River, you should consider crossing the soaring Astoria-Megler Bridge to explore sights on the Columbia's northern shore. There are both scenic and historical reasons to visit this remote corner of Washington State. The Lewis and Clark National and State Historical Parks aggregation includes a number of sites just across from Astoria in Washington, notably **Cape Disappointment State Park,** with views of the Columbia crashing into the ocean, as well as the Lewis and Clark Interpretive Center.

The **Long Beach Peninsula,** the thin sand spit just north of the mouth of the Columbia River, claims to have the world's longest beach. With 28 unbroken miles of beach, the boast has to be taken seriously. Like Seaside in Oregon, beach resorts at Seaview and Long Beach have a long pedigree, dating from the 1880s, when Portland families journeyed down the Columbia River by steamboat to summer at the coast. The bay side of the Long Beach sand spit creates **Willapa Bay,** known to oyster-lovers around the country for the excellent bivalves that grow in this shallow inlet, which is fed by six pristine rivers. Most of Willapa Bay is protected as a national wildlife refuge, and it's an excellent bird-watching site. **Oysterville,** a tiny village along the bay, stands largely unchanged since the 1880s, and the entire town has been placed on the National Register of Historic Places. The tip of the peninsula is preserved as 807-acre **Leadbetter Point State Park,** with informal hiking trails along both sandy beaches and the reedy bay.

SCANDINAVIAN MIDSUMMER FESTIVAL

The legacy of the thousands of Scandinavians who arrived to work in area mills and canneries in the late 19th and early 20th centuries is still strong in Astoria. For many locals, the summer's biggest event is the **Scandinavian Midsummer Festival** (503/325-6136, www.astoriascanfest.com, $8 adults, $3 ages 6-12), which usually takes place Friday-Sunday on the third weekend of June. Local Danes, Finns, Icelanders, Norwegians, and Swedes come together to celebrate their heritage; visitors and musicians from the old countries keep the festivities authentic. Costumed dancers weave around a flowered midsummer pole (a fertility rite), burn a bonfire to destroy evil spirits, and have tugs-of-war pitting Scandinavian nationalities against each other. Food, dancing, crafts, musical concerts, and a parade bring the whole town out to the Clatsop County Fairgrounds on Walluski Loop, just off Highway 202.

ASTORIA REGATTA WEEK

A tradition since 1894, **Astoria Regatta Week** (http://astoriaregatta.com) is considered the Pacific Northwest's longest-running festival. Held on the waterfront in mid-August, the five-day event kicks off with the regatta queen's coronation and reception. Attractions include live entertainment, a grand street parade, historic home tours, ship tours and boat rides, sailboat and dragon boat races, a classic car show, a salmon barbecue, arts and crafts, food booths, a beer garden, and a twilight boat parade.

SHOPPING

On Sundays between Mother's Day weekend and early October, follow local tradition and take a leisurely stroll up and down 12th Street between Marine Drive and Exchange Street for the **Astoria Sunday Market** (10am-3pm), where vendors offer farm-fresh produce, plants, crafts, and specialty foods.

A local store worth noting is **Finnware** (1116 Commercial St., 503/325-5720, www.finnware.com, 10am-5pm Mon.-Sat.,

11am-4pm Sun.), which stocks Scandinavian crystal and glassware, jewelry, books, and kitchen tools. This is a store that takes its Finnish roots seriously.

Art Galleries

Astoria has a well-deserved reputation as an art center, with many downtown storefronts now serving as art galleries. Not to miss is **RiverSea Gallery** (1160 Commercial St., 503/325-1270, http://riverseagallery. squarespace.com, 11am-5:30pm Mon.-Sat., 11am-4pm Sun.), with a large and varied selection of work by local painters, glass artists, jewelry makers, and craftspeople. For a more quixotic art scene, go to **Imogen Gallery** (240 11th St., 503/325-1566, http:// imogengallery.com, 11am-5pm Mon.-Tues. and Thurs.-Sat., 11am-4pm Sun.), dedicated to contemporary and conceptual art by local artists. **Lightbox Photographic Gallery** (1045 Marine Dr., 503/468-0238, http:// lightbox-photographic.com, 11am-5:30pm Tues.-Sat.) is the region's gallery for fine art photography. A special stop is **Ratz and Company** (260 10th St., 503/325-2035, www. ratzandcompany.com), which shows the work of Dave McMacken, an artist and graphic designer who was responsible for some of the great album covers of the 1970s and 1980s (think Frank Zappa). He now creates beautifully rendered, slightly unnerving images depicting the Pacific Northwest, though the incredible range of his commercial art is also available for sale at the gallery.

The second Saturday of each month is the **Astoria Art Walk** (5pm-9pm), when most galleries and shops in downtown stay open late.

Bookstores

Several bookstores in town invite serious browsing, buying, and intellectual stimulation. **Lucy's Books** (348 12th St., 503/325-4210, 10am-5:30pm Tues.-Sat., 11am-3pm Sun.) is a small but bighearted locally owned bookshop with an emphasis on Pacific Northwest regional subjects. On the next block, **Godfather's Books and Espresso** (1108 Commercial St., 503/325-8143, 9am-6pm daily) sells a mix of new and used books and has a case of excellent antique maps and prints depicting the Columbia River and north coast.

FOOD

Remember that in addition to options listed here, brewpubs also serve food. For riverfront dining, our favorite spot is **Buoy Beer Company,** listed in Nightlife under Brewpubs.

Pacific Northwest Cuisine

A good restaurant with an inspiring motto ("Eat well, laugh often, and love much") is the easygoing **T. Paul's Urban Cafe** (1119 Commercial St., 503/338-5133, http:// tpaulsurbancafe.com, 11am-9pm Mon.-Sat., $12-20). The menu of hip diner food with fresh Pacific Northwest twists includes towering turkey sandwiches, bay shrimp ceviche, Caribbean jerk quesadillas, prawn pasta, and clam chowder. Quesadillas are the specialty, with about a dozen innovative varieties served. T. Paul's has a second downtown location, ★ **The Supper Club** (360 12th St., 503/325-2545, http://tpaulssupperclub.com, 11am-9pm Mon.-Thurs., 11am-10pm Fri.-Sat., $15-32), with a wide-ranging menu, a rather swank dining room, and some of the most reliably delicious food in Astoria. Top choices are pasta dishes, burgers, salads, and fresh seafood. The tiny bar is the perfect spot for a cocktail.

As quirky and well loved as it is small, the **Columbian Cafe** (1114 Marine Dr., 503/325-2233, www.columbianvoodoo.com, 8am-2pm Mon.-Fri., 9am-2pm Sat.-Sun., $15-25, cash only) is an Astoria institution. The menu changes according to the season and the chef's whim (be daring and order the "chef's mercy") but generally includes a good selection of pastas, chilies, crepes, and fresh catch of the day, and always a selection of homemade garlic, jalapeño, and red-pepper jellies.

Breakfast is a highlight here. If this is your first visit to the Columbian Cafe, don't let the tiny, slightly seedy-looking venue put you off. Expect to be here for a while—the Columbian is not a fast-food dining experience.

Seafood

Settle in for some excellent seafood and river views at **Bridgewater Bistro** (20 Basin St., 503/235-6777, http://bridgewaterbistro.com, 11:30am-close Mon.-Sat., 11am-close Sun., $11-36), where you can graze on tapas (small plates menu 3pm-5pm) or order regular-size. The soaring ceiling and riverside setting of the historic building next to the Cannery Pier Hotel are almost as compelling as the food.

Although many locals just stop by **Albatross & Co.** (225 14th St., 503/741-3091, 5pm-11pm Tues.-Thurs., 5pm-midnight Fri.-Sat., $12-27) for an after-work drink, this low-key locavore spot is the place to go for fresh, local oysters and other seafood. The focused menu also features meats and vegetables from nearby Puget Island, in the Columbia River.

Indian

★ **Himani Indian Cuisine** (1044 Marine Dr., 503/325-8171, www.himaniic.com, lunch buffet 11am-3pm Sun.-Fri., dinner 5pm-9pm Sat.-Thurs. $13-20) serves a wide selection of Indian cuisine, with a specialty in southern Indian fare such as tandoori dishes (including tandoori salmon) and masala *dosa*. The naan breads are equally delicious. A buffet ($12) is available most days during lunch. Himani also serves food from its original stall at the Astoria Sunday Market. No alcohol is served.

Eastern European

There aren't a lot of Bosnian restaurants around, and the **Drina Daisy** (915 Commercial St., 503/338-2912, www.drinadaisy.com, 11am-3pm and 5pm-8pm Wed.-Sun., $11-23) is worth a stop to sample foods from an unfamiliar part of the world. The cuisine, which promises "a taste of Sarajevo," is a cross between Greek and Central European cooking. You can't go

wrong with the appetizers or salads, many of which come with smoked sausages and phyllo-wrapped goodies.

International

With the classiest dining room in Astoria, **Carruthers Restaurant** (1198 Commercial St., 503/975-5305, 11am-9pm Mon.-Thurs., 11am-11pm Fri.-Sat., 9am-5pm Sun., $18-29) is also on the city's busiest corner. This is a great spot for cocktails and appetizers before a show at the Liberty Theater; the all-day happy hour includes good blackened rockfish tacos and Thai-spiced brussels sprouts.

Bakeries and Cafés

At the collectively run ★ **Blue Scorcher Bakery Cafe** (1493 Duane St., 503/338-7473, www.bluescorcher.coop, 7am-2:30pm daily, $6-12), the motto is "delicious food, joyful work, strong community," and it's all true. Settle in with a tasty veggie sandwich (if the tempeh Reuben is on the menu, don't turn up your nose) and watch the Astorians—any one of whom would make an excellent new friend—come and go. A personal favorite are the cardamom almond rolls, an old-fashioned Swedish treat that's perfect with a cup of coffee on a brisk morning. A wide variety of freshly prepared dishes also appears seasonally, from nettle soup in spring to pumpkin-black bean chili in the fall. If it's all too healthy and wholesome for you, there's a brewpub next door.

Food Carts

Astoria features a number of food carts—there's a pod at **13th and Duane Streets** (in front of a handy brewpub for drinks) and another at **14th and Duane Streets.** Most notable is **Bowpicker Fish and Chips,** with really good fish-and-chips served out of a converted boat near the corner of Duane and 17th Streets.

Markets

In addition to the restaurants and cafés listed here, you'll find do-it-yourself options at local markets. Established in 1920 in a false-front clapboard building near the waterfront, **Josephson's Smokehouse** (106 Marine Dr., 503/325-2190, www.josephsons. com, 9am-6pm Mon.-Fri., 9:30am-6pm Sat., 10am-6pm Sun.) is Oregon's most esteemed purveyor of gourmet smoked fish, producing Scandinavian cold-smoked salmon without dyes or preservatives. On foggy days, there's nothing finer than a cup of Josephson's thick clam chowder. A good stop for fresh produce, health food, and deli items is the big new site of the **Astoria Co+op** (23rd St. and Marine Dr., 503/325-0027, 8am-8pm daily). To shop the daily catch, which can include Dungeness crab, wild salmon, halibut, albacore tuna, sardines, sole, and rockfish, go to **Warrenton Deep Sea Fish Market** (45 NE Harbor Place, Warrenton, 503/861-3911, 8:30am-5:30pm Mon.-Sat., 10am-4pm Sun.). It carries the largest selection of locally caught fish in the area, and you'll find a variety of smoked fish and seafood here as well. You can also browse the fresh options at the **Astoria Sunday Market** (12th St. between Marine Dr. and Exchange St., 10am-3pm Sun.).

ACCOMMODATIONS

The prices noted are for high season (summer) double-occupancy rooms. Rates fall by as much as half off-season. Also note that Astoria has many festival weekends, and on those occasions, rooms can be limited and prices high. In summer, plan your trip to avoid weekends if you're trying to save on lodging costs.

$50-100

Astoria's **Commodore** (258 14th St., 503/325-4747, http://commodoreastoria.com, $99-199) has simple but stylishly decorated rooms in a renovated downtown hotel. The least expensive rooms ("cabins") are just sleeping chambers with a sink and a flat-screen TV and DVD player, with shared toilets and handsome tiled showers at the end of the hallway. Suite rooms are larger and include a private bath. The Commodore is popular with hip young travelers, especially its coffee

shop on the ground floor. Be aware that the Commodore is on a busy downtown corner, so if traffic noise will bother you, bring earplugs.

Another vintage Astoria hotel made over into hip lodgings is the **Norblad Hotel and Hostel** (443 14th St., 503/325-6989, http:// norbladhotel.com, $34 hostel beds, $85-149 rooms and suites). Owned by the same local team that runs the Commodore, the Norblad has the same youthful, stylish vibe, with crisply designed "Euro-style" rooms, nearly all with baths down the hall. For the price, you can't beat the quality and the downtown location, though budget travelers looking for a real hostel experience might be disappointed with the perfunctory shared kitchen and lounge areas (though dozens of restaurants and pubs are just steps away).

$100-150

Clementine's Bed and Breakfast (847 Exchange St., 503/325-8005, www. clementines-bb.com, 2-night minimum, $139-289), a handsome two-story 1888 home built in the Italianate style, stands in good company across the street from the Flavel House and is itself on Astoria's Historic Homes Walking Tour. From the gardens around the house come the fresh flowers that accent the guest rooms and common areas and the herbs that spice the delicious gourmet breakfasts. In addition to five guest rooms, two suites are available in the **Moose Temple Lodge,** adjacent to the main house. Built in 1850, this is one of the oldest extant buildings in Astoria; it was the Moose Temple in 1900-1940 and later served as a Mormon church. Renovated with skylights, wood floors, fireplaces, small kitchens, and several beds, these suites are ideal for families or groups. Pets are welcome.

$150-200

Stay right downtown in the beautifully renovated ★ **Hotel Elliott** (357 12th St., 877/378-1924, www.hotelelliott.com, $179-279), a small boutique hotel that's an easy walk from good restaurants and the river. The Elliott first opened in 1924, and its current incarnation

has preserved much of the original charm of its Craftsman-era details, including the mahogany-clad lobby, handcrafted cabinetry, and wood and marble fireplaces. An original banner painted across the hotel's north side proudly proclaims, "Hotel Elliott—Wonderful Beds." The new Elliott has made a point of living up to this claim, with goose-down pillows, luxurious 440-thread-count Egyptian cotton sheets, feather beds, and top-of-the-line mattresses to ensure a memorable slumber. In addition to standard rooms, the Elliott has a variety of suites, including the five-room Presidential Suite with access to a rooftop garden. The rooftop is open to all and is a fine place to enjoy a glass of wine and the sunset.

The **Astoria Riverwalk Inn** (400 Industry St., 503/325-2013, $159-399), right above the west marina, isn't the fanciest place in town, but its many rooms have balconies over the harbor. The higher-priced rooms are decorated in a classy, subdued style, while others are bold and energetic. All come with great views and free breakfast.

Over $200
★ **Cannery Pier Hotel** (10 Basin St., 503/325-4996, www.cannerypierhotel.com, $329-399) is a modern luxury hotel on the former site of a historic cannery, jutting 600 feet out into the Columbia below the Astoria-Megler Bridge. The opulently furnished rooms have dramatic views, even from the shower; all rooms have balconies, fireplaces, and beautiful hardwood floors. Complimentary continental breakfast is included in the rates, as are hors d'oeuvres and wine in the afternoon. There's also a day spa in the hotel, plus a Finnish sauna, a fitness room, and a hot tub.

Camping
Families flock to **Fort Stevens State Park** (100 Peter Iredale Rd., Hammond, reservations 800/452-5687, www.oregonstateparks.org, year-round, $22 tent camping, $32-34 RV camping, $48-58 yurts, $93-103 cabins). With over 500 sites, the campground is the largest in the state park system, and it's incredibly popular. The park's many amenities and attractions make it the perfect base camp from which to take advantage of the region.

INFORMATION AND SERVICES
The **Astoria Chamber of Commerce** (111 W. Marine Dr., 503/325-6311 or 800/875-6807, www.travelastoria.com, 9am-5pm Mon.-Fri., 10am-5pm Sat.-Sun. May-Sept., 9am-5pm Mon.-Fri. Oct.-Apr.) operates the Oregon Welcome Center at its offices, providing an abundance of brochures and maps for visitors to Astoria and other destinations on the north Oregon coast and southwest Washington.

With 10,000 people, Astoria is the largest city and the media hub of the north coast. The local newspaper, the *Daily Astorian* (www.dailyastorian.com), is sold around town and worth a look. The free monthly *Hipfish* is a publication in the great tradition of the alternative press of the 1960s. Whether you agree with its take on regional politics or not, the thoughtful and lively articles and complete entertainment listings will enhance your visit to the north coast.

Throughout the north coast, **KMUN** (91.9 FM in Astoria and Seaside, 89.5 FM in Cannon Beach) is a public radio station with excellent community-based programming. Folk, classical, jazz, and rock music, public affairs, radio drama, literature readings, children's bedtime stories, and National Public Radio news will keep your dial set on this frequency. A sister station, KCPB, broadcasts classical music in addition to NPR news.

The **Astoria Post Office** is located in the Federal Building (750 Commercial St.). Useful numbers to know include the **county sheriff** (503/225-2061), the **U.S. Coast Guard** (2285 Airport Rd., Warrenton, 503/861-6220), and **Columbia Memorial Hospital** (2111 Exchange St., 503/325-4321).

1: Rogue Ales Public House **2:** Liberty Theatre

TRANSPORTATION

Northwest Point (888/846-4183, www.oregonpoint.com, $18) runs buses twice daily between the north coast and Portland's Union Station. Board the coach in Astoria at the downtown transit center (900 Marine Dr.). The bus also stops at Cannon Beach, Seaside, and Warrenton.

Car rentals are available from **Enterprise** (261 W. Marine Dr., 503/325-6500). For visitors willing to let go of their cars for a while, the Sunset Empire Transportation District, better known as **The Bus** (503/861-7433 or 800/776-6406, www.ridethebus.org), provides reasonably frequent transportation around Astoria and along the coast to Warrenton, Gearhart, Seaside, and Cannon Beach.

Seaside and Gearhart

Seaside is Oregon's quintessential, and oldest, family beach resort. The beach is long and flat, sheltered by a scenic headland, with a boardwalk winding through the dunes. Ice cream parlors, game arcades, eateries, and gift shops crowd shoulder to shoulder along the main drag, Broadway. The aromas of cotton candy and french fries lend a heady incense to the salt air, and the clatter of bumper cars and other amusements can induce sensory overload. Atlantic City it's not—thank goodness—but on a crowded summer day the town evokes the feeling of a carnival midway by the sea. During spring break, when Pacific Northwest high school and college students arrive, the town's population of 6,200 can quadruple almost overnight.

Neighboring Gearhart, a mainly residential community (pop. 1,100) just to the north, has a few lodgings away from the bustle of Seaside as well as a venerable 18-hole golf course.

Located along the Necanicum River, in the shadow of majestic Tillamook Head, Seaside has attracted tourists since the early 1870s, when transportation magnate Ben Holladay sensed the potential for a resort hotel near the water. But better transportation was needed to get customers to the place. At that time, the way to get to Seaside was first by boat from Portland down the Columbia River to Skipanon (now Warrenton), and from there by carriage south to Seaside. To speed the connection, Holladay later constructed a railroad line from Skipanon to Seaside.

To escape Portland's summer heat, families in the late 19th century would make the boat and railroad journey to spend their summer in Seaside. Most men would go back to Portland to work during the week, returning to the coast on Friday to visit the family. Every weekend the families would gather at the railroad station to greet the men, then see them off again for the trip back to Portland. It wasn't long before the train became known as the "Daddy Train." As roads between Portland and the coast were constructed, the car took over, and the railroad carried its last dad in 1939.

SIGHTS
The Promenade and Broadway

Sightseeing in Seaside means bustling up and down Broadway and strolling leisurely along the Prom. This three-mile-long concrete walkway, extending from Avenue U north to 12th Avenue, was initially constructed in 1908 to protect ocean properties from the waves. A pleasant walk alongside the beach, the boardwalk offers a fine vantage point from which to contemplate the sand, surf, frolicking beach lovers, and the massive contours of 1,200-foot-high Tillamook Head to the south. The Prom is also popular for jogging, bicycle and surrey riding, and in-line skating.

Midway along the Prom is the **Turnaround,** a concrete-and-brick traffic circle that is the western terminus of Broadway. A bronze statue of Lewis and Clark gazing ever seaward proclaims this point the

Seaside and Gearhart

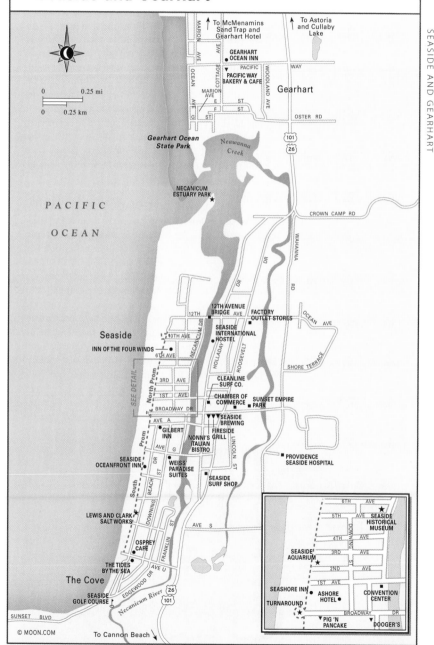

N

0   0.25 mi

0   0.25 km

To McMenamins
Sand Trap and
Gearhart Hotel

To Astoria
and Cullaby
Lake

MARION AVE

OCEAN AVE

COTTAGE AVE

PACIFIC WAY

WOODLAND AVE

GEARHART
OCEAN INN

PACIFIC WAY
BAKERY & CAFE

Gearhart

MARION AVE

E ST

F ST

G ST

ST

ST

OSTER RD

101
26

*Gearhart Ocean
State Park*

Neawanna
Creek

PACIFIC

OCEAN

NECANICUM
ESTUARY PARK ★

CROWN CAMP RD

DR

DR

WAHANNA RD

OCEAN AVE

SHORE TERRACE

12TH AVENUE
BRIDGE

12TH AVE

FACTORY
OUTLET STORES

Seaside

10TH AVE

SEASIDE
INTERNATIONAL
HOSTEL

INN OF THE FOUR WINDS

6TH AVE

NECANICUM DR

HOLLADAY

ROOSEVELT

North Prom

3RD AVE

1ST AVE

BROADWAY DR

CLEANLINE
SURF CO.

CHAMBER OF
COMMERCE

SUNSET EMPIRE
PARK

SEE DETAIL

AVE A

▼▼▼ SEASIDE
BREWING

Prom

GILBERT
INN

NONNI'S
ITALIAN
BISTRO

FIRESIDE
GRILL

AVE G

LINCOLN ST

SEASIDE
OCEANFRONT INN

South Prom

BEACH DR

WEISS'
PARADISE
SUITES

PROVIDENCE
SEASIDE HOSPITAL

SEASIDE
SURF SHOP

DOWNING

LEWIS AND CLARK
SALT WORKS

FRANKLIN ST

AVE S

OSPREY
CAFE

THE TIDES
BY THE SEA

The Cove

AVE U

SEASIDE
GOLF COURSE

EDGEWOOD DR

26
101

Necanicum River

SUNSET BLVD

© MOON.COM

To Cannon Beach ↓

6TH AVE

5TH

SEASIDE
HISTORICAL
MUSEUM ★

4TH

DOWNING ST

3RD AVE

AVE

SEASIDE
AQUARIUM ★

2ND AVE

1ST AVE

SEASHORE INN

TURNAROUND ★

ASHORE
HOTEL

CONVENTION
CENTER

BROADWAY

DR

PIG 'N
PANCAKE ▼

DOOGER'S

end of the trail for their expedition, though in fact they explored a bit farther south, beyond Tillamook Head. Eight blocks south of the Turnaround, between Beach Drive and the Prom, is a replica of the Lewis and Clark salt cairn.

Heading east from the Turnaround, Broadway runs 0.5 mile to Roosevelt Avenue (U.S. 101) through a dizzying gamut of tourist attractions, arcades, restaurants, and bars. Along Broadway, in a four-block area west of U.S. 101 and bordered by the Necanicum River, 1st Avenue, and Avenue A, you'll find some fancy Victorian frame houses, a few of the old buildings that survived the 1912 fire that destroyed much of the town.

Today, the most notable sight in this busy section of Seaside is the enormous $73.3 million WorldMark Seaside time-share condo development containing nearly 300 units. Condos in this outsize structure aren't available for rent directly from WorldMark, though vacation property rental companies can handle sublets.

Seaside Aquarium

Right on the Prom north of the Turnaround is the **Seaside Aquarium** (200 N. Promenade, 503/738-6211, www.seasideaquarium.com, 9am-7pm daily Mar.-Oct., 9am-5pm Wed.-Sun. Nov.-Feb., $8.50 adults, $7.25 seniors, $4.25 ages 6-13). It's not quite the Oregon Coast Aquarium (find that in Newport), but if you're not going to make it that far south, it's an okay introduction to sealife for young children. Back in the era of the Daddy Train, this place served as a natatorium, but was converted to its current use in 1937. Today the pool is filled with raucously barking seals. In addition, a hundred species of marinelife here include 20-ray sea stars, crabs, ferocious-looking wolf eels and moray eels, and octopuses.

Lewis and Clark Salt Works

Near the south end of the Prom at Lewis and Clark Way are the reconstructed **salt works** of Lewis and Clark. While camped at Fort Clatsop during the winter of 1805-1806, the captains sent a detachment south to find a place suitable for rendering salt from seawater. Their supply was nearly exhausted, and the precious commodity was a necessity for preserving and seasoning their food on the expedition's return journey. At the south end of present-day Seaside, five men built a cairn-like stone oven near a settlement of the

Seaside is a good spot to test-drive a surrey bike.

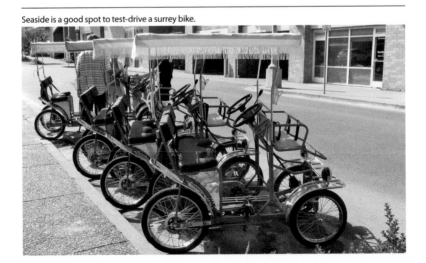

Clatsop and Killamox people and set about boiling seawater nonstop for seven weeks to produce 3.5 bushels (about 314 pounds) of salt for the trip back east.

RECREATION
Hiking

From the south end of Seaside, walk in the footsteps of Lewis and Clark on an exhilarating hike over Tillamook Head. In January 1806, neighboring Native Americans told of a beached whale lying several miles south of their encampment. William Clark and a few companions, including Sacajawea, set off in an attempt to find it and trade for blubber and whale oil, which fueled the expedition's lanterns. Climbing Tillamook Head from the north, the party crested the promontory. Clark was moved enough by the view to later write about it in his journal:

> I beheld the grandest and most pleasing prospect which my eyes ever surveyed. Immediately in front of us is the ocean breaking in fury. To this boisterous scene the Columbia with its tributaries and studded on both sides with the Chinook and Clatsop villages forms a charming contrast, while beneath our feet are stretched the rich prairies.

Today, you can experience the view that so impressed Clark on the **Tillamook Head National Recreation Trail,** which runs a little over six miles to Ecola State Park. Prior to setting out, you could arrange to have a friend drive south to Ecola's Indian Beach to pick you up at the end of this 3-5-hour trek. As you head up the forested trail on the north side of Tillamook Head, look back over the Seaside town site. In about 20 minutes, you'll be gazing down at the ocean from cliffs 1,000 feet above. A few hours later, you'll hike down onto Indian Beach.

To get to the trailhead from Seaside, drive south, following Avenue U past the golf course to Edgewood Street, and turn left; continue until you reach the parking lot at the end of the road.

Bicycling

Riding the beach on a fat-tired cruiser is great fun, and Seaside has a bumper crop of places that rent bicycles, as well as skates and surreys, all for similar rates, around $12-15 per hour for a bike. The **Prom Bike Shop** (622 12th Ave., 503/738-8251, http://prombikeshop. com, noon-5pm Wed.-Sun.) is a full-service bike shop. Rent cruisers, surreys, mopeds, and novelty bikes at **Wheel Fun Rentals** (151 Ave. A, 503/738-7212, 11am-sunset Mon.-Fri., 10am-sunset Sat.-Sun Memorial Day-Labor Day), with four locations in Seaside, this one closest to the boardwalk.

Wildlife-Watching

Bird-watchers gather at **Necanicum Estuary Park,** at the 1900 block of North Holladay Drive across the street from Seaside High School. Local students have built a viewing platform, stairs to the beach, a boardwalk, and interpretive signs. Great blue and green herons and numerous migratory bird species flock to the grassy marshes and slow tidal waters near the mouth of the Necanicum River. During the fall and winter, buffleheads and mergansers shelter in the estuary, while in summer the waters are often thronged with pelicans. Occasionally Roosevelt elk, black-tailed deer, river otters, beavers, mink, and muskrats can also be sighted.

Boating and Fishing

Just because you're smack-dab in the middle of a family resort town doesn't mean you can't enjoy some of nature's bounty: Anglers can reel in trout, salmon, and steelhead from the Necanicum River right in the center of downtown. The **12th Avenue Bridge** is a popular spot for fishing and crabbing.

Cullaby Lake, on the east side of U.S. 101 about four miles north of Gearhart, offers fishing for crappies, bluegills, perch, catfish, and largemouth bass. At 88 acres, Cullaby is the largest of the many lakes on the Clatsop Plains. Two parks on the lake, **Carnahan Park** and **Cullaby Lake County Park,** have boat ramps, picnic areas, and other facilities.

Cullaby is the only practical place to water-ski in the area.

Sunset Beach State Recreation Site, 0.5 mile west of U.S. 101 on Neacoxie Lake (also known as Sunset Lake), has a boat ramp, picnic tables, and a playground. Anglers come for warm-water fish species, plus the rainbow trout stocked in the spring. From Astoria, drive south 10 miles on U.S. 101 and turn west on Sunset Beach Road.

At **Quatat Park** (503/440-1548), beside the Necanicum River in downtown Seaside, rent kayaks, canoes, and pedal boats for exploring the waterway.

Surfing

The best surfing spot in the Seaside area is the beach just south of town, simply referred to as **The Cove,** directly north of Tillamook Head and reached from parking areas along Sunset Boulevard. While prevailing winds favor winter surfing rather than summer, this is in fact a popular destination year-round. Local surfers can be impatient with beginners, so this probably isn't a good spot for novices.

Seaside Surf Shop (1116 S. Roosevelt Dr., 503/717-1110, www.seasidesurfshop. com, 10am-6pm Mon.-Fri., 9am-6pm Sat., 9am-5pm Sun.) and **Cleanline Surf Co.** (60 N. Roosevelt Dr., 503/738-7888, www. cleanlinesurf.com, 9am-6pm daily) rent and sell surfboards as well as wetsuits, boots, and flippers; Cleanline Surf also offers instruction. **Northwest Women's Surf Camps** (503/440-5782, www.nwwomenssurfcamps. com) will give you a bit of land training (the camp includes yoga to get you limbered up and in the right frame of mind) and then accompany you into the waves. Although most of its programs are designed for women, co-ed clinics for surfing and bodyboarding are also offered.

Swimming

Swimming at Seaside's beach isn't exactly comfortable, unless you're used to the North Sea. Gearhart boasts a quieter beach than Seaside's, although the water is every bit as cool. Warm-blooded swimmers can head to the facilities at **Sunset Empire Park** (1140 E. Broadway, Seaside, 503/738-3311, daily), which includes three pools, waterslides, a 15-person hot tub, and fitness equipment.

Golf

The British-links-style course at **Gearhart Golf Links** (1157 N. Marion St., Gearhart, 503/738-3538, www.gearhartgolflinks.com, $85 for 18 holes in summer) was established in 1892, making it Oregon's oldest, and one of the oldest west of the Mississippi River.

ENTERTAINMENT AND EVENTS

Seaside predates any other town on the Oregon coast as a place built with good times in mind. A zoo and racetrack were among Seaside's first structures, and arcades are still thriving near the foot of Broadway.

The **Seaside Brewing Company** (851 Broadway, 503/717-5451, http:// seasidebrewery.com, 8am-9pm Mon.-Thurs., 8am-10pm Fri.-Sun., $13-15) makes great ales and has a handsome location in Seaside's old 1914 city hall and jail. In addition to the usual pub burgers, sandwiches, and pizza, Seaside Brewing serves breakfast. At the Gearhart Golf Links, the old clubhouse now houses the McMenamins' **Sand Trap Pub** (1157 N. Marion Ave., 503/717-8159, 7am-11pm Sun.-Thurs., 7am-1am Fri.-Sat., $13-29); it has been decorated with the McMenamins' trademark whimsical artwork and serves the local chain's decent (not great, but always edible) upscale pub food. Free live music is featured in the pub most Friday evenings, open to all ages.

The town celebrates the **Fourth of July** with a parade, a picnic and social at the Seaside Historical Society Museum (570 Necanicum Dr.), and a big fireworks show on the beach. In early September, **Wheels and Waves** (503/717-1914) brings over 500 classic hot rods and custom cars (1965 and earlier, please) to downtown and the **Civic and Convention Center** (1st Ave. at Necanicum Dr.).

FOOD

While a stroll down Broadway might have you thinking that cotton candy, corn dogs, and saltwater taffy are the staples of Seaside cuisine, several eateries here can satisfy more refined palates as well. But there's no disputing the fact that Seaside, despite being one of Oregon's most popular Pacific-front towns, is not a mecca of fine dining.

Should the frenetic ambience of Seaside on a holiday weekend begin to wear thin, try Gearhart's ★ **Pacific Way Bakery and Cafe** (601 Pacific Way, Gearhart, 503/738-0245, www.pacificwaybakery-cafe.com, bakery 7am-1pm Thurs.-Mon., restaurant 11am-3:30pm and 5pm-9pm Thurs.-Mon., dinner $14-32, dinner reservations recommended). Pasta, crusty pizzas, and seafood dishes (including thick seafood cioppino) as well as Dungeness crab sandwiches with aioli pop up at lunch and dinner. Rib-eye steak and local razor clams are other frequent dinner-time highlights in the surprisingly urbane little café hidden behind a rustic old storefront. In the morning, the bakery side of the operation is *the* place to be for coffee and pastries.

Dooger's (505 Broadway, 503/738-3773, http://doogersseafood.com, 11am-9pm daily, $16-31), which also has an outlet in Cannon Beach, is a popular Broadway mainstay known for its clam chowder. Although it's kind of a frumpy-looking place, it serves good seafood. Local clams and oysters, fresh Dungeness crab legs, sautéed shrimp, and marionberry cobbler are the basis of Dooger's reputation.

The menu at **Nonni's Italian Bistro** (831 Broadway, 503/738-4264, www.nonnisitalianbistro.com, 3pm-9pm Thurs.-Mon., $13-30) extends from meatball sandwiches to crab- and salmon-rich cioppino, with a selection of pasta dishes in between. This small and popular restaurant doesn't accept reservations, so it's wise to dine on the early side.

If you're traveling with kids, you'll almost inevitably end up eating at **Pig 'N Pancake** (323 Broadway, 503/738-7243, www.pignpancake.com, 6am-8pm Sun.-Thurs., 6am-9pm Fri.-Sat., $8-13), where the Swedish pancakes and crab-and-cheese omelets are tops at breakfast, and the Frisbee-size cinnamon rolls will launch your blood sugar to new heights.

An excellent destination for breakfast and brunch is the **Osprey Café** (2281 Beach Dr., 503/739-7054, 7:30am-3pm Thurs.-Tues., $9-14), with breakfast all day (classic egg dishes plus Mexican fare and Indonesian *nasi goreng* as well) and sandwiches for lunch. The Osprey is south of downtown, near the end of the boardwalk, near some of Seaside's more affordable hotels.

ACCOMMODATIONS

Whatever your price range, you'll have to reserve ahead for a room in Seaside during the summer and on weekends and holidays (especially spring break). If you do, chances are you'll be able to find the specs you're looking for, given the area's array of lodgings and over 1,800 hotel rooms. The **Seaside Visitors Bureau** (www.seasideor.com) has a helpful website with comprehensive listings and a handy booking engine for last-minute rooms.

Generally speaking, there are three lodging areas in Seaside. First are several modern motels along busy U.S. 101, about eight blocks from the beach. If you're just passing through or waited too long to call for reservations, these offer inexpensive rooms, but little in the way of beachside charm. A second grouping of hotels is in the center of Seaside, along the Necanicum River. These have a quieter riverside setting but still aren't beachfront (though you won't have to cross U.S. 101 to get to the beach). Finally, there are numerous hotels that face directly onto the beach or are just a short stumble to the strand. Even here, there's quite a difference in price between rooms that face the beach and those that face the parking lot.

Under $50

The cheapest place in town is the quite nice **Seaside International Hostel** (930 N. Holladay Dr., 503/738-7911, www.seasidehostel.net, dorm-style bunk $40 pp, private rooms $79-99), with special touches such as kayak rentals. Unlike many hostels, it doesn't close down during the day, and there's no curfew at night. There's an espresso bar on-site, and the Necanicum River runs through the backyard. Close by is the Necanicum Estuary Park.

$100-150

There's a clutch of motels south of the Broadway-Prom axis that offer easy beach access at fair prices—and a much quieter beach-front experience than in the town center. **The Tides by the Sea** (2316 Beach Dr., 503/738-6317 or 800/548-2846, www.thetidesbythesea.com, $123-281) is a well-located older motel that has converted its large guest rooms and cottages into condos. About a quarter of the units face onto the Prom, but those that don't are just seconds away from the beach. If you can live without an ocean view, you'll save a bundle here. Each of the units is different, but most have kitchens and fireplaces. In high season, there is a two-night minimum stay.

Farther north, the **Tradewinds Condo Hotel** (1022 N. Promenade, 503/738-9468, www.seaside-tradewinds.com, $149-169) doesn't look like much from the outside, but the rooms are very nice and represent some of the best values in Seaside, particularly off-season, when room prices can drop by half. All the rooms are individually decorated and come in different configurations, from studios with kitchenettes to one-bedroom condos with full kitchens and living areas. Book well in advance: This is a popular spot.

$150-200

Seaside's most stylish rooms are at the ★ **Inn of the Four Winds** (820 N. Promenade, 503/738-9524 or 800/818-9524, www.innofthefourwinds.com, $199-329). This 14-room boutique hotel has comfortable rooms furnished with taste and panache. Each guest room has a microwave, a coffeemaker, a fridge, an MP3 player, a gas fireplace, and a deck or balcony with an ocean view. Best of all, the inn faces directly onto the beach eight blocks north of the frenetic Broadway strip.

A charmingly refurbished lodging just three short blocks from the beach, ★ **Weiss' Paradise Suites** (741 S. Downing St., 503/738-6691, www.seasidesuites.com, $179-199) is south of the Broadway action but offers homey, upgraded units with lots of extras, including full kitchens, decks, two TVs, free DVDs, and robes. If you're looking for a cottage rental, ask about the two vacation houses available from this proprietor.

While motels dominate the lodging scene in Seaside, a few B&Bs and small inns offer an alternative. The **Gilbert Inn** (341 Beach Dr., 503/738-9770 or 800/410-9770, www.gilbertinn.com, $189-209) is a well-preserved 1892 Queen Anne just a block south of Broadway and a block from the beach. Period furnishings adorn the 11 guest rooms, which all have private baths, down comforters, and other nice touches, including breakfast. The 3rd-floor "Garret" sleeps up to four in a queen and two twin beds, with ocean views from the dormer window. All guests must be 18 or older.

If you're looking for a hotel with character, consider **Ashore Hotel** (125 Oceanway, 503/568-7506, $152-217), a fairly basic older motor-court hotel that's been renovated with a hip, urban industrial vibe. All the rooms are dog-friendly, and there are free bikes to borrow, a sauna and saltwater soaking pool, and a small café and bar.

Just north of the Necanicum River's mouth, Gearhart offers a respite from the bustle of Seaside. The ★ **Gearhart Ocean Inn** (67 N. Cottage St., Gearhart, 503/738-7373, www.gearhartoceaninn.com, $170-375) offers a choice of 12 New England-style wooden cottages with comforters, wicker chairs, and throw rugs, and the beaches are a short walk away. The two-story deluxe units have kitchens and hardwood floors. Pets are allowed in some units. Especially during the off-season, this spruced-up old motor court is one of the best values on the north coast. Also in Gearhart is the ★ **Gearhart Hotel** (1157 N. Marion Ave., Gearhart, 503/717-8159 or 855/846-7583, $185-270), a boutique hotel developed out of the historic Gearhart Golf Links clubhouse by the McMenamins local chain of hotels and breweries. It has all the trademark comfortable funkiness of other McMenamins properties, with the added benefits of sitting on the oldest golf course in Oregon and Pacific beaches just across the street. Rooms have private baths (though in the cheapest ones you'll sleep in a bunk bed), and there's a lively pub on the main floor.

Over $200

The rooms at **Seashore Inn** (60 N. Promenade, 503/738-6368 or 888/738-6368, www.seashoreinnor.com, $159-369) are right in the thick of it along the Promenade. Half the guest rooms face the beach, but half don't. These rooms are just steps from the beach but are a fraction of the cost of rooms on the other side of the building. All guest rooms have microwaves and mini-fridges, and some have full kitchens and balconies. There's also an indoor pool in case the weather turns foul.

Vacation Rentals

A good option for many travelers is one of the several dozen vacation rentals. Options range from tiny cottages for less than $100 per night (minimum stays are often required, especially in summer) to large homes that can host groups of 10-12. Check with the **Seaside Visitors Bureau** (7 N. Roosevelt St., 503/738-3097 or 888/306-2326, www.seasideor.com, 8am-5pm daily), or contact **Beachhouse Vacation Rentals** (503/738-9068, www.beachhouse1.com) or **Oceanside Vacation Rentals** (503/738-7767 or 800/840-7764, www.oceanside1.com).

INFORMATION AND SERVICES

The **Seaside Visitors Bureau** (7 N. Roosevelt St., 503/738-3097 or 888/306-2326, www.seasideor.com) is open 8am-5pm daily. **Providence Seaside Hospital** (725 S. Wahanna Rd., 503/717-7000) has 24-hour service and an emergency room.

GETTING THERE

Sunset Empire Transportation District operates **The Bus** (503/861-7433 or 800/776-6406, www.ridethebus.org), serving Cannon Beach, Seaside, Astoria-Warrenton, and points between. **Northwest Point** (888/846-4183, www.oregon-point.com, $17) buses pass through twice daily on their run between Portland and Astoria.

Cannon Beach and Vicinity

In 1846, the USS *Shark* met its end on the Columbia River Bar. The ship broke apart, and a section of deck bearing cannons and an iron capstan drifted south, finally in 1894 washing ashore south of the current city limits at Arch Cape. And so this town got its name, which it adopted in 1922. In the winter of 2008, during an especially low tide, two additional cannons were revealed. After a thorough study by historians and archivists at Texas A&M University, the cannons are now on display at Astoria's Columbia River Maritime Museum.

In 1873, stagecoach and railroad tycoon Ben Holladay helped create Oregon's first coastal tourist mecca, Seaside, while ignoring its attractive neighbor in the shadow of Haystack Rock. In the 20th century, Cannon Beach evolved into a bohemian alternative to the hustle and bustle of the family-oriented resort scene to the north. Before the recent era of development, this place was a quaint backwater attracting laid-back artists, summer-home residents, and the overflow from Seaside.

Today, the low-key charm and atmosphere conducive to artistic expression have in some part been quashed by development and the attendant massive visitor influx and price

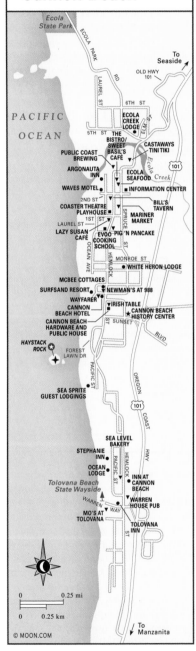

Cannon Beach

Ecola State Park

PACIFIC OCEAN

To Seaside

To Manzanita

© MOON.COM

increases. While such vital signs as a first-rate theater, a good bookstore, cheek-by-jowl art galleries, and fine restaurants are still in ample evidence, your view of them from the other side of the street might be blocked by a convoy of giant SUVs.

Nonetheless, the broad three-mile stretch of beach dominated by the impressive monolith of Haystack Rock still provides a contemplative experience. And if you're patient and resourceful enough to find a space for your wheels (try the free municipal lot one block east of the main street), the finest gallery-hopping, crafts, and shopping on the coast await. Wood shingles and understated earth tones dominate the architecture of tastefully rendered galleries, bookstores, and bistros. The city is small enough for strolling, and its location, removed from U.S. 101, spares it the kind of traffic blight seen on the main drags of other coastal tourist towns.

SIGHTS

★ Haystack Rock

Haystack Rock looms large above the long, broad beach. This is the third-tallest sea stack in the state, measuring 235 feet high. As part of the Oregon Islands National Wildlife Refuge, it has wilderness status and is off-limits to climbing. Puffins and other seabirds nest on its steep faces, and intertidal organisms thrive in the tide pools around the base. The surrounding tide pools, within a radius of 300 yards from the base of the monolith, are designated a "marine garden"; they are open to exploration, but with strict no-collecting (of anything) and no-harassment (of any living organisms) protections in effect. Flanking the monolith are two rock formations known as the Needles. These spires had two other counterparts at the turn of the 20th century that have gradually been leveled by weathering and erosion. Old-timers will tell you that the government dynamited a trail to the top of Haystack in 1968 to keep people off this bird rookery. It also reduced the number of intrepid hikers trapped on the rock at high tide.

Volunteers from the **Haystack Rock Awareness Program** (503/436-8060) are often on the beach with displays, spotting scopes, and answers to many of your questions. Spend some time chatting with these folks, but don't forget to listen to the beach's own distinctive voices. You can't miss the cacophony of seabirds at sunset and, if you listen closely, the winter phenomenon of "singing sands" created by wind blowing over the beach.

Beach access is available at the west end of any public east-west street. From downtown, Harrison Street works well; south of downtown, Tolovana Beach Wayside has a large parking area and easy beach access.

Ecola State Park

Ecola State Park (off U.S. 101, 800/551-6949, www.oregonstateparks.org, $5 day-use) is two miles north of Cannon Beach. Thick conifer forests line the access road to Ecola Point. This forested cliff has many trails leading down to the water. The view south takes in Haystack Rock and the overlapping peaks of the Coast Range extending to Neahkahnie Mountain. This is one of the most photographed views on the coast. Out to sea, the sight of sea lions basking on surf-drenched rocks (mid-Apr.-July) or migrating gray whales (Dec. and Mar.) and orcas (May) are seasonal highlights.

From Ecola Point, a steep, narrow road and a similarly steep trail lead north to horseshoe-shaped **Indian Beach,** a favorite with surfers. From Indian Beach, the 2.5-mile Clatsop Loop Trail goes up Tillamook Head, considered by Lewis and Clark the region's most beautiful viewpoint. Ambitious hikers can do the first half of the loop, then continue another four miles north to Seaside.

The name Ecola means "whale" in Chinook and was first used as a place-name by William Clark, referring to a creek in the area. Lewis and Clark journals note a 105-foot beached whale found somewhere within present-day Ecola Park's southern border at

Crescent Beach. This area represents the southernmost extent of Lewis and Clark's coastal Oregon travels.

Saddle Mountain State Natural Area

A good reason to head east from Cannon Beach is the hike up 3,283-foot Saddle Mountain at **Saddle Mountain State Natural Area** (off U.S. 26, 800/551-6949, www.oregonstateparks.org, free). On a clear day, hikers can see some 50 miles of Oregon and Washington coastlines, including the Columbia River. Also possible are spectacular views of Mounts Rainier, St. Helens, and Hood, and miles of clear-cuts. On the upper part of the trail, plant species that pushed south from Alaska and Canada during the last ice age still thrive. The cool, moist climate here keeps them from dying out as they did at lower elevations. Some early blooms include pink coast fawn lily, monkeyflower, wild rose, wood violet, bleeding heart, oxalis, Indian paintbrush, and trillium. Cable handrails provide safety on the narrow final 0.25-mile trail to the summit.

To get to the trailhead, take U.S. 26 from its junction with U.S. 101 for 10 miles and turn left on the prominently signed Saddle Mountain Road. (Although it's paved, this road is not suitable for RVs or wide-bodied vehicles.) After seven twisting miles, you'll come to the trailhead of the highest peak in this part of the Coast Range. The trail itself is steep, gaining more than 1,600 feet in 2.5 miles. Wet conditions can make the going difficult (allow four hours round-trip), and the scenery en route is not always exceptional unless you look down for the lovely May-August wildflower display; the view from the top is worth the climb.

The campground at Saddle Mountain is tiny and rustic and offers a secluded option for campers not attracted to the busy family scene at nearby Fort Stevens State Park.

Beaches

Stunning beaches don't end with Cannon Beach. Sandy expanses stretch seven miles

south to the Arch Cape tunnel on U.S. 101, indicating the entrance to Oswald West State Park. Several of these beaches are reached via state park waysides. As you head south, views of **Hug Point State Recreation Site** (off U.S. 101, 800/551-6949, www.oregonstateparks.org, free) and pristine beaches will have you ready to pull over. In summer, this can be a good escape from the crowds at Cannon Beach. Time your visit to coincide with low tide, when all manner of marinelife will be exposed in tidal pools. Also at low tide, you may see remains of an 800-foot-long Model T-size road blasted into the base of Hug Point, an early precursor to U.S. 101. The cliffs are gouged with caves and crevasses that also invite exploring, but be mindful of the tides so that you don't find yourself stranded. Hug Point got its name in the days when stagecoaches used the beach as highway; they had to dash between the waves, hugging the jutting headland to get around.

RECREATION
Bicycling
Family Fun Cycles (1160 S. Hemlock, 503/436-2247, 10am-6pm Tues.-Sun., $20 for 90 minutes) rents all manner of bikes, including mountain bikes, road bikes, beach cruisers, and three-wheeled recumbent "fun cycles," which zip up and down the hard-packed sand when the tide is out.

Horseback Riding
Sea Ranch Stables (415 N. Fir St., 503/436-2815, 9am-4:30pm daily mid-June-Labor Day, 9am-4:30pm Sat.-Sun. mid-May-mid-June, $95-140), at an RV park off U.S. 101 near the north entrance to Cannon Beach, offers a number of 1-2-hour guided rides, including sunset rides. Rides to Haystack Rock start at 9am, before the beach gets crowded.

Surfing
The area around Cannon Beach has several good surfing beaches. The most popular, and

1: Haystack Rock 2: Indian Beach at Ecola State Park

the best bet for beginners, is **Short Sands Beach,** at the end of the trail to the beach at Oswald West State Park, south of Arch Cape. It's a bit of a hike down to the beach, but the sheltered cove is a great place to spend the day, even if you're just bobbing around in the waves.

Another good spot for somewhat more advanced surfers (and surf kayakers) is **Indian Beach** at **Ecola State Park** (off U.S. 101, 800/551-6949, www.oregonstateparks.org, $5 day-use). Rent a board and wetsuit at **Cleanline Surf Co.** (171 Sunset Blvd., 503/436-9726, 9am-7pm daily).

ENTERTAINMENT
Brewpubs
Bill's Tavern (188 N. Hemlock St., 503/436-2202, 11:30am-10pm daily, bar open later, $7-13), once a legendary watering hole, is now a more traditional brewpub. Sweet thick onion rings, good fries, one-third-pound burgers, sautéed prawns, and grilled oysters are on the menu.

Realize that you've left your flashlight at home? And by the way, ready for a beer? Known locally as the "Screw and Brew," **Cannon Beach Hardware and Public House** (1235 S. Hemlock St., 503/436-4086, www.cannonbeachhardware.com, 10am-10pm Thurs.-Tues., $11-20) is a large hardware store with good food (the fish-and-chips are worth ordering, even at $20), local beers, and a fun, casual vibe.

Farther south near Tolovana, the **Warren House Pub** (3301 S. Hemlock St., 503/436-1130, 11:30am-1am Wed.-Mon., 4pm-1am Tues., $15-36) serves local beers from Bill's Tavern, but in an English pub setting. The menu includes good smoked ribs, burgers, and seafood; in summer the backyard beer garden is a lovely spot to relax. Kids are allowed on the restaurant side of the pub.

The **Public Coast Brewing Co.** (264 3rd St., 503/436-0285, http://publiccoastbrewing.com, noon-9pm daily, $13-16) is a block away from busy downtown Cannon Beach, but this spacious brewpub offers good food and excellent beers at good prices. Along with burgers, you can find fish tacos and fish-and-chips. A dozen beers (plus a house-brewed root beer) are usually on tap; the '67 Blonde Ale commemorates the 1967 Oregon Beach Bill, which ensured that Oregon's entire coastline remains open to the public.

The Arts

Going strong since 1972, the **Coaster Theatre Playhouse** (108 N. Hemlock St., 503/436-1242, www.coastertheatre.com, $20-25) stages a varied bill of musicals, dramas, mysteries, comedies, concerts, and other entertainment. It's open year-round in a building that started in the 1920s as a skating rink-turned-silent movie house.

Festivals and Events

The half-dozen or so other sand-sculpting contests that take place on the Oregon coast pale in comparison to Cannon Beach's annual **Sandcastle Contest** (503/436-2623, late June, call to confirm dates). In 1964 a tsunami washed out a bridge, and the isolated residents of Cannon Beach organized the first contest as a way to amuse their children. Now in its sixth decade, this is the state's oldest and most prestigious competition of its kind. Tens of thousands of spectators show up to watch 1,000-plus competitors fashion their sculptures with the aid of buckets, shovels, squirt guns, and any natural material found on the beach. The resulting sculptures are often amazingly complex and inventive. This event is free to spectators, but entrants pay a fee. Recent winners included Egyptian pyramids and a gigantic sea turtle. This collapsible art show usually coincides with the lowest-tide Saturday in June and takes place north of Haystack Rock. Building begins in the early morning; winners are announced at noon.

Writers, singers, composers, painters, and sculptors take over the town for the **Stormy Weather Arts Festival** (503/436-2623), usually held the first weekend of November. Events include music in the streets, plays, a Saturday afternoon art walk, and the Quick

Draw, in which artists have one hour to paint, complete, and frame a piece while the audience watches. The art is then sold by auction.

SHOPPING

Besides the beach, much of the attraction of Cannon Beach is window shopping up and down Hemlock Street, which, in addition to galleries, is lined with clothing stores and gift shops. Cannon Beach supports a fine kite store, **Once Upon a Breeze** (240 N. Spruce St., 503/436-1112, 10am-6pm daily) and one of the better bookstores on the coast, the **Cannon Beach Book Company** (130 N. Hemlock St., 503/436-1301, http://cannonbeachbooks.com, 10:30am-6:30pm daily); it's the place to pick up regional titles or a good novel (lots of mysteries) for that rainy weekend.

Art Galleries

Cannon Beach has long attracted artists and artisans, and here art lovers and shoppers will find nearly two dozen galleries and shops with high-quality works. Most of the Cannon Beach galleries and boutiques are concentrated along Hemlock Street, where you can hardly swing a Winsor & Newton No. 12 hog-bristle brush without hitting one. Not surprisingly, the seashore itself is the subject and inspiration of many works you'll see here, with Haystack Rock frequently depicted in various media. The **Cannon Beach Information Center** (201 E. 2nd St., 503/436-2623, www.cannonbeach.org, 11am-5pm Mon.-Sat., 10am-4pm Sun.) lists all the galleries in town on its website, or you can just stroll and discover them for yourself.

At the north end of town, **Northwest by Northwest Gallery** (232 N. Spruce St., 503/436-0741, www.nwbynwgallery.com, 11am-6pm daily) showcases photography, painting, sculpture, and ceramics and glass by noted regional artists. **White Bird Gallery** (251 N. Hemlock St., 503/436-2681, www.whitebirdgallery.com, 11am-5pm daily, call for winter hours), founded in 1971 and one of Cannon Beach's oldest galleries, casts a wide net with paintings, sculpture, prints, photography, glass, ceramics, and jewelry. Nearby, the **Bronze Coast Gallery** (224 N. Hemlock St., 503/436-1055, www.bronzecoastgallery. com, 10am-5pm daily) shows both traditional Western bronzes and innovative bronze works and paintings that may appeal to those who aren't crazy about traditional Western art. In midtown, **Icefire Glassworks** (116 E. Gower St., 503/436-2359, 10am-5pm Thurs.-Mon.) is a working glass studio where you can watch glassblowers and artists shape their work and then shop for unique pieces in the gallery.

DragonFire Gallery (123 S. Hemlock St., 503/436-1533, www.dragonfirestudio.com, 10am-6pm Mon.-Sat., 10am-5pm Sun.) shows the work of a wide variety of artists.

FOOD
Pacific Northwest Cuisine
Whether or not you're staying at the **Stephanie Inn** (2740 S. Pacific St., 503/436-2221 or 855/977-2444, www.stephanie-inn. com, 5pm-9pm daily, $45-50), you are welcome to join guests in the dining room for creative Pacific Northwest cuisine (reservations required for nonguests). The atmosphere boasts mountain views, open wood beams, and a river-rock fireplace. Since guests get first shot at tables, those staying elsewhere should reserve well ahead of time.

The Irish Table (1235 S. Hemlock St., 503/436-0708, www.theirishtable.com, 5:30pm-9pm Fri.-Tues., $25-30) makes the most of the Pacific Northwest bounty and hearty Irish cooking traditions, with meat pastries, grilled salmon, braised mussels, and variations on local lamb, including Irish lamb stew. The bar offers a wide selection of Scotch and Irish whiskies, plus Irish ales.

Seafood
Somewhat oddly, few of Cannon Beach's top restaurants have a view of the beach, so if excellent vistas of Haystack Rock and breaking waves are important to you, call to reserve a table at **The Wayfarer** (1190 Pacific Dr., 503/436-1108, www.wayfarer-restaurant.

com, 8am-9pm daily, dinner $34-42), tucked above a beach entrance at Gower Street. The food, which is good but not as memorable as the views, features seafood main courses and classic steaks. The lounge here is a good spot for a drink.

New American
While it's not a traditional restaurant, the **EVOO Cannon Beach Cooking School** (188 S. Hemlock, 503/436-8555, http://evoo. biz, cooking classes 6pm-9pm daily, $149 pp) is one of Cannon Beach's favorite "dinner theaters," where a small group of guests watch their meals cooked before their eyes. Dinners focus on seasonal ingredients and include a starter plus a three-course dinner, dessert, and one glass of wine. You don't need to help prepare the food, though special "hands-on" dinners are sometimes offered. Check the website for occasional midday lunch classes ($89).

Southern
Castaways (316 N. Fir St., 503/436-4444, 5pm-9pm Wed.-Sun., $22-29) describes its cooking as global, but many of the best dishes spring from Creole or New Orleans traditions. Several dishes are based on local seafood, such as Caribbean curried prawns and Bahamian crusted mahimahi. This is a busy spot, also popular for exotic cocktails.

International
Cozy and refined, **The Bistro** (263 N. Hemlock St., 503/436-2661, www. thebistrocannonbeach.com, 5pm-8:30pm Wed.-Sun., $20-25) is tucked back in a maze of shops and gardens in downtown Cannon Beach. The menu reflects international flavors, while the atmosphere is charmingly country French. The cioppino seafood stew is a wonderful blend of Pacific Northwest fish and shellfish prepared with Asian zest, and the locally sourced pork chops, served with goat milk polenta and Italian *agrodolce* sauce, are out of this world. The dining room is truly tiny and the food superlative, so reservations are mandatory.

Newman's at 988 (988 S. Hemlock St., 503/436-1151, www.newmansat988.com, 5pm-9pm daily July-mid-Sept., 5pm-9pm Tues.-Sun. Oct.-Nov. and May-June, 5pm-9pm Tues.-Sat. Dec.-Apr., $26-33) is a good special-occasion restaurant in a tiny house, with an elegant atmosphere and excellent food. The chef-owner takes great pride in using fresh local ingredients to prepare seasonal menus with French and Italian influences, featuring such dishes as seared duck breast with foie gras and truffle oil or grilled portabella mushroom with spinach, tomato, gorgonzola, and carrot juice.

Breakfast and Lunch

If all you need is excellent coffee and delicious fresh-baked goods, go to **Sea Level Bakery** (3116 S. Hemlock St., 503/436-4254, 7am-5pm daily, $4-12), where you'll find great bread for picnics, plus pastries and lunches that include a charcuterie plate, soups, quiche, and sandwiches.

Markets

If you're on a budget or renting a cottage, find fixings at the **Mariner Market** (139 N. Hemlock St., 503/436-2442, 8am-9pm Sun.-Thurs., 8am-10pm Fri.-Sat.), a dimly lit old grocery that's fully stocked with fresh meat, fruit, vegetables, and deli items. At the south end of town, **Fresh Foods** (3401 S. Hemlock St., 503/436-0945, 6:30am-10pm daily) has basic needs, tilted toward the gourmet end, with plenty of wine.

ACCOMMODATIONS

Cannon Beach is very popular in summer. Make reservations as early as possible in the spring to even get a room. By Memorial Day weekend, many of the most popular spots will be completely booked for the summer and early fall. Plan well ahead if you have your heart set on staying here in July and August. On the other hand, prices drop by as much as half for midweek off-season stays. If the prices in Cannon Beach are too daunting, consider staying a few miles away in Seaside.

$150-200

Just a few minutes' walk from downtown, **Ecola Creek Lodge** (208 E. 5th St., 503/436-2776 or 800/873-2749, www.ecolacreeklodge.com, $139-249) is a Cape Cod-style inn with 22 unique units set in four buildings. Accommodations range from simple queen-bed studios to two-bedroom suites. Special features include stained glass, lawns, fountains, flower gardens, and a lily pond. Les Shirley Park and Ecola Creek separate the lodge from the beach.

Over $200

The ★ **Surfsand Resort** (148 W. Gower St., 503/436-2274, www.surfsand.com, $279-409) offers a great combination of location and amenities, with Haystack Rock right out the door and spacious, nicely furnished suites. The 95-room resort has an indoor pool and spa and on-site massage services; pets are permitted in some rooms. The popular Wayfarer Restaurant is adjacent.

The fabulously expensive (for Oregon) ★ **Stephanie Inn** (2740 S. Pacific St., 503/436-2221 or 800/633-3466, www.stephanie-inn.com, $519-609) offers attentive B&B-style service (breakfast buffet and evening wine gathering included), attention to detail, and luxury-level rooms with a low-key, not-too-fussy Oregonian touch. All guest rooms have balconies, fireplaces, wet bars, jetted tubs, fine linens, and all the extras you'd expect in an upscale resort hotel, including a fine-dining restaurant. The Stephanie is a romantic, adult-focused inn; children under 12 are not permitted.

The handsome **Inn at Cannon Beach** (3215 S. Hemlock St., 503/436-9085 or 800/321-6304, www.innatcannonbeach.com, minimum stay in summer, $269-329) has large and stylish cottage-like rooms in a beautifully landscaped garden setting with a courtyard pond, just a block from the beach. All guest rooms include a gas fireplace, a fridge,

---

1: The Irish Table restaurant **2:** Sea Level Bakery
3: Hug Point State Recreation Site

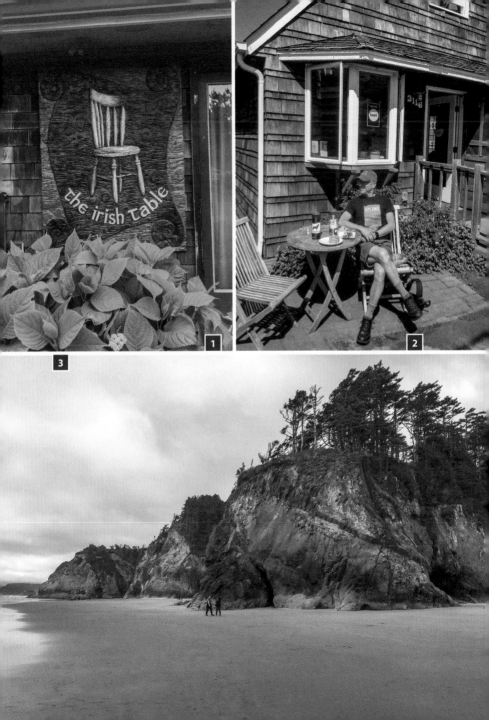

a microwave, a coffeemaker, and a TV/DVD combo; some rooms can accommodate pets.

The **Ocean Lodge** (2864 S. Pacific Dr., 503/436-2241 or 888/777-4047, www.theoceanlodge.com, $309-459) feels like a long-established beach getaway, though in fact it opened in 2002. The high-end furnishings also give a clue that despite its venerable design, this rambling lodge isn't soaked in tradition. Rooms all have balconies, fireplaces, microwaves, and fridges. Lower-cost rooms don't have ocean views, though all are just steps from the beach.

Cannon Beach Hotel Lodgings (503/436-1392, www.cannonbeach hotellodgings.com) comprise several properties, all booked through a central website or phone. The **Cannon Beach Hotel** (1116 Hemlock St., $247-293) is a converted 1910 loggers' boardinghouse with 30 rooms and a small café and restaurant on the premises. The most expensive rooms have fireplaces, whirlpools, and partial ocean views. Meals are available in the restaurant adjacent to the lobby. The pet-friendly **McBee Cottages** (888 S. Hemlock St., $125-258) are 1940s-era semidetached motel units that have been nicely renovated. The rooms are simple, but the McBee is nonetheless a favorite of many visitors looking for cozy accommodations, and it's just a minute from the beach and within walking distance of downtown. The charming attached cabins at the **Hearthstone Inn** (108 E. Jackson St., $234-258) are just across the street from the McBee and have basic kitchens and stone fireplaces, and pets are allowed.

Other homey spots include the **Argonauta Inn** and **The Waves Motel,** which share an office (188 W. 2nd St., 503/436-2205, www.thewavescannonbeach.com). The Argonauta ($199-330) is made up of four houses in the middle of downtown and has five furnished units just 150 feet from the beach. A cluster of six beachfront buildings makes up **The Waves** ($159-295), with units to fit the needs of families, couples, or larger groups. These are not cookie-cutter units, but the kind of individual lodgings you'd expect to find in Oregon. Under the same management, the **White Heron Lodge** (356 N. Spruce St., 2-night minimum stay in summer, $369) comprises six fully furnished oceanfront one-bedroom suites with a wall bed in the living room, so all can sleep up to four.

There aren't many inexpensive lodging options in Cannon Beach, but "mountain-view" rooms at the enormous **Tolovana Inn** (3400 S. Hemlock St., 503/436-2211 or 800/333-8890, www.tolovanainn.com, minimum stay in summer, $119-159 mountain view, $249-249 ocean view) hotel complex at the southern end of the Cannon Beach sprawl offer a good location at a fairly reasonable price. To make up for the rather cookie-cutter design and furnishings, you'll get a swimming pool, a spa and sauna, a number of restaurants sharing the same parking lots, and the beach right out the front door. Most oceanfront rooms have private patios or balconies; one- and two-bedroom suites are also available.

Vacation Rentals

Several local property management companies offer a large selection of furnished rentals, ranging from grand oceanfront homes to quaint secluded cottages. **Cannon Beach Property Management** (3188 S. Hemlock St., 503/436-2021 or 877/386-3402, www.cbpm.com) and **Cannon Beach Vacation Rentals** (503/436-0940 or 866/436-0940, www.visitcb.com) both have good websites. During the summer, many beach houses are only available for weekly rentals.

Camping

Camping offers easier access to Cannon Beach's natural wonders at a bargain price. Although camping is not permitted on the beach or in Cannon Beach city parks, there are plenty of options for RV, tent, and outdoor enthusiasts.

Unlike most private campgrounds, the small family-run **Wright's for Camping** (334 Reservoir Rd., 503/436-2347, www.wrightsforcamping.com, $45) is geared toward tent campers, though small RVs (less than 25 feet, no hookups available) can be accommodated in some sites. It's just east of U.S. 101 and has 22 sites with picnic tables and fire rings as well as restrooms and a laundry. Wright's is wheelchair accessible; leashed pets are allowed.

Roughly 20 miles east of Cannon Beach off U.S. 26 is **Saddle Mountain State Natural Area** (800/551-6949, www.oregonstateparks. org, Mar.-Oct., $11 tents), which offers 10 first-come, first-served tent camping sites at the base of 3,283-foot Saddle Mountain, one of the highest peaks in Oregon's Coast Range. This more primitive and remote campground (although there are flush toilets and piped water, in addition to picnic tables and fire pits) might just be the tonic if you're weary of the crowds along the beach.

INFORMATION AND SERVICES

The chamber of commerce operates the **Cannon Beach Information Center** (207 N. Spruce St., 503/436-2623, www.cannonbeach. org, 10am-5pm daily). This facility is close to the public restrooms (2nd St. and Spruce St.) and basketball and tennis courts.

Providence Cannon Beach Clinic (171 N. Larch St., 503/717-7000) offers medical care and minor emergency services. It's located in Sandpiper Square behind the stores on the main drag.

TRANSPORTATION

From U.S. 101, there's a choice of four entrances to the beach loop (also known as U.S. 101 Alternate, a section of the old Oregon Coast Highway) to take you into town. As you wade into the town's shops, galleries, and restaurants, the beach loop becomes Hemlock Street, the main drag of Cannon Beach. Sunset Empire Transportation District operates **The Bus** (503/861-7433 or 800/776-6406, www. ridethebus.org), which serves Cannon Beach, Seaside, Astoria-Warrenton, and points between. **Parking** can be hard to come by, especially on weekends, but you'll find public lots south of town at Tolovana Park and in town at Hemlock and 1st Streets and on 2nd Street.

The **Cannon Beach Shuttle** (10:30am-6pm Mon.-Fri., $1) runs every half hour on a 6.5-mile loop, from Les Shirley Park on the north end of town to Tolovana Park.

Northwest Point (888/846-4183, www. oregon-point.com, $17) runs two buses daily between Portland's Union Station and Cannon Beach, continuing on to Seaside and Astoria. The bus stops at 1170 South Hemlock Street, near the Cannon Beach Hotel.

Nehalem Bay Area

MANZANITA AND VICINITY

Just south of Arch Cape, Neahkahnie Mountain towers nearly 1,700 feet up from the edge of the sea. U.S. 101 climbs up and over its shoulder to an elevation of 700 feet, and the vistas from a half-dozen pullouts (the highest along the Oregon coast) are spectacular—but do try to keep your eyes on the snaking road until you've parked your car.

This stretch of the highway, built by the Works Progress Administration in the 1930s, was constructed by blasting a roadbed from the rock face and buttressing it with stonework walls on the precarious cliffs. The fainthearted or acrophobic certainly couldn't have lasted long on this job. The handiwork of these road builders and masons can be admired at several pullouts, along with the breathtaking vistas of Manzanita Beach and Nehalem Spit, stretching some 20 miles south to Cape Meares. Much of Neahkahnie Mountain and its rugged coastline are preserved in Oswald West State Park, one of the state's finest.

Immediately to the south, huddled along an expansive curve of beach at the foot of

Neahkahnie Mountain, quiet Manzanita (pop. 650) makes a pleasant stop for lunch or for the weekend. When adjacent coastal areas are fogbound, the seven-mile-long Manzanita Beach often enjoys sunshine because of the shelter of Neahkahnie Mountain. As one of the few towns along the north Oregon coast that's not located directly on U.S. 101, Manzanita feels more peaceful and secluded than most others; like Cannon Beach, it's also a relatively wealthy and stylish town.

Just two miles south of Manzanita on U.S. 101, tiny Nehalem occupies just a few blocks along U.S. 101 on the north bank of the Nehalem River. It's a lovely location with a few Old West-style storefronts. Sizable runs of spring and fall Chinook salmon and winter steelhead make this, and nearby Wheeler, popular destinations for anglers.

★ Oswald West State Park

Most of Neahkahnie Mountain and the prominent headlands of Cape Falcon are encompassed within the 2,500-acre gem of **Oswald West State Park** (off U.S. 101, 800/551-6949, www.oregonstateparks.org, free). Whether or not you believe in the stories of lost pirate wealth buried somewhere on the mountain, there is real treasure today for all who venture here in search of the intangible currency of extraordinary natural beauty. The state park bears the name of Governor Oswald West, whose farsighted 1913 beach bill was instrumental in protecting Oregon's virgin shoreline.

Several hiking trails weave through the park, including the 13 miles of the **Oregon Coast Trail** linking Arch Cape to the north with Manzanita. From the main parking lot on the east side of U.S. 101, a 0.5-mile trail follows Short Sands Creek to **Short Sands Beach,** a relatively sheltered beach that's popular with surfers year-round. Rainforests of hemlock, cedar, and gigantic Sitka spruce crowd the secluded boulder-strewn shoreline. From Short Sands Beach, hike north on the three-mile old-growth-lined **Cape Falcon Trail** to spectacular views.

From the trail to the beach, it's also possible to turn south and hike to **Neahkahnie Mountain** (4 miles one-way) with some stiff climbing. Shave about 1.3 miles off the hike by starting a mile south of the main Oswald West parking lot, where there's an access road to the Neahkahnie Mountain Summit Trail on the east side of the highway. It's not well marked; look for a subdivision on the golf course to the west. Drive up the gravel road 0.25 mile to the trailhead parking lot and begin a moderately difficult 1.5-mile ascent. Allow at least 45 minutes to get to the top. The summit view south to Cape Meares and east to the Nehalem Valley ranks as one of the finest on the coast.

Food

A couple of miles down the highway from town, ★ **Wanda's** (12880 H St., Nehalem, 503/368-8100, 8am-2pm daily, $8-15) is the area's favorite breakfast hangout. New owners have refurbished the building and expanded seating (yay!), but kept the menu pretty unchanged, including dreamy baked goods like the cinnamon swirl French toast.

The local bakery, **Bread and Ocean** (154 Laneda Ave., 503/368-5823, 7:30am-3pm Wed., 7:30am-3pm and 5pm-8pm Thurs.-Sat., 8am-3pm Sun., $8-12), is a good bet for breakfast pastries, quiche, and lunchtime sandwiches. Dinners ($20-25) are less of a forte.

Up near the highway, **Big Wave Cafe** (822 Laneda Ave., 503/368-9283, 11am-8pm Fri.-Tues., $13-32) is a good choice for dinner. The menu is pretty standard, ranging from burgers to seafood and steaks, all simply cooked but well executed from fresh ingredients.

For relaxed fine dining, the best option is **Neah-Kah-Nie Bistro** (519 Laneda Ave., 503/368-2722, www.nknbistro.com, 5pm-9pm Tues.-Sat., $16-35), a small dining room serving local seafood and meats with up-to-date continental preparations. True cod is pan-seared and served with lemon butter over manchego and asparagus risotto, while grilled pork chops come with brie and rosemary-pear jam.

Just a couple of blocks from the beach, Marzano's (60 Laneda Ave., 503/368-3663, www.marzanospizzapie.com, 4pm-9pm Thurs.-Tues. summer, check website for off-season hours, large pies $25-30) serves the area's best pizza, though it's only available for takeout (not a big problem since most Manzanita visitors are renting a house or camping nearby). The roasted vegetable pizza is recommended, and the smoked prosciutto with aged montegrappa cheese is another winner.

House renters, campers, and picnickers can take advantage of the excellent produce and impressive (for a coastal market) grocery section at Manzanita Grocery & Deli (193 Laneda Ave., 503/368-5362, 7am-10pm Mon.-Sat., 8am-10pm Sun. summer, 7am-9pm Mon.-Thurs., 7am-10pm Fri.-Sat, 8am-9pm Sun. winter).

Accommodations

Manzanita is a small town without an abundance of lodgings. Advance reservations are a must, especially in summer, and many accommodations require two- or three-night stays during the high season and on some holidays. A good alternative to motels for families here are the rentals available from the several property management agencies in town. Among these is Manzanita Beach Getaway (503/368-2929 or 855/368-2929, www.manzanitabeachgetaway.com), with fully furnished homes to rent, running $100-325 per night; most require weekly rentals in July and August.

If you're looking for a quiet retreat, the cedar-clad Inn at Manzanita (67 Laneda Ave., 503/368-6754, www.innatmanzanita.com, $179-225) is set in a Japanese-accented garden just a short walk from the beach. Each of its 14 wood-paneled guest rooms features a gas fireplace and a two-person tub; most rooms have a balcony, offering glimpses through the evergreens of the nearby beach. Fresh flowers daily, robes, and other amenities help you feel pampered. Despite being in the middle of town near restaurants and

the beach, a feeling of luxurious seclusion prevails.

Six blocks from the beach, the spacious, stylish, and airy cabins of Coast Cabins (635 Laneda Ave., 503/368-7113, www.coastcabins.com, 2-night minimum stay summer and weekends, $325-575) comfortably sleep two, though some are designed for up to four people and offer kitchenettes or full kitchens, satellite TV, and goose-down pillows and comforters. The Coast Cabins folks also rent out a few sophisticated one- and two-bedroom condos in downtown Manzanita.

For a more standard motel experience, the Sunset Surf (248 Ocean Rd., 503/368-5224 or 800/243-8035, www.sunsetsurfocean.com, $93-218) offers guest rooms (many with kitchens and some pet friendly) in three oceanfront units that share an outdoor pool. Rooms are older and pretty basic, but the setting is great.

Another upgraded older motel, the Spindrift Inn (114 Laneda Ave., 503/368-1001 or 877/368-1001, www.spindrift-inn.com, $109-165) has rooms that are nicer than the rather plain exterior. It's a short walk to the beach, and permits pets in some rooms.

CAMPING

Just south of Manzanita and occupying the entire sandy appendage of Nehalem Spit is scenic, sprawling Nehalem Bay State Park (reservations 800/452-5687, www.oregonstateparks.org, year-round, $31 tents or RVs, $47-57 yurts, $5 day-use for non-campers), a favorite with bikers, beachcombers, anglers, horse owners, and pilots (yes, there's a little airstrip and a fly-in campsite). Sandwiched between the bay and a beautiful four-mile beach stretching from Manzanita to the mouth of the Nehalem River is a vast campground with hot showers. Sites are a little bit close together, with few trees to screen the neighbors; dunes separate campers from the ocean. As big as this park is, it does fill up in summer, so reservations (www.reserveamerica.com) are advised, especially in July and August. To get there, turn south at Bayshore Junction just before U.S. 101

1

2

heads east into the town of Nehalem. Even if you don't bring your own horse to the park's horse camp (sites with little corrals), you can sign up for a ride with **Oregon Beach Rides** (day-use area of park, 971/237-6653, www.oregonbeachrides.com, $95 for 1 hour, $120-155 for 2 hours).

WHEELER

Wheeler (pop. 440) is a little town flanking the Nehalem River.

Oregon Coast Railriders (130 Marine Dr., 541/786-6574, http://ocrailriders.com, Wed.-Sun. summer, $26 adults, $16 children under 12, reservations required) offers recumbent quadricycle (four-wheeled bike) rides departing Wheeler at 9am and 3pm and heading north along the Nehalem River; a noon ride follows the bay to the south. Rides are 9-10 scenic miles along out-of-service railroad tracks.

Between Wheeler and Rockaway Beach is the **Jetty Fishery** (27550 U.S. 101 N., 503/368-5746, www.jettyfishery.com), a combo fishing camp and fresh fish shop where you have the choice of renting a boat and going crabbing near the mouth of the Nehalem River, or buying a just-cooked fresh crab to take out or eat right there at picnic tables on the pier. This isn't a fancy spot, but it sure is authentic.

Food

In a tiny cottage just off the main drag, the ★ **Rising Star Cafe** (92 Rorvik St., 503/368-3990, www.risingstarcafe.net, 5pm-8pm Wed.-Sat., 10am-2pm Sun., $20-30, cash or check only) is a sweet spot for excellent pasta, sandwiches, and chowder; the always-changing menu offers some of the best food on the coast, and the atmosphere is comfortable and friendly. This popular restaurant is tiny, though in good weather there's more seating on the patio; be sure to call ahead unless it's Thursday night, when the Rising Star offers

1: the wide beach at Manzanita 2: the Nehalem River

a $12.50 per person first-come, first-served pasta dinner.

The **Salmonberry Saloon** (380 Marine Dr., 503/714-1423, www.salmonberrysaloon.com, noon-9:30pm Wed.-Sun., $12-25) has a coveted spot right on the Nehalem River and delivers good food and drinks in addition to eye-popping views above the marina. The seafood earns a James Beard Smart Catch certification, and the fish tacos and fish-and-chips are both delicious.

Accommodations

Most of Wheeler's accommodations are low-cost efficiencies for visiting fisherfolk, but the 10 guest rooms of the **Wheeler on the Bay Lodge and Marina** (580 Marine Dr., 503/368-5858 or 800/469-3204, www.wheeleronthebay.com, $179-229), on U.S. 101 on the shore of Nehalem Bay, have more appeal. These are anything but cookie-cutter rooms and are clean and appealing. Most guest rooms have at least partial bay views, and several have jetted tubs. Kayak rentals are right out your door, and staff can help arrange fishing charters.

Rooms at the **Old Wheeler Hotel** (495 U.S. 101, 503/368-6000 or 877/653-4683, www.oldwheelerhotel.com, $135-190), a 1920s landmark across the road from the bay, may remind you of your great-aunt's guest room. They're old-fashioned in a down-to-earth way. Although all guest rooms have private baths, some baths are down the hall from their rooms.

ROCKAWAY BEACH

This town of 1,400 was established as a summer resort in the 1920s by Portlanders who wanted a coastal getaway. And so it remains today—a quiet spot without much going on besides walks on the seven miles of sandy beach, a **kite festival** in mid-May, and an **arts and crafts fair** in mid-August. Shallow **Lake Lytle,** on the east side of the highway, offers spring and early summer fishing for trout, bass, and crappie. While the town of Rockaway is singularly unattractive from U.S.

101—a lengthy stretch of tacky shops, modest motels, and big new condos—the beach is quite nice, anchored at the south by the impressive Twin Rocks formation. The **visitors information center** (503/355-8108, www.rockawaybeach.net), lodged in a bright red caboose in the center of town, can fill you in on other goings-on.

Food

The **Offshore Grill and Coffeehouse** (122 U.S. 101 N., 503/355-3005, 9am-5pm Mon., 8am-9pm Wed.-Thurs., 7am-9pm Fri.-Sun., $14-23) is one of the classier dining places in town (don't worry, flip-flops and a sweatshirt will get you by), bringing well-prepared comfort food to Rockaway Beach. The menu extends from grilled meatloaf to pan-roasted duck breast; specials usually include local seafood and fish in interesting preparations (think crab and artichoke ravioli with pork belly). Breakfasts are excellent.

Accommodations

Rockaway's motels are basic and family-oriented; if you are planning in advance, take a moment to check out the beach houses and condos available for rent on the **chamber of commerce website** (www.rockawaybeach.net).

The following motels are on the ocean side of busy U.S. 101, which dominates this long string bean of a town. **Surfside Resort Motel** (101 NW 11th Ave., 503/355-2312 or 800/243-7786, www.surfsideocean.com, $90-158 no ocean view, $146-180 ocean view) is a large beachfront complex with an indoor pool. Some guest rooms with kitchens are available, and some rooms are pet-friendly. **Silver Sands Oceanfront Resort** (215 S. Pacific Ave., 503/355-2206 or 800/457-8972, www.oregonsilversands.com, $138-164) is also right on the beach, with fairly basic rooms—some with kitchenettes and some that are pet-friendly—an indoor pool and hot tub, and a sauna.

About a mile south of town, **Twin Rocks Motel** (7925 Minehaha St., 503/355-2391 or 877/355-2391, www.twinrocksmotel.net, $229-249) is a small cluster of dog-friendly two-bedroom oceanfront cottages. If you're looking for a simple, quiet getaway with family or a couple of friends, this might be your place.

Tillamook Bay

GARIBALDI

Tillamook Bay's commercial fishing fleet is concentrated in this little port town (pop. 800) near the north end of the bay. Garibaldi, named in 1879 by the local postmaster for the Italian patriot, is a fish-processing center: Crabs, shrimp, fresh salmon, lingcod, and bottom fish (halibut, cabezon, rockfish, and sea perch) are the specialties. At the marina, **Garibaldi Cannery** (606 Commercial Dr., 503/322-3344, 9am-6pm Mon.-Thurs., 7am-6pm Fri.-Sun. summer, call for winter hours) and **The Spot** (304 Mooring Basin, 503/322-0080, 9am-5pm Wed.-Mon.) get crab, fish, and other seafood right off the boats, so the selection is both low-priced and fresh. If you want it fresher, you'll have to catch it yourself.

In addition to dock fishing, guide and charter services offer salmon and halibut fishing, bird-watching, and whale-watching excursions. North of Garibaldi on U.S. 101, the bay entrance is a good place to see brown pelicans, harlequin ducks, oystercatchers, and guillemots. The Miami River marsh, south of town, is a bird-watching paradise at low tide, when ducks and shorebirds hunt for food.

Garibaldi Maritime Museum

The small but interesting **Garibaldi Maritime Museum** (112 Garibaldi Ave., 503/322-8411, http://garibaldimuseum.org, 10am-4pm Thurs.-Mon. Apr.-Oct., $4 adults, $3 seniors, $4 ages 11-18) retells the history of this longtime fishing village. It also focuses on the late 18th-century sailing world and the British sea captain Robert Gray and his historic vessels, the *Lady Washington* and the *Columbia Rediviva*, which explored the Pacific Northwest in 1787 and 1792. Among the museum displays are models of these ships, an eight-foot-tall reproduction of the *Columbia* figurehead, a half model of the *Columbia* showing how the ship was provisioned for long voyages, and reproductions of period musical instruments and typical sailors' clothing.

Oregon Coast Explorer Trains

The **Oregon Coast Scenic Railroad** (503/842-8206, www.oregoncoastscenic.org, basic tours $22 adults, $20 seniors, $15 ages 3-12) operates a number of rail excursions on a train pulled by a 1910 Heisler Locomotive Works steam engine between Garibaldi and Rockaway Beach. The basic tour is 1.5 hours round-trip; trains depart Garibaldi at 10am, noon, and 2pm, with opportunities to board in Rockaway Beach at 11am and 1pm. The train operates weekends only mid-May-mid-June and late September, and daily mid-June-Labor Day, as well as assorted holidays throughout the year. Dinner trains are also offered.

Oregon Coast Railriders

Just south of Garibaldi, **Oregon Coast Railriders** (5400 Hayes Oyster Dr., Bay City, 541/786-6165, http://ocrailriders.com, 9am, noon, and 3pm Fri.-Tues. summer, $26 adults, $16 children under 12, reservations required) offers rides along out-of-service railroad tracks from Bay City to Tillamook via four-wheeled pedal-powered railriders (recumbent quadricycles). You'll cruise along Tillamook Bay and through tidal flats on this easygoing 12-mile round-trip.

Fishing

The town's fishing and crabbing piers attract visitors looking to catch their own. Rent fishing boats, crab traps, and other gear at the

Garibaldi Marina (302 Mooring Basin Rd., 503/322-3312, www.garibaldimarina.com).

The **Miami River** and **Kilchis River,** which empty into Tillamook Bay south of Garibaldi, get the state's only two significant runs of chum salmon, a species much more common from Washington northward. There's a catch-and-release season for them mid-September-mid-November. Both rivers also get runs of spring chinook and are open for steelhead most of the year.

Several charter companies have offices at the marina. **Garibaldi Charters** (607 Garibaldi Ave., 503/322-0007, www.garibaldicharters.com) offers fishing excursions. A full day of light-tackle bottom fishing runs about $105, with guided bay crabbing ($65 pp), salmon ($200), and tuna ($325) fishing also offered, and wildlife-viewing or whale-watching trips (Mar.-Apr., $40 pp). One-hour bay tours (late May-early Aug. and mid-Sept.-Oct., $40 pp) are also offered.

Food

One of the joys of eating on the Oregon coast is getting really good fish-and-chips from rough-edged dives on the docks. In Garibaldi, the **Fisherman's Korner Restaurant** (306 Mooring Basin, 503/322-2033, 7:30am-8pm Thurs.-Sun., 7:30am-3pm Mon., $7-16) is right on the wharf and offers absolutely fresh fish-and-chips. Breakfasts here are massive—meant for hungry sailors.

If you need a break from fried fish, **Garibaldi Portside Bistro** (606 Blak Ave., 971/265-1567, 11:30am-2:30pm Wed., 11:30am-8pm Thurs.-Sat., $6-25) has great burgers (try the one topped with goat cheese and blueberry sauce!) as well as a grilled fish sandwich.

Just north of Garibaldi, **Pirate's Cove Restaurant** (14170 U.S. 101 N., 503/322-2092, noon-9pm Mon.-Tues., 8am-9pm Wed.-Sat., 8am-8pm Sun., dinner $25-35) is one of the better restaurants between Manzanita and Lincoln City, with a dramatic vista of the mouth of Tillamook Bay. Try the local oysters and razor clams. Lunches ($13-20) are a better deal than the rather expensive dinners.

Four miles south at the little enclave of Bay City is another temple to seafood. **Pacific Oyster** (5150 Hayes Oyster Dr., Bay City, 503/377-2323, 11am-7pm daily, $5-16) is mostly an oyster-processing center, but it's also an excellent spot for a few oyster shooters or a quick meal. Although there are a variety of seafood choices, the main draw is the oysters, which are both a meal and entertainment here. As you eat, you can watch the oyster shuckers in action next door, as the dining area overlooks the oyster-processing area.

Accommodations and Camping

If you want to wake up on the docks, spend the night at the simple but sweet **Harbor View Inn & RV Park** (302 S. 7th St., 503/322-3251, www.harborviewfun.com, $129-139), a motel popular with fishers and sports enthusiasts. RV camping ($44) is geared toward larger rigs, but sites have good access to the beach, the pier, and a kayak launch site.

Garibaldi House Inn (502 Garibaldi Ave., 503/322-3338 or 877/322-6489, www.garibaldihouse.com, $159-259) is a more standard motel up the highway with pleasant rooms as well as an indoor pool, a hot tub, a sauna, and a fitness room. It offers complimentary breakfast and snacks, including clam chowder on Friday and Saturday evenings.

In nearby Bay City, **Sheltered Nook** (7860 Warren St., Bay City, 503/805-5526, www.shelterednook.com, $175) offers lodging in tiny homes; these 385-square-foot cabins are nicely fitted out with custom kitchens and sleeping lofts (easily sleeping four). Guests (and, often, their dogs) share a fire pit and access to a disc golf course.

TILLAMOOK

Without much sun or surf, what could possibly draw enough visitors to the town of Tillamook (pop. 5,200) to make it one of Oregon's biggest tourist attractions? Superficially speaking, cheese factories and a World War II blimp hangar, in a town flanked by mudflats and rain-soaked dairy country, shouldn't pull in more than a million tourists per year. But they do. And after a drive down U.S. 101 or along the scenic Three Capes Loop, you too will be mysteriously drawn to the huge white, blue, and gold building proffering bite-size samples of cheddar, not to mention ice cream.

Tillamook County is home to many more cows than people. They're the foundation of the Tillamook County Creamery Association's famous cheddar cheese and other dairy products, which generate about $800 million in annual sales—dwarfing the region's other important contributors to the local economy, fishing and oyster farming.

In 1940-1942, partially in response to a Japanese submarine firing on Fort Stevens in Astoria, the U.S. Navy built two blimp hangars south of town, the two largest wooden structures ever built, according to *Guinness World Records*. One of five naval air stations on the Pacific coast, the Tillamook blimp guard patrolled the waters from Northern California to Washington's San Juan Islands and escorted ships into Puget Sound. While all kinds of blimp stories abound in Tillamook bars, only one wartime encounter has been documented. Declassified records confirm that blimps were involved in the sinking of what was believed to be two Japanese submarines off Cape Meares. In late May 1943, two of the high-flying craft, assisted by U.S. Navy subchasers and destroyers, dropped several depth charges on the submarines, which are still lying on the ocean floor.

Until 1946, when the station was decommissioned, the naval presence here created a boomtown. Bars and businesses flourished, and civilian jobs were easy to come by. After the war years, Tillamook County returned to the economic trinity of "trees, cheese, and ocean breeze" that has sustained the region to the present day.

1: Garibaldi seafood spot **2:** Tillamook Creamery

Sights
TILLAMOOK CREAMERY

With over a million visitors a year, the **Tillamook Creamery** (4165 U.S. 101 N., 503/815-1300, www.tillamook.com/creamery, 8am-8pm daily mid-June-early Nov., 8am-6pm Mon.-Fri., 8am-8pm Sat.-Sun. early Nov.-mid-June, free) is far and away the county's biggest draw. The plant welcomes visitors with a reproduction of the *Morningstar*, the schooner that transported locally made butter and cheese in the late 1800s and now adorns the label of every Tillamook product. The quaint vessel symbolizing Tillamook cheesemaking's humble beginnings stands in contrast to the technology and sophistication that go into making this world-famous lunchbox staple today.

New in 2018, the grand 38,500-square-foot visitors center accommodates the roughly 1.5 million visitors who now stop by annually to peer down into the cheese-processing factory, where placards describe what the workers are doing. Tillamook produces tens of millions of pounds of cheese annually, including monterey jack, swiss, and multiple variations of the award-winning cheddar.

Although it's quite absorbing to watch the cheese-making process, the biggest crowds gather around the cheese-sampling station and migrate to the huge gift shop, where the selection of cheese goes way beyond what's shipped to grocery stores. Tillamook also makes pretty good ice cream, and most visitors walk out with an ice cream cone.

BLUE HERON FRENCH CHEESE COMPANY

A quarter-million people per year visit Tillamook County's *second*-most-popular attraction, **Blue Heron French Cheese Company** (2001 Blue Heron Dr., 503/842-8281, www.blueheronoregon.com, 8am-8pm daily Memorial Day-Labor Day, 8am-6pm daily Labor Day-Memorial Day), a store located about a mile south of the Tillamook Creamery. Housed in a large white barn, Blue Heron is famous for its brie-style cheese

(though it's not produced on-site). In addition to cheeses and other gourmet foods, the shop sells gift baskets; over 120 varieties of Oregon wines are available in the wine-tasting room. A deli serves lunches of homemade soups and salads. For kids, there's a petting farm with the usual barnyard suspects.

TILLAMOOK AIR MUSEUM

South of town off U.S. 101, you can't possibly miss the enormous Quonset hut-like building east of the highway. The world-class aircraft collection of the **Tillamook Air Museum** (6030 Hangar Rd., 503/842-1130, www.tillamookair.com, 10am-5pm daily, $10.50 adults, $9.50 seniors, $7.20 ages 7-16, $3.50 ages 1-6) is housed in and around Hangar B of the decommissioned Tillamook Naval Air Station. At 1,072 feet long, 206 feet wide, and 192 feet high, it's the largest wooden structure in the world, and it's worth the price of admission just to experience the enormity of it. During World War II, this and another gargantuan hangar on the site (which burned down in 1992) sheltered eight K-class blimps, each 242 feet long.

s) and photos and artifacts from the naval air station days. Check out the cyclo-crane, a combination blimp, plane, and helicopter. This was devised in the 1980s to aid in remote logging operations; it ended up an $8 million bust.

To get here from downtown, take U.S. 101 south two miles, make a left at the flashing yellow light, and follow the signs.

TILLAMOOK COUNTY PIONEER MUSEUM

East of the highway in the heart of downtown, **Tillamook County Pioneer Museum** (2106 2nd St., 503/842-4553, www.tcpm.org, 10am-4pm Tues.-Sun., $5 adults, $4 seniors, $2 ages 7-10) is famous for its taxidermy exhibits as well as memorabilia from pioneer households. Particularly intriguing are hunks of ancient beeswax with odd inscriptions recovered from near Neahkahnie Mountain, which are thought to be remnants from 18th-century

The Lost Treasure of Neahkahnie Mountain

Is there pirate gold on Neahkahnie Mountain? Local Native American legends tell of Spanish pirates burying a treasure here. One story relates that the crew of a shipwrecked Manila galleon salvaged its cargo of gold and beeswax (a valuable commodity in trade with Asia) by burying it in the side of the mountain. To deter local people from going to the site, the pirates killed a man and buried him on top of the cargo. While this account, taken from Native American histories, has never been substantiated, a piece of crudely inscribed beeswax retrieved from the Neah-kahnie region, carbon-dated to 1500-1700 and on display at the **Tillamook County Pioneer Museum,** keeps speculation alive.

Further intrigue was added by the 1993 discovery of an ancient wooden rigging block. Found in the mud at the mouth of the Nehalem River, it was determined by a Spanish maritime expert to have been from a Manila galleon during that same time period. Lewis and Clark's 1805 reports of an indigenous Chinook person with red hair, and similar accounts from the Vancouver Expedition's 1792 encounter with a redheaded indigenous man who claimed his late father had been a shipwrecked Spanish sailor, would tend to corroborate the shipwreck and treasure stories passed down in oral histories.

shipwrecks. The old courtroom on the 2nd floor has one of the best displays of natural history in the state. There are many beautiful dioramas, plus shells, insects, and nests. The Beals Memorial Room houses a large rock, mineral, and fossil collection.

MUNSON CREEK FALLS

The highest waterfall in the Oregon Coast Range is lovely **Munson Creek Falls,** which drops 266 feet over mossy cliffs surrounded by an old-growth forest. A steep 0.25-mile trail leads to the base of the falls, while another, slightly longer trail leads to a higher viewpoint; wooden walkways clinging to the cliff lead to a small viewing platform. This is a spectacle in all seasons, but in winter the falls pour down with greater fury.

To reach the falls, drive seven miles south of Tillamook, turn east from U.S. 101 on Munson Creek Road, and then drive 1.5 miles on a well-signed but very narrow and bumpy dirt access road that leads to the parking lot. Note that motor homes and trailers cannot get into the park; the lot is too small.

TILLAMOOK STATE FOREST

A series of intense forest fires in the 1930s and 1940s burned vast amounts of land in the northern Coast Range. Most of this land was owned by private timber companies, who walked away from the seemingly worthless "Tillamook Burn," leaving property rights to revert to the counties, who then handed the land over to the state. A massive replanting effort ensued, and in 1973 the Tillamook Burn became the **Tillamook State Forest.**

The **Tillamook Forest Center** (45500 Wilson River Hwy., 503/815-6800 or 866/930-4646, www.tillamookforestcenter. org, 10am-5pm Wed.-Sun. Memorial Day-Labor Day, reduced hours spring and fall, closed Dec.-Feb., $5 donation suggested), housed in a soaring timbered building in the middle of the now-lush forest, is a good place to learn about the local ecosystem. Stop in to see the short movie about the area's history; the vivid fire scenes are a bit frightening—a sensation that's enhanced when the smell of smoke is released into the auditorium. Don't leave without walking out through the center's back door, crossing the footbridge, and taking at least a short hike, where you'll see an assortment of native wildflowers, shrubs, and trees. If you head west from the bridge, Wilson Falls is about two miles away.

Recreation

HIKING

The Tillamook State Forest offers plenty of recreational opportunities. From a distance, the forest seems like a tree plantation, but hidden waterfalls, old railroad trestles from the days of logging trains, and moss-covered oaks in the Salmonberry River Canyon will convince you otherwise. Bird-watchers and mushroom pickers can easily penetrate this thicket, thanks to 1,000 miles of maintained roads and old railroad grades.

Two challenging trails off Highway 6, **Kings Mountain** (25 miles east of Tillamook) and **Elk Mountain** (28 miles east of Tillamook) climb through lands affected by the Tillamook Burn, but with scenic views throughout. Thanks to salvage logging in the wake of the disaster and subsequent replanting, myriad trails crisscross forests of Douglas and noble fir, hemlock, and red alder. Stop at the visitors center for maps and trail descriptions.

WILDLIFE-VIEWING

Bird-watchers flock to Tillamook Bay June-November to view pelicans, sandpipers, tufted puffins, blue herons, and a variety of shorebirds. Prime time is before high tide, but step lively, because this waterway was originally called "quicksand bay."

FISHING

Among Oregon anglers, Tillamook County is known for its steelhead and salmon. Motorists along U.S. 101 can tell the fall chinook run has arrived when fishing boats cluster outside the Tillamook Bay entrance at Garibaldi. As the season wears on, the fish—affectionately called "hogs" because they sometimes weigh in at more than 50 pounds—make their way inland up the five coastal rivers—the Trask, Wilson, Tillamook, Kilchis, and Miami—that flow into Tillamook Bay. At their peak, the runs create such competition for favorite holes that the process of sparring for them is jocularly referred to as "combat fishing," as fishing boats anchor up gunwale to gunwale to form a fish-stopping palisade called a "hogline." Smokehouses and gas stations dot the outer reaches of the bay to cater to this fall influx.

Entertainment

In recent years, Tillamook has substantially upped its game in terms of brewpubs. For sour-beer geeks, the most notable tasting room is **de Garde Brewing** (114 Ivy Ave., 503/815-1635, www.degardebrewing.com, 3pm-7pm Thurs.-Fri., noon-7pm Sat., 11am-5pm Sun., no minors or pets), one of Oregon's most notable wild-yeast breweries (note that these unusual beers will not please everyone). The only place to taste de Gard's wild beers on tap is at the brewery, and it's the best place to buy the brewery's limited selection of bottled beer.

A couple of blocks west of downtown is the **Pelican Brewing Company Pub** (1708 1st St., 503/842-7007, 11am-9pm daily, $12-17), where you'll find the bottling plant for popular Pelican beers, plus a pub that offers burgers, fish-and-chips, tacos, and other pub favorites. The tap room overlooks the brewery's 50,000-barrels-per-year production facility. If you'd like to check out how it's all done, ask about tours.

Food and Accommodations

To sample the county's freshest produce, visit the **Tillamook Farmers Market** (2nd St. and Laurel Ave., 9am-2pm Sat. mid-June-late Sept.) in downtown Tillamook.

Some of the best food in Tillamook is found at food trucks. Most are just north of downtown along U.S. 101. **Recess** (1910 Main Ave. N., 503/812-0308, 11am-7pm Mon.-Sat., $8-12) is a cheery little truck that turns out burgers and wraps to match any restaurant in town, and the Cobb salad with cornbread waffle croutons is a special treat.

In downtown Tillamook, attempts to open fine-dining restaurants have faltered in recent years. The latest, and best bet, is **Pacific Restaurant** (205 Main Ave., 503/842-0019, www.pacific-restaurant.com, 9am-3pm and 5pm-9pm Mon.-Thurs., 9am-3pm and

5pm-11pm Fri., 5pm-11pm Sat., $13-31), a large, classy room serving more seafood entrées than most of the local competition—think *furikake* (Japanese seasoning) salmon salad or miso-glazed halibut with mustard greens—as well as both fish-and-chips and oysters-and-chips. Swing by before lunchtime to pick up some bread from the restaurant's bakery

La Mexicana (2203 3rd St., 503/842-2101, 11am-9pm Mon.-Fri., noon-9pm Sat., $9-24) is the town's best Mexican restaurant, housed in a vintage home on the edge of downtown. Going way beyond tacos and burritos, La Mexicana prepares local fish and seafood with south-of-the-border zest and finesse.

Most travelers seem to pass through Tillamook on their way to someplace else, and there are plenty of chain motels available all along the busy U.S. 101 strip north of town. A good local choice along this strip is **Ashley Inn** (1722 N. Makinster Rd., 503/842-7599, www.ashleyinntillamook.com, $125-180), close to the cheese factory. Rooms have a fridge and microwave; amenities include an indoor pool, a sauna, a hot tub, and continental breakfast.

Transportation

The **Tillamook County Transportation District** (503/815-8283, www.nworegontransit.org) offers public bus transportation around Tillamook County, and also runs a couple of buses of interest to travelers. The service offers twice-daily buses north to and from Cannon Beach, with service to points north, including Astoria, and also four buses a day south to and from Lincoln City. The district also offers two buses a day to and from the Greyhound station in Portland ($15). The Tillamook Transit Center is at 2nd and Laurel Streets.

Information

The **Tillamook Chamber of Commerce** (208 Main Ave., 503/842-7525, www.tillamookchamber.org, 9am-5pm Mon.-Fri.) can help you with any business-related question about Tillamook and vicinity.

Three Capes Scenic Loop

The Three Capes Scenic Loop, a 35-mile byway off U.S. 101 between Tillamook and Pacific City, stays close to the ocean, which U.S. 101 does not. And although the beauty of Capes Meares, Lookout, and Kiwanda certainly justifies leaving the main highway, it would be an overstatement to portray this drive as a thrill-a-minute detour on the order of the south coast's Boardman State Park or the central coast's Otter Crest Loop. Instead of fronting the ocean, the road connecting the capes winds mostly through dairy country, small beach towns, and second-growth forest. What's special here are the three capes themselves, and unless you get out of the car and walk on the trails, you'll miss the aesthetic appeal and distinctiveness of each headland's ecosystem. The wave-battered bluffs of Cape Kiwanda, the precipitous overlooks along the Cape Lookout Highway, and the curious Octopus Tree at Cape Meares are the perfect antidotes to the inland towns along this stretch of U.S. 101. The majority of the Three Capes lodging and dining options are clustered in Netarts and Oceanside and at the other end in Pacific City. In between, it's mostly sand dunes, isolated beaches, rainforest, and pasture. To reach the Three Capes Scenic Loop from the north, turn west at Tillamook and follow signs to Cape Meares. From the south, follow signs north of Neskowin to Pacific City.

Three Capes Scenic Loop

CAPE MEARES STATE SCENIC VIEWPOINT

With stunning views, picnic tables, a newly restored lighthouse, and a uniquely contorted tree a short walk from the parking lot, **Cape Meares State Scenic Viewpoint** is the most effortless site to visit on the Three Capes Loop. It was named for English navigator John Meares, who mapped many points along this coast in a 1788 voyage. The famed **Octopus Tree** is less than 0.25 mile up a forested hill. The tentacle-like extensions of this Sitka spruce have also been compared to candelabra arms.

The 45-foot diameter of its base supports 5-foot-thick trunks, each of which is large enough to be a single tree. Scientists have propounded several theories for the cause of its unusual shape, including everything from wind and weather to insects damaging the spruce when it was young. A Native American legend about the spruce contends that it was shaped this way so that the branches could hold the canoes of a chief's dead family. Supposedly, the bodies were buried near the tree. This was a traditional practice among the indigenous people of the area, who referred to species formed thusly as "council trees."

Beyond the tree you can look south at Oceanside and Three Arch Rocks Wildlife Refuge. The sweep of Pacific shore and offshore monoliths makes a fitting beginning (or finale, if you're driving from the south) to your sojourn along the Three Capes Scenic Loop. Also be sure to stroll the short paved trail down to the lighthouse, which begins at the parking lot and provides dramatic views of an offshore wildlife refuge, **Cape Meares Rocks.** Bring binoculars to see tufted puffins, pelagic cormorants, seals, and sea lions. The landward portion of the refuge protects rare old-growth evergreens.

Cape Meares Lighthouse (503/842-3182, tours 11am-2pm and 2:30pm-4pm daily May-Sept., free) was built in 1890. This beacon was replaced as a functioning light in 1963 by the automated facility behind it, and it now houses a gift shop in its restored interior.

Volunteer tour guides might tell you about how the lighthouse was built here by mistake and perhaps offer a peek into the prismatic Fresnel lenses.

OCEANSIDE

The road between Cape Meares and Netarts heads into the beach-house community of Oceanside (pop. about 350). Many of the homes are built into the cliff overlooking the ocean, Sausalito-style. This maze of steep, narrow streets reaches its apex atop Maxwell Point. You can peer several hundred feet down at **Three Arch Rocks Wildlife Refuge** (www.fws.gov), part-time home to one of the continent's largest and most varied collections of shorebirds. A herd of sea lions also populates this trio of sea stacks from time to time. Oceanside's nearly complete lack of cell phone service means that this is a place to really get away from it all.

Food and Accommodations

A popular draw for hungry Three Capes travelers, ★ **Roseanna's Cafe** (1490 Pacific Ave. NW, 503/842-7351, www.roseannascafe.com, 11am-8pm Thurs.-Mon., $11-30) garners high marks from just about everyone. At first, the weather-beaten cedar-shake exterior might lead you to expect an old general store, as indeed it was decades ago. Once you're inside, however, the ornate decor leaves little doubt that this place takes its new identity seriously. From an elevated perch above the breakers, you'll be treated to expertly prepared local oysters, excellent chowder, fresh salmon, a bevy of chicken dishes, and interesting pastas, such as gorgonzola and pear with penne noodles. Save room for blackberry cobbler; order it warm so the Tillamook Vanilla Bean ice cream on top melts down the sides, and watch the waves over a long cup of coffee.

Blue Agate Cafe (1610 Pacific Ave., 503/815-2596, 9am-2pm Mon.-Fri., 8am-3pm Sat.-Sun., $8-15) is a happening little eatery in the center of Oceanside with fun breakfasts (try the Dungeness crab scramble), crab cakes, and excellent fish tacos.

There aren't many lodging options in Oceanside. While low prices and a window on the water can be found at **Ocean Front Cabins** (1610 Pacific Ave., 503/842-6081 or 888/845-8470, www.oceanfrontcabins.com, $80-165), the older, smallish guest rooms here might give upscale travelers pause. Nonetheless, for as little as $80 for a sleeping unit without a kitchenette—or $165 for a two-bed room with a full kitchen—you'll find yourself literally a stone's throw from Oceanside's beachcombing and dining highlights. Pets are accepted in some cabins.

Perched across the road from the ocean, but with good views, the **Three Arch Inn** (1440 Pacific Ave., 503/842-2961 or 800/347-2972, www.threearchinn.com, $144-192) includes a couple of suites that are like small apartments, as well as four guest rooms, most of which permit dogs. This is a self-check-in inn (a key code allows you to enter your room), and except for one suite, all rooms are on the 2nd and 3rd floors.

Considerably more upscale are the condo-like accommodations at **Oceanside Inn** (1440 Pacific Ave., 503/842-2961 or 800/347-2972, www.oceansideinn-oregon.com, $83-561), 11 different units perched right above the beach. These are comfortable lodgings, all with full kitchens and some with two bedrooms. Rates can swing wildly between weekday and weekend, so check your dates on the website in case a low rate is available.

NETARTS

Netarts (pop. about 750) has an enviable location overlooking Netarts Bay and the Pacific beyond. Along with nearby Oceanside, it's the closest coastal settlement to Tillamook and makes for a fine quiet getaway. Netarts Bay and seven-mile-long Netarts Spit are popular with clam diggers and crabbers, who can launch boats from Netarts Landing at the northeast corner of the bay. **Netarts Bay RV Park and Marina** (2260 Bilyeu St., 503/842-7774) and **Big Spruce RV Park** (4850 Netarts Hwy. W., 503/842-7443) rent out motorboats and crabbing supplies.

South of Netarts, follow the signs to the **Jacobsen Salt Co.** (9820 Whiskey Creek Rd., 503/719-4973, 10am-5pm daily Apr.-Oct., 10am-4pm daily Nov.-Mar.), an artisan salt works with the world's cutest gift shop perched just above the bay. Although tours of the salt works aren't offered, this is a good place to pick up a jar of finishing salt or some salty caramels for the folks back home.

Food and Accommodations

The view of Cape Lookout is tops at **The Schooner** (2065 Netarts Bay Rd., 503/815-9900, www.theschooner.net, 11:30am-8pm Mon.-Thurs., 11:30am-9pm Fri.-Sat., $16-28), and the "fresh, local, seasonal" food is a nice surprise also. Stop by for some steamer clams, fresh oysters, or a smoked and wood-oven-roasted pork chop.

The **Terimore** (5105 Crab Ave., 503/842-4623, www.terimoremotel.com, $85-225) is situated a short walk from the water at the north end of Netarts Bay. Other than some units with fireplaces and kitchens, there are few frills in these cabins and motel rooms, but for fair rates you'll find yourself close to the water, within easy driving distance of the Cape Lookout Trail, and a beach walk away from Roseanna's, the best restaurant on the Three Capes Scenic Loop.

TOP EXPERIENCE

CAPE LOOKOUT STATE PARK

One of the scenic highlights of the Three Capes route, **Cape Lookout State Park** (off U.S. 101, www.oregonstateparks.org, $5 day-use) juts out nearly a mile from the mainland, like a finger pointing out to sea. The cliffs along the south side of the cape rise 800 feet from the Pacific's pounding waves. The best way to take in the vista and the thrill of the location is on foot.

★ Hiking

Hiking to the end of mile-wide Cape Lookout is one of the top coastal hikes in Oregon. The trail begins either at the campground, where it climbs 2.5 miles up to a ridgetop trailhead with a parking lot, or from the Three Capes road at a well-signed trailhead. An orientation map at the trailhead details the options. The main 2.5-mile trail out to the end, along the narrowing finger of land, can give hikers the impression that they're on the prow of a giant ship suspended 500 feet above the ocean on all sides. Here, more than anywhere else on the Oregon coast, you get the sense of being on the edge of the continent. Giant spruces, western red cedars, and hemlocks surround the gently hilly trail to the tip of the cape. In March, Cape Lookout is a popular vantage point for whale-watching. June-August, a bevy of wildflowers and birds further enhance the rolling terrain en route to the tip of this headland, and in late summer red huckleberries line the path.

Halfway to the overlook, there are views north to Cape Meares over the Netarts sand spit. Even if you settle for a mere 15-minute stroll down the trail, you can look southward beyond Haystack Rock to Cascade Head. Right about where the trees open up, look for a bronze plaque commemorating the crash of a World War II plane and nearly a dozen casualties, which is embedded in the rock wall bordering the right-hand (north) side of the trail at eye level. If you're unable to take this hike, two unmarked turnouts along the Three Capes road between the sand dunes and Cape Lookout parking lot let you survey the terrain south to Cape Kiwanda. Don't be surprised if you see hang gliders and paragliders.

Another popular trail in the state park heads north from the campground through a variety of estuarine habitats along the sand spit separating Netarts Bay from the Pacific. It's a popular site for agate hunters, clammers, and crabbers.

Camping

At the southern end of Netarts Spit is the state park's **campground and beach extension** (13000 Whiskey Creek Rd. W., 503/842-4981, reservations 800/452-5687, www.reserveamerica.com, $5-7 reservation fee), which also encompasses the entire cape and the seven-mile-long Netarts Spit within its boundaries. The campground has 173 tent sites ($21) and 38 full-hookup sites ($34), as well as 13 yurts ($47), three cabins (with bath, kitchen, and TV/video player, $88-101), and a hiker-biker camp ($8); discounts apply October-April. Some yurts accept pets ($10). Amenities include showers, flush toilets, and evening programs. Reservations and a deposit are almost always required at this popular campground.

South of Cape Lookout, the terrain suddenly changes. Extensive sand dunes surrounding the Sand Lake Estuary suddenly appear, drowning the forest in sand. The dunes and beach attract squadrons of dune buggy enthusiasts. Camping is available year-round at **Sand Beach Campground** (Galloway Rd., 5 miles south of Cape Lookout, 503/392-3161, reservations 877/444-6777, www.recreation.gov, $25), a part of the Siuslaw National Forest, which has basic sites for tents and RVs. This dramatic area is also popular with hikers.

As you approach the shore in Pacific City, the sight of **Haystack Rock** will immediately grab your attention. At 327 feet, this sea stack is nearly 100 feet taller than the similarly named rock in Cannon Beach. Standing a mile offshore, this monolith has a brooding, enigmatic quality that constantly draws the eye. Look closely, and you'll understand why some folks call it Teacup Rock.

The tawny sandstone escarpment of Cape Kiwanda juts half a mile out to sea from Pacific City and frames the north end of the beach. In storm-tossed waters, this cape is the undisputed king, if you go by coffee-table books and calendar photos. While other sandstone promontories on the north coast have been ground into sandy beaches by the pounding surf, it's been theorized that Kiwanda has endured thanks to the buffer of Haystack Rock. In any case, paragliding aficionados are glad the cape is here. They scale its shoulders and set themselves aloft off the north face to glide above the beach and dunes.

The small town of Pacific City, with about 1,000 residents, is at the base of Cape Kiwanda. It attracts growing numbers of vacationers and retirees, but remains true to its

Pacific City

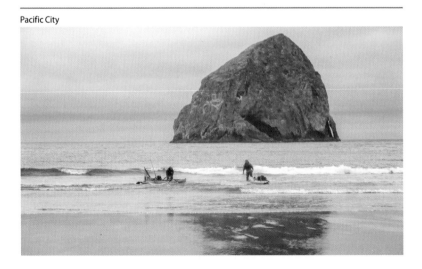

19th-century origins as a working fishing village. In addition to the knockout seascapes and recreation, if you come here at the right time of day, you may be treated to a unique spectacle—the launch or return of the **dory fleet.**

It's a tradition dating back to the 1920s, when gillnetting was banned on the Nestucca River to protect the dwindling salmon runs. To retain their livelihood, commercial fishers began to haul flat-bottomed double-ended dories down to the beach on horse-drawn wagons, then row out through the surf to fish. These days, trucks and trailers get the boats to and from the beach, and outboard motors have replaced oar power, enabling the dories to get 50 miles out to sea. If you come around 6am, you can watch them taking off. The fleet's late-afternoon return attracts a crowd that arrives to see the dory operators skidding their craft as far as possible up the beach to the waiting boat trailers. Others meet the dories to buy salmon and tuna.

The Pacific City area is also besieged by surfers, who enjoy some of the longest waves on the Oregon coast.

Recreation

If you want to join the anglers for a summertime ocean fishing trip on a dory, contact **Haystack Fishing** (503/679-9028), across from the beach near the Inn at Cape Kiwanda. Four- to six-hour salmon and bottom fishing trips start at $225 per person.

Robert Straub State Park, just south of town, offers access to Nestucca Bay and to the dunes and a long, uninterrupted stretch of beach. Pacific City surfers should use *extreme* caution when the dories are returning to the beach. Rent a board and wetsuit from **Moment Surf Co.** (33280 Cape Kiwanda Dr., 503/483-1025, www.momentsurfco.com, $60).

Rent a kayak or paddleboard from **Nestucca Adventures** (34650 Brooten Rd., 503/965-0060, http://nestuccaadventures. com, 10am-4pm Mon.-Thurs., 10am-6pm Fri.-Sun., $20-35/hour) and tour the quiet Nestucca River.

Festivals and Events

In mid-July, **Dory Days** celebrates the area's fleet. The three-day fete includes craft and food booths, a fish fry, a fishing derby, and other activities. For more information, call the **chamber of commerce** (503/965-6161).

Food

A popular and well-known Pacific City hangout is the ★ **Pelican Pub and Brewery** (33180 Cape Kiwanda Dr., 503/965-7007, 10:30am-10pm Sun.-Thurs., 10:30am-11pm Fri.-Sat., $6-23). Although there are now Pelican outposts in Cannon Beach and Tillamook, the original Pacific City pub is set in a most enviable spot right on the beach opposite Cape Kiwanda and Haystack Rock, and boasts the best coastal views of any brewpub in Oregon. Sweet potato-quinoa cakes, dory-caught fish-and-chips, flatbreads, and cioppino with a cream ale broth are some of the standouts. The pub's brews, including Tsunami Stout, Doryman's Dark Ale, India Pelican Ale, and MacPelican's Scottish Style Ale, have garnered stacks of awards.

South of Cape Kiwanda, find the **Grateful Bread Bakery** (34085 Brooten Rd., 503/965-7337, www.gratefulbreadbakery.com, 8am-3pm Thurs.-Mon., $7-15), where the challah bread, carrot cake, marionberry strudel, and other homemade baked goods deserve special mention. The breakfast menu offers a range of tasty pancakes, scrambles, and omelets served with oven-roasted spuds. Lunch sandwiches, quesadillas, and rice bowls include a wide range of vegetarian options.

Accommodations and Camping

Cape Kiwanda is the only place on the Three Capes Scenic Loop with luxurious accommodations.

At the large ★ **Inn at Cape Kiwanda** (33105 Cape Kiwanda Dr., 503/965-6366 or 888/965-7001, www.yourlittlebeachtown.com/inn, $279-369), all rooms face a beautiful beach and Cape Kiwanda's giant sand dune. If it's too rainy to go outside, fireplaces and spacious, well-appointed rooms make for great storm-watching. Whirlpool tub rooms are available, and pets are permitted in some rooms.

Even closer to the beach is the extra-comfortable **Headlands Coastal Lodge and Spa** (33000 Cape Kiwanda Dr., 503/483-3000, http://headlandslodge.com, $420-580), a beautiful hotel in high Pacific Northwest style, with a timbered entrance, wood-burning fireplace in the lobby, Pendleton blankets on the beds, cast-iron soaking tubs, cruiser bikes to ride, views from every well-appointed room, and a friendly, down-to-earth staff. The lodge, which invites guests to "head out or stay in" offers yoga classes and full spa services, and a concierge can set up outdoor excursions.

The Instagram-ready **Hart's Camp** (33145 Webb Park Rd., 503/965-7006, www.

hartscamp.com, $269-319 Airstreams, $49 RVs) is an RV park that also rents out Airstream trailers. It's tucked behind the Inn at Cape Kiwanda, so it's just a short walk to the beach. Airstreams come with bikes, linens, and cookware and have baths and indoor and outdoor showers. Most are pet-friendly, and there's even a small dog park (as if the beach weren't a giant dog park!).

A more genuine camping experience can be had about 4.5 miles north of Pacific City on the Three Capes Scenic Loop, where the **Clay Meyers Natural Area at Whalen Island** (25210 Sandlake Rd., Cloverdale, 503/965-6085, www.co.tillamook.or.us, $22-27) has a small campground run by Tillamook County. It's an open, sandy spot with a boat launch and flush toilets; nearby hiking trails traverse wetlands and provide a great look at the coastal Sand Lake Estuary.

Neskowin and Cascade Head

NESKOWIN

The tiny vacation village of Neskowin (rhymes with "let's go in," pop. 130) has a quiet appeal based on a beautiful beach and a golf course in the shadow of 1,500-foot-high Cascade Head. It's the polar opposite of busy Lincoln City, 15 miles south. There's not much to do here but relax on the uncrowded beach and enjoy the views of Cascade Head and the dark beauty of **Proposal Rock,** a stony, forested hillock that stands right at the edge of the surf, with Neskowin Creek curving around it. The feature was named by Neskowin's first postmistress, whose daughter received a marriage proposal nearby. Neskowin has a reputation as a beach town for old-money, in-the-know Portland families.

During especially low tides, a "ghost forest" emerges from the beach south of Proposal Rock. The Sitka spruce stumps, some of which are 2,000 years old, were covered when an earthquake dropped the land they were growing on and landslides or a tsunami covered

them with mud and debris. Tremendous storms during the winter of 1997-1998 scoured the debris, leaving the trees to emerge when the tides recede.

The sleepy town has only one art gallery, and it's a good one. **Hawk Creek Gallery** (48460 U.S. 101 S., 503/392-3879, www.hawkcreekgallery.com, 11am-5pm daily summer, 11am-5pm Sat.-Sun. spring and fall) is the studio and showroom for the works of painter Michael Schlicting, who exhibits his work internationally but has made the Hawk Creek Gallery his home base since 1978.

Food and Accommodations

Waits can be long at the tiny **Cafe on Hawk Creek** (4505 Salem Ave., 503/392-4400, www.cafeonhawkcreek.com, 8am-9pm daily, call for winter hours, $15-29), particularly at breakfast, but the food is worth it. Count on filling omelets for breakfast; sandwiches, burgers, and wood-fired pizza for lunch; and grilled fish and steaks for dinner. Hidden

behind the general store is **Beach Club Bistro** (48880 Hwy. 101 S., 503/392-3035, http://beachclubbistro.com, 4pm-9pm Wed.-Sun., $19-32), a friendly spot with a selection of small plates for grazing, and main courses such as crab and Parmesan ravioli with seared scallops and prawns for serious dining.

Proposal Rock Inn (48988 U.S. 101 S., 503/392-3115, www.proposalrockneskowin. com, $74-249) backs up on Hawk Creek and commands a fine view of the beach and the eponymous rock. Two-room ocean-view suites with a full kitchen fetch higher prices than the standard no-view guest rooms, but all are right on the beach.

Many of the available rental units in Neskowin are handled by **Grey Fox Vacation Rentals** (48900 Hwy. 101 S., 503/392-4355, www.neskowinbeachvacations.com, $149-375). Rooms are available at several condo complexes as well as in individual houses scattered around town.

CASCADE HEAD
Cascade Head Scenic Research Area

About 10 miles north of Lincoln City, the 11,890-acre Cascade Head Experimental Forest was set aside in 1934 for scientific study of typical coastal Sitka spruce and western hemlock forests found along the Oregon coast. In 1974, Congress established the 9,670-acre **Cascade Head Scenic Research Area** (www.fs.usda.gov/recarea/siuslaw/recreation), which includes the western half of the forest, several prairie headlands, and the Salmon River estuary. In 1980, the entire area was designated a biosphere reserve as part of the United Nations Biosphere Reserve system.

The headlands, reaching as high as 1,800 feet, are unusual for their extensive prairies still dominated by native grasses: red fescue, wild rye, and Pacific reedgrass. The Nechesney people, who inhabited the area as long as 12,000 years ago, purposely burned forest

---

1: Three Arch Rocks Wildlife Refuge at Oceanside
2: secluded beach at Neskowin

tracts around Cascade Head, probably to provide browse for deer and to reduce the possibility of larger uncontrollable blazes. These human-made alterations are complemented by the inherent dryness of south-facing slopes, which receive increased exposure to the sun. In contrast to these grasslands, the northern part of the headland is the domain of giant spruces and firs because it catches the brunt of the heavy rainfalls and lingering fogs. Endemic wildflowers include coastal paintbrush, goldenrod, streambank lupine, rare hairy checkermallow, and blue violet, a plant critical to the survival of the Oregon silverspot butterfly, a threatened species found in only six locations. Deer, elk, coyotes, snowshoe hares, and the Pacific giant salamander find refuge here, while bald eagles, great horned owls, and peregrine falcons may be seen hunting above the grassy slopes. Today, in addition to its biological importance, the area is a mecca for some 6,000 hikers annually, and for anglers who target the salmon and steelhead runs on the Salmon River.

On the north side of the Salmon River, turn west from U.S. 101 onto **Three Rocks Road** for a scenic driving detour on the south side of Cascade Head. The paved road curves about 2.5 miles above the wetlands and widening channel of the Salmon River estuary, passes Savage Road, and ends at a parking area and boat launch at Knight County Park. From the park, the road turns to gravel and narrows (not suitable for RVs or trailers), and continues about another 0.5 mile to its end at a spectacular overlook across the estuary.

HIKING

Cascade Head offers some outstanding scenic hikes, with rainforest pathways and wildflower meadows giving way to dramatic ocean views.

A short but brisk hike to the top of the headland on a **Nature Conservancy trail** begins near Knight County Park. Leave your car at the park and walk 0.5 mile up Savage Road to the trailhead. It's 1.7 miles one-way, with 1,100 feet of elevation gain. No dogs or bicycles are allowed on the trail, which is open year-round.

Two trails are accessible from Cascade Head Road (Forest Rd. 1861), a gravel road open seasonally (July 16-Dec. 31) that heads west off U.S. 101 about three miles north of Three Rocks Road, near the highway summit of Cascade Head. Travel this road four miles west of U.S. 101 to the **Hart's Cove trailhead.** The first part of the trail runs through arching red alder treetops and 250-year-old Sitka spruces with five-foot diameters. The understory of mosses and ferns is nourished by 100-inch rainfalls. Next the trail emerges into open grasslands. The five-mile round-trip hike loses 900 feet in elevation on its way to an oceanfront meadow overlooking Hart's Cove, where the barking of sea lions might greet you. This trail can have plenty of mud, so boots are recommended as you tromp through the rainforest.

An easier trail accessible from Cascade Head Road heads to a viewpoint on the Nature Conservancy's preserve. (Again, no dogs or bikes are allowed on Nature Conservancy land.) The 1-mile trail starts about 3.5 miles west of U.S. 101 and heads to a big meadow and an ocean overlook. It's possible to continue from the overlook, heading downhill to join up with the lower Nature Conservancy trail described above.

The **Cascade Head Trail** runs six miles roughly parallel to the highway, with a south trailhead near the intersection of Three Rocks Road and U.S. 101 and a north trailhead at Falls Creek, on U.S. 101 about one mile south of Neskowin. It passes through old-growth forest and is entirely inland, without the spectacular ocean views of other trails in the area.

Sitka Center for Art and Ecology

The region in the shadow of Cascade Head can be explored in even greater depth thanks to the **Sitka Center for Art and Ecology** (56605 Sitka Dr., Otis, 541/994-5485, www. sitkacenter.org, 10am-5pm Mon.-Fri.), located off Savage Road on the south side of the headland. Workshops (May-Sept.) are offered, focusing on art and nature, with an emphasis on the strong relationship between the two. Experts in everything from local plant communities to the baskets of the Siletz people conduct outdoor workshops on the grounds of Cascade Head Ranch. Classes can last from a couple of days to a week, and fees vary accordingly.

Central Coast

Oregon's central coast, from Lincoln City to Reedsport and Winchester Bay, embraces such contrasts that it's difficult to generalize about the region.

In the north, Lincoln City's dense mix of lodgings and outlet shopping, combined with its Native American casinos, generates the coast's worst traffic jams, especially on holidays and weekends. The sprawling town isn't everyone's first choice for a quiet getaway, but it's a longtime favorite with families. Depoe Bay—built around the world's smallest navigable natural harbor—is headquarters for the coast's busiest whale-watching fleet, and one of its largest and most sprawling condo developments.

A necklace of small state parks adorns the shore every couple of

Highlights

Look for ★ to find recommended sights, activities, dining, and lodging.

★ **Whale Watching Center:** Spot gray whales from an onshore viewing station in Depoe Bay, free and staffed by volunteers (page 112).

★ **Oregon Coast Aquarium:** Explore the life of Oregon's shores and the ocean at this excellent aquarium (page 116).

★ **Yaquina Head Outstanding Natural Area:** A soaring lighthouse stands above a tide-pool-studded inlet at this small park, the quintessence of the Oregon coast (page 121).

★ **Cape Perpetua:** One of the most dramatic natural areas along the Oregon coast is a top spot for hiking and exploring tide pools (page 131).

★ **Heceta Head Lighthouse and Devil's Elbow:** Climb to the top of this whitewashed lighthouse for wonderful views—or stay in the lighthouse keeper's house, now a B&B (page 137).

★ **Sea Lion Caves:** Take an elevator ride down to the caves at cliff's bottom to get a close look at the Steller sea lion rookery (page 137).

★ **John Dellenback Trail:** Explore 400-foot-high dunes in the Oregon Dunes National Recreation Area (page 149).

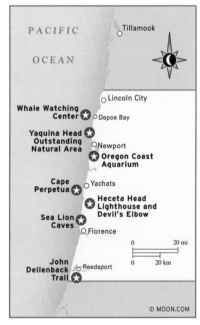

PACIFIC

OCEAN

Tillamook

Lincoln City

Whale Watching Center ★ ○ Depoe Bay

Yaquina Head Outstanding Natural Area ★ ○ Newport

★ Oregon Coast Aquarium

Cape Perpetua ★ ○ Yachats

★ Heceta Head Lighthouse and Devil's Elbow

Sea Lion Caves ★ ○ Florence

John Dellenback Trail ★ ○ Reedsport

0   20 mi
0   20 km

© MOON.COM

miles all the way from southern Lincoln City southward; inland, the Siuslaw National Forest safeguards several wilderness areas and groves of rare old-growth coastal forest, beckoning hikers to explore the primeval landscapes. Just north of Newport, Yaquina Head Outstanding Natural Area offers excellent vantage points for up-close whale-watching and bird-watching, plus tide pools accessible to wheelchair users.

The bustling harbor at Newport is home to both commercial fishing and recreational fleets, the latter of which runs charters year-round for rockfish and seasonally for salmon, tuna, and halibut. Newport also boasts the state-of-the-art Oregon Coast Aquarium and the bohemian resort community of Nye Beach, which has been attracting visitors since the 19th century.

Just south of Yachats, the panoramic view from Cape Perpetua can, on a clear day, extend 75 miles in each direction. Down at sea level, the tide pools here are some of the most fascinating on the coast. At Sea Lion Caves, a touristy but unique experience between Yachats and Florence, the world's largest sea cave is the only mainland rookery of Steller sea lions in the lower 48 states. Close by, photographers spend more time trying to capture the perfect image of Heceta Head Lighthouse than any other sight along the entire coast.

PLANNING YOUR TIME

It's easy to spend a few days exploring the central coast. Although Lincoln City has abundant hotel rooms and is a good fallback during busy times of the year, tiny Depoe Bay is a great place to spend a night, perhaps with an early rise to take a fishing or whale-watching trip. And though Newport is a big city by Oregon coast standards, it's definitely worth spending a couple of nights here. In fact, if you're looking for a base for central coast explorations, Newport is well situated to visit sites from Lincoln City down to Florence. While in Newport, you may simply want to poke around the Nye Beach and Bayfront neighborhoods, beachcomb on Agate Beach,

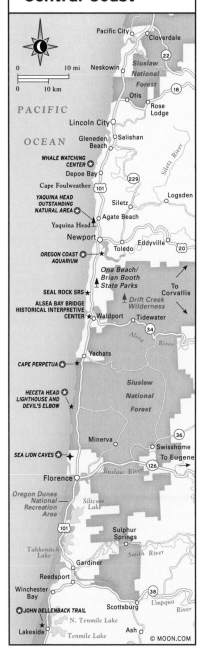

Central Coast

and check out the tide pools and lighthouse at the Yaquina Head Outstanding Natural Area; or you might decide to devote a day to the Oregon Coast Aquarium and the nearby Oregon State University Hatfield Marine Science Center.

Personally, when we have the opportunity to plunk down at the coast for a long weekend, we almost always head to **Yachats** to enjoy the low-key atmosphere, the incredible natural beauty, and the good restaurants of this tiny town. If you are touring the coast, we think it (and the incredible Cape Perpetua coastline just south) is worth a full day and night of your time.

Florence is a short hop from Yachats and is a good alternative if you'd rather stay in a slightly larger town with a lively Old Town and easy access to the north end of the Oregon Dunes National Recreation Area, a fantastic landscape of dazzling white-sand mountains and jewel lakes stretched along nearly 50 miles of shoreline.

Although anglers may want to stay at **Winchester Bay,** for most coast travelers this little town is a good stop for fish-and-chips, but not an overnight destination. Nearby, **Reedsport** is in the heart of the dune country and a good place to camp while exploring the dunes.

Lincoln City

Back in 1964, five burgs that straddled seven miles of beachfront between Siletz Bay and the Salmon River came together and incorporated as Lincoln City. In commemoration, a 14-foot bronze statue of President Abraham Lincoln was donated to the city by an Illinois sculptor. *The Lank Lawyer Reading in His Saddle While His Horse Grazes* originally occupied a city park; today the statue stands in a nondescript lot at NE 22nd Street and Quay Avenue. Look for the sign on U.S. 101 near the Dairy Queen.

What were once discrete towns have grown and melded into an uninterrupted conurbation with a population of about 9,000 (which can balloon to 30,000 on a busy weekend). While the resulting sprawl and heavy traffic on U.S. 101 can be maddening at times, once you get off the highway, Lincoln City has some charming neighborhoods (check out the Taft area at the south end of town); wide sandy beaches; superlative wildlife-viewing around Siletz Bay; the large, freshwater Devils Lake; one of the state's most noted resorts at Salishan, just south of the city; and two Native

American casinos. Add prime kite-flying, some of the coast's better restaurants, and bibliophilic and antiquing haunts, and it's clear that there's more to the area than the pull of saltwater taffy and outlet malls.

SIGHTS AND RECREATION
Lincoln City Beach

Lincoln City boasts seven uninterrupted miles of sandy beach. From Siletz Bay north to Road's End State Recreation Area, there are more than a dozen access points. You can head west from U.S. 101 on just about any side street to get there, though high coastal bluffs lining the north-central portion of town may mean a climb down (and back up) long flights of stairs cut into the cliff. For something approaching solitude on a crowded day, follow Logan Road west from the highway near the north end of town to **Road's End State Recreation Area;** tide pools and a secluded cove add to the allure. This stretch is also popular with kiteboarders and surfers.

Tide pool explorers should also check

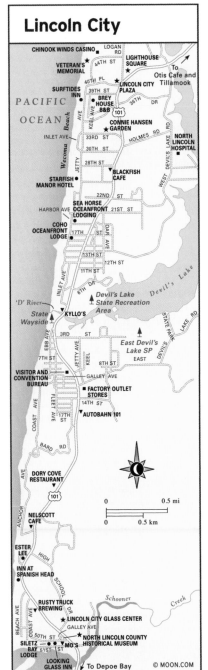

Lincoln City

out the **rock formations** at SW 11th Street (Canyon Drive Park), NW 15th Street, and SW 32nd Street.

The **D River Wayside,** a small park on the beach in more or less the middle of town, is a state park property where you can watch what locals claim is the "world's shortest river" empty into the ocean. Flowing just 120 feet from its source, Devils Lake, to its mouth at the Pacific, it's short, all right; despite its unspectacular appearance, it was a cause célèbre when *Guinness World Records* withdrew the D's claim to fame in favor of a Montana waterway, the Roe. Local schoolkids rallied to the D's defense with an amended measurement, but the Roe, at a mere 53 feet long, carries the *Guinness* imprimatur as the shortest river. In addition to seeing the D River flow from "D" Lake into "D" ocean, you can fly a kite on the beach. It's one of the easier beach access points between stretches of high, motel-topped bluffs, so it can get a little crowded.

Another convenient beach access is off SW 51st Street at the south end of town, just before **Siletz Bay.** A large parking area here in what's known as the Taft District stands beside the driftwood-strewn shore of the bay, where you can often see a group of harbor seals chasing their dinner or coming in for a closer look at you. It's a short walk to the ocean.

At one time it was common for storms and currents to wash up that ultimate beachcomber's prize—**glass fishing floats**—on the Oregon coast. Lincoln City improves the beachcomber's odds with its Finders Keepers program, in which the city distributes nearly 3,000 glass floats along its beaches mid-October-Memorial Day. Handcrafted by Pacific Northwest glass artists, each of the colorful floats is signed and numbered and placed by volunteers on the beaches above the high-tide line. If you find one, it's yours to keep; you can call or stop in at the visitors center for a certificate and information about the artist who created it.

The Legacy of Ken Kesey

Two miles south of Lincoln City, you'll come to the turnoff for Highway 229 along the Siletz River. If you drive down the north side of the river about 1.25 miles, on the opposite shore you'll notice a showy Victorian-ish house. It was constructed for the movie version of *Sometimes a Great Notion*. The 1971 film, a so-so adaptation of Ken Kesey's memorable novel, starred Paul Newman, Lee Remick, Henry Fonda, and Michael Sarrazin. The plot concerns the never-say-die spirit of an antiunion timber baron, his not-always-supportive family, and life in the mythical Coast Range logging community of Wakonda. A huge porch once fronted the riverbank, heavily reinforced against the elements. It was taken down in the decade after the movie was made, but it lives on in the pages of the book. Much of the movie was shot in this area, with café scenes taking place at Mo's on Newport's Bayfront. Other scenes were shot near Florence.

Devils Lake

Devils Lake, just east of the highway, is the recreation center of Lincoln City. In addition to windsurfing and hydroplaning, you can fish here—the lake is stocked with hatchery trout, and there's also a population of wild coho salmon (catch-and-release only) as well as lampreys. There's good bird-watching on and around this shallow 678-acre lake, which attracts flocks of migratory geese, ducks, and other waterfowl. Species to look for include canvasbacks, Canada geese, widgeons, gadwalls, grebes, and mallards. Bald eagles and ospreys nest in the trees bordering the lake.

The lake takes its name from a local Native American legend. The story goes that when Siletz warriors paddled a canoe across the lake one moonlit night, a tentacled beast erupted from the still water and pulled the men under. It's said that boaters today who cross the moon's reflection in the middle of the lake tempt the same fate, but the lake's devil has remained silent for years.

Of the five access points, East Devils Lake Road off U.S. 101 northeast of town offers a scenic route around the lake's east side before rejoining U.S. 101 near the day-use portion of the state park at the south end of the lake. To reach the camping area of Devils Lake State Recreation Area, take NE 6th Drive east from U.S. 101, about 0.25 mile north of the D River. The day-use area has a boat ramp, and there's a moorage dock across the lake adjacent to the campground.

Mountain bikes, canoes, fishing boats, and Jet Skis can be rented at Blue Heron Landing (4006 W. Devils Lake Rd., 541/994-4708, www.blueheronlanding.net, 9am-7pm daily).

Drift Creek Falls

Although it requires a drive inland, it's worth heading about 10 miles east to hike to Drift Creek Falls (503/392-3161, $5 NW Forest Pass to park). The relatively easy but steadily downhill 1.5-mile trail passes through a forest with mostly second growth, a little old growth, lots of big stumps, and an understory of lovely native plants, and it leads to a dramatic 240-foot-high suspension bridge overlooking the 75-foot falls. The bridge, built in 1998, is as much an attraction as the falls—it sways a little bit as you walk out to view the falls. From the bridge, the trail continues another 0.25 mile to the base of the falls.

From Highway 18, turn south at Rose Lodge onto Bear Creek Road (which becomes Forest Rd. 17) and follow it for about nine miles. At the fork with Schooner Creek Road, go left (uphill); a rustic sign notes that it's the way to "Drift Creek Camp."

From U.S. 101, turn east onto Drift Creek Road (at the south end of Lincoln City), then south onto South Drift Creek Road. Turn east onto Forest Road 17 and follow it for about 10 miles.

Siletz River

The **Siletz Bay National Wildlife Refuge** preserves coastal estuaries and wetlands on either side of U.S. 101 at the south end of Lincoln City. The skeleton trees here are reminders of times when the salt marsh was diked to provide pasture for dairy cows. Now these snags are used by red-tailed hawks, bald eagles, and other birds of prey. The wetlands provide habitat for great blue herons, egrets, and other waterbirds.

During the summer, refuge rangers lead a small number of **paddle trips** along the Siletz estuaries. Trips are free, but participants must register well beforehand (541/867-4550, www.fws.gov/refuge/siletz_bay) and provide their own canoe or kayak. **Siletz Moorage** (82 Siletz Hwy., 541/765-2109) rents kayaks ($40 for 3 hours) from its location on the north bank of the river just east of the highway.

Casinos

One of the biggest draws in town is the **Chinook Winds Casino** (1777 NW 44th St., 541/996-5825 or 888/244-6665, www.chinookwindscasino.com, 24 hours daily), operated by the Confederated Tribes of Siletz Indians, near the north end of town. In addition to slots, blackjack, poker, keno, bingo, craps, and roulette, the casino has a hotel, two on-site restaurants, a golf course, and a busy schedule of big-name (or formerly big-name) entertainment.

About 25 miles east of Lincoln City is the state's largest casino, **Spirit Mountain Casino** (21700 SW Salmon River Hwy., Grand Ronde, 503/879-2350, http://spiritmountain.com, 24 hours daily), operated by the Confederated Tribes of Grand Ronde. Games of chance include slots, craps, blackjack, poker, keno, and bingo. No matter what you think of the casino, it should be noted that the Grand Ronde people have done a great job at getting their tribal status officially reinstated after the U.S. government terminated it in 1954, leaving it with not much more than the tribal cemetery and a shed. They have amassed land and established a community fund that is a substantial supporter of non-profit organizations in Oregon; 6 percent of the casino's proceeds go into this charitable fund. A hotel and restaurants are on-site.

North Lincoln County Historical Museum

The modest **North Lincoln County Historical Museum** (4907 SW U.S. 101, 541/996-6614, www.northlincolncountyhistoricalmuseum.org, 11am-4pm Wed.-Sun. June-Aug., 11am-4pm Wed.-Sat. Sept.-Dec. 15 and Feb.-May, free) tells the story of this area through exhibits of old-time logging machinery, homesteading tools, fishing, military life, and Native American history. A highlight is the great collection of Japanese glass fishing floats.

Connie Hansen Garden

Tucked into the neighborhood between busy U.S. 101 and the beach, the **Connie Hansen Garden** (1931 NW 33rd St., 541/994-6338, www.conniehansengarden.com, dawn-dusk daily, free) is a great example of a coastal rainforest garden. The late Connie Hansen bought the land because its dampness seemed well suited to growing irises, her favorite plants, but she soon expanded her vision, working with the site's ecology and her own artistic talents to create a horticultural showcase. Guided tours are available for a small fee with advance notice, and there's a gift shop (10am-2pm Fri.-Sun. and Tues. Mar.-mid-Dec.).

Glass Art

Spend a rainy day learning to blow a glass float or paperweight at the **Lincoln City Glass Center** (4821 SW U.S. 101, 541/996-2569, www.lincolncityglasscenter.com, 10am-6pm daily, classes $65-185, reservations required). Kids ages eight and older may participate with parental supervision. Wear closed-toe shoes, and no fleece!

About four miles south of town, near Salishan, you can watch the glass blowers at **Alder House** (611 Immonen Rd., 541/996-2483, www.alderhouse.com, 10am-5pm daily

May-Oct.) and buy floats, paperweights, or other glass creations at reasonable prices. Call ahead to confirm opening hours.

Salishan Aerial Park

Explore the forests surrounding the **Salishan Resort** (7760 N. U.S. 101, Gleneden Beach, 800/452-2300, www.salishan.com, 10:30am and 2pm Fri.-Sun., $59) from treetop level. The aerial park has 15 platforms and 21 "challenge elements" such as bridges, cables, and Tarzan ropes that canopy explorers can take on or skip, depending on fitness level and courage. Participants must be at least eight years old and able to reach six feet high.

Golf

The area's most prestigious golf resort is seven miles south of Lincoln City at Gleneden Beach. **Salishan Resort** (7760 N. U.S. 101, Gleneden Beach, 541/764-3632, www.salishan.com, $84-99 for 18 holes) is an award-winning 18-hole course set in the foothills of the Coast Range and bordered by Siletz Bay and the sea. This challenging 6,470-yard, par-71 championship layout course was redesigned by Oregon golf superstar Peter Jacobsen and includes stunning ocean views. Keep in mind that this is a Scottish links course, where the roughs are really rough.

ENTERTAINMENT

Brewpubs

The **Lighthouse Brew Pub** (4157 U.S. 101 N., 541/994-7238, 11am-11pm Sun.-Thurs., 11am-midnight Fri.-Sat., $8-20) is a welcome rehash of the successful McMenamins formula. Just look for a lighthouse replica in a parking lot on the northwest side of U.S. 101 across from McDonald's. Pizza, burgers, sandwiches, and salads can be washed down with McMenamins' own ales as well as hard cider and wine.

To find **Rusty Truck Brewing** (4649 SW U.S. 101, 541/994-7729, http://rustytruckbrewing.com, 4pm-9pm Mon.-Thurs., noon-11pm Fri.-Sat., noon-9pm Sun. $8-20), look for the old Chevy pickup parked in front of Roadhouse 101. In addition to a brewpub, there's a tap room out back; they alternate days off, but within the hours posted you'll find a variety of beers, categorized as being hoppy, fruity, malty, or seasonal.

The Arts

Lincoln City's homegrown theater company, **Theatre West** (3536 SE U.S. 101, 541/994-5663, www.theatrewest.com), stages half a dozen productions each year, with an emphasis on comedies, musicals, and drama. Visit the website for a list of current plays and their synopses.

Festivals and Events

Lincoln City calls itself the kite capital of the world, pointing to its position midway between the pole and the equator, which gives the area predictable wind patterns. The town holds not one but two kite fiestas at the D River Wayside each year. The summer **Kite Festival** (541/994-3070 or 800/452-2151) takes place the last weekend in June; the fall festival is held the first weekend in October. The event is famous for giant spin socks, some as long as 150 feet.

SHOPPING

To sample the work of area artists, check out the **Pacific Artists' Co-Op Gallery** (620 NE U.S. 101, 541/557-8000, 10am-5pm daily), which represents the work of some 40 artists and craftspeople in the Lincoln City area. At the south end of town, the **Freed Gallery** (6119 SW U.S. 101, 541/994-5600, 10am-5pm Mon.-Sat., noon-5pm Sun.) shows the work of over 100 artists in media ranging from jewelry to large metal sculptures.

South of town at Salishan, the high-end **Gallery at Salishan** (7755 U.S. 101 N., 541/764-3687, 11am-4pm Wed.-Sun.) has an eclectic selection of art by regional artists.

With some 65 shops, the **Tanger Outlet Center** (1500 SE East Devils Lake Rd., 541/996-5000), near the south end of town,

1: Mo's restaurant 2: D River Wayside

is the largest outlet mall on the Oregon coast and has become something of a regional destination. Shops here include the ones you'd expect—Coach, Chico's, Eddie Bauer—plus the Oregon-based **Pendleton Woolen Mills** (541/994-2496, www.pendleton-usa.com).

Northwest Winds (130 SE U.S. 101, 541/994-1004, 10am-5pm daily) sells and repairs kites just across the highway from the D River Wayside, Lincoln City's kite-flying hub.

FOOD

Lincoln City offers many dining options, most of them busy and family-focused. There are several fine-dining and ethnic options, however, and the general quality of food is high.

Pacific Northwest Cuisine

The ★ **Blackfish Cafe** (2733 NW U.S. 101, 541/996-1007, www.blackfishcafe.com, 11:30am-3pm and 5pm-close Wed.-Mon., $14-33) is a great find. The chef has long-standing relationships with local farmers, anglers, and mushroom foragers, and the Blackfish Cafe is dedicated to fairly priced and delicious regional cooking. The emphasis is on what's fresh, homegrown, and creative, such as grilled Willamette Valley pork brisket rubbed with coriander and cumin and troll-caught Chinook salmon with fennel-lime butter. There is no shortage of humbler fare, either, such as the self-proclaimed best clam chowder on the coast, Pacific City dory-caught fish-and-chips, and amazing fish tacos.

The Salishan Resort has had its ups and downs over the years, but with new owners it seems to be on an upswing, and it's quite possible to find a good meal in an attractive setting at the **Sun Room Restaurant** (7760 N. U.S. 101, Gleneden Beach, www.salishan. com, 7am-11am and 5pm-9pm daily, $23-39). This casual restaurant is less elaborate and less expensive than Salishan's signature **Dining Room** (5pm-9pm daily, $28-49), but its cuisine comes from the same kitchen. The specialties are local seafood, meat, and game. The wine list here is one of the largest in the state, and if you plan ahead, you can arrange for your meal to be served in the resort's wine cellar.

The **Bay House** (5911 SW U.S. 101, 541/996-3222, www.thebayhouse.org, 5pm-9pm Wed.-Sun., $32-50) combines views of Siletz Bay with exquisite Pacific Northwest cuisine. Moscovy duck breast is served with black lentils, celeriac puree, and poached bing cherries. An $84 five-course tasting menu is available, but must be ordered by everyone at the table. For a more casual and less expensive light dinner, eat from the small-plates menu in the lounge; the three-course $30 menu is a great deal. In either dining area, oenophiles will want to look at the wine list, praised by *Wine Spectator*.

A half mile south of Salishan (five miles equidistant from Depoe Bay and Lincoln City) is a Gleneden Beach eatery with considerable appeal. The airy yet cozy-feeling dining room at the **Side Door Café** (6675 Gleneden Beach Loop, 541/764-3825, www.sidedoorcafe.com, 11am-9pm Tues.-Sat., $10-30) is a perfect complement to the Oregon coast casual-meets-elegance atmosphere. The Side Door features a menu where honey mustard and herb-rubbed salmon with marionberry glaze exemplifies the offerings.

Seafood

If coastal restaurants are eating a hole in your wallet, there's always tried-and-true **Mo's** (860 SW 51st St., 541/996-2535, www. moschowder.com, 10:30am-9pm daily, $9-19). As at all Mo's locations, the view is great, and the seafood more than serviceable.

The chowder is a little tastier at the **Dory Cove Restaurant** (2981 SW U.S. 101, 541/557-4000, www.dorycove.com, 8am-8pm Sun.-Thurs., 8am-9pm Fri.-Sat., $9-28), but the views from this simple restaurant are out onto the highway. The Dory Cove's secret weapon is breakfast: Try a crab-and-cheese omelet or grilled razor clams with eggs.

Kyllo's Seafood Grill (1110 NW 1st Court, 541/994-3179, www.kyllosrestaurant. com, 11:30am-8:30pm Sun.-Thurs., 11:30am-9pm Fri.-Sat., $16-30) specializes in broiled, sautéed, and baked seafood, plus excellent pasta, sandwiches, and homemade desserts served with Oregon microbrews and wines. The restaurant is visible from U.S. 101 right in the middle of Lincoln City as you drive by the D River Wayside. With views of the water on all sides, this restaurant is a good place to linger, though waits can be long in the evening since no reservations are taken.

Classic American

If you're en route to the wine country or the Willamette Valley or just want a respite from coastal traffic, a place that appeals to everybody is ★ **Otis Cafe** (1259 Salmon River Hwy., 541/994-2813, www.otiscafe.com), at the Otis Junction on Highway 18, five miles northeast of Lincoln City. It's our favorite pie stop and a good place for a hearty breakfast.

The perfect homey spot for a traditional breakfast is the **Nelscott Café** (3237 SW U.S. 101, 541/994-6100, 7:30am-1pm Mon. and Wed.-Sat., $7-12). The breakfast standards such as omelets and French toast are well prepared (don't deny yourself a cinnamon roll), and there are good burgers and sandwiches for lunch. This is a small place and can get busy on weekends.

German

If gluey Oregon clam chowder is wrecking your appetite, perhaps you're ready for **Autobahn 101** (1512 SE U.S. 101, 541/614-1811, 11:30am-10pm Sun.-Thurs., 11:30am-midnight Fri.-Sat., $10-15), a German pub with seven German beers on tap and a big menu of Teutonic bar food. Check out the schnitzel dinners and the house-made *weiss-wurst* (white sausage) with sauerkraut.

ACCOMMODATIONS

Lincoln City has more hotel rooms than any other coastal Oregon city. There are plenty to choose from, and many are similar—basic (usually pet-friendly) hotel rooms within walking distance of the beach. However, there are some distinctions. Unless severely constrained by budget, one would not purposefully choose to stay on the east side of U.S. 101, necessitating an unpleasant fording of that great vehicular river just to walk to the beach, so, with one exception (Salishan), all the following hotels are on the beach side of the highway. Also, just because a hotel is newer doesn't mean that it's preferred over older models. Many vintage hotels and motels have the best locations, and their slightly worn-in atmosphere is perfect for a summer holiday. For one-stop room shopping, the local visitors association **Central Oregon Coast** (www.oregoncoast.org) has a booking service with good rates.

$100-150

The **Ester Lee** (3803 SW U.S. 101, 541/996-3606 or 888/996-3606, www.esterlee.com, $126-149) is a decades-old family motel complex, with some cottages and motel units on a bluff above miles of beachfront. All rooms have ocean views and fireplaces; some have kitchens and hot tubs. Pets are allowed in some of the cottage units, most of which have kitchens and fireplaces. It's not a fancy place, but it's clean and pleasant, with a great location and a good value.

The **Siletz Bay Lodge** (1012 SW 51st St., 541/996-6111, http://siletzbaylodgelincolncity.com, $139-165), on the north end of Siletz Bay on a driftwood-strewn beach, is a family- and dog-friendly, wheelchair-accessible lodging in a location ideal for bird-watching and viewing seals. About half of the standard rooms of this older hotel have balconies, with views of the bay and the sunset over Salishan Spit. In-room amenities include microwaves, fridges, and coffeemakers, and a continental breakfast is offered.

Another good spot on the north end of Siletz Bay in Lincoln City's historic Taft area is the **Looking Glass Inn** (861 SW 51 St., 541/996-3996, www.lookingglass-inn.com, $124-169), an attractive place that would be quiet and tucked away if it weren't for the busy Mo's restaurant just across the road. Most rooms have kitchenettes, and most are dog-friendly.

Close to the beach at the north end of town, Brey House B&B (3725 NW Keel Ave., 541/994-7123, www.breyhouse.com, $114-164) is one of the oldest bed-and-breakfasts on the Oregon coast. The B&B is a three-story Cape Cod-style home built in 1940 with four bedrooms, all with private baths and entrances. The excellent breakfast is served in a light-filled room overlooking the ocean. Rooms are for adults only.

$150-200

A longtime, and now remodeled, Lincoln City motel, the Coho Oceanfront Lodge (1635 NW Harbor Ave., 541/994-3684 or 800/848-7006, www.thecoholodge.com, $156-199) has guest rooms with a sleek and sophisticated modern look. An indoor pool and steam room are available for guests to use, and breakfast is included in the stay.

A small oceanfront luxury hotel near the popular D River Wayside, the Shearwater Inn (120 NW Inlet Court, 541/994-4121 or 800/869-8069, www.theshearwaterinn.com, $149-289) offers 30 units with balconies and gas fireplaces. Guests meet in the lobby every afternoon to sample Oregon wine. The hotel provides concierge and massage services and a continental breakfast, and accepts pets. The building is also wheelchair accessible.

On the bluff above the beach, with fine views and easy access to the sand, Seahorse Oceanfront Lodging (2039 NW Harbor Dr., 541/994-2101 or 800/662-2101, www.seahorsemotel.com, $120-260) has a dizzying selection of lodging options, from simple motel rooms to cottages, houses, and two- and three-bedroom units, all in an extensive and quiet oceanfront compound. While it's a bit hard to generalize, most rooms have kitchens, some have fireplaces, and all guests are welcome at the breakfast bar, indoor pool, and outdoor hot tub, which overlooks the beach. There are a handful of discounted partial or no-view rooms available. This friendly and venerable operation is one of the reasons Lincoln City is so popular with families.

Over $200

More a small boutique hotel than the sprawling motel complex that typifies Lincoln City, ★ Starfish Manor Hotel (2735 NW Inlet Ave., 541/996-9300 or 800/972-6155, www.onthebeachfront.com, $199-299) has just 17 oceanfront guest rooms and suites perched above the beach. All units have large oceanview whirlpool tubs, fireplaces, oceanfront decks, kitchenettes, tasteful furnishings, and fine linens. Some units have two bedrooms.

Salishan Resort is designed to meld into the landscape.

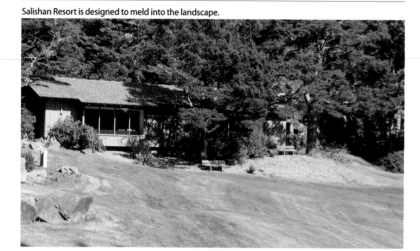

The Starfish is in a quiet part of town, perfect for a romantic getaway. The folks who own the Starfish have three other small boutique hotels with condo-like accommodations and similar prices; see the Starfish website.

A landmark that has had a recent makeover is the **Surftides** (2945 NW Jetty Ave., 541/994-2191 or 800/452-2159, www.surftideslincolncity.com, $170-280), a large complex hugging the beach at the northern edge of Lincoln City. All the oceanfront guest rooms have balconies, and most have fireplaces. All rooms include a small fridge, microwave, and coffeemaker. The inn has an indoor pool, a decent restaurant, a lounge, and meeting rooms. Prices vary by view; ask about partial- or no-view rooms, which are up to 30 percent cheaper. Pets are accepted in some rooms.

If you've been fantasizing about rolling out of bed, slipping on your robe, and walking out—coffee in hand—onto a semiprivate stretch of beach, then the **Inn at Spanish Head** (4009 SW U.S. 101, 541/996-2161 or 800/452-8127, www.spanishhead.com, $239-375) may be your best bet. Built right on the beach, the inn takes its place—large and looming—against the backdrop of rugged cliffs. Whether a suite, studio, or bedroom unit, every room has an ocean view. On-site amenities include a heated outdoor pool, saunas, a spa, and an exercise room.

When asked to choose *the* place to stay on the Oregon coast, many Oregonians would select the ★ **Salishan Resort** (7760 N. U.S. 101, Gleneden Beach, 541/764-3600 or 800/452-2300, www.salishan.com, $219-750), a few miles south of Lincoln City. While there are distant Siletz Bay views, Salishan isn't a beachfront resort, but most folks quickly learn to appreciate the peace of the forest and the golf course. This paradigm shift is facilitated by art and landscape architecture that convey the vision of John Gray, who built Salishan and such other Pacific Northwest properties as Skamania Lodge (on the Washington side of the Columbia Gorge) and Sunriver (south of Bend) from native materials with respect for the surrounding environment. In high season,

Salishan attracts well-heeled nature lovers, corporate expense-account clientele, folks enjoying a special occasion, and serious golfers. You'll also find everyday folks and seminar attendees on winter weekend specials at half the summertime rates. Ask about multiday packages for big savings on your room rate.

Vacation Rentals

To rent vacation homes throughout Lincoln County, contact the **Lincoln City Visitor and Convention Bureau** (800/452-2151, www.oregoncoast.org), or try **Meredith Lodging** (541/996-2955 or 877/778-9055, www.meredithlodging.com), which features a selection of vacation home rentals.

Camping

Devils Lake State Recreation Area (1452 NE 6th St., 541/994-2002, reservations 800/452-5687, www.reserveamerica.com, $21 tents, $32-34 RVs, $47-57 yurts, $8 hiker-biker) is the main public campground in Lincoln City. This campground is right in town, just off U.S. 101 at the northeast end, so it's hardly a quiet wilderness retreat, but it does provide easy access to swimming or boating on Devils Lake.

INFORMATION

The **Lincoln City Visitors Center** (540 NE U.S. 101, 541/994-3302, www.oregoncoast.org, 10am-4pm Mon.-Sat.) has a website that's full of helpful information.

TRANSPORTATION

Lincoln County Transit (541/265-4900, www.co.lincoln.or.us/transit) buses stop in town for service Monday-Saturday. The line goes as far south as Yachats and does not run on major holidays.

Peak traffic times in Lincoln City can result in 25,000 cars a day crawling through town. As an alternative to rush hour on U.S. 101, you could try detouring on NE West Devils Lake Road or NE East Devils Lake Road, which are themselves pretty slow, but bypass the worst congestion.

Depoe Bay

With its dramatic keyhole harbor—claimed to be the world's smallest natural harbor—Depoe Bay has long been a popular tourist destination. At least since the establishment of the town: For all intents and purposes, the town didn't really exist until the completion of the Roosevelt Highway (now U.S. 101) in 1927, which opened the area up to car travelers. Prior to that time, the area had been occupied mainly by a few Siletz people. One worked at the U.S. Army depot and called himself Charlie Depot. The town was named after him, eventually taking on the current spelling.

Regardless of what you think of the busy commercial strip and the enormous time-share resort along the highway, the scenic appeal of Depoe's location is impossible to ignore. The rocky outer bay, flanked by headlands to the north and south, is pierced by a narrow channel through the basalt cliffs leading to the inner harbor. It's home to an active sportfishing fleet as well as the whale-watching charters that have earned Depoe Bay its distinction as the whale-watching capital of the state. Depoe Bay's harbor was scenic enough to be selected as the site from which Jack Nicholson commandeered a yacht for his mental-patient crew in the classic 1975 film *One Flew Over the Cuckoo's Nest*.

SIGHTS AND RECREATION

The Bayfront and Harbor

Depoe Bay is situated along a truly beautiful coastline that cannot be fully appreciated from the highway. A quarter-mile-long seawall and promenade invite a stroll. For a panorama of the harbor, continue along the sidewalks across the gracefully arching concrete bridge, designed by Conde McCullough and built in 1927. Other photogenic perspectives are offered from residential streets west of U.S. 101; try Ellingson Street, south of the bridge, and Sunset Street, at the north end of the bay. Two "spouting horns," natural blowholes in the rocks north of the harbor entrance, can send plumes of spray 60 feet into the air when the tide and waves are right.

East of the bridge is Depoe Bay's claim to fame, the world's smallest navigable natural harbor. This boat basin is also exceptional because it's a harbor within a harbor. This topography is the result of wave action cutting into a fissure in the basalt cliffs over eons, finally creating a 50-foot passageway leading to a six-acre inland lagoon. In addition to whale-watching, folks congregate on the bridge between the ocean and the harbor to watch boats maneuver into the enclosure.Sights

TOP EXPERIENCE

★ Whale Watching Center

Stop in at the **Whale Watching Center** (119 SW U.S. 101, 541/765-3304, www.oregonstateparks.org, 10am-4pm daily summer, 10am-4pm Wed.-Sun. winter, free) where volunteers can help you spot whales and answer your questions about them. The center, right on the seawall, is an ideal viewing spot. Peak viewing times are mid-December-January, when whales are migrating south; late March-early June, when they're traveling north (mothers and babies generally come later in the season); and mid-July-early November, when resident whales feed off the coast. The least likely times to see whales from the central Oregon coast are mid-November-mid-December and mid-January-mid-March.

Whale, Sea Life & Shark Museum

The private **Whale, Sea Life & Shark Museum** (234 S. U.S. 101, 541/912-6734, www.oregonwhales.com, 11am-3pm daily, $5 adults, $3 ages 3-12) on the harbor side of the highway, 100 feet south of the bridge, is run in conjunction with the business Whale Research Eco Excursions, which offers whale-watching tours in Zodiac craft. The museum, which is free with a whale-watching trip, features models of marine mammals, a large collection of shark jaws, and lots of photos of whales.

Boiler Bay State Scenic Viewpoint

Boiler Bay, half a mile north of Depoe Bay, is so named because of the boiler left from the 1910 wreck of the *J. Marhoffer.* The ship caught fire three miles offshore and drifted into the bay. The remains of the boiler are visible at low tide. This rock-rimmed bay is a favorite spot for rock fishing, birding, and whale-watching. A trail leads down to some excellent tide pools.

Whale Cove

This picturesque bay 1.5 miles south of Depoe Bay has been scooped out of the sandstone bluffs. The tranquility of this calendar photo come to life is deceptive. There's considerable evidence to suggest that this tiny embayment—and not California's Marin County—was the site of Francis Drake's 1579 landing, but the jury is still out. During Prohibition, bootleggers used the protected cove as a clandestine port.

Rocky Creek State Scenic Viewpoint (800/551-6949, www.oregonstateparks.org, free) overlooks Whale Cove. There are picnic tables, and it's a good spot for whale-watching, but there's no beach access.

Otter Crest Loop

The rocky bluffs of this coastal stretch take on an even more dramatic aspect as you leave the highway at the **Otter Crest Loop,** a winding three-mile section of the old Coast Highway, two miles south of Depoe Bay. The northernmost part of the loop, down as far as Cape Foulweather, is one-way southbound, with a generous bike lane.

From atop **Cape Foulweather,** the visibility can extend 40 miles on a clear day. The view south to Yaquina Head and its lighthouse is a photographer's fantasy of headlands, coves, and offshore monoliths. Bronze plaques in the parking lot tell of Captain Cook naming the 500-foot-high headland during a bout with storm-tossed seas on March 7, 1778.

The Lookout (milepost 131.5, U.S. 101, 541/765-2270, www.oregonstateparks.org, 10am-4pm daily, free), a longtime gift shop on the north side of the promontory, is operated

the Whale Watching Center at Depoe Bay

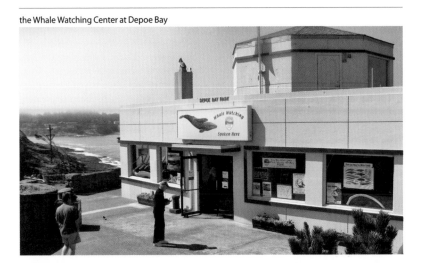

by Oregon State Parks. The million-dollar view from inside the shop is easily one of the most spectacular windows on the ocean to be found anywhere.

A mile south, in the hamlet of **Otter Rock,** you'll find another of the Oregon coast's several diabolically named natural features, the **Devil's Punchbowl.** The urn-like sandstone formation, filled with swirling water, has been sculpted by centuries of waves flooding into what had been a cave until its roof collapsed. The inexorable process continues today, thanks to the ebb and flow of the Pacific through two openings in the cauldron wall. A state park viewpoint gives you a ringside seat for this frothy confrontation between rock and tide. When the water recedes, you can see purple sea urchins and starfish in the tide pools of the **Marine Gardens** 100 feet to the north.

Back on U.S. 101, a mile's drive south brings you to Beverly Beach State Park.

TOP EXPERIENCE

Whale-Watching Tours

With the ocean minutes from Depoe Bay's port, seeing a whale is possible as soon as you leave the harbor.

Carrie Newell, a marine biologist and whale researcher, offers whale-watching tours with her company **Whale Research Eco Excursions** (234 S. U.S. 101, 541/912-6734, www.oregonwhales.com, 1.5 hours $45 adults, $35 ages 2-12) in inflatable Zodiac craft, which hold just six passengers. Carrie and her team offer insights into the local ecosystem and the life cycles of the local gray whales.

Most charter operators here also offer whale-watching excursions. **Dockside Charters** (541/765-2545 or 800/733-8915, http://docksidedepoebay.com) offers one-hour whale-watching trips ($20 adults) aboard its 50-foot excursion boat. **Tradewinds Charters** (541/765-2345 or 800/445-8730, www.tradewindscharters.com) hosts one- and two-hour trips ($20-35 adults).

Fishing

Most charter operators here also offer fishing excursions. Bottom-fishing trips average $80 for a five-hour run; salmon fishing (available only when salmon season is open) are about $150 for a seven- or eight-hour day; tuna and halibut fishing trips are available in season. In addition to whale-watching cruises. **Dockside Charters** (541/765-2545 or 800/733-8915, http://docksidedepoebay.com) and **Tradewinds Charters** (541/765-2345 or 800/445-8730, www.tradewindscharters.com) both offer fishing trips.

Surfing

If you're itching to actually get into the water and catch a few waves, the beach at **Otter Rock,** a few miles south of Depoe Bay, is a good place to surf. Park in the lot at Devil's Punchbowl and walk down the long flight of steps to the beach, which is relatively protected and has a large area where beginners tend to hang out. There's also a section that gets bigger waves and better surfers. **Pura Vida Surf Shop** (845 1st St., Otter Rock, 541/264-8793, http://pvsurfshop.com, 9am-6pm daily) offers rentals ($30/half-day) and lessons ($65-80).

ENTERTAINMENT AND EVENTS

The **Horn Public House and Brewery** (110 SE U.S. 101, 541/764-6886, http://thehorn.pub, 11am-9pm Sun.-Thurs., 11am-10pm Fri.-Sat., $11-15) offers a dozen brews on tap. From the 2nd-story dining room, you'll have great views of the harbor and the boats negotiating the narrow passage to the Pacific. The menu offers typical pub grub, including good versions of the coastal standards: chowder and fish-and-chips.

The **Depoe Bay Classic Wooden Boat Show, Crab Feed, and Ducky Derby** is held the third weekend in April. Several dozen wooden craft, both restored and newly constructed vessels, including kayaks, skiffs, dinghies, and larger fishing boats, are displayed in the harbor and the adjacent Depoe Bay City

Park. Rowing races, boatbuilding workshops, crab races, and other activities are scheduled. The big Crab Feed (11am-5pm Sat., 11am-3pm Sun., $15-25) sees some 2,000 pounds of crab plus side dishes devoured at the Community Hall. The Ducky Derby is a raffle in which you purchase "tickets" in the form of rubber duckies that race down the harbor's feeder stream vying for prizes. For more information, contact the **Depoe Bay Chamber of Commerce** (223 SW U.S. 101, 541/765-2889 or 877/485-8348, www.depoebaychamber.org, 11am-3pm Mon.-Sat.).

The **Fleet of Flowers** happens each Memorial Day in the harbor to honor those lost at sea and in military service. Thousands come to witness a blanket of blossoms cast upon the waters.

The **Depoe Bay Salmon Bake** ($25 adults, $12 children) takes place on the third Saturday of September (11am-4pm) at Depoe Bay City Park, flanking the rear of the boat basin. Some 3,000 pounds of fresh ocean fish are caught, cooked Native American-style on alder stakes over an open fire, and served with all the trimmings, to be savored to the accompaniment of live entertainment. It always seems to rain on the day of this event, but that's life on the Oregon coast.

FOOD

Of Depoe Bay's several restaurants, **Tidal Raves** (279 NW U.S. 101, 541/765-2995, www. tidalraves.com, 11am-9pm daily, $15-34) has the best combination of flavor, views, and casual ambience. A number of seafood dishes take on an Asian twist, such as Thai red curry barbecued shrimp. A pasta dish features crab, shrimp, lingcod, snapper, and more on a bed of linguine with your choice of sauce. The Dungeness crab mac and cheese is also noteworthy.

★ **Restaurant Beck** (2345 S. U.S. 101, 541/765-3220, http://restaurantbeck.com, 5pm-8pm daily, $29-34), in the Whale Cove Inn south of town, is Depoe Bay's only really elegant restaurant. It has a great view and excellent food, much of which originates on nearby farms and waters. Be prepared to

experiment: Pork belly confit and pickled sea beans are paired with miso ice cream; king salmon may be served with popcorn, corn puree, and beet tops. Seasonal ingredients figure prominently—in June, Rainier cherries pair with ancho chilies atop a lamb loin.

ACCOMMODATIONS

Lodgings in popular Depoe Bay require advance reservations on most weekends and holidays.

The ★ **Channel House** (35 Ellingson St., 541/765-2140 or 800/447-2140, www. channelhouse.com, rooms $125-330) features both standard B&B rooms and spacious suites boasting expansive views of the ocean, private decks with outdoor whirlpool tubs in most rooms, fireplaces, plush robes, and other amenities. This bluff-top B&B (there isn't a beach below, just miles of ocean and surrounding cliffs) may not look prepossessing from the outside, but inside, the place is all windows and angles—imagine *Architectural Digest* in a nautical theme. This is one of the best places on the Oregon coast to commune with whales, passing boats, winter storms, and the setting sun. A continental breakfast with tasty baked goods in an ocean-side dining area is included in the rates.

The **Inn at Arch Rock** (70 NW Sunset St., 541/765-2560 or 800/767-1835, www. innatarchrock.com, $99-349) is a cluster of white clapboard buildings that overlook Depoe Bay from a cliff-top perch at the north end of town. Most rooms have ocean views and are in the $150-200 range; a no-view room goes for much less. Pets are permitted in several rooms.

About a mile south of town, perched above scenic Whale Cove, find the boxy new **Whale Cove Inn** (2345 S. U.S. 101, 541/765-4300 or 800/628-3409, www.whalecoveinn.com, $480-650), a small boutique property that's a sister hotel to the Channel House. Here you can lounge in the hot tub on your private deck or on the Tempur-Pedic mattress in your bedroom alcove. All accommodations are in spacious suites; the top-end suites sleep six. Fine dining is available in the inn's Restaurant Beck. This is as high-end as the Oregon coast gets; kids 16 and older are welcome, but pets are not.

About three miles south of Depoe Bay, at one of the most scenic spots on the central coast, is the **Inn at Otter Crest** (301 Otter Crest Loop, Otter Rock, 541/765-2111 or 800/452-2101, www. innatottercrest.com, $140-230), a large condo resort perched near the sandstone bluffs at the ocean's edge. Hotel rooms have a king or two queen beds, a fridge, a coffeemaker, and a private deck with picture windows. Studios have a queen Murphy bed or a regular bed, a full kitchen, a fireplace, and a dining area; larger one- and two-bedroom suites are also available. The least expensive rooms have a forest view.

INFORMATION

On the east side of the highway, opposite the seawall, the **Depoe Bay Chamber of Commerce** (223 SW U.S. 101, 541/765-2889 or 877/485-8348, www.depoebaychamber.org) offers literature about the town and the central coast in general.

GETTING THERE

Lincoln County Transit (541/265-4900, www.co.lincoln.or.us/transit) runs buses, four times daily, north to Lincoln City and south to Yachats.

Newport

In January 1852, a storm grounded the schooner *Juliet* near Yaquina (pronounced yah-KWIN-nah) Bay, where her captain and crew were stranded for two months. When they finally made their way inland to the Willamette Valley, they reported their discovery of an abundance of tiny sweet-tasting oysters in the bay. Within a decade, commercial oyster farms were established—the first major impetus to growth and settlement in Newport. The tasty morsels, a Pacific Northwest species called Olympias, that delighted diners in San Francisco and at New York City's Waldorf-Astoria Hotel were almost harvested to extinction, but the oyster industry continued by introducing Japanese species. Dedicated oyster farmers have reestablished the briny Olympias in Oregon waters. They can now be found in select restaurants around the state.

In 2011, Newport (pop. 10,000) became the National Oceanic and Atmospheric Administration's Pacific Marine Operations Center, managing a fleet of research ships. During the summer, these ships are usually out at sea conducting oceanographic research, but when they're in port, the large white vessels are easy to spot in the harbor.

The port also bustles with the activity of Oregon's commercial and recreational fishing fleets. Factories to process *surimi* (a fish paste popular in Japan) and whiting have provided jobs, and a state-of-the-art aquarium that once housed Keiko the whale (from the movie *Free Willy*) brings in tourists. Wildlife observation facilities and access to tidal pools north of town at Yaquina Head make this park a highlight of the coast. The shops, galleries, and restaurants along Newport's historic Bayfront District, together with the Newport Performing Arts Center and quieter charm of Nye Beach, keep up a tourism tradition that goes back to when this town was the "honeymoon capital of Oregon."

SIGHTS

TOP EXPERIENCE

★ Oregon Coast Aquarium

There are 6,000 miles of water between the Oregon coast and Japan—the largest stretch of open ocean on earth. You can hear our side of the story at the **Oregon Coast Aquarium** (2820 SE Ferry Slip Rd., 541/867-3474, www. aquarium.org, 10am-6pm daily Memorial Day-Labor Day, 10am-5pm daily Labor Day-Memorial Day, $25 adults, $20 seniors and ages 13-17, $15 ages 3-12), one of the state's most popular attractions.

One of the gems of the aquarium is Passages

Newport

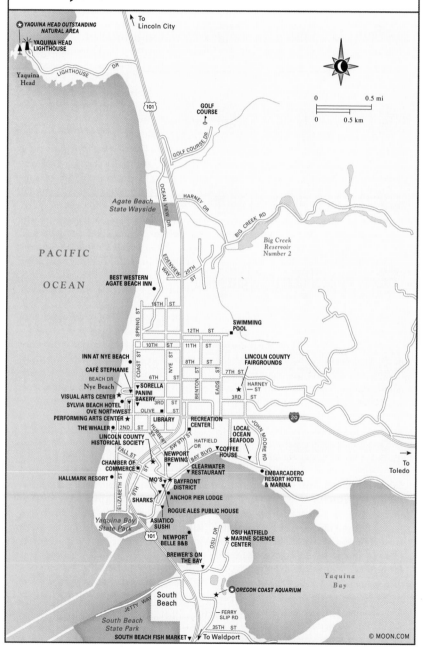

Yaquina Head

PACIFIC

OCEAN

To Lincoln City

YAQUINA HEAD OUTSTANDING NATURAL AREA

YAQUINA HEAD LIGHTHOUSE

Yaquina Head

LIGHTHOUSE DR

GOLF COURSE

GOLF COURSE DR

Agate Beach State Wayside

OCEAN VIEW DR

HARNEY DR

BIG CREEK RD

Big Creek Reservoir Number 2

EDENVIEW WAY

20TH ST

BEST WESTERN AGATE BEACH INN

15TH ST

SPRING ST

12TH ST

SWIMMING POOL

10TH ST

NYE ST

11TH ST

LINCOLN COUNTY FAIRGROUNDS

COAST ST

8TH ST

INN AT NYE BEACH

CAFÉ STEPHANIE

BEACH DR

Nye Beach

6TH ST

BENTON ST

EADS ST

7TH ST

HARNEY ST

SORELLA

PANINI BAKERY

VISUAL ARTS CENTER

3RD ST

3RD ST

SYLVIA BEACH HOTEL

OVE NORTHWEST

OLIVE ST

PERFORMING ARTS CENTER

LIBRARY

HUMBER ST

2ND ST

THE WHALER

RECREATION CENTER

LINCOLN COUNTY HISTORICAL SOCIETY

SW 9TH ST

JOHN MOORE RD

20

LOCAL OCEAN SEAFOOD

To Toledo

FALL ST

HATFIELD DR

BAY BLVD

NEWPORT BREWING

COFFEE HOUSE

CHAMBER OF COMMERCE

ELIZABETH ST

ST

CLEARWATER RESTAURANT

HALLMARK RESORT

EMBARCADERO RESORT HOTEL & MARINA

MO'S

9TH ST

BAYFRONT DISTRICT

SHARKS

ANCHOR PIER LODGE

Yaquina Bay State Park

ROGUE ALES PUBLIC HOUSE

ASIATICO SUSHI

101

NEWPORT BELLE B&B

OSU DR

OSU HATFIELD MARINE SCIENCE CENTER

BREWER'S ON THE BAY

Yaquina Bay

South Beach

OREGON COAST AQUARIUM

JETTY WAY

South Beach State Park

FERRY SLIP RD

35TH ST

SOUTH BEACH FISH MARKET

To Waldport

0   0.5 mi

0   0.5 km

© MOON.COM

of the Deep, a 200-foot-long acrylic tunnel offering 360-degree underwater views in three diverse habitats, from Orford Reef to Halibut Flats to Open Sea, where you're surrounded by free-swimming sharks. The jellyfish exhibit is a surprising highlight; it showcases several dozen kinds of jellyfish in an almost psychedelic display. And the "Seapunk" exhibit is a steampunk-inspired fantasy chronicling a fictitious inventor's underwater survival, complete with quirky mechanical inventions.

Of the several hundred species of Pacific Northwest fish, birds, and mammals on display in the rest of the facility, don't miss the sea otters, wolf eels, leopard sharks, lion's mane jellyfish, and tufted puffins. Kids will enjoy the sea cave with simulated wave action and a resident octopus. Simulations of indigenous ecosystems help visitors immerse themselves in the region's biology.

In addition to the regular exhibits, the aquarium offers hour-long Behind the Scenes tours (age 6 and over only, 12:30pm daily, $15), which show how keepers care for the over 15,000 animals that live here. Skip the extra fee and check the website to see animal feeding times (sea otters eat three times during the day!).

Advance tickets, available online, are recommended on weekends, major holidays, and during the summer. The facility also includes a couple eateries and a gift shop. To get here from U.S. 101 south of the Yaquina Bay Bridge, turn east on OSU Drive or 32nd Street and follow Ferry Slip Road to the parking lot.

OSU Hatfield Marine Science Center

Just south of the Yaquina Bay Bridge, head east on the road that parallels the bay to the **OSU Hatfield Marine Science Center** (2030 SE Marine Science Dr., 541/867-0100, http://hmsc.oregonstate.edu, 10am-5pm daily summer, 10am-4pm Thurs.-Mon. winter, 10am-4pm daily spring and winter break, $5 donation). This research and education facility is a low-key but interesting complement to the nearby Oregon Coast Aquarium.

The center has a "hands-on" area where you can experience the feel of starfish, anemones, and other sea creatures, plus tanks that represent different sea ecosystems. The back hallway has educational dioramas, and a theater shows marine science films throughout the day. Perhaps the biggest thrill is watching the octopus eat—it's fed at 1pm each Monday, Thursday, and Saturday.

Lincoln County Historical Society

The **Lincoln County Historical Society** has two facilities in Newport. For a glimpse into the rich past of Lincoln County, stop at the **Burrows House** (545 SW 9th St., 541/265-7509, http://oregoncoasthistory.org, 11am-4pm Thurs.-Sun., $5 donation), which incorporates a Queen Anne-style former boardinghouse, built in 1895, and the adjacent Log Cabin Museum. It's a half block east of the chamber of commerce on U.S. 101. The logging, farming, pioneer life, and maritime exhibits (particularly Newport shipwrecks) are interesting, but the Siletz baskets and other Native American artifacts steal the show.

Here you can learn the heartbreaking story of the hardships—forced displacement, inadequate housing, insufficient food, and poor medical facilities—that plagued the diverse Native American groups that made up the Confederated Siletz Reservation.

The historical society also runs the **Pacific Maritime & Heritage Center** (333 SE Bay Blvd., 11am-4pm Thurs.-Sun., $5 adults, free under age 12), which occupies a huge old mansion overlooking the Bayfront. Local residents have donated everything from ships' wheels to vintage surfboards to this museum, which is worth visiting for the setting and the building alone.

Bayfront District

Newport's **Old Town Bayfront District** can be easy to miss if you're not alert. At

1: a mini submarine at OSU Hatfield Marine Science Center 2: Passages of the Deep at the Oregon Coast Aquarium

The Spirit of Innovation

the north end of the **Yaquina Bay Bridge,** look for the signs pointing off U.S. 101 that lead down the hill to **Bay Boulevard,** the Bayfront's main drag. Alternatively, turn southeast off the highway a few blocks north onto Hurbert Street; it runs into Canyon Way, which ends at Bay Boulevard. On summer weekends, forget about parking anywhere near here unless you arrive early. Spots close by the boulevard can often be found, however, along Canyon Way, the hillside access route to downtown.

Until 1936, ferries shuttled people and vehicles to and from Newport's waterfront. With the completion of the Yaquina Bay Bridge that year, however, traffic bypassed the Old Town area. Commerce and development moved to the highway corridor, and the Bayfront faded in importance. Within the last couple of decades, the pendulum has swung back, and the Bayfront District is now one of Newport's prime attractions, with some of its best restaurants and watering holes, shopping, and tourist facilities.

One of the first things that'll strike you about the Bayfront today is that it's still a working neighborhood, not a sanitized recreation of a real seaport. Chowder houses, galleries, and shops stand shoulder to shoulder with fish-processing plants and canneries, and the air is filled with the cries of fishmongers and the barking of sea lions and harbor seals. On the waterfront, sport anglers step off charter boats with their catches, and vessels laden with everything from wood products to whale-watching tourists ply the bay. Unfortunately, the severe catch limits and cost of equipment make this less of a working port every year.

Yaquina Bay State Recreation Site

In 1871 a lighthouse was built here on a bluff overlooking the mouth of Yaquina Bay, and the lighthouse keeper, his wife, and seven children moved into the two-story wood-frame structure. It soon became apparent, however, that the location was not ideal, as the light could not be seen by ships approaching the harbor from the north. The station was abandoned after just three years once the nearby light at Yaquina Head was completed. The building was slated for demolition in 1934, when local residents formed the Lincoln County Historical Society to preserve it. In 1997 the government decided to turn Yaquina Bay's beacon back on.

Today, the handsome restored structure and surrounding grounds make up **Yaquina Bay State Recreation Site** (541/265-5679 or 800/551-6949, www.oregonstateparks.org, lighthouse hours noon-4pm daily, free), in a beautiful location at the north end of the Yaquina Bay Bridge. The last wooden lighthouse on the Oregon coast is also the oldest building in Newport. The living quarters, replete with period furnishings, are open to the public. Ask the volunteers about the resident ghost.

From the parking area, you have an excellent photo op of the bay and the bridge. The park is a good place to have a picnic, or you can descend the trails to the beach.

Nye Beach

The 1890s-era tourism boom that came to Newport's Bayfront spilled over into Nye Beach. In 1891, the city built a wooden sidewalk connecting the two neighborhoods, and soon "summer people" were filling the cedar cottages. In the next century, thanks to an improved river-and-land route from Corvallis, health faddists (who came for hot seawater baths in the sanatorium) and honeymooners soon joined the mix.

A mile north from the Bayfront, to the west of U.S. 101 (look for signs on the highway), this onetime favorite retreat for wealthy Portlanders has undergone a revival in recent years. Rough times and rougher weather had reduced luxurious beach houses here to a cluster of weather-beaten shacks until a performing arts center went up in 1988. On the heels of the development of this first-rate cultural facility, the conversion of a 1910 hotel into a kind of literary hostel encouraged other restorations and plenty of new construction. Culture vultures, beach lovers, and people-watchers now flock to Nye Beach, which feels a world away from the Coast Highway commercial strip just a few blocks to the east.

★ Yaquina Head Outstanding Natural Area

Five miles north of Newport, rocky Yaquina Head juts out to sea. Tools dating back 5,000 years have been unearthed at Yaquina Head. Many were made from elk and deer antlers and bone, as well as stone. Clam and mussel shells from middens in the area evidence a diet rich in shellfish for the area's ancient inhabitants.

Today, much of the headland is encompassed in the **Yaquina Head Outstanding Natural Area** (750 NW Lighthouse Dr., 541/574-3100, www.blm.gov, $7/vehicle), managed by the federal Bureau of Land Management. "Outstanding" is indeed the word for this place. Where the pounding ocean meets the land in a series of cliffs and tide pools, a visitor could easily spend several hours exploring all the site has to offer.

At its outer tip stands **Yaquina Head Lighthouse** (guided tours 11am-2pm daily July-mid-Sept., weather permitting, reserve at www.recreation.gov), the coast's tallest beacon. In the early 1870s, materials intended for construction of a lighthouse several miles north at Otter Crest were mistakenly delivered here. The 93-foot tower began operation in 1873, replacing the poorly located lighthouse south of here, at the mouth of Newport's harbor. When tours are offered, walk up the 114 cast-iron steps for a spectacular panorama of the headland and surrounding coast.

Below, an observation deck provides views of seals, sea lions, gray whales, and seabirds. Of the half-dozen varieties of pelagic birds that cluster on Colony Rock—a large monolith in the shallows 200 yards offshore—the tufted puffin is the most colorful. It's sometimes called a sea parrot because of its large yellow-orange bill. Puffins arrive here in April and are most visible early in the day on the rock's grassy patches. The most ubiquitous species are common murres, pigeon guillemots, and cormorants. The murre's white breast and belly contrast with its darker bill and elongated back. The guillemot resembles a pigeon, with white wing patches and bright red webbed feet, while the cormorant looks like a prehistoric pelican.

Down a flight of steps from the observation area is Cobble Beach, covered with surprisingly round stones. At low tides, the tide pools at Cobble Beach are teeming with sea stars, purple urchins, anemones, and hermit crabs.

On the way to the lighthouse, the large **interpretive center** (541/574-3116, 10am-5pm daily July-mid-Sept., 10am-4pm daily mid-Sept.-June) features exhibits on local ecosystems, Native American culture, and historical artifacts such as a 19th-century lighthouse keeper's journal. Other highlights include a life-size replica of the Fresnel lens that shines from the top of the nearby lighthouse, statues of birds and harbor seals, and information on tide pool inhabitants.

Beaches

The beach at **Yaquina Bay State Recreation Site** (541/265-5679 or 800/551-6949, www.oregonstateparks.org) is accessible via a trail from the bluff-top parking area. This is a popular spot for clam digging (permit required) and agate hunting. There's also easy beach access from the Nye Beach neighborhood, with a large parking lot at the end of NW Beach Street. Two miles south of the Yaquina Bay Bridge, **South Beach State Park** (541/867-4715 or 800/551-6949, www.oregonstateparks.org) draws beachcombers, anglers, surfers, campers, and picnickers to its miles of broad, sandy beach.

North of town along U.S. 101, **Agate Beach** is a wide swath of coastline famed for its agate-hunting opportunities and views of nearby Yaquina Head, as well as easy access surfing access. In addition to the semi-precious stones, the contemplative appeal of Agate Beach inspired no less a figure than Ernest Bloch, the noted Swiss composer, who

Agate Hunting

Hunting for agates after winter storms is a passion at several Oregon beaches, particularly around Newport. Deep in the earth, metals, oxides, and silicates fused together to create this type of quartz. Red, amber, blue, and other tones sometimes form stripes or spots in the translucent rocks. One of the best places to find these treasures is on the beach near the Best Western Agate Beach Hotel, not surprisingly called **Agate Beach.** Nearby **Moolack Beach** and the beach at **Seal Rock,** north of Waldport, as well as area estuaries and streambeds, are spots more worth a look October-May.

lived here from 1940 until his death in 1959. Famed violinist Yehudi Menuhin spoke of Bloch and the locale thusly: "Agate Beach is a wild forlorn stretch of coastline looking down upon waves coming in all the way from Asia to break on the shore, a place which suited the grandeur and intensity of Bloch's character."

Moolack Beach, two miles north of Yaquina Head, is a favorite with kite flyers and agate hunters. **Beverly Beach,** 1.5 miles farther north, is a place where 20-million-year-old fossils have been found in the sandstone cliffs above the shore. Beverly Beach also attracts waders, unique for Oregon's chilly waters. Offshore sandbars temper the waves and the weather, so it's not as rough or as cold as many coastal locales. This long stretch of sand (panoramic photos are best taken from Yaquina Head Lighthouse looking north) is connected via an under-highway passage to a large state park campground.

RECREATION
Fishing

Newport is one of the top spots on the coast for charter fishing, and opportunities abound at the home port of Oregon's second-largest recreational fleet. Bottom fishing (year-round), tuna fishing (Aug.-Oct.), crabbing (year-round), and salmon and halibut fishing (seasonal) are all possible. Typical rates are $80 for a half day and $125 for a full day of bottom fishing, $130 for an 8-hour Chinook salmon outing, $225 for 12 hours of tuna fishing, and $200 for an all-day halibut charter. Whale-watching tours go for about $30.

Newport Marina Store and Charters

(2128 SE Marine Science Dr., South Beach, 541/867-4470, www.nmscharters.com), **Newport Tradewinds** (653 SW Bay Blvd., 541/265-2101, www.newporttradewinds. com), and **Captain's Reel Charters** (343 SW Bay Blvd., 541/265-7441, www.captainsreel. com) are reliable local operators. In addition to a full menu of fishing excursions, these Newport operators also offer whale-watching charters.

For those who prefer to take matters into their own hands, the clamming and Dungeness crabbing can be good in Yaquina Bay. If you haven't done this before, local tackle shops, such as the Newport Marina Store in South Beach, rent crab pots or rings and offer instruction. The best time to dig clams is at extremely low tide. At that time, look for clammers grabbing up cockles in the shallows of the bay. Tide tables are available from the chamber of commerce and many local businesses; they're also easy to find online.

Whale-Watching

The best company on the coast in terms of state-of-the-art equipment and natural history interpretation is **Marine Discovery Tours** (345 SW Bay Blvd., 541/265-6200, www.marinediscovery.com, $42 adults, $28 ages 4-12). The two-hour SeaLife tour is narrated by naturalist guides and includes, depending on the time of year, whale-, seal-, and bird-watching, an oyster-bed tour, estuary and ocean exploration, and a harbor tour. The 65-foot *Discovery* features video cameras that magnify the fascinating interplay between smaller life-forms, but the real attractions can be appreciated by the naked eye. Landlubbers will especially relish the full crab pots pulled up from the deep and the resident pod of whales often visible north of Yaquina Bay off Yaquina Head.

During the prime whale-watching weeks of late December and late March, trained volunteers from Whale Watching Spoken Here (an Oregon Parks and Recreation Department program) staff the **Don A. Davis City Kiosk** in Nye Beach to answer questions and help you spot whales.

ENTERTAINMENT

In the Bayfront District, **Mariner Square** (250 SW Bay Blvd., 541/265-2206, 10am-7pm daily July-Aug., 10am-5pm daily June and Sept., usually 10am-4pm daily Oct.-May, $15/attraction adults, $8 ages 5-12) has two attractions that mostly appeal to kids: **Ripley's Believe It or Not!** and **The Wax Works.**

Brewpubs

Rogue Bayfront Public House (748 SW Bay Blvd., 541/265-3188, 11am-midnight Sun.-Thurs., 11am-1am Fri.-Sat., $7-18) is a lively pub along the bay in Old Town with 35 taps and outdoor seating. In addition to pouring some of Oregon's finest ales, the public house serves seafood salads, shrimp-melt sandwiches, pizza, and fish-and-chips (salmon or halibut). Besides the renowned Rogue ales, there's Rogue's draft root beer—a creamy concoction laced with honey and vanilla. Another Rogue Ales brewery, called **Brewers on the Bay** (2320 OSU Dr., 541/819-0202, 11am-8pm Sun.-Thurs., 11am-9pm Fri.-Sat., $8-18), is a pub and brewery complex across Yaquina Bay, near the Oregon Coast Aquarium. This is where the actual brewing is now done; tours (1pm, 3pm, and 5pm Thurs.-Mon.) are available.

Between the highway and Bayfront is one of the area's most anticipated new brewpubs, the **Newport Brewing Company** (1118 SW Canyon Way, 541/272-5120, 11am-10pm Mon.-Thurs., 11am-11pm Fri.-Sat., noon-9pm Sun., $15-20), opened in 2019. In addition to beers ranging from lagers to a hazy double IPA, there's a full bar.

The Arts

Overlooking the sea in Nye Beach, the **Newport Performing Arts Center** (777 W. Olive St., 541/265-2787, www.coastarts.org), the central coast's largest performance venue, hosts local and national entertainment in the 400-seat Alice Silverman Theatre and the smaller Studio Theatre. At the same address is the **Oregon Coast Council for the Arts,** which puts out a free monthly newsletter and has ticket information on the center venues. It also has updates on the **Newport Visual Arts Center** (777 NW Beach Dr., 541/265-6540), right above the beach two blocks north at the Nye Beach turnaround. Two floors and two galleries—**Runyan Gallery** (11am-5pm Tues.-Sun.) and **Upstairs Gallery** (noon-4pm Tues.-Sat.)—offer art education programs and exhibition space for paintings, sculpture, and other works, often with a maritime theme. All exhibits are free.

Festivals and Events

The biggest bash (and one of the largest events of its kind in the country) is late February's **Newport Seafood and Wine Festival** (541/265-8801 or 800/262-7844, www.seafoodandwine.com, $8-40), which features dozens of food booths and scores of Oregon wineries serving up palate pleasers, along with music and crafts, at the **South Beach Marina** (across Yaquina Bay from the Bayfront). A huge tent joins the exhibition hall, where festivalgoers wash down delights from the deep with Oregon vintages. The event is open only to the 21-and-over crowd.

FOOD

This is a town for serious diners—folks who know good food and don't mind paying a tad more for it. It's also the kind of place where wharf-side vendors supply fresh fish on the cheap. May-October, you can pick up the freshest garden produce the area has to offer,

1

2

3

OYSTERS

ALMO

GRAB
COOKE

TUNA HALIBUT
& COD FILLETS
PRAWNS & SCALLOPS
CALAMARIA   CLAMS
CRAB COCKTAILS
POPCORN SHRIMP

plus baked goods, honey, and other delectables, at the Lincoln County Small Farmers Association's **Saturday Farmers Market,** held in the parking area of the **Newport City Hall** (U.S. 101 and Angle St., 9am-1pm Sat. May-Oct.).

About seven miles east of the Bayfront, the **Oregon Oyster Farms** (6878 Yaquina Bay Rd., 541/265-5078, www.oregonoyster. com, 9am-5pm daily) is the only remaining commercial outlet for Yaquina Bay oysters. Visitors are welcome to observe the farming and processing of these succulent shellfish. Try oysters on the half-shell, or sample smoked oysters on a stick. To get there, follow Bay Boulevard east six miles from the Embarcadero Resort.

Seafood

If you're hankering for a broad selection of fresh local seafood but don't need a fancy dining room to enjoy it in, ★ **Local Ocean Seafoods** (213 SE Bay Blvd., 541/574-7959, http://localocean.net, 11:30am-9pm Sun.-Thurs., 11:30am-9:30pm Fri.-Sat., $13-35) is the place for you. Part fish-market, part seafood grill, this bright and bustling restaurant spotlights sustainably caught, impeccably fresh fish and offers a lively atmosphere; now there's a 2nd-story dining area. Each item in the fish case is identified by name, where it was caught, how it was harvested, and who caught it. The menu items change depending on what's fresh, and though you can count on great fish-and-chips here, you may want to step up to the albacore tuna mignon or the fishwives seafood stew with crab, shrimp, clams, and scallops.

Also in the Old Town harbor area, tiny **Sharks Seafood Bar & Steamer Co.** (852 SW Bay Blvd., 541/574-0590, http:// sharksseafoodbar.com, 4:15pm-9pm Sun.-Wed., 4:15pm-9:30pm Fri.-Sat., $10-25) specializes in steamed seafood. But don't

worry—this isn't tasteless health food. The Catalina bouillabaisse packs a wallop, with 1.5 pounds of seafood in every spice-filled bowl. You'll also find a savory seafood gumbo, oyster stew, and a mix of stewed and sautéed fish called a pan roast. Fresh fish gets the steam treatment—in season, try halibut, salmon, and rockfish steamed and served with the chef's special sauces. Sharks is a fun, quirky place; the proprietors provide not just dinner, but a show. Sidle up to the bar in front of the cooking area to watch the chef in action.

The Newport Bayfront is where Mohava Niemi first opened the original **Mo's** (622 SW Bay Blvd., 541/265-2979, www.moschowder. com, 11am-9pm Mon.-Thurs., 11am-10pm Fri.-Sun., $7-21) in 1946. Mo's small, homey place soon had more business than it could handle. In response to the overflow, **Mo's Annex** (657 SW Bay Blvd., 541/265-7512, 11am-7pm Sun.-Fri., 11am-8pm Sat.) was created across the street. While both establishments feature old-fashioned favorites, such as oyster stew, fried fish, and peanut butter cream pie, the Annex bay windows have the best view.

With three tiers of seating, one of them outdoors, right above Newport's fishing docks, **Clearwater Restaurant** (325 Bay Blvd, 541/272-5551, www.clearwaterrestaurant. com, 11am-9:30pm Mon.-Thurs. 11am-11pm Fri.-Sat., $16-38) offers postcard views along with upscale dining. Fresh local seafood leads the menu, such as baked halibut with mango-papaya salsa. You'll also find a selection of burgers and beef and lamb dishes.

In Nye Beach, **Ove Northwest** (749 NW 3rd St., 541/264-2990, http://ovenorthwest. com, 11:30am-2pm and 5pm-8pm Tues.-Thurs. 11:30am-2pm and 5pm-8:30pm Fri.-Sat., $16-30) doesn't have an ocean view, but you won't want to turn away from the lovely food at this friendly (and relatively affordable) restaurant. Ling cod (not typically our first pick) is delicious when combined with manila clams and chorizo and bathed in a saffron cream sauce. The wine list (mostly Oregon wines) is as thoughtful as the wonderful food.

1: riverfront dining at Clearwater Restaurant
2: Yaquina Head Lighthouse **3:** South Beach Fish Market

With both indoor and outdoor seating at a prime harbor-front location, **Asiatico Waterfront Fusion Sushi** (875 SW Bay Blvd., 541/265-8387, 11:30am-8:30pm Wed.-Sun., $11-30) serves up fresh fish and seafood in a variety of rolls, sushi, *nigiri,* and sashimi. Add in a compelling cocktail menu and you've found a great spot to experience Newport's legendary seafood.

There are ample opportunities to buy fresh fish or crab along the bayfront in Newport. About half a mile south of the bridge, the **South Beach Fish Market** (3640 S. U.S. 101, 541/867-6800, 7am-7pm daily, $9-15) sells fresh fish, cooked and uncooked. Stop here for fresh, non-greasy fish-and-chips and a generous helping of local color after a visit to the aquarium.

Italian

If Depoe Bay's Restaurant Beck is a little beyond your means, the same chef-owners have opened the more casual ★ **Sorella** (526 NW Coast St., 541/265-4055, www.sorellanyebeach.com, 3pm-9pm daily, sandwiches $5-12) in Nye Beach. In addition to the regular menu, which features handmade and sophisticated pastas and pizzas, Sorella's specials include $10 spaghetti and meatballs (Tues.) and $12 pizza (Thurs.).

Bakeries and Cafés

Down along the Bayfront, the **Coffee House** (156 SW Bay Blvd., 541/265-6263, www.thecoffeehousenewport.com, 7am-2pm daily, $8-16) serves up scones, muffins, and brunch fare such as a wild mushroom omelet, crab cakes Florentine, and oysters lightly breaded with Japanese panko breadcrumbs. In fair weather, the outside deck is a relaxing spot for soaking up some rays while you gaze out on the harbor.

In the Nye Beach neighborhood, a charming spot for breakfast (including a good breakfast burrito) and sandwiches is **Café Stephanie** (411 Coast St., 541/265-8082, 7:30am-2pm daily, $6-13), a bustling cubbyhole with friendly service. Here both breakfast and lunch are served during open hours; consider starting your day with a bowl of smoked salmon chowder.

Nearby, the tiny **Panini Bakery** (232 NW Coast St., 541/265-5033, 7am-7pm daily, sandwiches $5-12) is a great spot for a chocolate panini, a ginger scone, a slice of pizza, and the local vibe. It's the best bakery in town and has a few tables.

ACCOMMODATIONS

Most of Newport's lodgings run $150-200, with sometimes dramatics shifts upward on summer weekends and downward during the winter.

The ★ **Hallmark Resort** (744 SW Elizabeth St., 541/265-2600 or 888/448-4449, www.hallmarkinns.com, $159-349) is a large hotel complex sitting atop the Newport bluffs, looking westward over the Pacific and miles of sandy beach. Of the many modern hotels that share this vista, the Hallmark is one of the nicest, with large, well-maintained guest rooms. Facilities include an indoor pool, a spa, and a restaurant. Many guest rooms are pet-friendly.

At the center of Nye Beach dining and arts activities, the ★ **Inn at Nye Beach** (729 NW Coast St., 541/265-2477, www.innatnyebeach.com, $167-281) is a stylish and comfortable hotel just steps from Pacific beaches. Rooms have gas fireplaces and balconies or patios, and guests share a fire pit and a beach-view infinity hot tub.

For location, you can't beat **The Whaler** (155 SW Elizabeth St., 541/272-3630 or 833/212-5815, www.whalernewport.com, $159-202). Each of the 73 rooms has a view, and some have fireplaces, wet bars, and private balconies. Guests can use the pool and exercise facilities; continental breakfast is served. Dogs are permitted in some guest rooms.

Stay right above the Bayfront harbor at **Anchor Pier Lodge** (345 SW Bay Blvd., 541/265-7829, http://anchorpierlodge.com, $175-235), up a long flight of stairs from street level, where you'll truly be living "above the store" (there's a gift shop below). The rooms are simple, with wood-plank floors, but tastefully and individually decorated. Although the Bayfront can be a little noisy with carousing people and sea lions, the inn provides earplugs. Rooms that overlook the bay have balconies; they're the ones to go for.

The **Best Western Plus Agate Beach Inn** (3019 N. Coast Hwy., 541/265-9411 or 800/547-3310, www.agatebeachinn.com, $135-163) is a tall oceanfront hotel with a fine view overlooking Yaquina Head Lighthouse and Agate Beach. Rooms are comfortable standard-issue hotel rooms, and although it's a little bit of a hike down to the beach, it is one of Newport's best beaches. Pets are permitted in some guest rooms.

North of town and above a great stretch of beach, the **Moolack Shores Motel** (8835 N. U.S. 101, 541/265-2326, http://moolackshores.com, $149-169) is a quiet spot, even though its parking area is just off the highway. The rooms are individually decorated and more than a little bit quirky, but most have good ocean views, and the beach is just down a long flight of wooden stairs from the motel.

The **Sylvia Beach Hotel** (267 NW Cliff St., 541/265-5428, www.sylviabeachhotel. com, $135-260) is a favorite of many Oregonians, thanks to its literary theme and old-fashioned (chic?) shabbiness. The 21 guest rooms, named after different authors, are furnished with decor evocative of each respective literary legacy. The Edgar Allan Poe Room, for instance, has a pendulum guillotine blade and stuffed ravens, while the Agatha Christie Room drops such clues as shoes underneath the curtains and capsules marked "Poison" in the medicine cabinet.

Most of the rooms ("best-sellers") run $185, with several oceanfront suites ("classics") featuring a fireplace and a deck going for $260. "Novels" go for $150 (no ocean view, but still quite charming). All rates include a full breakfast and reflect double occupancy. At breakfast, you have a choice of entrées and share a table with eight other guests, so misanthropes beware. Reservations are required for dinner in the hotel's Tables of Content, where a fixed-price family-style dinner is served at 7pm daily. No smoking, pets, or radios are allowed on the premises, and small children are discouraged.

You may not find any riverboat gamblers aboard the **Newport Belle Bed & Breakfast** (2126 SE Marine Science Dr., 541/867-6290, www.newportbelle.com, mid-Feb.-Sept., $165-175), a sternwheeler designed as a floating inn, but this 97-foot-long B&B moored on the H Dock of the Newport Marina evokes the ambience of the sternwheeler heyday. Choose from five generous staterooms, each with its own personality and private bath. Most have fabulous vistas of the bustling marina and bridge area. In the evening, guests can retire to their staterooms, enjoy the open afterdeck, or socialize in the main salon, where a gourmet breakfast is served every morning. Children are not permitted; pets are allowed in one room. Soft-soled shoes are required.

Camping

The campgrounds at Beverly Beach State Park and South Beach State Park are among the most popular on the Oregon coast. Their proximity to Newport, the absence of other camping in the area, and the special features of each explain their appeal.

Beverly Beach State Park (541/265-9278, reservations 800/452-5687, www.reserveamerica.com, $21 tents, $31-34 RVs, $47-57 yurts, $8 hiker-biker) is a huge multiple-loop campground set seven miles north of Newport on the east side of the highway in a mossy glade. A pedestrian tunnel passes under the highway and leads to a long, wide beach that is, unfortunately, directly bordered by the road. Devil's Punchbowl and Otter Crest are one and two miles up the highway, respectively.

It's just a hop over the sand dunes to the beach at **South Beach State Park** (541/867-4715 or 800/551-6949, reservations

800/452-5687, www.reserveamerica.com, $21 tents, $31 RVs, $47-57 yurts, $8 hiker-biker), just south of the Yaquina Bay Bridge. The long beach has opportunities for fishing, agate hunting, windsurfing (for experts), horseback riding, and hiking; a paved bike trail (bike rentals at the park's info center) runs down the long jetty. Sign up in advance (541/867-6500) for kayak tours of nearby Beaver Creek.

INFORMATION AND SERVICES

The **Greater Newport Chamber of Commerce** (555 SW U.S. 101, 541/265-8801 or 800/262-7844, http://discovernewport.com, 8:30am-5pm Mon.-Fri. year-round, 10am-2pm Sat. summer) is just off the highway.

Samaritan Pacific Communities Hospital (930 SW Abbey St., 541/265-2244) is the central coast's only major hospital.

TRANSPORTATION

Lincoln County Transit (541/265-4900, www.co.lincoln.or.us/transit) runs buses, several times daily Monday-Saturday, north to Lincoln City and south to Yachats, with numerous stops en route through Newport. In addition, the county also offers the Coast to Valley Express, a four-times-daily bus service to and from Corvallis and Albany (with connections to Amtrak) in the Willamette Valley.

A **shuttle bus** (www.co.lincoln.or.us/transit, 7:15am-5pm daily) travels up and down the length of Newport on streets just east and west of U.S. 101, going as far south as the Newport Business Plaza in South Beach and north to NE 73rd Street. The wheelchair-accessible bus is equipped with a bike rack. It's free for those with a pass from their Newport hotel and $1 for others. The route is not straightforward; it helps to check the transit website for a map and schedule.

Waldport and Vicinity

Originally a stronghold of the Alsea Native Americans, Waldport also has had incarnations as a gold rush town, salmon-canning center, and lumber port. This town of about 2,000, whose name means "forest port" in German, is pretty quiet today, with a nondescript main drag that gives no hint of the surrounding beaches and prime fishing and crabbing spots. Waldport provides a low-cost alternative to the big-name destinations; you won't have to fight for a parking spot or make reservations months in advance.

SIGHTS AND RECREATION
Ona Beach State Park
Beaver Creek flows into the ocean at **Ona Beach State Park** (800/551-6949, day-use only). A 0.25-mile trail starts at the parking area and crosses a footbridge over the creek before landing at a fine stretch of beach.

Brian Booth State Park
Beaver Creek State Natural Area runs through **Brian Booth State Park** (541/563-6413, visitors center 10am-4pm daily June-Aug., noon-4pm daily Sept.-May); the visitors center is two miles east of Ona Beach, up Beaver Creek Road. This coastal wetland area has good paddling on ranger-led, four-hour kayak tours (http://store.oregonstateparks.org, 8am Thurs.-Mon. July-Labor Day, reservations required, $20) and wildlife-watching, both from the creek and from a viewing blind that's just a short walk from the road. If you're not prepared to paddle, a seven-mile network of hiking trails starts near the visitors center.

Seal Rock State Recreation Site
Four miles north of Waldport, **Seal Rock** (800/551-6949, day-use only) attracts beachcombers and agate hunters as well as folks who come to explore the tide pools and observe the

seals on offshore rocks. The park's name derives from a seal-shaped rock in the cluster of interesting formations in the tidewater. The picnic area is set in a shady area behind the sandy beach. During Christmas and spring breaks, the volunteers of Whale Watching Spoken Here are on hand to help visitors spot passing grays 10am-1pm daily.

Alsea Bay Bridge Historical Interpretive Center

The small museum and visitors center known as the **Alsea Bay Bridge Historical Interpretive Center** (620 NW Spring St., 541/563-2133 www.oregonstateparks.org, 9am-4pm Tues.-Sat. summer, 10am-4pm Thurs.-Mon. winter, free), operated by the Oregon Parks and Recreation Department and Waldport Chamber of Commerce, stands along the highway on the south side of the river. Exhibits here tell the story of how the sleek 1991 bridge replaced the aging Conde McCullough span across the bay, which has since been demolished. Displays about transportation methods along the central coast since the 1800s, information on the Alsea Native American people, and a telescope trained on the seals and waterfowl on the bay are worth a quick stop.

On summer weekends, Oregon Parks and Recreation gives clamming and crabbing demonstrations (locations and times vary according to the tides; see the website for a calendar).

Drift Creek Wilderness

Seven miles east of Waldport are the nearly 5,800 acres of the **Drift Creek Wilderness,** which protects the Coast Range's largest remaining stands of old-growth rainforest. Here you can see giant Sitka spruce and western hemlock hundreds of years old, nourished by up to 120 inches of rain per year. These trees are the "climax forest" in the Douglas fir ecosystem. They seldom reach old-growth status because the timber industry tends to replant fir seedlings after logging operations. The forest provides habitat for spotted owls along with bald eagles, Roosevelt elk, and black bears. Drift Creek sustains wild runs of chinook, steelhead, and coho salmon, which come up the Alsea River.

Steep ridges and their drainages, as well as small meadows, make up the topography, which is accessed via a couple of hiking trails. The trailhead closest to Waldport is the 3.5-mile **Harris Ranch Trail,** which descends 1,200 feet to a meadow near Drift Creek. The

Ona Beach

local access to Harris Ranch Trail and the conjoining Horse Creek Trail is via Highway 34; turn north off 34 at the Alsea River crossing, seven miles east of Waldport. Here, pick up Risely Creek Road (Forest Rd. 3446) and Forest Road 346 to the trailhead.

Fishing

Waldport's recreational raison d'être is fishing. World-class clamming and Dungeness crabbing in Alsea Bay and the Alsea River's salmon, steelhead, and cutthroat trout runs account for a high percentage of visits to the area. Before commercial fishing on the river was shut down in 1957, as much as 137,000 pounds of chinook were netted in a season. The wild fall chinook run remains healthy and starts up in late August. Catch-and-release for sea-run cutthroats starts in mid-August, while steelhead are in the river December-March. Crabbers without boats can take advantage of the Port of Waldport docks. **Dock of the Bay Marina** (1245 NE Mill St., 541/563-2003) rents and sells crabbing and fishing supplies and can guide you to the best spots.

FOOD AND ACCOMMODATIONS

Dining options in Waldport are limited. We recommend heading about 10 miles south to Yachats for dinner. If you just need a loaf of artisanal bread or a pastry and time it right, **Pacific Sourdough** (740 NE Mill St., 541/563-3044, 10am-3pm Thurs. and Sat.) is the place to go. The bakers sell their bread to several restaurants in Yachats.

Midway between Waldport and Yachats, the **Sanderling Sea Cottages** (7160 SW U.S. 101, 541/563-3377, www.vacasa.com, $71-200) has simple guest rooms that range in style from modern to vintage and in size from basic budget motel size to two-bedroom units with kitchens. Although the guest rooms are not extravagantly furnished, they all have decks with nice views and easy access to the beach. Minimum stays may apply.

The vintage **Cape Cod Cottages** (4150 SW U.S. 101, 541/563-2106, www.capecodcottagesonline.com, $96-245) offers one- and two-bedroom oceanfront units with complete kitchens, fireplaces, spectacular views, and private decks. The least expensive units are basic motel rooms with no decks. Minimum stays may apply.

If a standard motel is more your style, the **Waldport Inn** (190 SW U.S. 101, 541/563-5750, www.thewaldportinn.com, $109-129) is a pleasant spot to spend the night. The innkeepers also offer a number of two- and three-bedroom apartments for rent.

Camping

Two campgrounds sit about four miles south of Waldport on U.S. 101 along the beach. **Beachside State Park** (541/563-3220, reservations 800/452-5687, www.reserveamerica.com, $21 tents, $31 RVs, $47 yurts, $57 pet-friendly yurt) is between the beach and the highway (some sites get highway noise) not far from Alsea Bay and the Alsea River. This is a paradise for rock fishers, surfcasters, clammers, and crabbers. Beachside fills up fast, so reserve early for space Memorial Day-Labor Day.

Half a mile south of Beachside, the Siuslaw National Forest's **Tillicum Beach** (reservations 877/444-6777, www.recreation.gov, reservations strongly advised in summer, $26 tents, $33 RVs with electricity) is set right along the ocean. U.S. Forest Service roads from here access Coast Range fishing streams. You'll also appreciate the strip of vegetation blocking the cool evening winds that whip up off the ocean.

Should Beachside and Tillicum be filled to overflowing, you might want to set up a base camp in the Coast Range along Highway 34—especially if you have fishing or hiking in the Drift Creek Wilderness in mind. Just go east of Waldport 17 miles on Highway 34 to the Siuslaw National Forest's **Blackberry Campground** (reservations 877/444-6777, www.recreation.gov, $22). The 33 sites are open year-round; most are right on the river. A boat ramp, flush toilets, and piped water are on-site.

INFORMATION

The Waldport Chamber of Commerce operates a **visitors center** (620 NW Spring St., 541/563-2133, www.waldport-chamber. com, 9am-4pm Tues.-Sat.) in the Alsea Bay Bridge Historical Interpretive Center, just south of the river. The **Siuslaw National Forest-Waldport Ranger Station** (1130 Forestry Ln., 541/563-8400) can provide information on area camping and hiking, including the trails in the Drift Creek Wilderness.

GETTING THERE

Highway 34 runs east from Waldport, following the Alsea River for several miles before veering northeast to Corvallis, about 65 miles away. This is one of the prettiest (and slowest) routes between the coast and the Willamette Valley.

The **Lincoln County Transit** (541/265-4900, www.co.lincoln.or.us/transit) buses run four times a day Monday-Saturday between Yachats and Newport.

Yachats and Cape Perpetua

Yachats (pronounced YAH-hots) is derived from an Alsea word meaning "dark waters at the foot of the mountain." The phrase aptly describes the location of this picturesque resort village of 700 people, clustered on the hillsides and coastal shelf beside the Yachats River mouth in the shadow of Cape Perpetua. Word of mouth has helped to spread the popularity of Yachats as a place for a quiet getaway and a base for enjoying the 2,700-acre Cape Perpetua Scenic Area and nearby beaches.

SIGHTS AND RECREATION

TOP EXPERIENCE

★ Cape Perpetua

The most notable sight near Yachats, indeed on the whole central coast, is the view from 803-foot-high Cape Perpetua. The name derives from Captain Cook's sighting of the promontory on March 7, 1778, St. Perpetua's Day. The road to the top of the cape affords 150 miles of north-south visibility from the top of the headland. On a clear day, you can also see nearly 40 miles out to sea.

Prior to hiking the 23 miles of foot trails or driving to the top of the cape, stop off at the **Cape Perpetua Visitor Center** (541/547-3289, 9:30am-4:30pm daily mid-June-Aug., 10am-4pm daily Sept.-mid-June, Northwest Forest Pass or $5/car), three miles south of Yachats on the east side of the highway. A picture window framing a bird's-eye view of rockbound coast, along with exhibits on forestry, marinelife, and monster storms, provide an introduction to the region. Stick around to watch the excellent 15-minute film about Oregon's intertidal biome. During the summer, rangers give talks and lead hikes; call for the schedule.

HIKING

Pick up a map or pamphlet about such trails as Cummins Creek, Giant Spruce, and Restless Waters, as well as directions for the drive (or stiff hike) to the summit of the cape, from which you can take the 0.25-mile **Whispering Spruce Trail** through the grounds of a former World War II U.S. Coast Guard lookout built by the Civilian Conservation Corps (CCC) in 1933. The southern views from the crest take in the highway and headlands as far south as Coos Bay. Halfway along the path, you'll come to a Works Progress Administration-built rock hut called the West Shelter, which makes a lofty perch for whale-watching. Beyond this

ridgetop aerie, the curtain of trees parts to reveal fantastic views of the shoreline between Yachats and Cape Foulweather.

To begin your auto ascent, from the visitors center drive 100 yards north on U.S. 101 and look for the steep, winding spur road (Forest Rd. 55) on the right. As you climb, you'll notice large Sitka spruce trees abutting the road. Halfway up the 2-mile route, you'll come to a Y in the road. Take a hard left and follow the road another mile to the top of Cape Perpetua. If you miss the left turn and go straight ahead, you'll soon find yourself on a 22-mile loop through the Coast Range to Yachats. Along the way, placards annotate forest ecology.

If you'd rather hike to the top of the cape, the awe-inspiring 1.5-mile **Saint Perpetua Trail** from the Cape Perpetua Visitor Center to the summit is of moderate difficulty, gaining 600 feet in elevation. En route, placards explain the role of wind, erosion, and fire in forest succession in this mixed-conifer ecosystem.

The actual cape is only half the attraction at Cape Perpetua. At least as fascinating are the rocky coast and its tide pools, churns, and spouting horns of water. Just north of the turnoff for the top of Cape Perpetua (Forest Rd. 55) and U.S. 101 is the turnout for **Devil's Churn,** on the west side of the highway. Here the tides have cut a deep fissure in a basalt embankment on the shore. You can observe the action from a vertigo-inducing overlook high above or take the easy switchbacking trail down to the water's edge. While watching the white-water torrents in this foaming cistern, beware of "sneaker waves," particularly if you venture beyond the boundaries of the **Trail of the Restless Waters.** The highlights here are the spouting horns and acres of tide pools. All along this stretch of the coast, many trees appear to be leaning away from the ocean, as if bent by storms. This illusion is caused by salt-laden westerlies drying out and killing the

buds on the exposed side of the tree, leaving growth only on the leeward branches.

Another hike from the Cape Perpetua Visitor Center goes down to a geological blowhole (called a spouting horn), where seawater is funneled between rocks and explodes into spray. This is the **Captain Cook Trail,** which runs six miles through a dense wind-carved forest and the remains of an old CCC camp under U.S. 101 to an ancient lava deposit on the shore. Given enough wave action, water bubbles up through fissures in the basalt. There are also Native American shell middens built up from 300-2,000 years ago in the area.

State Parks and Coastal Waysides

In this part of the coast, state parks and viewpoints abound with attractions. There's so much to see here that keeping your eyes on the road in this heavily traveled section is a challenge.

A mile north of Yachats, **Smelt Sands State Recreation Site** gives access to tide pools and the 0.75-mile **804 Trail,** which follows the rocky shore north to a broad, sandy beach, where it continues along the beach all the way north to Waldport (about seven miles). To the south, the 804 Trail cuts across the Adobe Lodge's lawn and passes a residential area on the way to the **Yachats State Recreation Area.** An alternate route to the wave-battered recreation area is from 2nd Street in downtown Yachats.

On the south bank of the Yachats River is a short but beautiful beach loop off U.S. 101 (going south, look for the "Beach Access" sign). The road runs between the landscaped grounds of beach houses and resorts on one side and the foamy sea on the other. A wide beach, tide pools, and blowholes on the bank by the river's mouth are a special treat.

A mile south of Cape Perpetua, **Neptune State Park** has a beautiful beach and is near the 9,300-acre **Cummins Creek Wilderness** east of U.S. 101. Just north of Neptune Park, Forest Road 1050 leads east to the Cummins Creek trailhead. Half a mile south, gravel

1: view from Cape Perpetua 2: enjoying a beer at Yachats Brewing

Forest Road 1051 can take you to a point where a moderately difficult 2.5-mile hike leads to Cummins Ridge trailhead. This pathway has some of the last remaining coastal old-growth Sitka spruce stands. Get maps and detailed directions for these and other area trails at the Cape Perpetua Visitor Center.

Close by, there's a chance to explore tide pools and sometimes observe harbor seals at **Strawberry Hill.** Scenic shorelines can also be found in the next few miles farther south at **Stonesfield Beach State Recreation Site** and **Muriel O. Ponsler State Scenic Viewpoint.**

FESTIVALS AND EVENTS

The little village of Yachats seems to be busy with some festival or other event just about every weekend. For a full schedule, see the local chamber of commerce website (www.yachats.org). What follows are some highlights.

In late March, the chamber-sponsored **Original Yachats Arts and Crafts Fair** (Yachats Commons, U.S. 101 and W. 4th St., 541/547-3530 or 800/929-0477, free) exhibits the work of some 75 Pacific Northwest artists and artisans.

Yachats pulls out all the stops for the **Fourth of July.** Events include the short and silly La De Da Parade at noon, a pie and ice cream social, lots of live music, and a fireworks show on the bay when darkness falls.

Fall is mushroom season on the coast, and the **Yachats Village Mushroom Fest** (541/547-3530 or 800/929-0477), held the third weekend in October, showcases the native mushrooms that abound in these temperate rainforests. Activities over the weekend include fungi feasts, mushroom cooking and growing lessons, talks on forest ecology, and guided mushroom walks.

SHOPPING

Yachats has long been a center for artists and bohemians, and for proof of this you need go no farther than **Earthworks Gallery** (2222 U.S. 101 N., 541/547-4300, http://earthworksgalleries.net, 10am-5pm daily). This excellent gallery displays the work of local painters, glass artists, and jewelers, as well as high-quality crafts. **Touchstone Gallery** (2118 U.S. 101 N., 541/547-4121, 10am-5pm daily) is another gallery with unique Pacific Northwest arts and crafts.

a giant spruce tree at Cape Perpetua

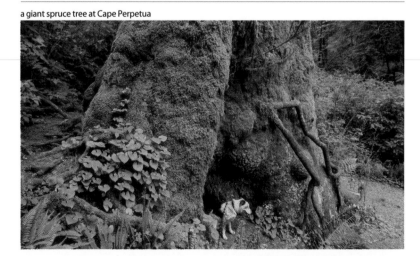

FOOD

For a town its size, Yachats has particularly good restaurant choices. Stop by ★ **Yachats Brewing** (348 U.S. 101 N., 541/547-3884, http://yachatsbrewing.com, 11:30am-9pm Sun.-Thurs., 11:30am-10pm Fri.-Sat., $10-16) for a pint or a meal. The beer, including seasonal sours made from local berries, is perfect after a hike or beach walk, and the food, including many fermented veggie dishes, is some of the best, and certainly most creative, in town.

If you're looking for fresh seafood, go to tiny ★ **Luna Sea Fish House** (153 NW U.S. 101, 541/547-4794, www.lunaseafishhouse.com, 8am-9pm daily summer, 8am-8pm daily winter, $10-17), a restaurant owned by a local fisherman. Don't let the simple decor put you off; the food here is *good*. Using locally caught (not farmed) fish and local ingredients, Luna Sea offers superlative fish-and-chips, fish tacos and sandwiches, and Slumgullion (cheesy shrimp and clam chowder). Breakfast omelets are also top-notch.

The carefully restored but easygoing and family-friendly **Drift Inn Pub** (124 U.S. 101 N., 541/547-4477, http://the-drift-inn.com, 8am-9pm daily summer, 8am-8pm daily winter, $12-32) offers seafood dishes, big salads, fish-and-chips, wood-fired pizza, and other well-prepared pub grub in a relaxed atmosphere. There's often really good live music, too, making this a lively spot whether you're here to eat or to quaff a pint or two. If you never want to leave, rooms are available for rent ($50-163) upstairs.

Start the day at **Green Salmon Bakery and Cafe** (220 U.S. 101, 541/547-3077, www.thegreensalmon.com, 7:30am-2:30pm daily, $3-12) for fresh breads and good pastries plus soup and sandwiches for lunch. Lines can be long and slow-moving at the counter, so come equipped with patience; the upside is that you'll probably be waiting with a bunch of friendly locals.

Beach Street Kitchen (84 Beach St., 541/547-4409, 8am-3pm Thurs.-Mon., $8-13) is a quintessential Yachats business. This tiny coffee shop and bakery also makes excellent salads, sandwiches, and fritattas. Everything is homemade, locally sourced, and served with charm and care.

The simply decorated bay-view **Ona Restaurant** (131 U.S. 101 N., 541/547-6627, www.onarestaurant.com, 11am-3:45pm and 4pm-8:30pm daily summer, 4pm-8:30pm Mon.-Fri., 11am-3:45pm and 4pm-8:30pm Sat.-Sun. winter, $12-37) serves grilled seafood, meatloaf, steak, and fresh pasta. For appetizers, you can choose between oysters, shrimp, clams, and crab cakes. Ona has a good happy hour (4pm-6pm Sun.-Thurs.), which is the best time to check out its offerings without emptying your wallet.

ACCOMMODATIONS
$50-100

For those looking for budget prices close to the center of town, try **Rock Park Cottages** (431 W. 2nd St., 541/547-3214, http://sweethomesrentals.com/rock-park-cottages, $50-175), adjacent to Yachats State Recreation Area. Consisting of five rustic cottages arranged around a courtyard, Rock Park has to be one of the better bargains on the coast. The kitchens are well equipped, and the vintage cottages couldn't be better located. This lodging also offers a two-bedroom A-frame and a three-bedroom house.

$100-150

Facing onto the beach loop south of town, the **Yachats Inn** (331 U.S. 101, 541/547-3456 or 888/270-3456, www.yachatsinn.com, $110-160) offers basic summer shelter with unfussy rooms that have little decks and TVs but no phones; some have kitchens and fireplaces. There's great access to the beach. Suites with full kitchens and fireplaces are newer, but they are set back from the beach and don't permit dogs. An indoor pool overlooks the beach.

Set back from U.S. 101 with a short walk to the beach, the **Dublin House Motel** (251 W. 7th St., 541/547-3703 or 866/922-4287, www.dublinhousemotel.com, $109-139) offers standard motel rooms and ocean views, each room having a microwave, fridge, coffeemaker, and cable TV; some kitchen units are also available. The indoor heated pool is especially nice in the winter months.

A little north of the town center, the imposing **Adobe Resort** (155 U.S. 101 N., 541/547-3141, www.adoberesort.com, $145 hillside view, $190 ocean view) overlooks Smelt Sands Beach. Although the Adobe isn't what you'd call luxurious, it is one of the few full-service resorts in the area, with a good on-site restaurant. All units have fridges, microwaves, satellite TV, DVD players, and a phone with voice mail. Pets are accepted in some guest rooms. Two-bedroom hot tub suites are 1,400 square feet and have all the comforts of a small home.

The **Fireside Motel** (1881 U.S. 101, 541/547-3636 or 800/336-3573, www.firesidemotel.com, $134-219) is known for its pet-friendly policies. The more expensive rooms have fireplaces, balconies, and views of tide pools; the cheaper rooms are pretty basic, but you're still located right next to a beachside trail.

Over $200

A mile north of Yachats, above a thrust of wave-pounded tide pools, ★ **Overleaf Lodge** (2055 U.S. 101, 541/547-4880 or 800/338-0507, www.overleaflodge.com, $199-345) offers the newest and nicest rooms in the Yachats area. Most guest rooms have balconies, hot tubs, and fireplaces, and all have fantastic views. Rates include a breakfast buffet plus access to a fitness area. A 3,000-square-foot spa has treatment rooms, steam rooms, and saunas, plus ocean-view hot tubs. Adjacent to the lodge are eight cottages ($295-415, 2-night minimum stay) tucked into the forest. With 2-4 bedrooms, these charming units with Craftsman-style decor have

full kitchens and everything a family or small group will need for a great beach vacation.

Vacation Rentals

If you'd rather settle into a house, check out **Yachats Village Rentals** (541/547-3501 or 888/288-5077, www.97498.com), which offers a varied stable of vacation homes ($140-350) for long- or short-term rental.

Camping

Set along Cape Creek in the Cape Perpetua Scenic Area, the Forest Service's **Cape Perpetua Campground** (reservations 877/444-6777, www.recreation.gov, May-Sept., $24), with 38 sites for tents, trailers, or motor homes up to 22 feet long, is a great base for exploring the wonderful Cape Perpetua area. Trails run from the campground to the top of the cape and to the beach. Flush toilets and piped water are available.

INFORMATION

The **Yachats Area Chamber of Commerce** (241 U.S. 101, 541/547-3530 or 800/929-0477, www.yachats.org, 10am-5:30pm daily mid-Mar.-Sept., 10am-5:30pm Fri.-Sun. Oct.-mid-Mar.) has a central location on the highway (next to Clark's Market) and enthusiastic staff. Ask them about fishing, rockhounding, bird-watching, and beachcombing in the area.

GETTING THERE

The bus stop is in the parking lot of the **Log Church** (328 W. 3rd St.). Here you can catch **Lincoln County Transit** (541/265-4900, www.co.lincoln.or.us/transit) buses, which run four times a day Monday-Saturday between Yachats and Newport, with connections north to Lincoln City and east to Corvallis.

Florence and Vicinity

If you study the map of the central Oregon coast, you'll see that Florence is oriented along the Siuslaw River; a spit of dunes reaches up from the south, barring quick access from downtown to the ocean. But don't dismiss this riverfront town for its lack of oceanfront real estate: The views onto the river are plenty scenic, and Old Town is charming and easy to navigate on foot.

SIGHTS

If first and last impressions are enduring, Florence is truly memorable. A short way to the north of town, U.S. 101 passes over Heceta Head, with great views of the lighthouse there. As you leave the city to the south, a graceful bridge over the Siuslaw ushers you away.

The **Siuslaw River Bridge** is an impressive example of Conde McCullough's Works Progress Administration-built spans. The Egyptian obelisks and art deco styling of McCullough's design are complemented by the views to the west of the coruscating sand dunes. To the east, the riverside panorama of Florence's Old Town beckons further investigation.

Old Town itself is a tasteful restoration, with all manner of shops and restaurants and an inviting boardwalk along the river. The quickest access to the beach and dunes is south of the bridge via South Jetty Road.

TOP EXPERIENCE

★ Heceta Head Lighthouse and Devil's Elbow

Twelve miles north of Florence, **Heceta Head Lighthouse** (541/547-3416, www.oregonstateparks.org, tours 11am-3pm daily summer, 11am-2pm daily winter, $5 day-use) is dramatically situated above a lovely cove at the mouth of Cape Creek and wedged into the flanks of 1,000-foot-high Heceta Head. The whitewashed lighthouse was completed in 1894 and beautifully restored in 2013; it's still in use, beaming the strongest light on the Oregon coast from its perch 205 feet above the pounding surf. A little below the lighthouse is Heceta House, where the lighthouse keepers used to live. Today, it serves both as a **gift shop** (11am-6pm daily Memorial Day-Sept.) and the **Heceta Head Lighthouse B&B** (92072 U.S. 101, 541/547-3696 or 866/547-3696, www.hecetalighthouse.com, $224-405). An easy 0.5-mile trail leads up from the lighthouse's picnic and parking area to the tower; a trail network stretches 7 miles. Other than the day-use fee, admission and tours are free.

Just south of the lighthouse, the graceful arc of Conde McCullough's Cape Creek Bridge spans a chasm more than 200 feet deep. From the lighthouse parking lot, a trail leads down to where Cape Creek meets the beach at **Devil's Elbow State Park.** Be conscious of tides here if you climb along the rocks adjoining the beach.

Heceta Head is said to be the most photographed lighthouse in the country; that may be difficult to verify, but it's impossible to quibble with the magnificent sight of the gleaming white tower and outbuildings on the headland, particularly when viewed from a set of highway pullouts just south of the bridge. The vistas from the lighthouse and network of trails on the headland are no less dramatic. See murres, tufted puffins, and other seabirds as well as sea lions on the rock islands below; bald eagles soaring overhead; and in spring, northbound female gray whales and their calves as they pass close to shore. A trail leading to the north side of Heceta Head offers views to Cape Perpetua, 10 miles to the north.

★ Sea Lion Caves

Eleven miles north of Florence, you can descend into a massive sea cave to observe the only U.S. mainland rookery of Steller sea lions (*Eumetopias jubatus*). **Sea Lion Caves** (91560

U.S. 101, 541/547-3111, www.sealioncaves. com, 9am-7pm daily, closed Thanksgiving and Christmas, $14 adults, $13 seniors, $8 ages 5-12, free under age 5) is home to a herd that averages 200 individuals, although the numbers change from season to season. These animals occupy the cave during the fall and winter, which are thus the prime times to visit. The Steller sea lions you'll see at those times are cows, yearlings, and immature bulls. In spring and summer, they breed and raise their young on the rock ledges just outside the cave; given this, note that in summer you may not see any sea lions in the cave, but might spot them with binoculars on the rocks outside the cave. In addition, California sea lions (*Zalophus californianus*), common all along the Pacific coast, are found at Sea Lion Caves late fall-early spring.

Enter Sea Lion Caves through the gift shop on U.S. 101. A steep downhill walk reveals stunning perspectives of the coastal cliffs as well as several kinds of gulls and cormorants that nest here. The final leg of the descent is by an elevator that drops an additional 208 feet. After stepping off the lift into the cave, your eyes adjust to the gloomy subterranean light, and you'll see sea lions on the rock shelves amid the surging water inside the enormous cave. Flash photography is forbidden, so study your camera's settings if you want to take pictures inside. A set of stairs leads up to a view of Heceta Head Lighthouse through an opening in the cave.

Steller sea lions were referred to as *lobos marinos* (sea wolves) in early Spanish mariners' accounts of their 16th-century West Coast voyages, and their doglike yelps might explain why. You'll notice several shades of color in the herd, which has to do with the progressive lightening of their coats with age. Males sometimes weigh more than a ton, and dominate the scene with macho posturing to scare off rivals for harems of as many as two dozen cows. Their protection as an endangered species angers many commercial anglers, who claim that the sea lions take a significant bite out of fishing revenues by preying on salmon. In any case, the close-up view of these huge sea mammals in the cavernous enclaves of their natural habitat should not be missed—despite an odor not unlike sweat-soaked sneakers.

If you can't observe the animals to your satisfaction in the cave, or if you want a free look from a distance, go 0.25 mile north of the concession entrance to the "rockwork" turnout, where the herd sometimes populates the rocky ledges several hundred feet below. It's also a good place to snap a shot of the picturesque Heceta Head Lighthouse across the cove to the north from the turnout.

Darlingtonia Botanical Gardens

Three miles north up the Coast Highway from Florence, in an area noted for dune access and freshwater lakes, are the **Darlingtonia Botanical Gardens** (east side of U.S. 101, 5 miles north of Florence, 800/551-6949, www.oregonstateparks. org, free). In a sylvan grove of spruce and alder is a series of wooden platforms that guide you through a bog where carnivorous *Darlingtonia californica* plants thrive. Shaped like a serpent's head, the *Darlingtonia* is variously referred to as the cobra orchid, cobra lily, or pitcher plant.

The plant produces a sweet smell that invites insects to crawl through an opening into a hollow chamber beneath the plant's hood. Inside, thin transparent "windows" allow light to shine inside the chamber, confusing the bug as to where the exit is. As the insect crawls around in search of an escape, downward-pointing hairs within the enclosure inhibit its movement to freedom. Eventually, the tired-out bug falls to the bottom of the stem, where it is digested. The plant needs the nutrients from the trapped insects to compensate for the lack of sustenance supplied by its small root system. If you still have an appetite after witnessing this carnage, you might want to enjoy lunch at one of the shaded picnic tables.

Siuslaw Pioneer Museum

To fill yourself in on the early history of Florence and the Siuslaw River Valley, and to get some notion of Native American and pioneer life, spend an hour or so at the **Siuslaw Pioneer Museum** (278 Maple St., 541/997-7884, www.siuslawpioneermuseum.com, noon-4pm Tues.-Sun., $5 adults, free under age 13). You'll find it in Old Town in a renovated school building dating from 1905. Along with exhibits on early logging and farming, read an account of how the U.S. government double-crossed the Siuslaw people, who sold their land to the feds and never received the promised recompense. The museum can also set you loose on a walking tour of historic Old Town buildings.

Jessie M. Honeyman Memorial State Park

Jessie M. Honeyman Memorial State Park (84505 U.S. 101 S., information 541/997-3641, reservations 800/452-5687, Oregon Coast Passport or $5 day-use), three miles south of Florence, has a spectacular dunescape and then some. Come here in May when the rhododendrons bloom along the short, sinuous road heading to the parking lot. A short walk west of the lot brings you to a 150-foot-high dune overlooking Cleawox Lake, which is a good place for a swim in the summer. From the top of this dune, look westward across the expanse of sand, marsh, and remnants of forest at the blue Pacific some two miles away. This is also a popular place to camp.

South Jetty

The northern boundary of the Oregon Dunes National Recreation Area is at the **South Jetty** (Northwest Forest Pass or $5 parking), where the Siuslaw River flows into the Pacific Ocean. May-September and on all weekends and holidays, the beach at the South Jetty is closed to motor vehicles, and even though there are no marked trails, it's a great place to explore the dunes in near solitude. The road into the jetty has several staging areas for off-highway vehicles; during the summer months, the area south of the road is open to motor vehicles. South Jetty Road is 0.5 mile south of the Siuslaw River Bridge.

RECREATION

Huckleberry picking is an attraction just outside Florence. Some prime pickings are found about five miles north of Florence along the Sutton Creek Trail, which begins in the

the Siuslaw River Bridge

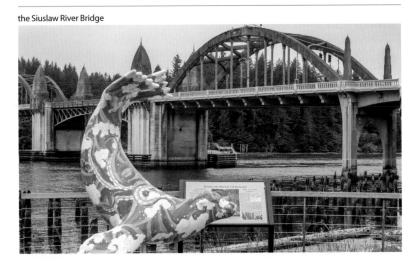

Sutton Campground just off U.S. 101. During late summer or fall, these berries flourish below the dense canopy of shore pines.

Hiking

You'll find incredibly scenic hiking in the area around **Carl G. Washburne State Park,** 14 miles north of Florence on U.S. 101. About a mile south of the park entrance, find the parking area for the **Hobbit Trail** on the east side of the highway. This salal-lined trail winds 0.4 mile through dense forest thickets of pine, fir, and rhododendrons to the secluded 3-mile-long beach. From the same trailhead, another path takes off uphill to the **Heceta Head Lighthouse.** In its 1.75-mile run, the trail gains quite a bit of elevation and passes some outstanding viewpoints. Also starting at the same U.S. 101 parking area, the **China Creek Trail** (a.k.a. the Valley Trail) runs 1.7 miles on the east side of the highway through a series of elk meadows to the Washburne Campground. If the parking area is full, head to the day-use lot across the highway from the campground, catch the Valley Trail near the campground entrance, and hike to the Hobbit and Heceta Head Trails.

Up the North Fork of the Siuslaw River is the **Pawn Old-Growth Trail,** a 0.5-mile pathway through 9-foot-thick, 275-foot-tall Douglas fir and hemlock trees that are several hundred years old. The trailhead, at the confluence of the North Fork of the Siuslaw and Taylor's Creek, is a good place to see salmon spawning in the fall and observe water ouzels (also called dippers). The trail follows the creek and offers interpretive placards along the way. At one point in the trail, visitors walk through fallen Douglas fir logs 21 feet in diameter. Placards explain the science of tree rings. From Florence, take Highway 126 east for 1 mile, then turn north onto Forest Road 5070 and take it 12 miles to Forest Road 5084; stay right and go another 5 miles to the trailhead.

An excellent and not terribly difficult introduction to dune hiking can be found about 10 miles south of Florence at the **Oregon Dunes Day-Use Area** ($5 day-use). The **Overlook Beach Trail** runs for about a mile from a viewing platform to the beach. Follow the blue-topped wooden posts that mark the trail through the sand. To turn this into a more strenuous 3.5-mile loop, continue 1 mile south along the beach, then head back inland (again following the posts) along the more rugged **Tahkenitch Creek Loop.** Find the turnoff from U.S. 101 near milepost 201.

Another good place to explore the dunes is along **Carter Dunes Trail** and **Taylor Dunes Trail.** Carter Dunes Trail starts near Carter Lake and heads west 1.5 miles to the beach. The first half of the mile-long Taylor Dunes Trail is wheelchair accessible; the trail passes some of the oldest (and gnarliest) conifers in the area. Both of these trails are good places to view wildlife, especially in the winter and spring, when the dunes take on wetland characteristics. The two trails link up, forming a Y rather than a loop. The turnoff for both trails is 7.5 miles south of Florence. Carter Lake also has a campground.

Hike the **Waxmyrtle Trail** along the Siltcoos River; the 1.5-mile trail travels along the estuary and ends up at the beach. The trail is closed March 15-September 15 to protect nesting snowy plovers. This is a good spot for bird-watching. Find the trailhead near the Waxmyrtle Campground about eight miles south of Florence at the Siltcoos Recreation Area.

Dune Rides

Ride into the dunes with the folks from **Sand Dunes Frontier** (83960 U.S. 101, 541/997-3544, http://sanddunesfrontier.com, 9am-6pm daily summer, 10am-4pm Tues.-Sat. mid-Dec.-mid-Mar.) on 30-minute, 20-person dune buggy rides ($14 adults, $11 ages 4-11). Or you can choose a zippier half-hour trip on a sand rail vehicle ($35), which is similar to a dune buggy. Protective goggles are provided, along with a driver. At the same location, **Torex ATV Rentals** (541/997-5363, http://torexatvrentals.com, $50-300/hour) rents vehicles for travel in specially designated areas

Dune Country: Florence to Coos Bay

a jumping-off point for trails in the Oregon Dunes, south of Florence

Even though the 47-mile stretch of U.S. 101 between Coos Bay and Florence does not overlook the ocean, your eyes will be drawn constantly westward to the largest and most extensive oceanfront dunes in the world.

How did they come to exist in a coastal topography otherwise dominated by rocky bluffs? A combination of factors created this landscape over the past 12,000 years, but the principal agents are the Coos, Siuslaw, and Umpqua Rivers. The sand and sediment transported to the sea by these waterways are deposited by waves on the flat, shallow beaches. Prevailing westerlies move the particulate matter exposed by the tide eastward up to several yards per year. Over the millennia, the dunes have grown huge, with some topping 500 feet.

Constantly on the move, the shifting sands have engulfed ancient forests, a fact occasionally corroborated by hikers as they stumble on the top of an exposed snag. The cross-section of sand-swept woodlands seen from U.S. 101 demonstrates that this inundation is still occurring. Nonetheless, the motorist gets the impression that the trees are winning the battle, because the dunes are only intermittently visible from the road.

within the Oregon Dunes National Recreation Area. Go in the morning, when the sand tends to blow around less.

Sandboarding

Dude, it's a natural! Wax up a board, strap it onto your bare feet, and carve your way down the dunes. On the outskirts of Florence, you can rent a board and try out the rails and jumps at **Sand Master Park** (5351 U.S. 101, 541/997-6006, www.sandmasterpark.com, 10am-5pm daily mid-June-mid-Sept., 10am-5pm Mon.-Tues. and Thurs.-Sat., noon-5pm Sun. Mar.-May and mid-Sept.-mid-Jan., board rentals $10-25, includes admission). If you're more of a do-it-yourselfer, a number of roadside shops rent sandboards, and the dunes are certainly plentiful.

Horseback Riding

Riding across the dunes into the sunset on a trusty steed sounds like a fantasy, but you can do it thanks to **C&M Stables** (90241 U.S. 101, 541/997-7540, www.oregonhorsebackriding. com, 10am-5pm daily). Rates range $65-175 per person for trips of 1-2 hours, with discounts for larger parties. The stables are open year-round and are located near 14 miles of horse trails that wind through the forest on a bluff above the beach. With beach rides, dune trail excursions, and sunset trips, there's something for everybody.

Fishing

Oregon's largest coastal lake, 3,100-acre **Siltcoos Lake,** six miles south of Florence, offers excellent fishing and other recreation. The lake is stocked with rainbow trout in the spring, and steelhead, salmon (the lake is closed to coho fishing), and sea-run cutthroat trout move from the ocean into the lake via the short Siltcoos River in late summer and fall. But the real excitement here is the fishing for warm-water species, which is some of the best in the Pacific Northwest. Bluegill, crappie, yellow perch, and brown bullhead action is good through the summer, while fishing for largemouth bass can be good year-round. Access points include several public and private boat ramps on the lake, as well as a wheelchair-accessible fishing pier at Westlake Resort.

Water Sports

Although only the hardiest swimmers go into the ocean without wetsuits, **Cleawox** and **Woahink Lakes** warm up sufficiently to make summertime swimming enjoyable. Cleawox, the smaller of the two, is especially well suited for swimming. A lodge (10am-5pm daily Memorial Day-Labor Day) by the swimming beach rents pedal boats, canoes, and kayaks. Both lakes are within Honeyman State Park (day-use $5/vehicle), three miles south of Florence.

Surfers head to the beaches at South Jetty, where the waves are best when small—they can often become overwhelming and unsuitable for novices. Look for more protection from the wind at the mouth of the river.

South of Florence, in the Oregon Dunes National Recreation Area, the three-mile **Siltcoos River Canoe Trail** is inviting to kayakers and canoeists. Meandering through

dunes, forest, and estuary, the Siltcoos is a gentle Class I paddle with no white water or rapids, although a small dam midway must be portaged. Wildlife that you may encounter along the way include mink, raccoons, otters, beavers, and even bears. In the estuary, sea lions and harbor seals are common. Rent a kayak from **Siltcoos Lake Resort** (82855 Fir St., Westlake, 541/999-6941, www.siltcooslakeresort.com, $45-65/day), six miles south of Florence.

Golf

Ocean Dunes Golf Links (3345 Munsel Lake Rd., 541/997-3232, www.threeriverscasino.com/golf, $48 for 18 holes), part of the Three Rivers Casino complex, lets you tee off with sand dunes (some more than 60 feet high) as a backdrop. The manicured 18-hole course has a driving range, a full pro shop, and equipment rentals on-site. For the ultimate in golfing by the dunes, however, try **Florence Golf Links** (1201 35th St., 541/997-1940, http://florencegolflinks.com, $64-79 for 18 holes). To get there, go west off U.S. 101 on 35th Street. In May and June rhododendrons line this drive, which heads into dune country as you move toward the sea. Follow the signs until you see a water tower not far from the pro shop. A 7,190-yard par-72 course, Florence Golf Links' layout features fairways lined with lakes, Douglas firs, and beach grass on gently undulating terrain; the inward nine holes are traditional links style. Coastal winds that kick up in the afternoon can figure prominently in your shot selection.

ENTERTAINMENT AND EVENTS

For current information on Florence area events, contact the **Florence Chamber of Commerce** (541/997-3128, www.florencechamber.com).

During the third weekend of May, Florence celebrates the **Rhododendron Festival,** coinciding with the blooming of these flowers, which proliferate in the area. It's a tradition that goes back to 1908, when the festival was started as a way to draw attention and commerce to the town. A parade, carnival, flower show, 5K "Rhody Run," and the crowning of Queen Rhododendra are highlights of the festivities. This is a popular event, attracting more than 15,000 visitors each year.

Fourth of July celebrations include live outdoor music and a barbecue in Old Town, along with a fireworks display over the river. Authors, publishers, and readers gather at the **Florence Festival of Books** (541/997-1994, www.florencefestivalofbooks.org), held at the Florence Events Center the last weekend of September. For general entertainment, the Coos, Lower Umpqua, and Siuslaw tribes run **Three Rivers Casino** (5647 Hwy. 126, 541/997-7529, www.threeriverscasino.com). Along with the slots and game tables, there's a hotel and golf course.

FOOD

Many Florence restaurants are along the Old Town waterfront. Walk along Bay Street and discover dozens of dining options, from casual to upscale.

Pacific Northwest Cuisine

The Oregon coast isn't really known for adventurous fine dining, but a handful of hip eateries are spicing up the scene. At the edge of Old Town, the ★ **Homegrown Public House** (294 Laurel St., 541/997-4886, http://homegrownpublichouse.com, 11am-9pm Tues.-Sat., 11am-8pm Sun., $9-23) is an easygoing place for a beer and a snack or a full meal—maybe wild salmon and barley risotto with wild mushrooms. As the name implies, much of the food is locally grown or gathered, and seasonal.

Seafood

No one will ever accuse the ★ **Waterfront Depot** (1252 Bay St., 541/902-9100, www.thewaterfrontdepot.com, 4pm-10pm daily, reservations recommended, $15-30) of lacking in personality; it's a friendly, bustling place with good views out onto the river and a delicious signature dish of crab-encrusted

halibut; you'll also find excellent steak and rack of lamb. This historic structure was formerly the rail station at nearby Mapleton before it was barged down the Siuslaw River to its current riverfront location.

The **Bridgewater Ocean Fresh Fish House and Zebra Bar** (1297 Bay St., 541/997-9405, 11am-10pm Wed.-Mon., $17-36) offers a broad menu that includes many seafood options in the heart of Old Town. You'll find fresh ahi, halibut, salmon, and shellfish, as well as classic steaks, fried chicken, and Cobb salads.

Eastern European

At ★ **Mari's Kitchen** (1277 Bay St., 541/305-2041, http://mariskitchenflorence.com, 8am-9pm daily, $17-14), a Romanian-born chef re-creates her homeland's highlight dishes such as a *musaca* (a tomato and beef casserole baked with sliced potatoes), as well as excellent local seafood and pasta.

Mexican

It doesn't look like much from the front, but the best reason to seek out the **Traveler's Cove** (1362 Bay St., 541/997-6845, 9am-9pm daily, $9-22) is the lovely back patio, with tables directly over the river. The food is eclectic, with homemade clam chowder, tempting salads and sandwiches, and a number of Mexican dishes. Fresh Dungeness crab makes an appearance here with crab quiche, crab enchiladas, and "crabby" Caesar salad.

Italian

A good place to take a break from chowder (though not necessarily seafood) is **La Pomodori Ristorante** (1415 7th St., 541/902-2525, www.lapomodori.com, 11:30am-2pm and 5pm-8pm Tues.-Fri., 5pm-8pm Sat., $15-24), an intimate northern Italian restaurant in a converted house. Specialties include brandy pan-fried fresh prawns, as well as traditional Italian classics like chicken or veal piccata.

Down in Old Town, **1285 Restobar** (1285 Bay St., 541/902-8338, www.1285restobar.com, 11am-8pm Sun.-Thurs., 11am-9pm

Fri.-Sat., $9-17) is a lively trattoria with a focus on good seafood entrées; pizza is also a popular choice. Have a seat at a sidewalk table and watch the action on Bay Street; the patio out back is more secluded.

Coffee and Tea

Under the bridge in Old Town, **Siuslaw River Coffee Roasters** (1240 Bay St., 541/997-3443, www.coffeeoregon.com, 7am-5pm daily, $2-6) serves good coffee and pastries. There's a little deck out back overlooking the river, and lots of books, gifts, and hobnobbing inside.

If you're visiting on a rainy afternoon, a good place to while away the time is **Lovejoy's Tea Room** (129 Nopal St., 541/997-0502, http://lovejoysrestaurant.com, 7am-5pm daily, $8-25), where you can share a pot of Earl Grey (or fine coffee), dine on a Cornish pasty or sausage roll, or go for high tea service with scones and clotted cream.

Dessert

After dinner, have dessert at one of the two locations of **BJ's Ice Cream Parlor** (2930 U.S. 101; 1441 Bay St., 541/997-7286, 11am-10pm daily, $2-6). BJ's churns out hundreds of flavors, with 58 on display at any given time. Full fountain service, ice cream cakes, cheesecakes, gourmet frozen yogurt, and pies complement the cones and cups.

ACCOMMODATIONS

Like just about everywhere else, there are budget motels on the main drag. We've selected a few with some character but urge you to consider one of the local B&Bs. Unless otherwise noted, prices listed are for high-season doubles.

$50-100

One of the best bargains in town is the **Lighthouse Inn** (155 U.S. 101, 541/997-3221 or 866/997-3221, http://lighthouseinnflorence.com, $90-150), a Cape Cod-style two-story motel on the highway close to the bridge and convenient to Old Town. With

neatly kept but aging rooms decorated with bric-a-brac and other homey touches, it may give you the feeling that you're spending the night at your grandmother's house. A pet-friendly suite includes a kitchenette, and most rooms have microwaves and fridges. Most guest rooms also have a queen or king bed and sleep two; some are considered suites, with two rooms and a connecting bath, sleeping up to five guests. A few rooms are designated as pet-friendly.

$100-150

For the best riverside setting in town, stay at the ★ **River House Inn** (1202 Bay St., 541/997-3933 or 888/824-2454, www.riverhouseflorence.com, $129-199). It's worth paying extra for a waterfront balcony ($169-199). This attractive motel has good views of the Siuslaw River Bridge and is just two blocks away from the heart of Old Town.

Just around the corner from Old Town and across the highway from the Lighthouse Inn, the pet-friendly **Old Town Inn** (170 U.S. 101 N., 541/997-7131 or 800/301-6494, www.old-town-inn.com, $124) provides guests with spacious rooms a short walk away from the river and Old Town. Although this motel is on U.S. 101, the guest rooms are fairly quiet.

At Heceta Beach, on the northern edge of Florence, **Driftwood Shores Resort** (5.2 miles north of Florence at 88416 1st Ave., 541/997-8263 or 800/422-5091, www.driftwoodshores.com, $143-226) is unique among Florence lodgings in that it is oceanside. It is also a huge complex and in a pretty isolated area, far from Old Town and restaurants (except the resort restaurant). All rooms face the ocean and have decks or patios, as well as microwaves and fridges; some suites have full kitchens. The resort also has an indoor aquatic center and playground.

If it's not important for you to be an easy walk from Old Town, consider staying three miles south at the charming and pet-friendly ★ **Park Motel** (85034 U.S. 101, 541/997-2634 or 800/392-0441, http://parkflorence.com, $134-170), a classic mom-and-pop place set well back from the highway in a stand of Douglas firs. The guest rooms are paneled in knotty pine and come in a variety of sizes and configurations, including a few cabins, making it a good place for families or groups of friends.

$150-200

★ **The Edwin K B&B** (1155 Bay St., 541/997-8360 or 800/833-9465, www.edwink.com, $175-200) has six guest rooms, all with private baths, as well as an apartment suite ($190-215). The Edwin K is just two blocks from Old Town, across the street from the Siuslaw River. River views, period antiques, and multicourse breakfasts with locally famous soufflés and home-baked breads served on fine china have established this gracious 1914 home as Florence's preeminent B&B. Add a private courtyard and waterfall in back, tea and sherry in the afternoon, and a restful atmosphere, and you'll understand the need to reserve well in advance.

Over $200

Twelve miles north of Florence and just a short walk from Heceta Head Lighthouse is **Heceta Head Lighthouse B&B** (92072 U.S. 101, 541/547-3696 or 866/547-3696, www.hecetalighthouse.com, $285-435), built in 1893. It used to be the lighthouse keeper's home; today it's a B&B with antique furnishings and vintage photos, which help re-create the lives of the keepers of the flame. Among the six bedrooms, the two Mariners rooms command the finest views. The current caretakers maintain a garden on the grounds, as did the actual lighthouse keepers of yesteryear, and they use some of the produce to turn out amazing seven-course breakfasts. The innkeepers are more likely to tell you about resident ghosts during breakfast than right before bedtime.

On the south bank of the river, just across the bridge from Old Town, the **Best Western Pier Point Inn** (85625 U.S. 101, 541/997-7191 or 800/435-6736, www.bwpierpointinn.com, $215-239) offers spacious rooms, an indoor pool, a restaurant and bar, great bay views, sand-dune hiking across the street, and a complimentary hot breakfast. Rates at this large and classy motel drop by about half in the off-season.

Camping

There are excellent campgrounds around Florence, several with recreational opportunities comparable to those at the nearby Oregon Dunes National Recreation Area but with more varied scenery.

Carl G. Washburne State Park (93111 U.S. 101 N., 541/547-3416, yurt reservations 800/452-5687, www.oregonstateparks.org, year-round, $21 tents, $31-33 RVs, $46 yurts, $56 pet-friendly yurts, $8 hiker-biker) is popular with Oregonians because of its proximity to beaches, tide pools, Sea Lion Caves, and hiking trails. The seven walk-in tent sites are secluded, and the remaining 57 sites have electricity and water (some also have sewer hookups); like almost all state park campgrounds, there are showers. Reservations are not accepted for regular sites, but the park's two yurts can be reserved. It's 14 miles north of Florence on U.S. 101 and 3 miles past Sea Lion Caves, then 1 mile west on a park road. This state park offers a number of good hiking trails and, via the Hobbit Trail, three miles of relatively isolated beach.

Three miles south of Florence's McCullough Bridge and on both sides of U.S. 101 is **Honeyman State Park** (84505 U.S. 101 S., 541/997-3641, reservations 800/452-5687, www.oregonstateparks.org, $21 tents, $31-33 RVs, $46 yurts, $56 pet-friendly yurts, $8 hiker-biker). This large and exceedingly popular campground gets crowded in the summer—reservations are a must—but it empties out enough during spring and autumn to make a stay here worthwhile. The park is popular with all-terrain vehicle (ATV) users, who camp in the H loop, where there's a two-mile ATV trail to the beach. Hiking from the campground to the beach is discouraged. In spring, pink rhododendrons line the highway and park roads.

If you're looking for something smaller and low-key, then two Siuslaw National Forest campgrounds just north of Florence might be the ticket. **Sutton Campground** (reservations 877/444-6777, www.recreation. gov, regular sites $22, with electricity $27) is four miles north of Florence, and in addition to 80 campsites amid the dunes, it features a *Darlingtonia* bog and a hiking trail network. In high summer season, about a quarter of the sites can be reserved; the rest are available on a first-come, first-served basis.

Just another mile north is **Alder Dune Campground** (reservations 877/444-6777, www.recreation.gov, $21) with two lakes with swimming beaches and trout fishing. Hiking trails lead out into the dunes and reach the Pacific beaches. During summer high season, all of the campground's 39 sites can be reserved. For more information on these campgrounds, contact the **Siuslaw National Forest** (541/271-6000, www. fs.fed.us).

INFORMATION AND SERVICES

The **Florence Area Chamber of Commerce** (290 U.S. 101, 541/997-3128, www.florencechamber.com, 9am-5pm Mon.-Fri., 10am-2pm Sat.) is three blocks north of the Siuslaw River Bridge.

Peace Harbor Hospital (400 9th St., 541/997-8412) is open 24 hours daily, with a handful of specialists and an emergency room. The **post office** (770 Maple St., 541/997-2533), near the junction of Highway 126 and U.S. 101, is close to the library.

GETTING THERE

Pacific Crest Bus Lines (541/344-6265, http://pacificcrestbuslines.com) offers bus service (Sun.-Fri.) between Coos Bay in the south and Eugene to the east, with connections to Bend. Eugene offers both Greyhound and Amtrak service, as well as air links to the rest of the country from Mahlon Sweet Field Airport (EUG).

Reedsport and Winchester Bay

If you're going fishing or coming back from a dunes hike, you'll appreciate a clean, low-priced motel room in Reedsport. Otherwise, this town of 5,000 people might seem like a strange mirage of cut-rate motels, taverns, and burger joints in the midst of the Oregon Dunes National Recreation Area. Reedsport is not a tourist town, to put it politely. But there's lots of fascinating recreation available in the Oregon Dunes NRA that encircles the town, and the Umpqua River is itself a destination for anglers.

Three miles southwest of Reedsport, Salmon Harbor Marina in **Winchester Bay,** a busy port for commercial sportfishing at the mouth of the Umpqua, has given the whole

area new life in recent years, following hard times precipitated by the decline in timber revenues. In many ways, Winchester Bay is the more interesting destination of the two side-by-side towns, with its busy harbor and collage of waterfront bars and restaurants.

SIGHTS
Oregon Dunes

A great place to start your explorations is the **Oregon Dunes National Recreation Area Visitor Information Center** (885 U.S. 101, Reedsport, 541/271-6100, www.fs.usda.gov/siuslaw, 8am-4pm Mon.-Fri. and some summer Sat.), at the junction of the Coast Highway and Highway 38. In addition to the printed information on hiking, camping, and recreation, the Siuslaw National Forest personnel are helpful. Note that a $5 day-use fee is charged per vehicle at most facilities and

1: Umpqua Discovery Center in Reedsport
2: the viewing platform at the Sea Lion Caves near Florence 3: Florence waterfront

access points within the NRA. You can purchase an annual pass at the Dunes Visitor Center for $30.

Because the dunes are difficult to see from the highway in many places, the most commonly asked question in the visitors center is "Where are the dunes?" To answer that question for everybody, the U.S. Forest Service opened **Oregon Dunes Overlook** just south of Carter Lake, midway between Florence and Reedsport, at the point where the dunes come closest to U.S. 101. In addition to four levels of railing-enclosed platforms connected by wooden walkways, there are trails down to the sand. It's only about 0.25 mile to the dunes and then 1 mile through sand and wetlands to the beach.

You can hike a loop beginning where the sand gives way to willows. Bear right en route to the beach. Once there, walk south 1.5 miles. A wooden post marks where the trail resumes. It then traverses a footbridge going through trees onto sand, completing the loop. If you go in February, this loop has great bird-watching potential.

Umpqua Discovery Center

In Reedsport's Old Town, on the south bank of the river, the **Umpqua Discovery Center** (409 Riverfront Way, 541/271-4816, www.umpquadiscoverycenter.com, 10am-5pm Mon.-Sat., noon-4pm Sun. June-Sept., 10am-4pm Mon.-Sat., noon-4pm Sun. Oct.-May, $8 adults, $4 ages 6-16) interprets the regional human and natural history through multimedia programs, dioramas, scale models, and helpful staff. The gift store is stuffed with local goodies. The boardwalk and observation tower give a good view of the broad lower reaches of the Umpqua.

Dean Creek Elk Viewing Area

Three miles east of Reedsport and stretching three miles along the south side of Highway 38, the **Dean Creek Elk Viewing Area** (48819 Hwy. 38, Reedsport, 541/756-0100, www.blm.gov) provides parking areas and viewing platforms for observing the herd of some 120 wild

Roosevelt elk that roam this 1,100-acre preserve. The elk move out of the forest to graze the preserve's marshy pastures, sometimes coming quite close to the highway. Elk can reach 1,100 pounds at maturity, and the majestic rack on a fully grown bull can spread three feet across. Early morning and just before dusk are the most promising times to look for them; during hot weather and storms, the elk tend to stay within the cover of the woods.

Umpqua Lighthouse State Park

Less than one mile south of Winchester Bay is **Umpqua Lighthouse State Park** (460 Lighthouse Rd., Winchester Bay, 541/271-4118, www.oregonstateparks.org). Tour the red-capped 1894 **lighthouse** (1020 Lighthouse Rd., 541/271-4631, 10am-5pm daily May-Oct., 10am-4pm daily Nov.-Dec. and Mar.-Apr., lighthouse tours $8 adults, $4 children 5-17) or admire it from the roadside. Next door, in a former U.S. Coast Guard building, a **visitors center and museum** has marine and timber exhibits; this is also where tours begin. Directly opposite the lighthouse, overlooking the mouth of the Umpqua and oceanfront dunes, is a whale-watching platform with a plaque explaining where, when, and what to look for.

The main part of the state park, which includes a campground and Lake Marie, is a five-minute drive from the lighthouse itself. The lake has a swimming beach and is stocked with rainbow trout. A one-mile forest trail around the lake makes for an easy hike. A trail from the campground leads to the second-highest dunes in the United States (elev. 545 feet), west of Clear Lake.

RECREATION

TOP EXPERIENCE

Hiking

There are three excellent state parks and a dozen Siuslaw National Forest campgrounds within the **Oregon Dunes NRA.** Although joyriding in noisy dune buggies and other off-road vehicles doesn't lack devotees, the best way to appreciate the interface of ecosystems is on foot. Dunes exceeding 500 feet in height, wetland breeding grounds for waterfowl and other animals, evergreen forests, and deserted beaches can be encountered in a march to the sea. Numerous designated hiking trails, ranging from easy 0.5-mile loops to 6-mile round-trips, give visitors a chance to star in their own version of *Lawrence of Arabia*. The soundtrack is provided by over 200 species of birds—along with your heartbeat—as you scale these elephantine promontories of sand. Deserted beaches and secret swimming holes are among the many rewards of the journey.

Before setting out, pick up the *Hiking Trails Recreation Opportunity Guide* from the **Oregon Dunes NRA Visitor Information Center** (885 U.S. 101, Reedsport, 541/271-6100, www.fs.usda.gov/siuslaw, 8am-4pm Mon.-Fri.). Carry plenty of water and dress in layers—there are hot spots in dune valleys and ocean breezes at higher elevations.

★ JOHN DELLENBACK TRAIL

This spectacular dunes landscape can be found 10.5 miles south of Reedsport and 0.25 mile south of the Eel Creek Campground near Lakeside. After you emerge from a 0.5-mile hike through coastal evergreen forest, you'll be greeted by dunes 300-400 feet high. It's said that dunes near here can approach 500 feet high and 1 mile long after a windblown buildup. The trail, marked by blue-banded wooden posts, continues another 2.5 miles to the beach. Note that dune hiking can be a bit disorienting. If you lose the trail, climb to the top of the tallest dune and scan for the trail markers.

A shorter and easier one-mile loop trail leads through woodlands to the dunes for a quick introduction to this landscape.

Skate Park

Near the south end of Reedsport in Lions Park is a world-class **skate park** (U.S. 101 and S. 22nd St.). Here you'll find a funnel-shaped full pipe and a 360-degree full loop, as well as many more approachable features.

Fishing

Winchester Bay and the tidewater reaches of the lower Umpqua River are Oregon's top coastal sturgeon fishery and one of the best areas for striped bass, particularly near the mouth of the Smith River, which enters the Umpqua just east of Reedsport. The best action for the Umpqua's spring chinook tends to be inland, below Scottsburg. Fall chinook enter the bay July-September. Other notable fisheries here are the huge runs of shad, which peak in May and June, and smallmouth bass offer action upstream from Reedsport. Crabbing and clamming are also popular and productive pastimes in Winchester Bay and the lower reaches of the river.

Fishing charter services operating in the area include **Living Waters** (541/584-2295, www.fishinglivingwaters.com) and **Winchester Bay Charters** (541/361-0180, www.winchesterbaycharters.com).

Water Sports

Ten miles south of Reedsport, the sleepy resort town of **Lakeside** hosted visits from Bob Hope, Bing Crosby, and the Ink Spots, among other luminaries, back in its 1930s and 1940s heyday. Today, it's still a popular destination, primarily for its proximity to the sprawling, many-armed Tenmile and North Tenmile Lakes. These large, shallow lakes offer waterskiing and excellent fishing for stocked rainbow trout and warm-water species, including crappie, yellow perch, bluegill, and lunker largemouth bass, which can grow up to 10 pounds. A 0.25-mile channel connects the two lakes, and a county park on Tenmile Lake has a paved boat ramp, fishing docks, a sandy swimming beach, and a picnic area.

FESTIVALS AND EVENTS

Every June over Father's Day weekend, chainsaw sculptors compete for $10,000 in prizes as they transform pieces of raw western red cedar into grizzly bears, giant salmon, and other rustic works of art during the **Chainsaw Sculpture Championships** (www.oregonccc.com) at the Rainbow Plaza in Old Town Reedsport, near North 2nd Street and Greenwood Avenue.

Dunefest (541/271-3495, http://dunefest. com) brings ATV riders to town for races, freestyle shows, a treasure hunt, and more at the end of July.

FOOD

Seek not cuisine in Reedsport—standard American fare is the norm in this hardscrabble town. The best bets for seafood are the wharf-side restaurants in Winchester Bay.

Reedsport

A popular diner on U.S. 101 is **Don's Diner & Ice Cream Parlor** (2115 Winchester Ave., 541/271-2032, 8am-7pm daily, $7-12), with burgers, fried chicken, and a parlor serving local Umpqua ice cream. This is the local favorite place for pie; the Pie Lover's special is half a sandwich, a cup of coffee, and a slice of pie.

The **Schooner Inn Café** (423 Riverfront Way, 541/271-3945, 10am-4pm Sun.-Wed., 10am-7pm Thurs.-Sat., $9-15), on the boardwalk next door to the Umpqua Discovery Center, has a pleasant riverside patio and a good selection of delicious salads and sandwiches. It's a quiet spot for an alfresco lunch overlooking the Umpqua.

Winchester Bay

For the best fresh seafood in the dune country, head down to the Salmon Harbor Marina at Winchester Bay, where there are a number of casual seafood restaurants within easy strolling distance.

Stop by **Sportsmen's Cannery and Smokehouse** (182 Bay Front Loop, 541/271-3293, shop 9am-5pm daily) to pick up cans of tuna. No kidding, it's worth the price and will make a great gift for the folks back home. While you're at this fish market, order an oyster shooter or shrimp cocktail and dine at a picnic table out front.

Another good bet for fresh seafood in an authentic, albeit indoor, dockside setting is **Crabby's Bar & Grill** (196 Bay Front Loop, 541/271-3474, 11am-midnight daily, $8-25), which offers excellent fish-and-chips, crab, and fish sandwiches in a woodsy dining room.

ACCOMMODATIONS

Just off U.S. 101 on the road to Winchester Bay, **Salmon Harbor Landing** (265 8th St., Winchester Bay, 541/271-3742, $65-75) is a simple but clean and friendly motel. This is a good place to stay if you don't need fancy amenities yet enjoy a personal touch. Each room is individually decorated, with many of the owner's antiques featured.

Anglers, or anyone who'd rather be in a location off the main drag, should consider the **Winchester Bay Inn** (390 Broadway, Winchester Bay, 541/271-4871 or 800/246-1462, www.winbayinn.com, $89-145), just across from the docks. Guest rooms are basic but clean, and some include kitchens. Even though this is a large, sprawling complex, reserve ahead of time in fishing season. Pets are permitted in some guest rooms.

The **Best Western Plus Salbasgeon Inn** (1400 U.S. 101, 541/271-4831 or 800/780-7234, $150-176) is Reedsport's largest and most full-service hotel, on U.S. 101 just south of the Umpqua River bridge. Amenities include an indoor pool, a fitness center, guest laundry, a hot tub, and breakfast included.

Camping

Choices abound in this recreation-rich area. Just south of Winchester Bay is **Umpqua Lighthouse State Park** (460 Lighthouse Rd., Winchester Bay, 541/271-4118, reservations 800/452-5687, www.oregonstateparks.org, $19-80). The campground alongside Lake Marie has firewood, flush toilets, showers, picnic tables, electricity, and piped water. The 20 RV sites go for $29-31; the 24 tent sites are $19; two basic yurts are $43-53; six deluxe yurts (with shower, small kitchen, fridge, microwave, and

TV/DVD player) are $82; and two rustic cabins are $43. The lake offers fishing, boating, and swimming. Trails from the campground lead to the second-highest dunes in the United States (elev. 545 feet), west of Clear Lake.

William A. Tugman State Park (541/759-3604, reservations 800/452-5687, www.oregonstateparks.org, $26 tents or RVs, $46 yurts, $56 pet-friendly yurts) is eight miles south of Reedsport, in the heart of dune country. This larger campground, with 115 sites, sits on the west shore of Eel Lake, east of U.S. 101, across from the widest point of the dunes and two miles from the sea.

Windy Cove Campground (541/271-4138, www.co.douglas.or.us/parks) is a county park with 24 full-hookup sites ($25) and 4 other sites with electricity only ($17). Located on the south side of Salmon Harbor Drive across from the Winchester Bay marina, it has restrooms, picnic tables, grass, and paved site pads. No reservations are accepted. It is legal to drive your off-highway vehicle (OHV) from this campground directly to the dunes, but that requires a couple of miles' drive on the pavement.

About nine miles south of Reedsport, set along Eel Creek near Eel and Tenmile Lakes, is **Eel Creek Campground** (reservations 877/444-6777, www.recreation.gov, $22-44), a Siuslaw National Forest facility with 51 basic tent and RV sites; reservations are advised. The Umpqua Dunes Trail offers access to the dunes and the beach.

Eight miles north of Reedsport, the **Tahkenitch Campground** (reservations 877/444-6777, www.recreation.gov, mid-May-Sept., $22-44) is another Forest Service facility set among ancient Douglas firs and conveniently located near Tahkenitch and other lakes, dunes, and ocean beaches. A network of trails branch out through the dunes, along Tahkenitch Lake, and to the beach. Just a mile away, another Forest Service campground is **Tahkenitch Landing Campground** (reservations 877/444-6777, www.recreation.gov, year-round, $22), which doesn't have piped water.

INFORMATION

The **Oregon Dunes NRA Visitor Information Center** (885 U.S. 101, Reedsport, 541/271-6100, www.fs.usda.gov/siuslaw) and **Reedsport Chamber of Commerce** (541/271-3495, www.reedsportcc.org) share a building at the junction of U.S. 101 and Highway 38, open 8am-4pm Monday-Friday year-round.

South Coast

Stretching from Coos Bay to the California bor-
der, the southern Oregon coast is far from the population centers of
Oregon's interior valleys, but amply rewards visitors who make the effort to get here. The foothills of the Klamath Mountains tumble down
the narrow coastal plain and fall off in precipitous headlands at the
ocean's edge. Close to shore, the waters are a rocky garden of sea stacks
and islets that are home to uncounted flocks of pelagic birds. With half
a dozen wild rivers slicing through the mountains to the sea, the south
coast is famed for its outstanding salmon fishing, especially on charters
from the harbors of Charleston, Gold Beach, Bandon, and Brookings.

In addition, the southern region is blessed with the fairest weather
on the Oregon coast and generally gets the most sunshine, the least

Highlights

Look for ★ to find recommended sights, activities, dining, and lodging.

★ **Shore Acres State Park:** The regal manor house is gone, but the formal gardens from a onetime private estate still thrive above an especially rugged stretch of beach (page 157).

★ **Bandon Dunes Golf Resort:** This links-style course on the coastal headlands is evocative of Scotland. Its four golf courses are expertly designed in a gorgeous setting (page 171).

★ **Cape Blanco State Park and Hughes House:** This is the only lighthouse in Oregon that allows visitors into the lantern room, with its massive Fresnel lens (page 177).

★ **Humbug Mountain:** On a hike to the top of this mountain, you'll pass a spectacular array of native plants and earn impressive views (page 177).

★ **Cape Sebastian:** Hike up Cape Sebastian for a front-row seat for springtime whale-watching (page 183).

★ **Rogue River Jet-Boat Ride:** Even die-hard paddlers won't regret succumbing to a jet-boat tour up the Rogue River. Boaters often get to see ospreys and eagles fishing along this stretch of river (page 183).

★ **Samuel H. Boardman State Scenic Corridor:** North of Brookings, the road winds

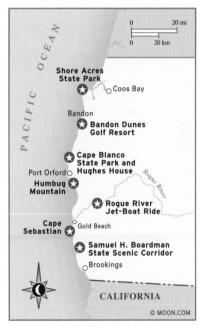

hundreds of feet above the surf, allowing you to peer down at one of the most dramatic meetings of rock and tide in the world (page 191).

rain, and the warmest temperatures—attributes as appealing to visitors as to the area's many retirees and other transplants.

Scenic highlights of the south coast include the weather-beaten bluffs and formal gardens at Cape Arago and Shore Acres State Parks, the gorgeous scenery of Boardman and Harris Beach State Parks, and just about every inch of the drive between Brookings and Port Orford. Outstanding courses draw golfers to Bandon; some of the coast's top windsurfing and kiting are found near Cape Sebastian; and popular jet-boat tours run up the Rogue River from Gold Beach.

PLANNING YOUR TIME

Plan to spend at least a day or two exploring the **Coos Bay-Bandon** region. Coos Bay is the only real city along the southern coast, and like Tillamook to the north, it's a gateway to some spectacular areas, but pretty workaday itself. Head west and south from town to explore the wonderful shoreline parks at Sunset Bay and Cape Arago.

Don't overlook the coastal wetlands, especially the coastal estuary at **South Slough National Estuarine Research Reserve,** south of Coos Bay. **Bandon Marsh National Wildlife Refuge** protects the largest remaining tract of salt marsh within the Coquille River estuary. Major habitats include undisturbed salt marsh, mudflat, Sitka spruce, and alder riparian communities, which provide resting and feeding areas for migratory waterfowl, shore and wading birds, and raptors.

Although **Bandon** is known for its world-class Bandon Dunes Golf Resort, the old downtown area still hums to counterculture vibes. Bandon's beachfront, along with the Coos Bay sand spit, the beaches on the western side of Humbug Mountain, and the isolated shorelines of Boardman State Park, are choice beachcombing spots.

Port Orford is often overlooked, but it's one of our favorite spots, with great ocean vistas from town and lots of hiking at nearby Humbug Mountain. It also doesn't hurt that

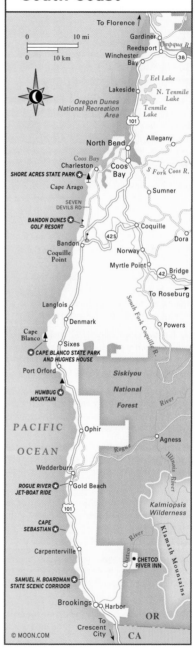

South Coast

© MOON.COM

there's good eating here. It's worth at least an afternoon stop.

Jet-boat tours start in **Gold Beach** and head up the Rogue River, offering those with just a morning to spare the chance to explore stunning river vistas—and perhaps help deliver the mail. Between Gold Beach and Brookings, save some serious time to explore beaches sequestered between steep cliffs and pounding surf at the 11-mile-long **Boardman State Scenic Corridor.**

Charleston, Coos Bay, and North Bend

The towns around the harbor of Coos Bay—Charleston, Coos Bay, and North Bend—refer to themselves collectively as the Bay Area. In contrast to its namesake in California, the Oregon version is not exactly the Athens of the coast. Nonetheless, visitors will be impressed by the area's beautiful beaches and three wonderfully scenic and historic state parks. Because much of this natural beauty is away from the industrialized core of the area and U.S. 101, it's easy to miss. All that many motorists see upon entering Coos Bay and North Bend on the Coast Highway are the dockside lumber mills and foreign vessels anchored at the onetime site of the world's largest lumber port.

The little town of Charleston to the southwest makes few pretenses of being anything other than what it really is—a bustling commercial fishing port. Processing plants here can or cold-pack tuna, salmon, crab, oysters, shrimp, and other kinds of seafood. The few restaurants and lodgings are good values, the Marine Life Center is worth a visit, and the area is the gateway to a trio of extraordinary state parks: Sunset Bay, Shore Acres, and Cape Arago.

SIGHTS
Coos Bay Harbor
A good place to take in the bustling bayfront is the **Coos Bay Boardwalk** (U.S. 101 and Anderson Ave.), where you can check out the oceangoing freighters, visit a restored tugboat, and learn of the harbor's history courtesy of interpretive placards. A 400-gallon saltwater aquarium holds fish and other marinelife of Coos Bay. This is the largest coastal harbor between San Francisco and Puget Sound.

Coos History Museum
The expansive **Coos History Museum** (1210 N. Front St., Coos Bay, 541/756-6320, www.cooshistory.org, 10am-5pm Tues.-Sat., $7 adults, $6 AAA or AARP, $3 ages 5-17), right on the waterfront at the north end of Coos Bay, is worth a visit for its visually compelling exhibits. The cedar-lined Welcoming Gallery invokes the look of a Pacific Northwest plank house. A logging display features a giant rotating band saw, and in the fishing area, a boat seems to sail right out of a wall. After traveling around the area, visitors may want to take a close look at the Fresnel lens from the Cape Arago Lighthouse or a section of the McCullough Bridge.

Coos Art Museum
The **Coos Art Museum** (235 Anderson Ave., Coos Bay, 541/267-3901, www.coosart.org, 10am-4pm Tues.-Fri., 1pm-4pm Sat., $5 adults, $2 seniors and students), in downtown Coos Bay, is the Oregon coast's only civic art museum and features primarily 20th-century and contemporary works by American artists, including pieces by Robert Rauschenberg and Larry Rivers. Etchings, woodcuts, serigraphs, and other prints make up a large part

SOUTH COAST
CHARLESTON, COOS BAY, AND NORTH BEND

Previous: Shore Acres State Park; Oregon Redwoods Trail; Fishermen's Seafood Market in Coos Bay.

Coos Bay and North Bend

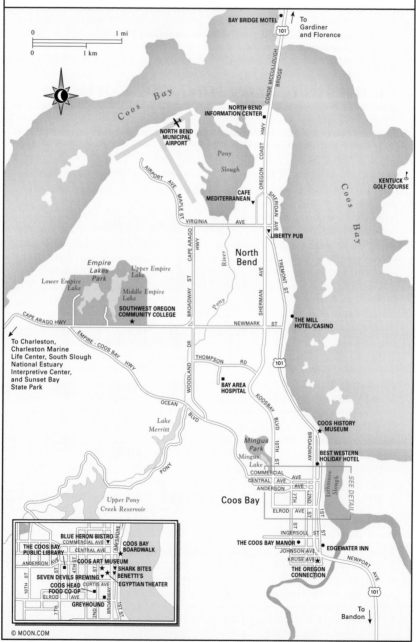

0   1 mi

0   1 km

BAY BRIDGE MOTEL

To Gardiner and Florence

Coos Bay

NORTH BEND
INFORMATION CENTER

NORTH BEND
MUNICIPAL
AIRPORT

KENTUCK
GOLF COURSE

Pony

Slough

CAFE
MEDITERRANEAN

Coos Bay

VIRGINIA   AVE

LIBERTY PUB

River

North
Bend

Empire
Lakes
Park

Upper Empire
Lake

Lower Empire
Lake

Middle Empire
Lake

SOUTHWEST OREGON
COMMUNITY COLLEGE

Pony

NEWMARK   ST

THE MILL
HOTEL/CASINO

CAPE ARAGO HWY

EMPIRE - COOS BAY HWY

To Charleston,
Charleston Marine
Life Center, South Slough
National Estuary
Interpretive Center,
and Sunset Bay
State Park

THOMPSON   RD

BAY AREA
HOSPITAL

OCEAN   BLVD

Lake
Merritt

COOS HISTORY
MUSEUM

Mingus
Park

Mingus
Lake

BEST WESTERN
HOLIDAY HOTEL

COMMERCIAL

CENTRAL   AVE

ANDERSON

SEE DETAIL

PONY

Coos Bay

ELROD   AVE

Upper Pony
Creek Reservoir

INGERSOLL   ST

THE COOS BAY MANOR

EDGEWATER INN

NEWPORT

JOHNSON AVE

KRUSE AVE

THE OREGON
CONNECTION

To
Bandon

BLUE HERON BISTRO

COMMERCIAL AVE

COOS BAY
BOARDWALK

THE COOS BAY
PUBLIC LIBRARY

CENTRAL AVE

ANDERSON

COOS ART MUSEUM

SHARK BITES

SEVEN DEVILS BREWING

BENETTI'S

COOS HEAD
FOOD CO-OP

CURTIS AVE

EGYPTIAN THEATER

ELROD   AVE

GREYHOUND

© MOON.COM

of the permanent collection, which includes several of Janet Turner's richly detailed depictions of birds in natural settings. Don't miss the Prefontaine Room on the 2nd floor of the museum. Photos, trophies, medals, and other memorabilia of native-son world-class runner Steve Prefontaine illustrate his credo: "I want to make something beautiful when I run."

In addition to the permanent collection, recurring events worth detouring for are the May-June juried show of artists from the western states.

Sunset Bay State Park

The Cape Arago Highway west of Charleston leads to some of the most dramatic beaches and interesting state parks on the coast. Among the several beaches on the road to Cape Arago, the strand at **Sunset Bay State Park** (13030 Cape Arago Hwy., 541/888-4902, reservations 800/452-5687, www.oregonstateparks.org, camping $19-29, yurts $43-53) is the big attraction because its sheltered shallow cove, encircled by sandstone bluffs, is warm and calm enough for swimming, a rarity in Oregon. Local legend tells that pirates hid out in this well-protected cove. In addition to swimmers, divers, surfers, kayakers, and boaters, many people come here to watch the sunset; the campground, just inland from the beach, is a good base for exploring the local parks.

A spectacular four-mile cliffside segment of the **Oregon Coast Trail** runs from Sunset Beach south to Cape Arago. Good views of **Cape Arago Lighthouse** across the water can be seen along this route. Listen for its unique foghorn. For a short hike, follow the signs from the mouth of Big Creek to the viewpoint overlooking Sunset Bay.

The Cape Arago Lighthouse is on Chief Island and was once linked to the mainland by a steel-truss bridge. For the local Coos people, Chief Island and the adjacent shoreline were a traditional burial ground, though after the building of the first lighthouse in 1866, the U.S. Coast Guard no longer allowed burials. However, the island continued to

have sacred significance for the Coos. After the lighthouse was decommissioned in 2006, the ownership of the island, the lighthouse, and the adjacent shoreline was transferred to the Confederated Tribes of the Coos, Lower Umpqua, and Siuslaw Indians. The bridge to Chief Island has been removed, and the lighthouse and Chief Island are currently not open to the public.

★ Shore Acres State Park

Less than one mile south of Sunset Bay at **Shore Acres State Park** (541/888-3732, 8am-sunset year-round, no pets outside vehicles, Oregon Coast Passport or $5/vehicle, free with camping receipt from Sunset Bay State Park), the grandeur of nature is complemented by human endeavor. The park is set on the grounds of lumber magnate and entrepreneur Louis J. Simpson's early-1900s mansion, which began as a summer home in 1906 and grew into a three-story mansion complete with an indoor heated swimming pool and large ballroom. Originally a Christmas present to his wife, Shore Acres became the showplace of the Oregon coast, with formal and Japanese gardens eventually added to the 743-acre estate. After a 1921 fire, a second, larger (two stories high and 224 feet long) incarnation of Simpson's "shack by the beach" was built. Over the following years the building fell into disrepair; the house and grounds were ceded to the state in 1942. Because of the high cost of upkeep, the mansion had to be razed, but the gardens have been lovingly maintained.

The gardens are compelling attractions, but the headland's rim is more dramatic. Perched near the edge of the bluff, on the site formerly occupied by the mansion, a glass-enclosed observation shelter makes a perfect vantage point from which to watch for whales or marvel at the crashing waves. When there's a storm, the waves slam into the sandstone reefs and cliffs, hurling up tremendous fountains of spray. It's not uncommon to feel the spray atop the 75-foot promontory. The history of the Simpson family is really the history of the

Bay Area, and their story is captioned beneath period photos in the observation gazebo and in the garden in a small enclosure at the west end of the floral displays.

In the seven acres of neatly tended gardens, set back from the sea, the international botanical bounty culled by Simpson clipper ships and schooners is still in its glory, complemented by award-winning roses, rhododendrons, tulips, and azaleas. A restored gardener's cottage with antique furnishings stands at the back of the formal gardens. It's open for special occasions and during the winter holidays. Also in the gardens, note the copper egret sculptures at the pond, and the greenhouse for rare plants from warmer climes.

Thanksgiving-New Year's, during the annual **Holiday Lights and Open House** (4pm-10pm daily), the gardens are decorated with 250,000 colored lights and other holiday touches. The gardener's cottage opens and serves free refreshments during this time.

If you bear right and follow the pond's contours toward the ocean, you'll come to the **Simpson Beach Trail.** Follow it north for cliffside views of the rock-studded shallows below. Southward, the trail goes downhill to a scene of exceptional beauty. From the vantage point of a small beach, you can watch waves crash into rocks with such force that the white spray appears to hang suspended in the air. Pursuits for the active traveler include exploring tide pools and caves as well as springtime swimming in a cove, formed by winter storms, on the south side of the beach.

Cape Arago State Park

A little more than one mile south of Shore Acres is **Cape Arago State Park** (800/551-6949, day-use only, free), at the end of the Cape Arago Highway. Locals have made much of the fact that this was a possible landing site of the English explorer Sir Francis Drake in 1579, and put a plaque here commemorating him.

Beachcombers can make their own discoveries in the numerous tide pools, some

of the best on the coast. The south cove trail (find it past the picnic shelter) runs down to a sandy beach and the better tide pools. The north cove trail leads to more tide pools, good spots for fishing, and views of the colonies of seals and sea lions at Shell Island, including the most northerly breeding colony of enormous elephant seals. Their huge pups when just a month old may already weigh 300-400 pounds. Note that the north trail closes March 1-June 30 to protect seal pups. The picnic tables on the headlands command beautiful ocean panoramas and are superbly placed for whale-watching.

Charleston Marine Life Center

Right on the docks of this fishing town, and directly across the road from the University of Oregon's Institute of Marine Biology, the **Charleston Marine Life Center** (63466 Boat Basin Rd., Charleston, 541/888-2581, www.charlestonmarinelifecenter.com, 11am-5pm Wed.-Sat., $5 adults, $4 seniors or AAA) is smaller and more intimate than the Oregon Coast Aquarium in Newport. In fact, it's so intimate that a volunteer will introduce you to the nudibranchs and other invertebrates housed in aquariums, and encourage you to plunge a hand into a tide-pool-like touch tank. Most of the creatures here were brought in by local fisherfolk or marine biology students who'd finished their experiments. In addition to these up-close encounters with the local fauna, visitors can look at underwater images of various places along the Oregon coast (they vary widely!) and live video feeds from deep-ocean exploration in the Pacific.

South Slough National Estuarine Research Reserve

Estuaries, where freshwater and saltwater interface, form some of the richest ecosystems on earth—capable of producing five times more plant material than a cornfield of comparable size while supporting great numbers

1: Shore Acres State Park **2:** on the Coos Bay Boardwalk

The Myrtlewood Tree

When exploring the southern Oregon coast, you'll soon discover that myrtlewood is popular hereabouts—nearly every town has a myrtlewood factory or showroom that peddles bowls, sculpture, furniture, and other products fashioned from this rare and unusual wood.

Myrtlewood is a member of the Lauraceae family of small trees and is a relative of the camphor, bay, and sassafras trees. Like these trees, the leaves and wood of the tree have a pungent odor, not unlike bay leaves. The myrtlewood tree grows only in a small area of southern Oregon and northern California, and it is large enough to harvest only after 100-150 years of growth. The wood is highly patterned, with the grain forming erratic bands of differing color in a single block of wood.

Myrtlewood is particularly popular for turning into bowls—salad and serving bowls make a lovely gift or keepsake of a trip to coastal Oregon. However, the tree and its wood have been used for myriad other functional and decorative purposes for many years. Hudson's Bay Company trappers used myrtlewood leaves to brew tea as a remedy for chills. In 1869 the golden spike marking the completion of the nation's first transcontinental railroad (near Promontory, Utah) was driven into a highly polished myrtlewood tie. Novelist Jack London was so taken by the beauty of the wood's swirling grain that he ordered an entire suite of furniture.

During the Depression, the city of North Bend issued myrtlewood coins after the only bank in town failed. The coins ranged $0.50 to $10 in value and are still redeemable, although they are worth far more as collectors' items.

of fish, birds, and other wildlife. The South Slough of Coos Bay is the largest such web of life on the Oregon coast. The **South Slough National Estuarine Research Reserve Interpretive Center** (61907 Seven Devils Rd., 541/888-5558, www.oregon.gov/dsl/SS, 10am-4pm Tues.-Sat., free), four miles south of Charleston, will help you coordinate a canoe trip (though you need to bring your own boat) through the estuary.

The center looks out over several estuarine arms of Coos Bay. These vital wetlands nurture a variety of life-forms, detailed by the placards captioning the center's exhibits. Eight miles of trails and boardwalks (open daily) form a loop with many shorter options. The coastal ecosystem is introduced by the "10-minute trail" behind the interpretive center. The various conifers and the understory are clearly labeled along the gently sloping 0.5-mile loop. Branch trails lead down toward the water for an up-close view of the estuary. Down by the slough, you may see elk grazing in marshy meadows and bald eagles circling above, while *Homo sapiens* harvest oysters and shrimp in these waters.

Horsfall Beach and the North Spit

On the spit north of North Bend, the Oregon Dunes taper down to wide sandy beaches and wetlands. **Horsfall Beach** is extremely popular with all-terrain vehicle (ATV) riders, but it's also a good place to enjoy nature. It's worth exploring on foot, especially in the winter, when storms can expose old shipwrecks.

RECREATION

Take a walk with a naturalist from **Wavecrest Discoveries** (541/267-4027, http://wavecrestdiscoveries.com) to explore forest trails, wetlands, or tide pools, and maybe even arrange for some clamming. Contact them to arrange a custom half-day excursion ($175) for groups ranging in size from 1-40.

Hiking

Although most hikers head to the coast, especially the four-mile stretch of the **Oregon Coast Trail** between Sunset Bay and Cape Arago, for a nice trail with spectacular views, it's also worth looking inland. Twenty-five miles northeast of Coos Bay in the Coast Range is **Golden and Silver Falls**

State Natural Area (800/551-6949, www.
oregonstateparks.org). Two spectacular waterfalls are showcased in this little-known gem of
a park. To find your way from Coos Bay, look
for the Allegany/Eastside exit from U.S. 101.
Beyond the community of Allegany, continue
up the East Fork of the Millicoma River to its
junction with Glenn Creek, which ultimately
leads to the park. The narrow, winding gravel
roads make this half-hour trip unsuitable for
a wide-body vehicle.

You can reach each waterfall by way of
two 0.5-mile trails. The 100-foot cataracts
lie about one mile apart, and although both
are about the same height, each has a distinct
character. For most of the year, Silver Falls is
more visually arresting because it flows in a
near semicircle around a knob near its top.
During or just after winter rains, however, the
thunderous sound of Golden Falls makes it
the more awe-inspiring of the two. Along the
trails, look for the beautifully delicate maidenhair fern.

Kayaking

From a canoe or sea kayak, as you pass tide
flats, salt marshes, forested areas, and open
water, you can really begin to grasp the rich-
ness of the estuarine habitat at the **South
Slough National Estuarine Research
Reserve** (541/888-5558, www.oregon.gov/
dsl/SS). The estuary here has two main
branches, offering plenty of territory for a
day of exploration.

Although the waters are placid, they are
strongly influenced by the tides—be sure to
consult tide tables when you plan an outing. Wind can also affect your trip: Know
that in the spring and summer, the prevailing winds are from the northwest; in the winter they're from the southwest. At all times of
year, the wind blows hardest in the afternoon.
South Coast Tours (541/373-0487, www.
southcoasttours.net, $80 single, $160 tan-
dem) offers 2.5-hour tours of South Slough,
as well as other southern Oregon coast rivers and bays.

Fishing

Spring Chinook salmon, which sometimes
exceed 30 pounds and are renowned as an
unrivaled dining treat, offer prime fishing
in Coos Bay. However, their population levels and fishing rules vary from year to year.
Mid-August-November, Isthmus Slough sees a
good return of fin-clipped hatchery cohos. In
saltwater, chinook and coho are usually found
in good numbers within a 1-2-mile radius of
the mouth of Coos Bay June-August, although
the legal season varies.

Coos Bay is also one of the premier areas
for crabbing and clamming. The Charleston
Fishing Pier is a productive spot for crabs,
while the best clamming spots are found along
the bay side of the North Spit.

Fishing charters, bay cruises, whale-
watching, and the like can be arranged
through a number of charter outfits based at the
Charleston Boat Basin. **Betty Kay Charters**
(541/888-9021 or 800/752-6303, www.
bettykaycharters.com) charges typical prices:
$85 per person for 5 hours of rock fishing; $200
for 12 hours of tuna or halibut fishing.

Surfing and Swimming

The best spot on the entire Oregon coast for
swimming is **Sunset Bay State Park** (13030
Cape Arago Hwy., Coos Bay, 541/888-4902).
The water is warm enough for most adults and
gentle enough for most kids.

Surfing is best just northeast of Sunset Bay,
at **Bastendorff Beach County Park** (63379
Bastendorff Beach Rd., Charleston, 541/888-
5353). Rent a board in downtown Coos Bay
at **Waxer's Surf & Skate** (240 S. Broadway,
Coos Bay, 541/266-9020, www.surfwaxers.
com, 11am-6pm Mon.-Sat., from $45).

ENTERTAINMENT
Brewpubs

Spend an evening on the patio at **Seven
Devils Brewing** (247 S. 2nd St., Coos Bay,
541/808-3738, www.7devilsbrewery.com,
11am-10pm Sun.-Mon. and Wed.-Thurs.,
11am-11pm Fri.-Sat., shorter hours in winter,

$8-14), where the fire pit is a good place to get the local vibe, listen to live music, and wash down an order of poutine fries with a hoppy Northwest-style ale.

Casinos

Occupying the former bayside site of the Weyerhaeuser mill alongside U.S. 101 in North Bend, the **Mill Casino** (3201 Tremont Ave., North Bend, 541/756-8800 or 800/953-4800, www.themillcasino.com) is operated by the Coquille Indian Tribe. Open 24 hours daily, the casino offers blackjack, lots o' slots, poker, and bingo. A large hotel, lounge, and several restaurants are on-site.

Festivals and Events

The first event of note in summer is the **Oregon Coast Music Festival** (541/267-0938, www.oregoncoastmusic.org), which runs for two weeks in mid-July and has been bringing music to the coast since 1978. Coos Bay is the central venue for these classical, jazz, pop, and world music concerts, but Bandon, North Bend, Charleston, and other neighboring burgs host some performances as well. Tickets to some events are free, with tickets to the majority of events under $25.

In late August, the ubiquitous Oregon blackberry is celebrated with the **Blackberry Arts Festival** (541/266-9706, https://blackberryartsfestival.com). Food and wine-tasting booths, a juried arts-and-crafts show, and entertainers fill the **Coos Bay Mall** (Central Ave. in downtown Coos Bay) for a weekend.

Polish up the spotting scope and head to the Oregon Institute of Marine Biology in Charleston during the last weekend of August or first weekend of September to see migratory shorebirds with the **Oregon Shorebird Festival** (541/867-4550). Guided trips on land and water are offered; a boat trip out to see albatross and other seldom-seen species that frequent the open ocean is a highlight. Other excursions visit the Bandon Marsh National Wildlife Refuge and Coos Bay to see plovers, loons, and a variety of other shorebirds.

In mid-September, perhaps the best-known Bay Area sports celebrity, Steve Prefontaine, is honored with a 10K race and two-mile walk in the annual **Prefontaine Memorial Run** (www.prefontainerun.com). Prefontaine was a world-class runner whose gutsy style of running and record performances made him a major sports personality until his premature death at age 24 in 1974. Many top-flight runners pay homage by taking part in the race. Events begin and end at the runner's alma mater, **Marshfield High School** (4th St. and Anderson Ave., Coos Bay).

FOOD

Oregon's Bay Area has many eateries where your nutritional needs can be met, if not in fine style then at least at the right price. With a couple of notable exceptions, in both Coos Bay and North Bend, you won't find it easy to dine on seafood—in these hardworking towns, eating well seems to require heartier fare. For fresh seafood, you're advised to head to the docks in Charleston.

Coos Bay

Nearly all the following are located along a two-block section of busy Broadway, which is the name given to southbound U.S. 101 as it passes through downtown Coos Bay. So just park the car and check out which of the following looks good.

One good spot for seafood in Coos Bay is ★ **SharkBites** (240 S. Broadway, 541/266-7582, www.sharkbites.cafe/home, 11am-9pm Mon.-Thurs., 11am-9:30pm Fri.-Sat., $8-26), a hip little eatery with a droll sense of humor and good, freshly prepared food, with several local seafood options. A variety of wraps and sandwiches—including tasty halibut tacos—as well as pasta and shrimp and crab salads are favorites. Best of all, prices are fair and quality is high.

If you're visiting the waterfront boardwalk and feel the hankering for seafood, stop by **Fishermen's Seafood Market** (200 S. Bayshore Dr., 541/267-2722, http://fishermensseafoodmarket.com, 10:30am-7pm

Mon.-Sat., $6-17), a boat anchored off the boardwalk that serves as a seafood store for a local fishing family, plus a casual spot for (mostly) carry-out seafood sandwiches, fish-and-chips, and chowder.

The **Blue Heron Bistro** (110 W. Commercial Ave., 541/267-3933, noon-8:30pm Mon.-Sat., 10am-8pm Sun., $17-25) is in the heart of downtown Coos Bay—with its Bavarian-style half-timbered exterior, you can't miss it. The specialty is traditional German cooking, such as sauerbraten, schnitzel, and sausages, although fresh salmon and seafood are also featured.

Coos Head Food Co-Op (353 S. 2nd St., 541/756-7264, 9am-7pm Mon.-Fri., 9am-6pm Sat., 10am-6pm Sun.) has the largest selection of certified organic produce and food on the south coast.

North Bend

If you've had enough of the standard coastal fare, try ★ **Cafe Mediterranean** (1860 Union St., 541/756-2299, www.cafemediterranean.net, 11am-9pm Mon.-Fri., 5pm-9pm Sat., $9-19) for Middle Eastern-style Mediterranean food, including a locally famed lentil soup, in a friendly relaxed setting. This is a good spot for sharing a meze platter, a Greek salad, and some kebabs.

Stop by the **Liberty Pub** (2047 Sherman Ave., 541/756-2550, www.thelibpub.com, 4pm-10pm Wed.-Sat., 4pm-9pm Sun., $10-13), with a good selection of Northwest beers on tap, tasty pizza, and live music on Wednesday evenings. Half of the restaurant is family-friendly (minors are allowed).

Charleston

You can't go too far wrong looking for a fresh seafood meal down at the docks—a number of casual restaurants and seafood vendors (some more like shacks) cluster here, including one spot where the crab cooker is always on. If you're an oyster lover, you'll certainly want to visit **Qualman's** (63218 Troller Rd., 541/888-3145, 10am-5:30pm Wed.-Sat.), which

sells incredibly fresh oysters from its nearby beds. Just look for the signs on the north side of the Charleston Bridge on the east side of the highway.

Part sports bar, part seafood restaurant, ★ **Miller's at the Cove** (63346 Boat Basin Rd., 541/808-2404, www.millersatthecove. rocks, 11am-midnight daily, $7-17) has seafood every bit as fresh as it should be. Don't expect anything fancy, but it's a good place for fish tacos or an oyster bacon burger. Kids are allowed until 9pm.

Close by, the classier **Portside** (63383 Kingfisher Rd., Charleston Boat Basin, 541/888-5544, www.portsidebythebay. com, 11:30am-11pm daily, $15-55) has a view of the water and a wide menu of rather old-fashioned, but delicious seafood specialties.

The casual **High Tide Cafe** (91124 Cape Arago Hwy., 541/888-3664, http://hightidecafeoregon.com, noon-8pm Sun. and Wed.-Thurs., 11am-8pm Fri.-Sat., $18-25) is a good place for seafood dinners such as cioppino, albacore tuna fish-and-chips, or a plate of pasta, including seafood pasta. If the weather's nice, sit outside, where there's a view of South Slough near its entrance to the bay.

For a coffee and a pastry, a breakfast burrito, a lunchtime sandwich, or a birthday cake, stop by **Crabby Cakes Bakery** (63345 Boat Basin Rd., 541/808-2388, 8:45am-3pm Wed.-Thurs., 8:45am-5pm Fri.-Sun., $3-10), a sweet family-run spot for a snack or a meal.

ACCOMMODATIONS AND CAMPING

Most of the lodgings in Coos Bay and North Bend stretch along busy U.S. 101, and most are of the mid-century motor-court variety, but the majority are well maintained and represent good value. Another option is staying in Charleston, particularly if your destination includes local state parks, ocean beaches, or South Slough. Charleston lodgings are pretty basic, but you'll stay near the fishing marina, not the highway.

Coos Bay

Best Western Holiday Hotel (411 N. Bayshore Dr., 541/269-5111, www. bestwestern.com, $162-180) is an older but well-kept and pet-friendly hotel within walking distance of the city center restaurants with a pool, a hot tub, and a hot breakfast buffet.

Coos Bay Manor (955 5th St., 800/269-1224, www.coosbaymanor.com, $155-245, full breakfast included) is a grand high-ceilinged, colonial-style home with eye-popping river views from the open-air 2nd-floor breakfast balcony. The B&B's five spacious rooms have distinctive decor; two of the rooms can be combined to make a suite for families.

The waterfront **Edgewater Inn** (275 E. Johnson Ave., 541/267-0423 or 800/233-0423, www.theedgewaterinn.com, $129-139) is located off the highway facing the working waterfront. Room decor is a bit dated, but many rooms have good views, and the pet-friendly motel also offers fitness equipment, an indoor pool, a spa and sauna, and a light complimentary breakfast.

Northwest of the Bay Area—2.5 miles north of the McCullough Bridge—is the Trans-Pacific Parkway, a causeway west across the water leading to Coos Bay's North Spit and the south end of the Oregon Dunes National Recreation Area, with four **U.S. Forest Service campgrounds** (541/271-6000, reservations 877/444-6777, www.recreation.gov, year-round, $22-25) and expansive dunes that draw ATV enthusiasts. The main **Horsfall Campground** is popular with crowds of noisy ATVs and RVs. It's the only campground on the spit with showers. For more quiet and privacy, continue another mile on Horsfall Beach Road to **Bluebill Lake.** There isn't ATV dune access from this campground, and it tends to attract trekkers who use their feet to explore. Ask the campground hosts about area trails and the nearby oyster farm for the ultimate in campfire fare. Close by, **Horsfall Beach Campground** is in the dunes next to the beach. ATV access and beachcombing are popular activities. A half mile away, **Wild Mare Horse Camp** has beach and dune access and a dozen primitive campsites, each with a single or double horse corral.

North Bend

One of the best values in the area is **Bay Bridge Motel** (33 Coast Hwy., 541/765-3151, www.baybridgemotel.com, $70-110), a small, older motel just north of the McCullough Bridge, with good views of the bay from the higher-priced rooms.

The Mill Hotel (3201 Tremont Ave., 541/756-8800 or 800/953-4800, www.themillcasino.com, $165-195) is just south of the Mill Casino along the waterfront in a new seven-story tower and a building that once housed a plywood mill. Owned and operated by the Coquille (pronounced ko-KWELL in the local dialect) Indian Tribe, the hotel seeks to express its owners' patrimony: The exterior of this three-story hotel is the same cedar that the Coquille people used to build their plank houses, and the fireplace in the lobby is made of Coquille River rocks. The canoe displayed behind the front desk was carved by Coquille community members and is part of an interpretive display that tells the story of the Coquille people. Guest rooms are nicely furnished, and waterfront views from the tower are especially dramatic. And, of course, all the pleasures of a modern casino are just a few feet away. In addition to gaming, the casino has restaurants, shops, and a performance center.

Charleston

There are a few basic motels in Charleston, but even better are the nearby campgrounds. The **Plainview Motel** (91904 Cape Arago Hwy., 541/888-5166 or 800/962-2815, www.stayhereandplay.com, $99-175) is easy to spot—it's covered with colorful murals of sealife. If you'd like to catch your own dinner, the Plainview is a good base for clamming expeditions or fishing trips. This small, older motel has rooms with kitchenettes, plus a cabin and a two-bedroom home.

If you want proximity to the area's parks, consider camping. Even though the crowds at **Sunset Bay State Park** (13030 Cape Arago

Hwy., 541/888-4902, reservations 800/452-5687, www.reserveamerica.com, $7-53) can make it seem like a trailer park in midsummer, the proximity of Oregon's only major swimming beach on the ocean keeps occupants of the 66 tent sites ($19) and 65 trailer sites ($29-31) happy. Yurts go for $43 each ($53 for a pet-friendly yurt), and primitive hiker-biker sites are $7 each. Facilities include the standard state park showers, and there is a boat launch at the north end of the beach. This site, three miles southwest of Charleston, is popular with anglers, who can cast into the rocky intertidal area for cabezon and sea bass. It's also a good base camp for hikers.

Bastendorff Beach County Park (63379 Bastendorff Beach Rd., Charleston, 541/888-5353, www.co.coos.or.us, year-round, campsites $20-30, camping cabin $45) is a conveniently and beautifully located park two miles west of Charleston, just off the Cape Arago Highway. It has camping with RV and tent sites as well as cabins and some hiker-biker sites. The campground has drinking water, flush toilets, and hot showers ($2). Fishing, hiking, and a nice stretch of beach are the recreational attractions, plus there's a good playground for toddlers.

INFORMATION AND SERVICES

The **Coos Bay Visitors Center** (50 E. Central Ave., Coos Bay, 541/269-0215 or 800/824-8486, http://oregonsadventurecoast.com, 9am-5pm Mon.-Fri., 11am-3pm Sat., 10am-3pm Sun. Memorial Day-Labor Day) is right downtown across from the Boardwalk. The *Coos Bay World* (www.theworldlink.com) is the largest daily paper on the south coast.

For health care and emergencies, the **Bay Area Hospital** (1775 Thompson Rd., Coos Bay, 541/269-8111), 0.5 mile west of U.S. 101 via Newmark Street, is the south coast's largest medical facility.

TRANSPORTATION

Improvements to Highway 42 make it possible to get to and from Roseburg, 87 miles from Coos Bay, in less than two hours.

Pacific Crest Bus Lines (541/269-7183, http://highdesert-point.com) operates daily bus service between Coos Bay and Bend via Reedsport and Florence. Eugene has Amtrak rail and regular Greyhound bus service, as well as an airport served by national carriers. **Coastal Express** (800/921-2871, www.currypublictransit.org) buses, operated by Curry County Transport, run Monday-Saturday between North Bend and Brookings to the south.

The **Southwest Oregon Regional Airport** (OTH, www.flyoth.com), at the north end of North Bend, offers scheduled flights to Portland, San Francisco, and Denver. Public transportation in the Bay Area is limited; one bus line, **Coos County Area Transit** (541/267-7111, www.coostransit.org), makes a loop in Coos Bay and North Bend.

Bandon and Vicinity

Between Coos Bay and Bandon, U.S. 101 veers inland through forests and bucolic farmland. The highway reencounters the Pacific at Bandon, near the mouth of the Coquille River. Bandon (pop. 3,000) is characterized by the style and grace of an earlier era, especially in Old Town, a picturesque collection of shops, galleries, and restaurants fronting onto a bustling waterfront.

Although logging, fishing, dairy products, and the harvest of cranberries have been the traditional mainstays of the local economy, in the early part of the 20th century Bandon also enjoyed its first tourism boom. In addition to being a summer retreat from the heat of the Willamette Valley, it was a port of call for thousands of San Francisco-to-Seattle steamship passengers. This era inspired such

Bandon

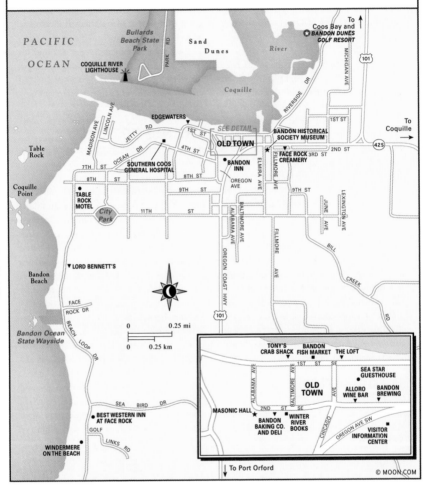

PACIFIC OCEAN

Bullards Beach State Park

Sand Dunes

River

Coquille

COQUILLE RIVER LIGHTHOUSE

PARK RD

MICHIGAN AVE

101

To Coos Bay and BANDON DUNES GOLF RESORT

RIVERSIDE DR

1ST ST

To Coquille

EDGEWATERS

LINCOLN AVE

MADISON AVE

JETTY RD

1ST ST

SEE DETAIL

OLD TOWN

BANDON HISTORICAL SOCIETY MUSEUM

425

4TH ST

OCEAN DR

Table Rock

7TH ST

SOUTHERN COOS GENERAL HOSPITAL

BANDON INN

FACE ROCK CREAMERY

2ND ST

3RD ST

ELMIRA AVE

FILLMORE AVE

8TH ST

8TH ST

OREGON AVE

9TH ST

Coquille Point

9TH ST

LEXINGTON AVE

TABLE ROCK MOTEL

City Park

11TH ST

ST

ALABAMA AVE

BALTIMORE AVE

JUNE AVE

Bandon Beach

LORD BENNETT'S

FILLMORE AVE

OREGON COAST HWY

BILL CREEK RD

FACE ROCK DR

101

Bandon Ocean State Wayside

BEACH LOOP DR

0   0.25 mi

0   0.25 km

SEA BIRD DR

BEST WESTERN INN AT FACE ROCK

GOLF

LINKS RD

WINDERMERE ON THE BEACH

OLD TOWN

TONY'S CRAB SHACK

BANDON FISH MARKET

THE LOFT

1ST ST SE

SEA STAR GUESTHOUSE

ALABAMA AVE

BALTIMORE AVE

ALLORO WINE BAR

BANDON BREWING

MASONIC HALL

2ND ST SE

BANDON BAKING CO. AND DELI

WINTER RIVER BOOKS

CHICAGO AVE

OREGON AVE SW

VISITOR INFORMATION CENTER

To Port Orford

© MOON.COM

tourist venues as the Silver Spray dance hall and a natatorium with a saltwater pool. The golden age that began with the advent of large-scale steamship traffic in 1900, however, came to an abrupt end following a fire in 1936 that destroyed most of the town. The blaze was started by the easily ignitable gorse weed, imported from Ireland (as was the town's name) in the mid-1800s.

The facelift given Old Town decades later, and the subsequent tourist influx, conjured for many the image of the mythical phoenix rising from its ashes to fly again. Today, Bandon is a curious mixture of provincial backwater, destination golf resort, and artists' colony.

SIGHTS

One of the appealing things about Bandon is that most of its attractions are within walking distance of each other. In addition, on the periphery of town is a varied array of things to see and do, including a beautiful stretch of beach just south of downtown.

Old Town

Bandon's **Old Town** is a half-dozen blocks of shops, cafés, and galleries squeezed in between the harbor and a steep bluff. The renovated waterfront invites relaxed strolling, and crabbers and anglers pull in catches right off the city docks. The small commercial fleet based here pursues salmon and tuna offshore.

Preservation buffs should check out **Masonic Hall,** one of the few buildings to have survived Bandon's 1914 and 1936 blazes. A photo in the local historical museum shows the same building and surrounding structures circa 1914. The photo depicts boardwalks leading to a woolen mill, old storefronts, a theater, and the Bandon Popular Hotel and Restaurant, outside which a horse and buggy await. The scene today has changed dramatically—the Masonic Hall now houses a good shoe store, the **Cobbler's Bench** (110 2nd St., 541/347-9012, www.bandoncobblersbench. com, 10am-6pm Mon.-Sat., 11am-5pm Sun.), but an early-1900s charm still pervades the neighborhood.

Throughout Old Town are artists and artisans pursuing their crafts and selling their wares. The **2nd Street Gallery** (210 2nd St., 541/347-4133, http://secondstreetgallery.net, 10am-5pm daily) has a little of everything, from functional and art pottery to blown glass to paintings and sculptures. **WinterRiver Books and Gallery** (170 2nd St., 541/347-4111, www.winterriverbooks. com, 10am-6pm daily) has a wide-ranging assortment of travel titles, photo essays, and fiction that makes this the best bookstore on the south coast. Close by, the **Bandon Driftwood Museum** (130 Baltimore Ave., 541/347-3719, 9am-5:30pm Mon.-Sat., 10am-5pm Sun., free) shows off an interesting collection of natural sculptures, from gnarly root balls to whole tree trunks. It's housed at the **Big Wheel General Store,** where you'll also find the Fudge Factory and 24 flavors of homemade ice cream and butter fudge.

As you enter Old Town, you may spot a giant fish sculpture. Take a closer look; it's made of plastic beach debris. The **Washed Ashore Project** (http://washedashore.org) draws attention to the problem of plastic pollution; the **Harbortown Events Center** (325 2nd St. SE, 541/329-0317, 11am-5pm Tues.-Sat.) hosts an exhibit of more beach litter art.

Bandon Historical Society Museum

The captivating **Bandon Historical Society Museum** (270 Fillmore St., 541/347-2164, http://bandonhistoricalmuseum.org, 10am-4pm daily June-Sept., 10am-4pm Mon.-Sat. Oct.-Dec. and Feb.-May, $3 adults, free for children), at the corner of U.S. 101 and Fillmore Street in Bandon's former city hall, traces the history of the Coquille people and their forebears. The chronology continues with the steamers and railroads that brought in white settlers. One room is devoted to Bandon's unofficial standing as the cranberry capital of Oregon. Black-and-white photos showing women stooping over in the bogs to harvest the ripe berries are captioned with such quips as this classic from an overseer: "I had 25 women picking for me, and I knew every one by her fanny." Color photos spanning five decades of Cranberry Festival princesses also adorn the walls.

Another room depicts Bandon's resort years, 1900-1931, when the town was called the "Playground of the Pacific." The most compelling exhibits in the museum deal with shipwrecks and the fires of 1914 and 1936.

Scenic Beach Loop

U.S. 101 follows an inland path for more than 50 miles between Coos Bay and Port Orford, but you can leave the highway in Bandon and take the four-mile Beach Loop for a lovely seaside detour south of town. Several access roads lead west from the highway to Beach Loop Drive (County Rd. 29), each about 0.25 mile from the others. Most people begin the drive by heading west from Old Town on 1st Street along the Coquille. Another popular approach is from 11th Street, which

1

Henry the Fish

Beer cans, water bottles, beach toys, plastic bags and food containers all litter the sand and sea life when set behind on the sand. Little from streak blows into rivers and ends every day and becomes a vital meal for fish as they search unknowingly for food. Bird cans and broken glass become sharp and dangerous to both sea creatures and humans.

Henry is made from debris that has landed on our beaches from near and far. Plastic particles in the ocean last forever and take time up to 200 years to degrade.

Bring Artists Create!

Washed Ashore is a non-profit community project to the public. The process of collecting and building litter into art structures.

Took part proudly to the community and to the children and visitors at large to enjoy.

2

3

leads to Coquille Point. The south end of the drive runs through the northern portion of **Bandon State Natural Area,** providing parking, beach access, and picnic tables.

The once-bucolic drive along the Beach Loop has changed a bit—trophy homes form pretty much the only view you have for the first mile or two. Still, there are state park parking areas that let you put the McMansions to your back and allow a look at the dramatic ocean views or a trek down the bluff to a gorgeous beach.

Along this fine stretch of beach are rock formations with such evocative names as Table Rock, Elephant Rock, Garden of the Gods, and Cat and Kittens Rocks. The whole grouping of sea stacks (rocks eroded away from their original cliffs by the sea), included within the Oregon Islands National Wildlife Refuge, looks like a surrealist chess set cast upon the waters. The most eye-catching of all is **Face Rock,** a basalt monolith that resembles the face of a woman gazing skyward. A Native American legend says that she was a princess frozen by an evil sea spirit. Look for the Face Rock turnout 0.25 mile south of Coquille Point on the Beach Loop. On select days (more frequently in summer), a volunteer group, Circles in the Sand (www. sandypathbandon.com), carves an elaborate labyrinth into the sand at the Face Rock beach; semi-organized mindfulness walks occur in the mornings when the labyrinth is intact. Check the website for the schedule.

Despite their scenic and recreational attractions, the beaches south of town can be surprisingly deserted, perhaps because of the long, steep trails up from the water along some parts. In any case, this dearth of people can make for great beachcombing. Agates, driftwood, and tide pools full of starfish and anemones are commonly encountered, along with bird-watching opportunities galore. Elephant Rock has a reputation as the Parthenon of puffins, while murres,

oystercatchers, and other species proliferate on the other offshore formations.

Bullards Beach State Park

Two miles north of Bandon, bordering the Coquille River estuary and more than four miles of beachfront, **Bullards Beach State Park** (541/347-2209 or 800/551-6949, www. oregonstateparks.org, most campsites $29-31, yurts $43-53) is a great place to fish, crab, bike, fly a kite, windsurf, picnic, or overnight in the large sheltered campground. The beach and lighthouse are reached via a scenic three-mile drive paralleling the Coquille River. Look for jasper and agates amid the heaps of driftwood on the shore. Equestrian trails and horse-camping facilities make this a popular destination for riders. The boat ramp gives anglers, kayakers, and canoeists access to the lower Coquille River and Bandon Marsh National Wildlife Refuge.

The riverside road going out to the Coquille's north jetty takes you through the dunes to the picturesque **Coquille River Lighthouse** (tours 11am-5pm daily mid-May-Sept., free), a squat tower with adjacent octagonal quarters. The last lighthouse built on the Oregon coast, it was completed in 1896, then abandoned in 1939 when the Coast Guard installed an automated light across the river. After years of neglect, the structure was restored in the late 1970s; its light is now solar-powered. Etchings of ships that made it across Bandon's treacherous bar—and some that didn't—greet you inside.

West Coast Game Park Safari

Seven miles south of Bandon is the **West Coast Game Park Safari** (46914 U.S. 101 S., 541/347-3106, www.westcoastgameparksafari. com, 10am-5pm daily Mar.-Nov., call for winter hours, $20.50 adults, $18 seniors, $13.50 ages 7-12, $10.50 ages 2-6), the self-proclaimed largest wild animal petting park in the country. There are 450 animals representing 75 different species, including tiger cubs, camels, zebras, monkeys, and snow leopards. Visitors may be surprised to see a lion and tiger caged

1: fish sculpture made entirely of beach debris, part of the Washed Ashore Project 2: Coquille River Lighthouse 3: Coos Bay Manor bed-and-breakfast

together, or a fox and a raccoon sharing the same nursery. The park tries raising different species together and often finds that animals can live harmoniously with their natural enemies. Free-roaming animals include deer, peacocks, pygmy goats, and llamas. An elk refuge is another popular area of the park. Even if you're not with a child, the opportunity to pet a pup, a cub, or a kit can bring out the kid in you. The park is open year-round, but call during winter because the hours of operation are restricted.

New River

In 1890, storm-blown sand blocked the outlet of Floras Lake (located south of Bandon), and floodwater flowed into a low channel just east of a dune paralleling the beach, forming the New River. The river runs north from the lake for nine miles, through a remote area with only a couple of roads leading to it and a trail along its length. Hikers and paddlers have the chance to see birds, animals, and plants that are otherwise rarely spotted. Some areas are set aside March 15-September 15 for nesting snowy plovers; check the information boards so you'll be sure to avoid these areas. A **nature center** (Croft Lake Ln., 541/756-0100, www.blm.gov, sunrise-sunset daily, free) located at Storm Ranch, 2 miles west of the highway and about 8.5 miles south of Bandon, is a good place to learn more about the area and access trails. The trail is also easy to reach at Floras Lake, west of the town of Langlois.

RECREATION
Horseback Riding
Bandon Beach Riding Stables (54629 Beach Loop Rd., 541/347-3423, year-round, $50-70) is four miles south of Face Rock on the Beach Loop. Several beach rides are offered daily, plus sunset rides in the summer. Riders of all abilities are welcome, including those with disabilities. Reservations are advised.

Wildlife-Viewing
Bird-watchers flock to the tidal salt marsh and the elevated observation deck of the **Bandon Marsh National Wildlife Refuge** (541/347-1470, www.fws.gov, sunrise-sunset daily), especially in the fall, to take in what may be the prime birding site on the coast. The extensive mudflats attract flocks of shorebirds, including red phalaropes, black-bellied plovers, long-billed curlews, and dunlins, as well as such strays from Asia as Mongolian plovers.

Reach Bandon Marsh by a short paddle across the river from the Bullards Beach State Park, or via Riverside Drive, which runs from Bandon to U.S. 101 on the south side of the Coquille River bridge. The refuge protects more than 700 precious acres of the Coquille estuary's remaining salt-marsh habitat along the southeastern side of the river. Migrating waterfowl, bald eagles, California brown pelicans, and other birds feast on the rich food sources. From U.S. 101 just north of Bandon, turn west onto Riverside Drive and continue for about one mile, where you'll reach the refuge.

Fishing
The Coquille River runs 30 miles from its Siskiyou headwaters before meandering leisurely through Bandon. The north and south jetties are popular spots for perch and rockfish, while the city docks right in Old Town yield catches of perch and crab April-October and smelt July-September. The spring chinook run pales in comparison to those in the Rogue and Chetco Rivers to the south, but the fall runs of chinook (Sept.-Oct.) and coho (Oct.-Nov.) are strong and productive. Steelhead usually arrive in November, and the run gathers steam in January-February. A boat is necessary for the best steelhead and salmon water, but bank anglers can fish the mouth of Ferry Creek, just off Riverside Drive in Bandon. Fishing guides and gear can be arranged through **Bandon Bait & Tackle** (110 1st St., 541/347-3905, 6am-6pm daily), across from the boat basin. The shop also rents crab rings and other gear and can point you to productive spots for catching Dungeness crab. It's also not a bad place to grab a plate of fish-and-chips.

Just off the south end of Beach Loop Drive,

30-acre **Bradley Lake,** protected from ocean winds by high dunes, offers good trout fishing and a boat ramp. Each spring the lake is stocked with trophy rainbows, averaging five pounds, reared at the Bandon Fish Hatchery east of town.

Golf

South of town, **Bandon Crossings Golf Course** (87530 Dew Valley Ln., 541/347-3232, www.bandoncrossings.com, $48-84 for 18 holes) is a forested, challenging, but fun course that's good for families, novices, and anyone looking for a less intense experience than at the Bandon Dunes Golf Resort.

★ BANDON DUNES GOLF RESORT
Bandon Dunes Golf Resort (57744 Round Lake Dr., 541/347-4380 or 800/742-0172, www.bandondunesgolf.com, May-Oct. greens fees $285 hotel guests, $335 nonguests, off-season $100-295, reduced rates for same-day 2nd round) has drawn accolades from the golf press and is by far the most spectacular place to golf in Oregon. The original Bandon Dunes course has 7 holes along the Pacific and unobstructed ocean views from all 18. Three other 18-hole courses, Pacific Dunes, Bandon Trails, and Old Macdonald (inspired by golf course architect C. B. Macdonald), give golfers a chance to stay for a few days and keep encountering new territory. Resort guests also have free access to the Punchbowl, an 18-hole putting course, and Shorty's, a 9-hole par-3 practice course.

In addition to the main courses, the 13-hole par-3 Bandon Preserve course ($100 peak season, $50-75 off-season) starts at the top of a sand dune and works its way down to the beach. Proceeds from this course go to the Wild Rivers Coast Alliance, an organization that supports conservation, community, and the economy along the southern Oregon coast. To preserve the natural surroundings along the ocean bluffs, this Scottish links course doesn't allow carts (the only amenity missing), so you'll have to hire a caddie or schlep your own bag (a practice that is frowned upon here). A luxurious resort with Pacific views, attentive staff, and a fine restaurant are also available for those who come to worship in the south coast's Sistine Chapel of golf.

Golfers who have never played on the Oregon coast should come prepared for wind, especially in the afternoon. Oregon golfers may know about the wind, but we have a special piece of advice for you—dress up. This is a rather formal place, and you'll feel out of place in your baggy cargo shorts and faded polo shirt. The resort is one mile north of the Coquille River. November-April, Oregonians are admitted at the guest rate. Caddies expect at least $100 per bag.

ENTERTAINMENT AND EVENTS
Bandon Brewing (395 2nd St. SE, 541/347-3911, www.bandonbrewingco.com, 11am-8pm daily, $8-14) is a lively brewpub in the heart of Old Town. This family- and dog-friendly pub with good wood-fired pizza and a friendly atmosphere is a fun place to sample local brews and chow down, perhaps on a Crabby Mozzarella pie.

A parade, cardboard boat races, and ice cream and apple pie are highlights of Bandon's **Fourth of July** celebration; at dusk, fireworks are launched across the Coquille to burst above the river.

The biggest weekend of the year for Bandonians comes the second weekend in September, when the **Cranberry Festival** (541/347-9616, www.bandon.com) brings everyone together in Old Town for a parade, a crafts fair, tours of a cranberry farm, and the Bandon High Cranberry Bowl—in which the local footballers take on traditional rival Coquille High.

FOOD
If you want an edible souvenir or gift, stop by the roadside stand **Misty Meadows Jams** (48053 U.S. 101 S., 541/347-2575, www.oregonjam.com, 9am-5pm daily) for a wide variety of jams and jellies, including products incorporating Bandon cranberries. In addition to

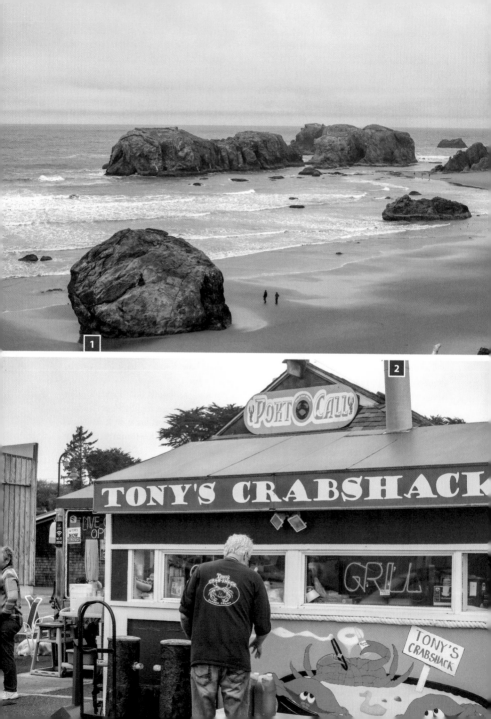

preserves, the shop sells olives and fruit-based barbecue sauce, syrup, honey, and salsa. Look here and in other shops in town for Vincent Family dried cranberries or cranberry juice, produced by three generations of Vincents.

Face Rock Creamery

For over a century, Bandon was Oregon's "other" cheese-making center, and cheeses from the Bandon Cheddar Cheese Factory rivaled those of Tillamook until the operation closed in 2002. Cheese making returned to Bandon in 2013 with the opening of the **Face Rock Creamery** (680 2nd St. SE, 541/347-3233, www.facerockcreamery.com, 9am-6:30pm daily summer, call for winter hours), just north of downtown Bandon on U.S. 101. Stop to watch cheese production and taste the many samples of cheese made from local milk (the Coquille River valley east of Bandon is lined with dairies). The creamery also sells a large selection of cheeses and gourmet food items from around the world—this is a good place to stock up for picnics—and it offers freshly made ice cream, deli sandwiches, and a wine bar as well.

Pacific Northwest Cuisine

From its 2nd-floor perch above the harbor, ★ **The Loft** (315 1st St. SE, 541/329-0535, www.theloftofbandon.com, 10am-3:30pm Thurs.-Sun., $12-22) serves some of the best brunches—and best views—in town, and with lovely vistas of the marina. Abundant use is made of local produce, and there's always lots of good seafood on the menu. The dining room is fairly small, so reservations are a good idea.

Although the initial attraction may be the views of the Coquille River and Lighthouse, the food is also very good at **Edgewater's** (480 1st St. NW, 541/347-8500, http://edgewaters.net, 5pm-9:30pm Mon.-Thurs., 11:30am-3pm and 5pm-9:30pm Fri.-Sun. June-Sept., 5pm-9:30pm Tues.-Thurs., 11:30am-3pm and 5pm-9:30pm Fri.-Sun.

Oct.-May, $15-30). Fresh fish is a highlight here—go for the halibut if it's in season—but there are also plenty of steak and pasta dishes, including a rich and delicious farfalle with smoked salmon.

A longtime favorite on the Beach Loop, **Lord Bennett's** (1695 Beach Loop Dr., 541/347-3663, http://lordbennett.com, 5pm-9pm Mon.-Sat., 10am-2pm and 5pm-9pm Sun. $15-31) offers a dramatic ocean view. The food does justice to these surroundings with elegantly rendered pasta, steak, chicken, and seafood dishes. Jazz on selected evenings in the lounge adds a nice touch.

The **Bandon Dunes Golf Resort** (57744 Round Lake Dr., 541/347-4380 or 888/345-6008, www.bandondunesgolf.com) offers a number of dining options. In the main lodge is **The Gallery** (6am-10am and 5pm-10pm daily, $24-60), a good place to eat an excellent steak, and the many seasonal fish and seafood preparations are always noteworthy. If you're not staying at the resort, lunch ($9-14) is an interesting time to get a feel for the place and to enjoy the views out onto the Bandon Dunes course. The Gallery doesn't serve lunch, but you can check out the adjacent Tufted Puffin Lounge or the Bunker Bar downstairs, which has a gentlemen's club vibe; both serve snacks and light meals.

Seafood

If you're looking for inexpensive street food, check along 1st Street near the Old Town Marina, where **Tony's Crab Shack** (155 1st St., 541/347-2875, http://tonyscrabshack.com, 10:30am-7pm daily, $9-16) sells crab sandwiches, fish tacos, grilled salmon, steamer clams, and lots more. As the name implies, it's not really a sit-down place, though there are a few picnic tables on the dock.

Line up for your fish-and-chips to go at the **Bandon Fish Market** (249 1st St. SE, 541/347-4282, www.bandonfishmarket.com, 11am-7pm daily, $5-20). Though it's takeout only, a picnic table outside near the harbor is the place to enjoy it all, with a trip across the street to **Cranberry Sweets** (280 1st St. SE,

---

1: on the Scenic Beach Loop **2:** Tony's Crab Shack

Bogged Down with Cranberries

From the vantage point of U.S. 101 between Port Orford and 10 miles north of Bandon, you'll notice what appears to be reddish-tinged ground in flood-irrigated fields. If you get closer, you'll see cranberries—small evergreen bushes that creep along the ground and send out runners that take root. Along the runners, upright branches 6-8 inches long hold pink flowers and, later, deep-red fruit.

These berries are cultivated in bogs to satisfy their tremendous need for water and to protect them against insects and winter cold. Bandon leads Oregon in this crop, with an output ranking third in the nation. Oregon berries are often used in cranberry juice production because of their deep-red pigment and high vitamin C content.

Fill up on cranberry confections at Cranberry Sweets. For sale are confections ranging from cranberry fudge to cranberry truffles. Other shops in town, including the local grocery store, stock Vincent Family (www.vincentcranberries.com) dried cranberries or cranberry juice. Three generations of Vincents have been tending cranberry bogs; they're committed to making the business sustainable and are working toward organic certification for their berries.

541/347-9475 or 800/527-5748, 9:30am-6pm Mon.-Sat., 9:30am-5pm Sun.) for dessert.

Italian

Although it's called a wine bar, ★ Alloro Wine Bar (375 2nd St., 541/347-1850, www.allorowinebar.com, 4:30pm-8:30pm Thurs.-Sun. Mar.-Dec., dinner $26-36) is the top choice in town for an Italian dinner. But don't come looking for basic spaghetti—the cuisine is much more upscale. Instead, expect dishes like pan-seared sea scallops with orange-zest spaetzle and pea puree or a Tuscan-style seafood stew. The food is excellent, and the pace is relaxed. The pasta is house-made, and most of the produce is local. If you don't want a full dinner, there's a small bar where you can taste a flight of wines and nibble on olives or Italian cheeses.

Bakeries

Grab a coffee and a tasty cinnamon roll at the Bandon Baking Co. and Deli (160 2nd St., 541/347-9440, www.bandonbakingco.com, 8am-4pm Tues.-Sat. Feb.-Dec.), which has the area's best baked goods.

ACCOMMODATIONS

For the best ocean views, often with nearby trails to the beach, look to the lodgings along the Beach Loop. If you want to be able to walk to dinner in Old Town, stay at one of the in-town locations. For the best of both worlds, bring a bike and cycle into town from a Beach Loop room. Bandon bills itself as the country's storm-watching capital, and special packages are often available October-March.

$50-100

On a bluff at the top of Beach Loop Road, find an assortment of motel rooms and small cottages at Table Rock Motel (840 Beach Loop Dr., 541/347-2700 or 800/457-9141, www.tablerockmotel.com, $80-169). The least expensive rooms are small, with no ocean views, but all are a short, steep walk away from one of the coast's prettiest beaches.

$150-200

Set on a bluff overlooking Old Town, the ★ Bandon Inn (355 U.S. 101, 541/347-4417 or 800/526-0209, www.bandoninn.com, $154-185) has spectacular views, comfortable rooms—all with balconies—and a path down to town. Pets are permitted in some rooms; a couple of suites ($259-279) are also available. This is a great spot to stay if you want the wining and dining of Old Town within walking distance.

A favorite place to stay on the Beach Loop is the older but refurbished Windermere on the Beach (3250 Beach Loop Rd., 541/347-3710, www.windermereonthebeach.com, $149-209), where baby-boomers can relive their childhood beach getaways in old-fashioned cottages or motel rooms (some with kitchens), situated on a bluff above a wind-swept beach. Housekeeping facilities and proximity to restaurants (Lord Bennett's) and the West Coast Game Park also make this an ideal family vacation spot.

Another popular place is the **Best Western Inn at Face Rock** (3225 Beach Loop Rd., 541/347-9441 or 800/638-3092, www.innatfacerock.com, $188-299). Part of its popularity has to do with the motel's location—set back from the road near the southern end of the Beach Loop, across the road from Bandon's coastline. Many of the modern, well-appointed guest rooms have magnificent ocean views. The indoor pool, fitness room, whirlpool, and restaurant also make this an especially good choice for travelers looking for amenities. Some suites have fireplaces, kitchenettes, and private patios. There is a short path to the beach.

Over $200

For avid golfers or those seeking upscale accommodations, amenities, and service, the **Bandon Dunes Golf Resort** (57744 Round Lake Dr., 541/347-4380 or 888/345-6008, www.bandondunesgolf.com, most rooms $220-450) is the place to stay. Lodging is in several different locations around the resort and includes single lodge or inn rooms in various sizes, two- or four-bedroom suites, and multiple-bedroom cottages (up to $1,900). View options vary from golf course and ocean to dune and surrounding woods. Bandon Dunes is 10 minutes from Bandon, 1 mile north of the Coquille River, and 27 miles (30 minutes' drive) from the North Bend Airport, which is served by daily flights from Portland, San Francisco, and Denver. Nongolfers can fish, take a meditative walk on the resort's labyrinth, or hike more wild trails.

Vacation Rentals

Bandon is an easy place to spend a weekend, and there are several property management companies that can help you find a house to rent.

Many of the places offered by **Exclusive Property Management** (541/347-3790 or 800/527-5445, www.visitbandon.com) are large and quite upscale, with great locations and lovely interior design. It also rents a few more modest homes, so don't be afraid to call or check the website. **Bandon Beach Vacation Rentals** (54515 Beach Loop Rd., 541/347-4801 or 888/441-8030, www.bandonbeachrentals.com) has several reasonably priced units available, including one that'll sleep 10 people.

Camping

Bullards Beach State Park (541/347-2209 or 800/551-6949, reservations 800/452-5687, www.oregonstateparks.org, campsites $29-31, horse camp $19, yurts $43-53, hiker-biker $7) is a large and busy state park, with over 200 tightly packed campsites in a great location between the Coquille River and four miles of beach. To get here, drive north of town on U.S. 101 for about one mile; just past the bridge on the west side of the highway is the park entrance. The beach is reached via a scenic two-mile drive paralleling the Coquille River. Electricity, picnic tables, and grills are provided.

INFORMATION AND SERVICES

The **Bandon Chamber of Commerce** (300 2nd St. SE, Bandon, 541/347-9616, www.bandon.com, 9am-5pm daily summer, 10am-4pm daily winter) in Old Town distributes a comprehensive guide and a large annotated pictographic map of the town.

Southern Coos General Hospital (900 11th St. SE, 541/347-2426) features an ocean view that is in itself therapeutic, as well as a 24-hour emergency room.

TRANSPORTATION

North- and southbound **Coastal Express** (800/921-2871, www.currypublictransit.org) buses run Monday-Saturday between North Bend and Brookings.

Port Orford and Vicinity

Port Orford marks the northernmost end of one of the most spectacular stretches of coastline in the United States. From Bandon, the highway runs inland; when it hits Port Orford, the road nearly runs into the Pacific. And what a splendid place to encounter the ocean: The beach is perfect for long treasure-hunting walks, and the bluffs just to the north are also fun to explore. A few miles north, blustery Cape Blanco is the second westernmost point of the continental United States; a short distance south, Humbug Mountain rises almost directly from the ocean. All of these places are great for a quick ogle and a snapshot, but even better for hiking and exploring. Port Orford is a good base for all of that, with a wide range of accommodations and a few good places to eat.

SIGHTS AND RECREATION

Port Orford has an ocean view from downtown that is arguably the most scenic of any town on the coast. A waterfront stroll lets you appreciate the cliffs and offshore sea stacks, as well as the unique sight of commercial fishing boats being hoisted by large cranes into and out of the harbor. With only a short jetty on its north side, Port Orford's harbor, the only open-water port in Oregon, is unprotected from southerly swells, so boats can't be safely moored on the water. When not in use, the fleet rests on wheeled trailer-like dollies near the foot of the pier.

A stroll or bike ride through town is a perfect way to visit Port Orford's impressive selection of art galleries. These are, by and large, much different and far more interesting than the typical seaside-town collections of landscape paintings and sunset photos. Expect to find high-quality crafts, glass art, sculpture, and computer-generated art.

Battle Rock Park

As you come into town on U.S. 101, it's hard to ignore imposing Battle Rock on the shoreline, the site of the 1851 conflict between local Native Americans and the first landing party of white colonists. If you can make your way through the driftwood and blackberry bushes surrounding its base, you can climb the short trail to the top for a heightened perspective on the rockbound coast that parallels the town. You'll also notice the east-west orientation of the harbor. The rock is also the site of a fireworks display at the **Fourth of July Jubilee Celebration.**

Even if you're not up for a scramble on Battle Rock, do take the short path down to the beach, which is relatively sheltered from the wind and a good place for a walk. It's also a good spot for beachcombing, with agates and fishing floats being the prize finds.

Port Orford Heads State Park

Another shoreline scene, featuring a striking panorama from north to south, is up West 9th Street at **Port Orford Heads State Park** (541/332-6774, www. oregonstateparks.org, free). If you go down the cement trail to the tip of the blustery headland, you look south to the mouth of Port Orford's harbor. To the north, many small rocks fill the water, along with boats trolling for salmon or checking crab pots. On clear days, visibility extends from Cape Blanco to Humbug Mountain.

Also here is the historic **Port Orford Lifeboat Station** (10am-3:30pm Wed.-Mon. Apr.-Oct., free), built by the U.S. Coast Guard in 1934 to provide rescue service to the southern Oregon coast. After it was decommissioned in 1970, the officers' quarters, the pleasingly proportioned crew barracks, and other outbuildings were converted into a museum depicting the work of the station. A trail leads down to Nellie's Cove, site of the former boathouse and launch ramp.

Port Orford Indian Wars

In 1850, the U.S. Congress passed the Oregon Donation Land Act, allowing white settlers to file claims on Native American land in western Oregon. This was news, of course, to the Native American nations of the region, who had not been consulted on the decision. William Tichenor, captain of the steamship *Gull*, hoping to exploit the new act, had ambitions to establish an outpost on the coast at what's now Port Orford. When Tichenor observed the hostility of the Quatomah band of the Tututni people in the tidewater, he put nine men ashore on an immense rock promontory fronting the beach because of its suitability as a defensive position. The Native Americans besieged the rock for two weeks before the colonists escaped under cover of night. Tichenor returned with a well-armed party of 70 men and succeeded in founding his settlement.

From this inauspicious beginning, Port Orford established itself as the first town site on the south coast. Shortly thereafter, the town became the site of the first fort established on the coast during the Rogue River Wars. This conflict started when gold miners and settlers came into Native American lands. As a result of the clashes, hundreds of local indigenous people were rounded up and sent to the Siletz Reservation near Lincoln City in 1856.

TOP EXPERIENCE

★ Cape Blanco State Park and Hughes House

Four miles north of Port Orford, west of U.S. 101, is **Cape Blanco,** whose remoteness gives you the feeling of being at the edge of the continent—as indeed you are here, at the westernmost point in Oregon. From the vantage of Cape Blanco, dark mountains rise behind you and the eaves of the forest overhang the tidewater. Below, driftwood and 100-foot-long bull kelp on slivers of black-sand beach fan out from both sides of this earthy red bluff. Somehow, the Spaniards who sailed past it in 1603 viewed the cape as having a *blanco* (white) color. It has been theorized that perhaps they were referring to fossilized shells on the front of the cliff.

With its exposed location, Cape Blanco really takes it on the chin from Pacific storms. The vegetation along the five-mile state park road down to the beach attests to the severity of winter storms in the area. Gales of 100-mph winds (record winds have been clocked at 184 mph) and horizontal sheets of rain have given some of the usually massive Sitka spruces the appearance of bonsai trees. An understory of salmonberry and bracken fern help evoke the look of a southeast Alaskan forest.

Atop the weathered headland is Oregon's oldest, most westerly, and highest lighthouse in continuous use. Built in 1870, the beacon stands 256 feet above sea level and can be seen some 23 nautical miles out at sea. **Cape Blanco Lighthouse** (541/332-6774, 10am-3:30pm Wed.-Mon. Apr.-Oct., $2 adults) also holds the distinction of having had Oregon's first female lighthouse keeper, Mabel E. Bretherton, who assumed her duties in 1903. Tours of the facility include the chance to climb the 64 spiraling steps to the top. This is the only operational lighthouse in the state that allows visitors into the lantern room to view the working Fresnel lens.

Near Cape Blanco on a side road along the Sixes River is the **Hughes House** (541/332-0248, 10am-3:30pm Wed.-Mon. Apr.-Oct., free), a restored Victorian home built in 1898 for rancher and county commissioner Patrick Hughes. Owned and operated today by the state of Oregon, the house offers an intriguing glimpse of rural life on the coast over a century ago.

★ Humbug Mountain

Some people will tell you that 1,756-foot-high Humbug Mountain, six miles south of Port Orford on U.S. 101, is the highest mountain rising directly off the Oregon shoreline. Because the criteria for such a distinction vary as much as the tides, let's just say it's a special place. There's more than one version of how the peak, formerly called Sugarloaf Mountain, got its name. According to one, gold miners drawn here in the 1850s by tales of gold in the black sands nearby soon discovered that the rumored riches proved to be "humbug."

Once the site of Native American vision quests, Humbug Mountain now casts its shadow upon a state park campground surrounded by myrtles, alders, and maples. Just north is a breezy black-sand beach. A three-mile trail to the top of Humbug rewards hardy hikers with impressive vistas to the south and a chance to see wild rhododendrons 20-25 feet high. Rising above the rhodies and giant ferns are bigleaf maples, Port Orford cedars, and Douglas and grand firs. Access the trail from the campground or from a trailhead parking area off the highway near the south end of the park. In addition, the **Oregon Coast Trail,** which follows the beach south from Battle Rock, traverses the mountain and leads down its south side to the beach at Rocky Point.

Prehistoric Gardens

What can we say about this unique roadside attraction, featuring a 25-foot-tall Formica-green *Tyrannosaurus rex* standing beside the parking lot? Is it kitsch, or is it educational? You decide. In any case, if you've got children in the car, unless they're sleeping or blindfolded, you're probably going to have to pull over. **Prehistoric Gardens** (36848 U.S. 101, 541/332-4463, www.prehistoricgardens.com, 9am-6pm daily summer, 10am-5pm daily spring and fall, call for winter hours, $12 adults, $10 over age 60, $8 ages 3-12), about 10 miles south of Port Orford, is the creation of E. V. Nelson, a sculptor and self-taught paleontologist who began fabricating life-size dinosaurs here back in 1953 and placing them amid the lush rainforest on the back of Humbug Mountain. Paths lead through the ferns, trees, and undergrowth to a towering brontosaurus, triceratops, and 20 other ferro-concrete replicas, painted in a dazzling palette of Fiestaware colors.

Grassy Knob Wilderness

The **Grassy Knob Wilderness** (Siskiyou National Forest, Powers Ranger District, 541/439-6200, www.fs.usda.gov) encompasses 17,200 acres of steep, rugged terrain and protects rare stands of Port Orford cedar. The wood of this majestic fragrant tree is light, strong, and durable. Its use in planes during World War II and in Japanese construction has made it highly valued, but a fatal root fungus spread by logging trucks accounts for its rarity and astronomically high price. (As you travel around the area, you may notice the dead or dying cedars.) During World War II, Japanese submarines used Cape Blanco Lighthouse as an orientation mark to aim planes loaded with incendiary bombs at the Coast Range. The Japanese hoped to ignite forest fires that would destroy the region's Port Orford cedar trees, which were used to construct airplanes. Because of the perennial dampness, the results were negligible. A short (0.8-mile) but moderately difficult trail leads to the summit of Grassy Knob. To get here, follow U.S. 101 north of Port Orford about four miles, then go east on County Road 196 to Forest Road 5105, which ends at the trailhead.

Bicycling

The **Wild Rivers Coast Scenic Bikeway** (www.rideoregonride.com) starts and ends in Port Orford, and over the course of 61 miles visits the Elk River, Cape Blanco State Park, Paradise Point, and Port Orford Heads State Park. It's easy to break this long ride down into shorter trips.

Boating and Waterskiing

In the northwest part of town, drive west of the highway on 14th or 18th Streets to 90-acre **Garrison Lake** for boating, waterskiing, and fishing for stocked rainbow and cutthroat trout. **Buffington Memorial City Park,** at

1: dinosaur at Prehistoric Gardens 2: Cape Blanco Lighthouse 3: the view south from Port Orford toward Humbug Mountain

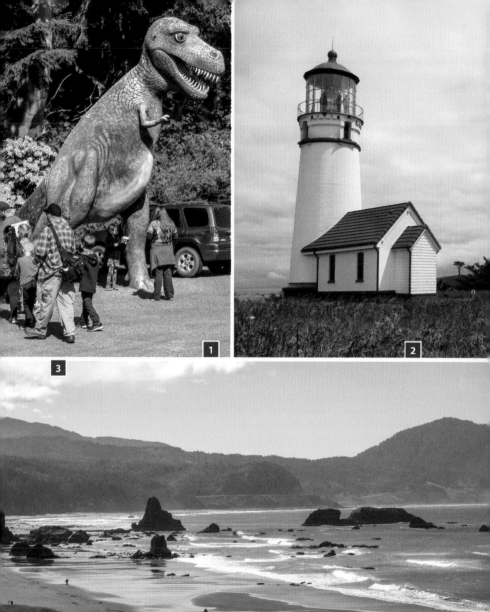

the end of 14th Street, has a dock for fishing or swimming, plus playing fields, tennis courts, picnic areas, hiking trails, and a horse arena. Half a mile north of the lake, look for agates on **Paradise Point Beach.**

Fishing

The **Elk River,** which empties on the south side of Cape Blanco, and the **Sixes River,** which meets the sea north of the cape, are two popular streams for salmon and steelhead fishing. Chinook and steelhead begin to enter both rivers after the first good rains of fall arrive, usually in November. Private lands limit bank access, with the exception of a good stretch of the Sixes that runs through Cape Blanco State Park. The salmon season runs to the end of the year, and steelhead through the following March. **Lamm's Guide Service** (541/784-5145, www.umpquafishingguide.com) leads trips on both rivers.

Surfing

The south-facing beach at **Battle Rock Beach,** in downtown Port Orford, can be okay for surfing during the winter, when northwesterly winds blow in. Otherwise, surfers tend to go about a mile south of town to the beach at **Hubbard Creek** (best in the spring). What these spots may lack in intensity, they make up for in scenery.

Windsurfing and Kiteboarding

Between Port Orford and Bandon (just southwest of Langlois) is **Floras Lake,** one of the southern Oregon coast's two great windsurfing and kiteboarding spots (the other is south of Gold Beach at **Pistol River**). The lake, just barely inland from the beach, catches incredible breezes. **Floras Lake Windsurfing & Kiteboarding** (541/348-9912, www.floraslake.com) offers lessons (1.5-hour windsurfing lesson $75, half-day kiteboarding lesson $300-350) and rentals (3 hours, windsurfing board $40, kiteboard $25, kiteboard harness $20). Reserve 3-4 weeks in advance July-August. The proprietors also have a nice B&B just above the lake. Also on the lake

is Boice Cope County Park, which has basic tent and RV sites and a boat ramp, making it a good base for windsurfers and kiteboarders.

FOOD

Port Orford doesn't have a lot of restaurants, but there are a few good places to eat, including two of the best fish-and-chips joints on the coast.

Make sure to visit Port Orford's docks, where **Griff's on the Dock** (303 Dock Rd., 541/332-8985, 10:30am-8pm Mon.-Sat., 10:30am-7:30pm Sun., $7-20), a weathered shack amid the boats and tackle shops, serves up excellent fish-and-chips. The fish here is as fresh as it gets, and the atmosphere, with crusty old anglers eating hot dogs and talking crabbing, is not your cookie-cutter idea of a fish-and-chips place.

There are more really good fish-and-chips up on the highway, where **The Crazy Norwegians** (259 6th St., 541/332-8601, 11:30am-8pm Tues.-Sun., $8-16) also serves tasty tuna melts, burgers, and chowder. It's a busy place, so expect to wait on a summer weekend.

The best views and most upscale dinners are at **Redfish** (517 Jefferson St., 541/366-2200, www.redfishportorford.com, 11am-9pm Mon.-Fri., 10am-9pm Sat.-Sun., $15-38). There's always fresh fish, perhaps halibut served over Israeli couscous with béarnaise sauce. The food is a little hit-or-miss, but the setting is almost worth the price (come 4pm-6pm Mon.-Fri. during happy hour). Adjoining the restaurant is an upscale gallery.

ACCOMMODATIONS

Port Orford is the kind of place where a room with a view will not break your budget, with one notable exception: The town's serene luxury resort, ★ **Wildspring Guest Habitat** (92978 Cemetery Loop, 866/333-9453, www.wildspring.com, $298-328, including continental breakfast). The small (five-cabin) resort is in a forested setting on a bluff high above the highway (but totally secluded from it), with views of the ocean from the main lodge and hot tub. The cabins are beautifully and meticulously designed and furnished (including a fridge, a massage table, and Wi-Fi access in each cabin, but no telephones or TVs) and are as comfortable as they are perfect-looking. The main guest hall has a kitchen that's available to guests as long as it's not being used to prepare breakfast. The well-tended grounds include a labyrinth and several meditation nooks, but perhaps the best place to hang out is the slate-lined hot tub, which looks out over treetops to the ocean. It's a good idea to take binoculars, as Wildspring is a stop along the Oregon Coast Birding Trail. This is a good place for a romantic retreat or a solo contemplative getaway.

In town, ★ **Castaway-by-the-Sea** (545 W. 5th St., 541/332-4502, www.castaway bythesea.com, $110-185) features ocean and harbor views from high on a bluff, fireplaces, and housekeeping units, and it allows pets. In addition to the rather basic motel rooms, the Castaway has a two-bedroom lodge that'll sleep up to seven (from $185). The rates on the upper-end lodgings go down significantly in the off-season. It's said that Jack London once stayed in an earlier incarnation of this place.

Just south of town, the **Seacrest** **Motel** (44 U.S. 101 S., 541/332-3040, www. seacrestoregon.com, $75-97) features views of coastal cliffs and a garden from a quiet hillside on the east side of the highway. Pets are welcome at this older motel.

North of Port Orford, the **Floras Lake House B&B** (92870 Boice Cope Rd., Langlois, 541/348-2573, www.floraslake.com, $175-195, includes breakfast) is perfectly suited for windsurfers or others who want to explore the beaches in this unpopulated area. The spacious light-filled house looks out onto Floras Lake and the ocean, and the proprietors also offer windsurfing and kiteboarding lessons.

Camping

Humbug Mountain State Park (541/332-6774, www.oregonstateparks.org, reservations 800/452-5687, www.reserveamerica.com), six miles south of Port Orford on U.S. 101, features 62 tent sites ($17) and 32 electrical sites for RVs ($24), along with wind-protected sites reserved for hikers and bikers ($7). Flush toilets, showers, picnic tables, water, and firewood are available. A short trail leads under the highway to the beach; a longer one goes up Humbug Mountain.

Reach **Cape Blanco State Park** (39745 U.S. 101 S., 541/332-6774, cabin reservations

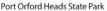

Port Orford Heads State Park

800/452-5687, $24 tents or RVs, $17 horse camp, $7 hiker-biker, $43-53 rustic cabins) by driving four miles north of Port Orford on U.S. 101, then heading northwest on the park road that continues five miles beyond to the campground. Sites are nestled into salal hedges where they're largely protected from the wind; picnic tables, water, and showers are available. For horseback riders, there's a seven-mile trail and a huge open riding area; horses are also allowed on the beach. Only cabins can be reserved; regular sites are first-come, first-served.

Boice Cope County Park (92850 Boice Cope Rd., Langlois, 541/247-3386, reservations 541/373-1555, www.co.curry.or.us, $15-25), on the shore of Floras Lake, is a good base for windsurfers and kiteboarders. The area is known for its wind.

INFORMATION

Begin your travels at **Battle Rock Information Center** (Battle Rock Wayside, 541/332-4106, www.enjoyportorford.com, 10am-3pm daily), on the west side of U.S. 101. The people here are especially friendly and helpful.

TRANSPORTATION

Curry County's **Coastal Express** (800/921-2871, www.currypublictransit.org) buses run up and down the south coast Monday-Saturday between North Bend and the California border, including local service in Port Orford.

Gold Beach and Vicinity

This town is one part of the coast where the action is definitely away from the ocean. To lure people from Oregon's superlative ocean shores, the Rogue estuary has been bestowed with many blessings. First, the gold-laden black sands were mined in the 1850s and 1860s. While this short-lived boom era gave Gold Beach its name, the arrival of Robert Hume, later known as the Salmon King of the Rogue, had greater historical significance. By the turn of the 20th century, Hume's canneries were shipping out some 16,000 cases of salmon per year and established the river's image as a leading salmon and steelhead stream. This reputation was later enhanced by outdoorsman and novelist Zane Grey in his *Rogue River Feud* and other writings. Over the years, Herbert Hoover, Winston Churchill, Ginger Rogers (who had a home on the Rogue), Clark Gable, Jack London, George H. W. Bush, and Jimmy Carter, among other notables, have come here to try their luck. During the last several decades, Rogue River boat tours focusing on the abundant wildlife, scenic beauty, and fascinating lore of the upstream region have hooked other sectors of the traveling public.

At the north end of town, just before the road gives way to Conde McCullough's elegant Patterson Bridge (illuminated at night by LED lights), the harbor comes into view on the left, full of salmon trawlers, jet boats, pelicans, and seals bobbing up and down.

SIGHTS
Beaches

The driftwood-strewn strand of **South Beach,** just south of Gold Beach's harbor, is convenient but only so-so. You'll find more exciting stretches both north and south of town. Two miles south, there's easy access to a nice beach and some tide-pooling at tiny **Buena Vista State Park,** at the mouth of Hunter Creek. Seven miles south of Gold Beach, there's more tide-pooling amid the camera-friendly basalt sea stacks at beautiful **Myers Creek Beach,** part of Pistol River State Park south of Cape Sebastian. The south side of Cape Sebastian and **Pistol River State Park,** a couple of miles farther south, are the best places on the Oregon coast for windsurfers to sail in the ocean. The beaches around Pistol River are also great places to find razor clams in season.

★ Cape Sebastian

Seven miles south of Gold Beach is **Cape Sebastian.** This spectacular windswept headland was named by explorer Sebastián Vizcaíno, who plied offshore waters here for Spain in 1602 along with Martín de Aguilar. At 720 feet above the sea, Cape Sebastian is the highest south coast overlook reachable by a paved public road. On a clear day, visibility extends 43 miles north to Humbug Mountain and 50 miles south to California. This is one of the best perches along the south coast for whale-watching. A trail zigzags through beautiful springtime wildflowers down the south side of the cape for about two miles until it reaches the sea. In April and May, Pacific paintbrushes, Douglas irises, orchids, and snow queens usher you along. In addition, Cape Sebastian supports a population of large-headed goldfields, a summer-blooming yellow daisy-like flower found only in coastal Curry County.

In 1942, a caretaker heard Japanese voices drifting across the water through the fog. When the mist lifted, he looked down from the Cape Sebastian trail to see a surfaced submarine. This sighting, together with the Japanese bombing at Brookings and the incendiary balloon spotted over Cape Blanco, sent shock waves up the south coast. But the potential threat remained just that, and local anxiety eventually subsided.

Museums and Books

At the **Curry County Historical Museum** (29419 S. Ellensburg Ave., 541/247-9396, www.curryhistory.com, 10am-4pm Tues.-Sat. Feb.-Dec., $2), the local historical society has assembled a small collection of exhibits. Particularly interesting are a realistic reconstruction of a miner's cabin, vintage photos, and Native American petroglyphs.

In the harbor area on the west side of U.S.

101, **Jerry's Rogue Jets** (29980 Harbor Way, 541/247-9737, 9am-9pm Mon.-Sat., 10am-9pm Sun. July-Aug., 9am-6pm Mon.-Sat., 10am-5pm Sun. Sept.-June, free) has assembled the best regional museum on the south coast in its gift shop. Centuries of natural and human history are depicted. Museum photos of early river runs—hauling freight, passengers, and mail—can impart a sense of history to your trip upriver or up the road.

And although it's not exactly a museum, **Gold Beach Books** (29707 Ellensburg Ave., 541/247-2495, http://goldbeachbooks.com, 7am-5:30pm Mon.-Sat., 8am-5pm Sun.) is an amazing treasure trove of mostly used and obscure books. Even on a nice day, it's hard to leave; on a rainy day, it's a place to grab a coffee from **Rachel's,** the in-house coffee shop, and settle in for a long browse.

Scenic Drives

From U.S. 101, two miles south of town, you can pick up **Hunter's Creek Road,** which loops north through the forest, finally following the course of the Rogue back into Gold Beach along Jerry's Flat Road. The three-hour drive follows Hunter's Creek inland for several miles, passing several picnic areas and campgrounds.

Other roads less traveled include the old **Coast Highway,** which you can pick up near Pistol River and Brookings; the **Shasta Costa Road,** paralleling the Rogue from Gold Beach to Galice; and an unpaved summer-only road into the **Rogue Wilderness** from Agness (a town upriver on the Rogue) to Powers. Despite most of these routes being paved (except the last one), they are all narrow, winding, and not suitable for trailers or motor homes. Be sure to travel with a good map; don't just rely on your GPS.

RECREATION

TOP EXPERIENCE

★ Rogue River Jet-Boat Ride

The most popular way to take in the mighty Rogue is on a jet-boat ride from

Gold Beach. It's an exciting and interesting look at the varied flora and fauna along the estuary as well as the changing moods of the river. Three different lengths of river tours are available. Most of the estimated 50,000 people per year who "do" the Rogue in this way take the 64-mile round-trip cruise. An 80-mile trip goes farther up the Rogue, and the most adventurous trip is the 104-mile excursion that enters the Rogue River canyon. Meals are not included in the cost of the cruise, and you can either bring your own food or have a meal at one of the secluded fishing lodges upriver, where the tours stop for meal breaks. The pilot-commentators are often folks who have grown up on the river, and their evocations of the diverse ecosystems and Native American and gold-mining history can greatly enhance your enjoyment. Bears, otters, seals, and beavers may be sighted en route, and anglers may hold up a big catch to show off. Ospreys, snowy egrets, eagles, mergansers, and kingfishers are also seen with regularity in this stopover for migratory waterfowl.

In the first part of the journey, idyllic riverside retreats dot the hillsides, breaking up stands of fir and hemlock. Myrtle, madrona, and impressive springtime wildflower groupings also vary the landscape. All the jet-boat trips out of Gold Beach focus on the section of the Rogue protected by the government as a Wild and Scenic River. Only the longer trips take you into the pristine Rogue Wilderness, an area that motor launches from Grants Pass do not reach. The 13 miles of this wilderness you see from the boat have canyon walls rising 1,500 feet above you. Geologists say this part of the Klamath Mountains is composed of ancient islands and seafloor that collided with North America. To deal with the rapids upstream, smaller and faster boats are used to skim over the boulders with just six inches of water between hull and the rock surface.

The season runs May-October 15. Remember that chill and fog near the mouth of the estuary usually give way to much warmer conditions upstream. These tour outfits have wool blankets available on cold days as well as complimentary hot beverages. Also keep in mind that the upriver lodges can be booked for overnight stays, and your trip may be resumed the following day.

Just south of the Rogue River Bridge, west of U.S. 101 on Harbor Way, is **Jerry's Rogue Jets** (29985 Harbor Way, 541/247-4571 or 800/451-3645, www.roguejets.com). Jerry's offers 64-mile ($50 adults, $25 ages 4-11), 80-mile ($70 adults, $35 ages 4-11), and 104-mile ($95 adults, $45 ages 4-11) trips. There are usually two departures for each trip daily: one in the morning and one near midday. This heavily patronized company is noted for personable, well-informed guides.

Hiking

The 40-mile **Rogue River Trail** (www.blm.gov/or) offers lodge-to-lodge hiking, which means you need little more in your pack than the essentials. The lodges here are comfortably rustic, serve home-style food in copious portions, and run $130-310 for a double room. They are also comfortably spaced, so extended hiking is seldom a necessity.

Before you go, check with the **Gold Beach Ranger Station** (29279 Ellensburg Ave., 541/247-3600, www.fs.usda.gov/rogue-siskiyou, 8am-5pm Mon.-Fri.) on trail conditions and specific directions to the trailhead. Pick up the western end of the trail 35 miles east of Gold Beach, about 0.5 mile from Foster Bar, a popular boat landing. Park there and walk east and north on the paved road until you see signs on the left marking the Rogue River Trail. Go in spring before the hot weather and enjoy yellow Siskiyou irises and fragrant wild azaleas. The trail ends at Grave Creek, 27 miles northwest of Grants Pass. Be careful of rattlesnakes, and note that summers are extremely hot on the trail.

Fishing

Fishing is a mighty big deal in Gold Beach, which has one of the highest concentrations of professional guides in the state. There's something to fish for just about year-round, but salmon and steelhead are the top quarry. When the spring chinook are running (Apr.-June), anglers will need to book guided trips well in advance to get a shot at them. Catches peak in May, though it's important to check in advance; if fish aren't plentiful enough, the season may be limited or closed. Summer steelhead and fall-run chinook usually arrive July-September, then it's hatchery coho September-November (sometimes as early as August). In December, the first of the winter steelhead make their appearance and continue into March.

The **Rogue Outdoor Store** (29865 Ellensburg Ave., 541/247-7142, 8am-5:30pm daily) is well stocked with fishing, camping, and other gear, and its staff can advise on where, when, and what to fish. Typical rates for guided salmon trips are $250-400 per person depending on the size of your group. Contact the **Gold Beach Visitors Center** (541/247-7526 or 800/525-2334, www.visitgoldbeach.com) for a list of over two dozen licensed guides. **Fish Oregon** (541/347-6338, www.fishoregon.com) is a well-established guide service; **Sportfishing Oregon** (541/425-1318, www.sportfishingoregon.com) also guides salmon and steelhead fishing trips. Both of these outfitters offer fishing trips on a number of southern Oregon rivers, and can take you where the fish are biting.

Windsurfing

Although beginners may want to hone their skills up north at Floras Lake, experienced windsurfers head out into the ocean near the debouchment of the **Pistol River.**

ENTERTAINMENT
Brewpubs

Arch Rock Brewing Company (28779 Hunter Creek Loop, 541/247-0555, 11am-6pm Tues.-Fri., 11am-5pm Sat.) doesn't offer a full brewpub experience, but you're welcome to stop by the brewery to taste the beers or fill up your growler. You can also find the brews in most local bars and restaurants.

Festivals and Events

The **Pistol River Wave Bash National Windsurfing Competition** (http://internationalwindsurfingtour.com) brings four days of competitive riding to Pistol River State Park each June. The **Curry County Fair** takes place at the **Event Center on the Beach** (29392 Ellensburg Ave., 541/247-4541, admission varies) in late July.

Since 1982, the **Pistol River Concert Association** (541/247-2848, www.pistolriver.com, $15 adults) has produced a top-notch **concert series,** encompassing bluegrass, folk, jazz, classical, and blues at the Pistol River Friendship Hall. Concerts are held roughly once a month throughout the year, and it's well worth fussing with your schedule in order to catch one. Past and present performers are a who's who of acoustic music, including Greg Brown, Mike Seeger, Peggy Seeger, Kevin Burke, Norman and Nancy Blake, Peter Rowan, and Tony Rice, to name a few. To get there from Gold Beach, take U.S. 101 for 10 miles south to the second Pistol River exit (Pistol River-Carpenterville), then take the first right. The Pistol River Friendship Hall is 0.5 mile ahead on the right.

FOOD

★ **Anna's By the Sea** (29672 Stewart St., at 3rd St., 541/247-2100, www.annasbythesea.com, 5pm-8pm Wed.-Sat., reservations recommended, $17-39), tucked into a residential neighborhood a couple of blocks east of busy Ellensburg Avenue, is a wonderfully quirky and intimate restaurant serving "nouvelle Canadian Prairie cuisine"—think Angus beef drizzled with black truffle oil or locally caught cod in a vegetable-based broth over dumplings. The chef-owner hates to make desserts; instead, enjoy an after-dinner drink (try an *eau de vie* from the excellent list of distilled fruit brandies) and some excellent housemade cheeses. Anna's is a tiny place—just 15 seats—so come early if you don't want to wait (in summer, there's more seating on the deck).

Drive a mile up the south bank of the Rogue to eat breakfast in a relaxed riverfront setting at **Indian Creek Café** (94682 Jerry's Flat Rd., 541/247-0680, 5:30am-2pm daily, $8-12). In good weather, there's seating on a deck overlooking Indian Creek, which flows into the Rogue here. Omelets, pancakes, and other traditional breakfast items are well prepared; lunch is mostly burgers and sandwiches.

Locals recommend the **Port Hole Café** (29975 Harbor Way, 541/247-7411, http://portholecafe.com, 11am-9pm daily, $9-20), with bay and river views in the Cannery building at the port, for hearty portions of fish-and-chips, chowder, and homemade pies at decent prices.

The squat, octagonal **Barnacle Bistro** (29805 Ellensburg Ave., 541/247-7799, www.barnaclebistro.com, 11:30am-8pm Mon.-Sat., $8-18) is a lively spot for light meals, offering sandwiches, burgers, and fish tacos. The salad greens are local and organically grown, and all the sauces and dressings are made in-house. This is also a good place to sample the excellent local Arch Rock Brewing Company beer.

The menu at **Spinner's Seafood, Steak and Chophouse** (29430 Ellensburg Ave., 541/247-5160, www.spinnersrestaurant.com, 4:30pm-9pm daily, $9-39) is wide-ranging and the dining room extremely pleasant. Look for fresh, well-prepared seafood and prime rib, along with choice beef and chops. A children's menu is available.

ACCOMMODATIONS

As in most coastal towns, there is no shortage of places to stay along the main drag, Ellensburg Avenue (a.k.a. U.S. 101). In fact, Gold Beach offers the largest number and widest range of accommodations on the south coast, with intimate lodges overlooking the Rogue as popular as the oceanfront motels. A discount of 20 percent or more on rooms is usually available during winter, when 80-90 inches of rain can fall.

$50-100

The best bet for a clean, inexpensive room is the **Wild Chinook Inn** (94200 Harlow St., 541/247-6675, http://chinookinn.com, $95-135), where you get clean, no-frills accommodations in a motor-court motel across from the fairgrounds. Rooms have Wi-Fi, a fridge, and a microwave; some full-kitchen units are available.

Ireland's Rustic Lodges

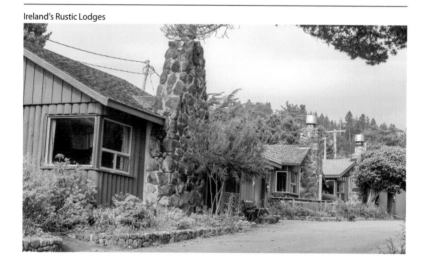

$100-150

Ireland's Rustic Lodges and the **Gold Beach Inn** are sister properties that operate out of the same office (29330 Ellensburg Ave., 541/247-7718, www.irelandsrusticlodges.com, cabins $104-174, lodge rooms $104-174, hotel rooms $99-194, includes breakfast buffet) and share parklike grounds lovingly landscaped with pine trees, flowers, and ocean views, with the sandy beach a short stroll to the west. Ireland's Rustic Lodges includes vintage (and pretty rustic) cabins, and also offers more modern lodge rooms perched above the beach. Many of the guest rooms have fireplaces, knotty pine interiors, and distinctive decor. The adjacent Gold Beach Inn is a more modern hotel; although the exterior is weather-beaten, the rooms are comfortable. On the way to the beach you'll pass a cluster of outdoor hot tubs and picnic areas. This sprawling operation also offers condos and beach houses; call to inquire.

$150-200

Three miles upriver from U.S. 101, the ★ **Rogue River Lodge at Snag Patch** (94966 N. Bank Rogue River Rd., 541/247-0101, www. rogueriverlodge.com, $150-280, includes breakfast) is a small lodge perched above the Rogue, with a couple of standard rooms and a variety of kitchenette suites, including one with three bedrooms ($580). All rooms have private decks, most have river views, and the grounds are as beautiful as the classy rooms.

For a more traditional oceanfront hotel, the **SureStay Plus Hotel Gold Beach** (29232 Ellensburg Ave., 541/247-7066, www.gbresort.com, $169-199) offers nicely furnished ocean-view rooms, all with balconies. Also part of this large complex, with easy beach access, are one- and two-bedroom condos, all with fireplaces. Facilities include an indoor pool and a fitness center; a complimentary continental breakfast is available.

Over $200

★ **Tu Tu Tun Resort** (96550 North Bank Rogue River Rd., 541/247-6664 or 800/864-6357, http://tututun.com, rooms $295-390, suites $450-530, house $560-1,195, closed in Jan.) is the most luxurious place to stay on the southern Oregon coast, where lucky guests take in river views through the floor-to-ceiling windows, enjoy a good book from the lodge's library in front of the massive river-rock fireplace, and savor delicious Pacific Northwest cuisine. As you sit on your patio overlooking the water along with the resident bald eagles, only the sounds of an occasional passing boat may intrude upon your Rogue River reverie. Rooms are graciously furnished, but not overly fussy—why interfere with the stunning views? The lodge is seven miles up the Rogue River from Gold Beach. The acclaimed retreat also offers a heated pool and other recreational facilities. A meal package ($80 pp) includes hors d'oeuvres, a gourmet four-course dinner, and breakfast; guests can also pay by the meal (dinner $65). Nonguests are welcome to dinner ($75) with reservations. Tu Tu Tun is not a secret, so reservations are required well in advance of your stay.

Upriver Lodges

Several lodges on the Rogue, some accessible only by boat or via hiking trails, lure visitors deep into the Rogue interior. Jet-boat trips can drop you off for an overnight or longer stay. Advance reservations are essential.

Accessible by road and boat, the authentically rustic **Lucas Lodge** (3904 Cougar Ln., Agness, 541/247-7443, www.lucaslodgeoregon.com, $50-100) is 32 miles east of Gold Beach. Some cabins here come equipped with kitchen options. Meals (daily May-mid-Oct., dinner $15-22) are served in the lodge—chicken, biscuits, and garden vegetables are standard fare. Reservations are required.

Accessible only by helicopter, boat, or on foot, the **Paradise Lodge** (541/842-2822 or 888/667-6483, www.paradise-lodge.com, May-Oct., $165-175 pp, $100 children, includes meals) attracts guests who want to immerse themselves in nature but still eat and sleep well. A huge on-site garden provides ingredients for home-cooked meals.

Another backcountry lodge, the **Clay Hill Lodge** (541/859-3772, www.clayhilllodge. com, $165 pp, $100 children, includes meals), is accessible via raft (from upstream), jet boat, or on foot. On foot, it's about three hours (six miles) up from the trailhead near Foster Bar, east of Gold Beach. The lodge also offers fishing and raft trips.

Camping

There are no public campgrounds along the coast between Humbug Mountain, just south of Port Orford, and Harris Beach, at the northern entrance to Brookings. But campsites east of town up the Rogue River provide wonderful spots to bed down for the night. Those taking the road along the Rogue should be alert for oncoming log trucks, raft transport vehicles, and other wide-body vehicles. In addition to the public campgrounds listed, there are *many* private RV resorts up the north bank of the Rogue.

Foster Bar Campground (Siskiyou National Forest, 541/247-6651, www.fs.usda. gov, year-round, flush toilets May-Oct., $10) is 30 miles east of Gold Beach on the south bank of the Rogue. Take Jerry's Flat Road east for 30 miles to the turnoff for Agness. Turn right on Illahe Agness Road and drive three miles to camp. Campsites here come equipped with drinking water, toilets, ADA-compliant facilities, picnic tables, fire rings, and a boat ramp. Sites are available on a first-come, first-served basis only. This is a popular spot from which to embark on an eight-mile inner-tube ride to Agness. It's also where rafters pull out, so the parking lot may be jam-packed. The rapids are dangerous—wear a life jacket. You are

also within walking distance of the trailhead for the Rogue River Trail.

Lobster Creek Campground (541/247-3600, www.fs.usda.gov, year-round, $10) is nine miles east of Gold Beach via Forest Road 33. This small campground with large grassy sites has flush toilets and drinking water. The Schrader old-growth trail is two miles from the campground via Forest Road 090. It is a gentle one-mile walk through a rare and majestic ecosystem. Also nearby is the world's largest myrtle tree.

INFORMATION AND SERVICES

The **Gold Beach Visitors Center** (94080 Shirley Ln., 541/247-7526 or 800/525-2334, www.visitgoldbeach.com, 8am-4pm daily) has an excellent and informative website. The **Gold Beach Ranger Station** (29279 Ellensburg Ave., 541/247-3600, www.fs.usda. gov/rogue-siskiyou, 8am-5pm Mon.-Fri.) can provide information on camping and recreation in the district.

The **post office** (541/247-7610) is at the port on Harbor Way. A modern building houses the **public library** (94341 3rd St., 541/247-7246, 10am-7pm Mon.-Thurs., 10am-5pm Fri.-Sat.), one block east of the highway in the north end of town. **Curry General Hospital** (94220 4th St., 541/247-6621) is the only hospital in the county.

TRANSPORTATION

Curry County's **Coastal Express** (541/412-8806 or 800/921-2871, www. currypublictransit.org) buses run up and down the south coast Monday-Saturday between North Bend and the California border, including local service in Gold Beach.

Brookings-Harbor and Vicinity

Brookings and Harbor sit on a coastal plain overlooking the Pacific six miles north of the California border, split by U.S. 101 (Chetco Ave.) and the Chetco River. Flowing out of the Klamath Mountains east of town, the Chetco drains part of the nearby Siskiyou National Forest and the Kalmiopsis Wilderness, extensive tracts encompassing some of the wildest country in the Lower 48 and renowned for their rare flowers and trees. The Kalmiopsis Wilderness is named for a unique shrub, the *Kalmiopsis leachiana,* one of the oldest members of the heath family (Ericaceae) that grows nowhere else on earth.

Don't form your opinion of Brookings by simply driving down U.S. 101. Just make your way past the somewhat drab main drag to Samuel Boardman State Park north of town, where 12 of the most scenic miles of the Oregon coast await you. Or head down to the harbor to embark on a boating expedition, with some of the safest offshore navigation conditions in the region. Or drive up the Chetco River, where the fog that frequently drenches the coastline during the summer months burns away a couple of miles inland, and hikers can find trails.

During winter, Brookings and its neighbor, Harbor, enjoy mild temperatures. Enough 60-70°F days occur during January and February in this south coast "banana belt" town that more than 50 species of flowering plants thrive—along with retirees, outdoor-sports lovers, and beachcombers. With two gorgeous state parks virtually inside the city and world-class salmon and steelhead fishing nearby, only the lavish winter rainfall, averaging over 73 inches a year, can cool the ardor of local outdoor enthusiasts. In the springtime, the area south of town is lush with lilies—it's the Easter lily capital of the world.

SIGHTS

In Brookings, camellias bloom in December, and flowering plums add color the next month. Daffodils, grown commercially on the coastal plain south of Brookings, bloom in late January and into February. Magnolia shrubs, some early azaleas, and rhododendrons bloom in late winter. The area also produces 90 percent of the world's Easter lily crop.

Azalea Park (640 Old Country Rd.) is a quiet place just off the main drag to picnic and enjoy the flowers. This Works Progress Administration-built enclave features 20-foot-high azaleas (which are several hundred years old), hand-hewn myrtlewood picnic tables, a playground, and a band shell that hosts summer concerts.

Harris Beach State Park

At the northern limits of Brookings, **Harris Beach State Park** makes up for all the strip-mall architecture you'll find on Chetco Avenue. Besides its stunning views, this state park offers many incoming travelers from California their first chance to actually walk on the beach in Oregon. You can begin directly west of the park's campground, where a sandy beach strewn with boulders often becomes flooded with intertidal life and driftwood. The early morning hours, as the waves crash through a small tunnel in a massive rock onto the shoreline, are the best time to look for sponges, umbrella crabs, solitary corals, and sea stars. In addition to beachcombing, you can picnic at tables above the parking lot, loll about in the shallow waters of nearby Harris Creek, or cast in the surf for perch.

Offshore, **Bird Island** (also called Goat Island) is the largest island along the Oregon coast and the state's largest seabird rookery. This outpost of Oregon Islands National Wildlife Refuge dispatches squadrons of cormorants, pelicans, tufted puffins, and other

Brookings-Harbor

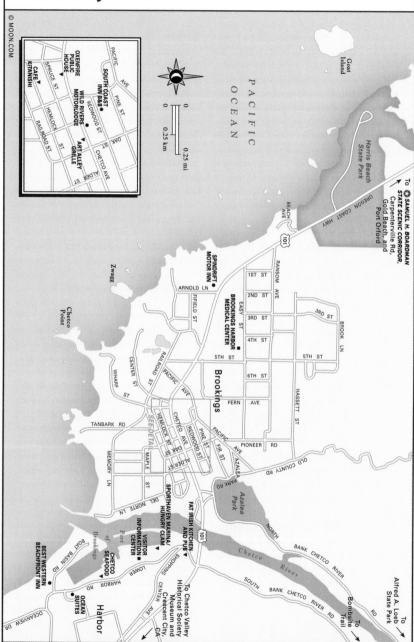

© MOON.COM

OXENFIRE PUBLIC HOUSE

SOUTH COAST INN B&B

WILD RIVERS MOTORLODGE

CAFE KITANISHI

ART ALLEY GRILLE

PACIFIC AVE

PINE ST

SPRUCE ST

REDWOOD ST

OAK ST

CHETCO AVE

HEMLOCK ST

RAILROAD ST

ALDER ST

PACIFIC OCEAN

Goat Island

Harris Beach State Park

To ☆ SAMUEL H. BOARDMAN STATE SCENIC CORRIDOR, Carpenterville Rd., Gold Beach, and Port Orford

BEACH AVE

OREGON COAST HWY

101

SPINDRIFT MOTOR INN

ARNOLD LN

Zwagg

Chetco Point

FIFIELD ST

1ST ST

2ND ST

RANSOM AVE

3RD ST

EASY ST

3RD ST

BROOK LN

BROOKINGS HARBOR MEDICAL CENTER

4TH ST

5TH ST

5TH ST

Brookings

6TH ST

CENTER ST

RAILROAD ST

PACIFIC AVE

WHARF ST

FERN AVE

HASSETT ST

TANBARK RD

SEEDETAIL

HEMLOCK ST

CHETCO AVE

REDWOOD ST

OAK ST

PINE ST

FIR ST

PACIFIC AVE

PIONEER RD

OLD COUNTY RD

MEMORY LN

ALDER ST

MAPLE ST

AZALEA RD

PARK RD

Azalea Park

DEL NORTE LN

SPORTHAVEN MARINA/ HUNGRY CLAM

FAT IRISH KITCHEN AND PUB

VISITOR INFORMATION CENTER

Port of Brookings

Brookings

BOAT BASIN RD

CHETCO SEAFOOD

LOWER HARBOR RD

SHOPPING

CENTER AVE

BEST WESTERN BEACHFRONT INN

OCEANVIEW DR

OCEAN SUITES

Harbor

To Chetco Valley Historical Society Museum and Crescent City, CA

101

NORTH BANK CHETCO RIVER

Chetco River

SOUTH BANK CHETCO RIVER RD

Alfred A. Loeb State Park

To Bombsite Trail

To RD

0   0.25 mi

0   0.25 km

waterfowl, which dive-bomb the incoming waves for food.

Chetco Valley Historical Society Museum

The **Chetco Valley Historical Society Museum** (15461 Museum Rd., 541/469-6651, www.chetcomuseum.org, noon-4pm Sat.-Sun. Memorial Day-Labor Day, donation), in the red-and-white Blake House, sits on a hill overlooking U.S. 101 two miles south of the Chetco River. The structure dates to 1857 and was used as a stagecoach way station and trading post before Abraham Lincoln was president. Oregon's largest Monterey cypress tree is located on the hill near the museum. The 130-foot-tall tree has a trunk diameter of more than 18 feet.

TOP EXPERIENCE

★ Samuel H. Boardman State Scenic Corridor

The stretch of highway from Brookings to Port Orford is known as the "fabulous 50 miles." Some consider the section of coastline just north of Brookings to be the most scenic in Oregon—and one of the most dramatic meetings of rock and tide in the world. The "fabulous 50" sobriquet is perhaps most apt in the dozen miles directly north of Brookings, encompassed by **Samuel H. Boardman State Scenic Corridor.** You'll want to have a camera close at hand and a loose schedule when you make this drive, because you'll find it hard not to pull over again and again, as each photo opportunity seems to outdazzle the last. Of the 11 named viewpoints that have been cut into the highway's shoulder, the following are especially recommended (all viewpoints are marked by signs on the west side of U.S. 101 and are listed here from north to south).

Near the north end of Boardman State Park, a short walk down the hillside trail leads you to the **Arch Rock** viewpoint, where an immense boomerang-shaped basalt archway

juts out of the water about a quarter mile offshore. This site has picnic tables within view of the monolith.

A few miles south, the sign for **Natural Bridges Cove** seems to front just a forested parking lot. However, the paved walkway at the south end of the lot leads to a spectacular overlook. Below, several rock archways frame an azure cove. This feature was created by the collapse of the entrance and exit of a sea cave. A steep trail through giant ferns and towering Sitka spruce and Douglas fir takes you down for a closer look. Thimbleberry (a sweet but seedy raspberry) is plentiful in late spring. As in similar forests on the south coast, it's important to stay on the trail. The rainforest-like biome is exceptionally fragile, and the soil erodes easily when the delicate vegetation is damaged.

Thomas Creek Bridge, the highest bridge in Oregon (345 feet above the water) as well as the highest north of San Francisco, has been used as a silent star in many TV commercials. A parking lot at the south end of the bridge offers the best views.

A couple miles south, the **Whaleshead Island** viewpoint and picnic area offer vistas and trails to an enchanting preserve, a bay-full of rocky islands and wave-pummeled beaches.

House Rock was the site of a World War II air-raid sentry tower that sat hundreds of feet above whitecaps pounding the rock-strewn beaches. To the north, you'll see one of the highest cliffs on the coast, Cape Sebastian. A steep, circuitous trail lined with salal goes down to the water. The path begins behind the Samuel Boardman monument on the west end of the parking lot. The sign to the highest viewpoint in Boardman State Park is easy to miss, but look for the turnout that precedes House Rock, called Cape Ferrelo (for Juan Cabrillo's navigator, who sailed up much of the West Coast in 1543).

Drive down to **Lone Ranch Beach,** where you can get down to water level with close-up views of offshore rocks.

Carpenterville Road

The current roadbed of U.S. 101 was laid in southern Oregon in 1961. The previous coastal route still exists along **Carpenterville Road,** which can be picked up near Harris Beach. It comes out near the Pistol River, where it descends in a series of switchbacks. Its highest point is 1,700 feet above sea level at Burnt Hill. Views of the Siskiyous to the east and the Pacific panoramas to the west make the sometimes-rough road worth the effort. In clear weather, it's possible to look back toward the southeast at Mount Shasta between the ridgelines. This route is best appreciated going south, and it makes for a great 20-mile bike ride, with a long climb to 1,700 feet above sea level.

Alfred A. Loeb State Park

Eight miles northeast of Brookings, on North Bank Chetco River Road (which follows the Chetco River), the **Alfred A. Loeb State Park** preserves 320 acres of old-growth myrtlewood, the state's largest grove. Many of these aromatic trees are much older than 200 years.

The 0.25-mile Riverview Trail passes numerous big trees to connect Loeb Park with the **Redwood Nature Trail.** This trail winds 1.2 miles through the northernmost stands of naturally occurring *Sequoia sempervirens.* This is Oregon's largest redwood grove and contains the state's largest specimens. Within the grove are several trees more than 500 years old, measuring 5-8 feet in diameter and towering more than 300 feet above the forest floor. One tree has a 33-foot girth and is estimated to exceed 800 years in age. When the south coast is foggy and cold on summer mornings, it's often warm and dry in upriver locations such as this one, inviting the possibility of swimming in the Chetco.

Kalmiopsis Wilderness

The Kalmiopsis Wilderness has been ravaged by wildfires in recent years, including the Klondike Fire (2018), Chetco Bar Fire (2017),

and Biscuit Fire (2002), the second-largest fire in recorded Oregon history. While the wilderness is open to hikers and other visitors, not all trails have been cleared and fire damage may make travel less pleasant or impossible for some time. For current road and trail information, contact the **Gold Beach Ranger Station** (29279 Ellensburg Ave., 541/247-3600) or check out the **Siskiyou Mountain Club website** (http://siskiyoumountainclub. org), which offers trail condition maps with current closures.

The **Kalmiopsis Wilderness** lures intrepid hikers despite the summer's blazing heat and winter's torrential rains. In addition to enjoying the isolation of the wilderness, they come to take in the pink rhododendron-like blooms of *Kalmiopsis leachiana* (in June) and other rare flowers. The area is also home to such economically valued species as Port Orford cedar and, in the past, illegal marijuana grows. (Cannabis is a leading cash crop in this part of the state.) During the fall there's a lucrative mushroom harvest; take care not to encroach on pickers, who may be quite territorial.

In any case, the Forest Service prohibits plant collection *of any kind* to preserve the region's special botanical populations. These include the insect-eating *Darlingtonia* plant and the Brewer's weeping spruce. The forest canopy is composed largely of the more common Douglas fir, canyon live oak, madrona, and chinquapin. Stark peaks top this red-rock forest, whose understory is choked with blueberry, manzanita, and dense chaparral.

Many of this wilderness's rare species survived the glacial epoch because the glaciers from that era left the area untouched. This, combined with the fact that the area was once an offshore island, has enabled the region's singular ecosystem to maintain its integrity through the millennia.

Even if you don't have the slightest intention of hiking in the Kalmiopsis, the scenic drive through the **Chetco Valley** is worth it. From Brookings, turn off U.S. 101 at the north end of the Chetco River Bridge. Follow this paved road upriver past Loeb State Park and continue along the river on County Roads 784 and 1376 until a narrow bridge crosses the Chetco. From here, turn right for 18 miles along Forest Roads 1909, 160, and 1917 to reach the Upper Chetco trailhead (just past the Quail Prairie Lookout). The driving distance from Brookings is 31 miles. If you're not hiking into the wilderness, you can continue west on Forest Road 1917 (portions are not paved), which will return you to the above-mentioned narrow bridge over the Chetco.

Crissey Field State Recreation Area

Crissey Field State Recreation Area lies south of Brookings, almost to the California border, and is set along the Winchuck River. The park, which was added to the state park system in 2008, is a great place to watch birds, harbor seals, California sea lions, and other wildlife. A trail leads through a huge pile of driftwood logs to dunes that shelter native plants, tiny wetlands, and old-growth Sitka spruce trees. Crissey Field is also the site of a spacious **visitors center.** Incidentally, the park's name has nothing to do with the San Francisco park (that's Crissy); it's in the heart of the lily-growing area and is named for a lily bulb grower.

RECREATION
Hiking
BOMBSITE TRAIL

Brookings takes a peculiar pride in having been bombed by the Japanese during World War II. In 1942, two incendiary bombs were dropped about 16 miles east of town, on the slopes of Mount Emily. Although they were intended to start a fire, conditions were wet, and the small blaze that resulted was easily controlled. A sort of mutual respect eventually developed between the Japanese pilot who dropped the bomb and the town of Brookings. The pilot was a guest of honor at one Azalea Festival, and his family later presented the town with his samurai sword, which he wore during the bombing and throughout the war.

The sword is now on exhibit at the local library (420 Alder St.).

The Mount Emily **Bombsite Trail,** 19 miles by road from town, commemorates the bombing. It's a 2-mile stretch with redwoods near the beginning and fire-dependent species such as knobcone pine and manzanita along the way. To reach the trail, head 8 miles east up South Bank Road and turn right onto Mount Emily Road. At the fork, turn onto Wheeler Creek Road and follow the signs.

OREGON REDWOODS TRAIL

In addition to the trail through redwood trees in Loeb Park, hikers can explore some not huge but still old-growth redwoods along the 1.7-mile **Oregon Redwoods Trail** southeast of town. The first 0.5 mile of the trail is wheelchair-accessible; a longer stretch leads downhill to a scattered collection of redwoods. Although redwoods here at the northern edge of their range aren't the monster trees that you see in California, this is a pretty trail.

Getting to this trailhead is half the fun of the hike. From U.S. 101, take the Winchuck River Road; turn right onto Forest Road 1101 and continue 4 miles up this narrow gravel road to the trailhead, which is 11 miles from town. It's best not to take a trailer or large RV on this road.

VULCAN LAKE TRAIL

Note: The massive Chetco Bar Fire burned in this area in 2017; at press time, the access road to the trailhead is closed. Contact the **Gold Beach Ranger Station** (29279 Ellensburg Ave., 541/247-3600) for the latest conditions.

If the trailhead is open, the one-mile hike to **Vulcan Lake** at the foot of Vulcan Peak is a good introduction to the Kalmiopsis Wilderness, and the major jumping-off point for trails into the area. It begins at Forest Road 1909 and takes off up the mountains past Pollywog Butte and Red Mountain Prairie. The open patches in the Douglas firs reveal a kaleidoscope of Pacific Ocean views and panoramas of the Chetco Valley and the Big Craggies. For the botanist in search of rare

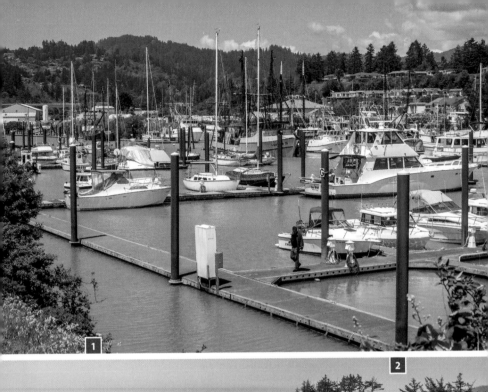

plants, however, the real show is on the trail; it's located in the area burned by the 2002 Biscuit Fire and shows the recovery since then. Despite steep spots, the walk from Forest Road 1909 to Vulcan Lake is not difficult.

To reach the trailhead from Brookings, turn east off U.S. 101 at the north end of the Chetco River Bridge, follow North Bank Road (County Rd. 784) and Forest Road 1376 along the Chetco River for six miles, and then turn right and follow Forest Road 1909 to its bumpy end. Driving distance from Brookings is 31 miles. Hikers should watch out for the three shiny leaves of poison oak, as well as for rattlesnakes, which are numerous. Black bears also populate the area, but their lack of contact with humans makes them shier than their Cascade counterparts.

Fishing

Fishing on the Chetco was once one of southern Oregon's best-kept secrets, but word has gotten out about the river's October run of huge chinook and its superlative influx of winter steelhead. The late-summer ocean salmon season out of Brookings may be the best in the Pacific Northwest. Boatless anglers can try their luck at the public fishing pier at the harbor and on the south jetty at the mouth of the Chetco. Chinook season generally runs mid-May-mid-September, but that's subject to change, so check the regulations.

Guided fishing trips for salmon, steelhead, and ocean-bottom fish can be arranged through **Wild Rivers Fishing** (541/813-1082, www.wildriversfishing.com) or **Tidewind Sportfishing** (16368 Lower Harbor Rd., 541/469-0337, www.tidewindsportfishing.com).

Surfing, Boogie Boarding, and Kayaking

The best surfing is usually found at **Sporthaven Beach,** at the north end of the jetty in Harbor. Reach it by driving to the end of Boat Basin Road to the RV park. There's plenty of parking at the very end of the road. Even if the surf is not spectacular (it's usually best in the winter), it's a pretty mellow place for beginners, and as a fringe benefit, it can be a good spot to see whales during their springtime or December migrations.

Boogie boarders tend to favor **Harris Beach State Park.** Fall-spring, the waves are big and dangerous, and the water is cold. If you know what you're doing, come on in.

South Coast Tours (541/373-0487, www.southcoasttours.net) leads kayak tours in the ocean ($95) or Chetco River ($80). The 3-4-mile trip heads out from the calm mouth of the Chetco at the boat basin into a fairly protected area of the ocean, making it accessible for even beginning sea kayakers.

If you'd rather rent a kayak and go at it yourself down the mostly mellow Chetco, head three miles up North Bank Chetco Road to the **Riverside Market** (98877 North Bank Chetco Rd., 541/661-3213, www.chetcokayaks.com), where you can rent a kayak or stand-up paddleboard ($30-45/day), and also arrange for a shuttle to pick you up downstream.

Golf

The beautiful 18-hole public **Salmon Run Golf Course** (99040 South Bank Chetco River Rd., 541/469-4888, http://salmonrun.net, $44 for 18 holes) was designed with environmentally sensitive imperatives to enable wildlife to thrive. Whether it's the chance to see salmon (usually after the first rains in November) and steelhead spawning (January), black bears, elk, and wild turkeys, or just the opportunity to play a first-rate course, golfers shouldn't overlook this one. Beginner and intermediate players may find the executive nine-hole ($35) course ideal. This par-34 course within a course is located on the back nine holes and measures 1,310 yards.

ENTERTAINMENT AND EVENTS

Follow the stairs down off busy Chetco Avenue to find a haven of ale and enchantment. **Misty Mountains Brewing** (625 Chetco Ave.,

---

1: Brookings-Harbor 2: a vista along the Samuel H. Boardman State Scenic Corridor

541/813-2599, http://mistymountainbrewing. com, 2pm-10pm Wed.-Sun., $5-9) has some of Brookings's best brews and a collection of Tolkien memorabilia. Check out the Grey Pilgrim Pale Ale or the Black Gate IBA, made with rye and dark malts.

Brookings's big event is the **Azalea Festival** (541/469-3181 or 800/535-9469, Memorial Day weekend), which celebrates the local flower with carnival rides, street food, a fun run, and a parade. Most of the action is down at the harbor, which is thronged with vendors, food stands, music, and giant inflatables. Brookings puts its windy weather to good use with its annual **Southern Oregon Kite Festival** (www.southernoregonkitefestival. com), held the third weekend in July. Individuals and teams display their aerial skills at the port of Brookings-Harbor.

FOOD

Brookings has a profusion of family-friendly, though unexciting, restaurants that serve large portions at a good value—this is not a fine-dining capital. For slightly more distinctive fare than the usual fast food and family-dining joints, check out the following places.

For Brookings's most sophisticated dining, head to ★ **Black Trumpet Bistro** (625 Chetco Ave., 541/887-0860, www. blacktrumpetbistro.net, 11am-9pm Mon.-Fri., 3pm-9pm Sat., 3pm-8pm Sun., $10-28), an attractive but informal spot where you can eat lighter dishes like sandwiches or salads, or get serious with excellent pasta (butternut squash ravioli) or bistro classics like chicken marsala or cioppino.

A pleasant surprise in downtown Brookings is the ★ **Oxenfre Public House** (631 Chetco Ave., 541/813-1985, www.oxenpub.com, 4pm-9pm daily dinner, bar until 11pm or later, $15-27), a self-proclaimed gastropub with a hip atmosphere and trendy meals such as Korean short-rib wraps with sesame cucumber relish and chili peanut slaw or fried chicken with Belgian waffle. Kids are welcome until 9pm.

For ocean-to-plate cooking, **Catalyst Seafood** (16182 Lower Harbor Rd.,

541/813-2422, 11am-9pm Wed.-Mon. $10-22) is the place to go in Brookings. It's not fancy—being more of a bar and grill along the harbor—but you can trust in the freshness of the fish: The restaurant owner also operates a fishing boat and offers the Pacific's freshest catches, including salmon, crab, black cod, and tuna in season, as well as well-prepared classics like fish-and-chips and daily specials like a lemon-crusted halibut with thyme rice.

Fish-and-chips, as well as burgers, salads, and a good selection of local beers, can be found near the entrance to the harbor at the fun and family-friendly **Fat Irish Kitchen & Pub** (16403 Lower Harbor Rd., 541/254-3292, www.fatirishpub.com, 11am-9pm Mon.-Thurs., 11am-10 Fri., 9am-10pm Sat., 9am-9pm Sun., $10-17).

Start your day at **First Rise Baking Company** (630 Fleet St., 541/254-9164, 7am-2pm Tues.-Fri., 8am-2pm. Sat., $5-10), a friendly spot with house-made bagels, pastries, and sandwiches.

ACCOMMODATIONS

Rooms in Brookings are generally rather expensive; there are more budget accommodations 29 miles north in Gold Beach. It's also harder to find pet-friendly lodgings here than in most other coastal towns.

$50-100

Just north of the Chetco River Bridge, **Wild Rivers Motorlodge** (437 Chetco Ave., 541/469-5361, www.wildriversmotorlodge. com, $96-110) is the most attractive roadside budget motel in town. Rooms come with fridges and microwaves; some are pet-friendly.

$100-150

A coastal gem one block north of the highway, the ★ **South Coast Inn B&B** (516 Redwood St., 541/469-5557 or 800/525-9273, www.southcoastinn.com, $119-159, minimum stays may apply) is a 1917 Craftsman building and was once the home of lumber baron William Ward. Designed by famed architect Bernard Maybeck and situated in the heart of old Brookings just blocks away from the beach and shopping, this 4,000-square-foot B&B offers four guest rooms, a guest cottage, and an apartment. All rooms have TVs with video players (and access to the inn's video library), private baths, and other amenities. An indoor spa with a sauna and a hot tub and an included breakfast featuring a health-conscious menu are additional enticements to book space early. Ask the friendly innkeepers about other Maybeck structures in town.

Perhaps the best value in Brookings lodgings is **Ocean Suites Motel** (16045 Lower Harbor Rd., 541/469-4004 or 866/520-9768, http://oceansuitesmotel.com, $135), at the Harbor end of town. These really are suites—each has a full kitchen (especially nice to have if you buy fresh fish at the harbor) and a living room.

$150-200

Stay up the river at **Mt. Emily Ranch B&B** (99847 South Bank Chetco Rd., 541/661-2134 or 541/469-3983, www.mtemilyranch.com, $195), a large, newer log home with a comfortable level of rusticity. Because the B&B is several miles from town, you may want to settle in and eat dinner ($24) as well as breakfast here. This is a real ranch, and dinner may feature ranch-raised beef or organic veggies from the garden.

Over $200

The best conventional hotel is south of the Chetco River in Harbor. The ★ **Best Western Beachfront Inn** (16008 Boat Basin Rd., Harbor, 541/469-7779, www.beachfrontinn.com, $263-290) sits right on the beach at the mouth of the Chetco River, just past the port and marina. All units feature private decks, microwaves, and fridges. Kitchenettes as well as suites with ocean-view hot tubs and an indoor pool are available. A limited number of pet-friendly rooms are also available.

Camping

Harris Beach State Park (1655 U.S. 101, 541/469-2021, www.oregonstateparks.org, reservations 800/452-5687, www.reserveamerica.com, year-round, $20 tents, $30-32 RVs, $45-55 yurts, $8 hiker-biker), on an ocean-side bluff two miles north of town, has over 150 sites. Reservations are definitely necessary Memorial Day-Labor Day. Flush toilets, electricity, water, sewer hookups, sanitary service, showers, firewood, and a playground are available. Whale-watching is particularly

the South Coast Inn B&B, designed by architect Bernard Maybeck

good here in January and May, and the birding is good year-round.

Alfred A. Loeb State Park (541/469-2021, www.oregonstateparks.org, campsites $24, cabins $42-52) is nine miles northeast of Brookings on North Bank Chetco River Road. There are 48 sites with electrical hookups for trailers and RVs (50 feet maximum) or tents, as well as three cabins. Electricity, piped water, and picnic tables are provided; flush toilets, showers, and firewood are available. The campground is in a fragrant and secluded myrtlewood grove on the east bank of the Chetco River. From here, the Riverview Trail takes hikers to the Siskiyou National Forest's Redwood Nature Trail, where nature lovers will marvel at 800-year-old redwood beauties. Although the cabins can be reserved (800/452-5687, www.reserveamerica.com), campsites are all first-come, first-served.

The Forest Service rents several cabins and fire lookouts ($40-50) for overnight stays; advance booking is required. Contact the **Gold Beach Ranger District** (541/247-3600, www.fs.usda.gov, reservations 877/444-6777, www.recreation.gov) for information about renting Packer's Cabin, Ludlum House, or the Quail Prairie Lookout.

INFORMATION

Pull off the highway and talk to the friendly folks at the **Crissey Field Welcome Center** (16633 U.S. 101 S., 541/469-4117, 9am-5pm daily Apr.-Oct., 9am-4:30pm Mon.-Fri. Nov.-Mar.), where you can gather information and brochures about the coast and the rest of the state.

TRANSPORTATION

It takes determination to get to Brookings using public transportation. Curry County's **Coastal Express** (800/921-2871, www.currypublictransit.org) buses run up and down the south coast Monday-Saturday between North Bend and the California border, including local service in Brookings. **Pacific Crest Bus Lines** (541/344-6265, http://pacificcrestbuslines.com) operates daily bus service between Coos Bay and Eugene via Reedsport and Florence. Eugene has Amtrak trains and regular Greyhound bus service, as well as an airport served by national carriers.

Background

The Landscape

The Oregon coast encompasses nearly 400 miles of beaches, rainforest, dunes, high-rise headlands, rocky sea stacks and islands, and tidal pools showcasing marine worlds in miniature. The narrow coastal plateau is hemmed in by the Klamath Mountains in the state's southern quarter and by the Coast Range between Coos Bay and Astoria to the north, which together form a palisade between the sea and the state's interior. Neither range is particularly high; the tallest peaks in each of these cordilleras barely top 4,000 feet. More than a dozen major rivers and scores of smaller streams cut through these mountain barriers

to the sea. The valleys that the rivers follow through the mountains are the same routes traversed now by the east-west highways that link the coast with the rest of the state.

GEOGRAPHY
Tectonics

Timeless as it may appear to the modern observer, the Oregon coast hasn't always been where or as we see it today. Titanic forces shaped—and continue to affect—this coastal region, and indeed the entire Pacific Northwest. The giant tectonic plates that make up the earth's crust slide under one another as they collide. In Pacific Northwest coastal regions, this takes place when the Juan de Fuca plate's marine layer is subducted, or pushed under, the continental North American plate. The stress of this collision heaved up the Klamath Mountains some 225 million years ago and created the Coast Range 20-50 million years ago. This subduction is ongoing, and the resulting geologic pressure that builds from it is released periodically in earthquakes, large and small.

With virtually every part of the coastline possessing seismic potential that hasn't been released in many years, the pressure along the fault lines is increasing. Scientists have unearthed discontinuities in rock strata and tree rings on the north Oregon coast that indicate that Tillamook County has experienced major tremors every few hundred years. They estimate that the next one could come within our lifetime and be of significant magnitude. In coastal areas, one of the greatest dangers associated with earthquakes is the possibility of tsunamis.

The ocean waves produced by seismic activity can be enormous and devastating. Ever since a tsunami (measured at 14.2 feet high at the mouth of the Umpqua River) unleashed by Alaska's Good Friday quake in 1964 resulted in four casualties in Beverly Beach and more

than $1 million in damage, local authorities have made seismic preparedness a priority.

Along the coast today, warning sirens stand ready. Visitors will also see blue evacuation signs pointing the way to higher ground and escape routes, acknowledging the imminent danger of a 30-foot wave that could strike within minutes of an offshore temblor. When a tsunami warning was issued following the 2011 Tohoku earthquake in Japan, coastal residents and visitors hurried to higher ground; the resulting waves were fairly small along most of the coast, but did cause serious damage to the harbor in Brookings. Debris from that event continues to wash up on the Oregon coast; the most significant was a 180-ton dock that landed on Newport's Agate Beach in 2012 (it was removed).

Ice and Fire

At the height of the most recent major glaciation, sea level of the world's oceans was some 300-500 feet lower than it is now. North America and Asia were connected by a land bridge across the Bering Strait. The Oregon seashore lay miles west of where it is now, and the Columbia River channel extended out past present-day Astoria.

As the glaciers melted, the sea rose. When that glacial epoch's final meltdown 12,000 years ago unleashed water dammed up by thick ice, great rivers were spawned and existing channels enlarged. A particularly large inundation was the Missoula Floods, which began with an ice dam breaking up in present-day Montana. Before it subsided, it carved out the contours of what are now the Columbia River Gorge and the Willamette Valley. Other glacial floodwaters found their outlet westward to the sea, flushing out silt-ridden estuaries in the process. Pacific wave action eventually washed this debris back up onto the land, creating beaches and sand dunes.

Like the rest of the state, the Oregon coast also shows off distinct remnants of Oregon's

---

Previous: rhododendrons.

volcanic past. The offshore waters are scattered with 1,477 volcanic islets. These rocky outcrops, as well as many of the headlands that separate the beaches, are made of erosion-resistant basalt, an extremely durable igneous material that has endured long after wind and waves have eroded the softer surrounding earth.

The Beach: Contours and Character

Most Oregon visitors who travel west of the Coast Range head straight to the beach. Despite Pacific temperatures cold enough to render swimming an at-your-own-risk activity, the cliffside ocean vistas, wildlife, beachcombing, and other attractions make the coast the state's number-one regional destination.

With rare exceptions, all beaches in Oregon below mean high tide are owned by the public. This is thanks largely to Governor Oswald West, who in 1913 pushed through legislation defining Oregon's ocean beaches as public highways (which in fact they were before real roads were built) and thus off-limits to private encroachment. Later, Oregon's Beach Bills of 1967 and 1972 were written to further guarantee public access to the state's gem of a coastline. In recent years, however, certain sections of this publicly owned paradise have increasingly become exclusive bailiwicks of the wealthy, with gated communities cutting off easy access to a few beaches.

Black sand, high in iron and other metals, is common on the coast, particularly south of Coos Bay. There was also enough gold in the black sands to spur a flurry of gold-mining activity on the south coast in the 1850s and 1860s. Scientists have known for decades of the placer deposits of heavy minerals washed ashore on prehistoric beaches thousands of years ago, when ocean levels were much lower. These beach sands now lie submerged.

Speaking of sand, the central Oregon coast has about 32,000 acres of shimmering white dunes, the largest oceanfront collection in North America and the highest in the world. Some hills top out at more than 500 feet

high. Oregon's Sahara is located along a 40-mile stretch between Coos Bay and Florence. Buffeted by winds, the dunes are continually on the move; in some places, roads are in danger of being engulfed by the shifting sands.

CLIMATE

Oregon's location equidistant from the equator and the North Pole subjects the state to weather from both tropical and polar airflows. This makes for a pattern of changeability in which calm often alternates with storm. Although it's difficult to predict daily weather patterns in western Oregon, there are definite seasonal climatic shifts. In winter, arctic and tropical air masses collide over the Pacific, producing much of the state's rain. During summer, the clashes are much less frequent. At that time, Oregon weather is most affected by Pacific Ocean temperatures and air pressure differences between inland and coastal areas.

Oregon's coastal weather can best be summed up as wet and mild. The coast as a whole receives roughly 70 inches of rain yearly on average. Most of that falls late fall-mid-spring, whereas May-September is generally fairly dry.

Lincoln City and vicinity tend to record the highest amounts of rain, with nearly 100 inches per year, while towns both north and south are generally less wet by comparison. Coast-bound travelers should bear in mind that inland from the coastal plateau, the Coast and Klamath Ranges receive substantially more precipitation, because as moisture-laden westerlies blow in from the Pacific, they slam into the mountain slopes and are pushed upward. As the clouds climb higher, they drop their moisture in the form of rain or snow because rising air cools, and cooler air can't hold as much moisture as warm air. As a consequence, precipitation averages 150 inches per year over the coastal mountains. Anyone driving through the Coast Range sees evidence of the siege mentality that sets in with each winter monsoon season—stacks of firewood covered in blue plastic tarps are

Summer Fog

Mark Twain reportedly once quipped that "the coldest winter I ever spent was summer in San Francisco." That's because he never spent time on the Oregon coast, where summer fogs can really put the chill into your summer vacation.

When the Willamette and other inland valleys are hot and sunny, and you're dreaming of perfect sun-drenched weather at the beach, it's often the case that the Oregon coast is encased in bone-chilling fog. High pressure inland pulls low-pressure marine mists in off the ocean, wrapping beaches and startled tourists in thick fog and 50°F temperatures. This can be annoying to photographers, who find lighthouse and sea stack vistas completely obscured by pea-soup conditions. Often the fog bank extends only half a mile inland, and it tends to burn off as the day proceeds, but the hotter the temperatures inland, the thicker and longer-lasting the fog.

There's not much you can do about it, except to remember to bring a jacket and long pants, *particularly* at the height of summer. When planning a summer trip, have a fallback plan for a cold and foggy day. For instance, when fog obscures the beach, plan a hike in the Coast Range—chances are that you'll leave the fog behind you as you drive inland.

common lawn ornaments here in the rainiest part of the state.

The moderating influence of the Pacific Ocean gives the coastal region an unusually mild climate for a state so far north. Coastal temperatures are fairly constant throughout the year, and extremes are rare. With infrequent freezes and rarely recorded snowfall, winters are mild. In fact, Coos Bay, for example, is often touted as having one of the mildest (in terms of absence of extremes) year-round climates in the United States. Even in winter, daytime highs along the coast tend to reach the mid-50s Fahrenheit, and nighttime lows generally drop into the 40s. Spring, summer, and fall see highs in the 60s and into the 70s, with overnight lows staying in the mid-40s to mid-50s. Summer highs above 90°F are unusual, although the mercury in south coast locations such as Brookings and Bandon has topped 100°F on rare occasions. Midwinter and spring dry spells with 60°F-plus temperatures commonly occur.

Any time of year, the coast can be very windy. Although that can make for terrific kite-flying, picnics aren't quite so much fun at those times. In winter, the winds typically blow from the south and southwest, whereas the gentler summer winds usually come from the northeast.

Plants and Animals

PLANTS

Although giant conifers and a profuse understory of greenery are the most noticeable traits of coastal Oregon's flora, this ecosystem represents only the most visible part of the region's bountiful botany. In addition to Brookings's Azalea Festival and Florence's Rhododendron Festival, coast-bound travelers come to take in such horticultural highlights as the insect-eating *Darlingtonia* plant, Oregon myrtle trees, and some remaining stands of ancient old-growth forest. Serious botanists might search out the pine mushroom (a.k.a. matsutake), found in the Oregon Dunes and a few other places across the state, or probe the Kalmiopsis Wilderness near the south coast, habitat to many rare plants.

Coos Bay marks the boundary between the Mediterranean beach flora found south into California and the subarctic species growing north from there into Washington and British Columbia.

Trees

Sandwiched between the mountains and the sea, the mixed-conifer ecosystem of western Oregon's wet lowlands, comprising primarily fir, western hemlock, Sitka spruce, and cedar, is the most productive belt of evergreens in the world. The conifers are broken up by pockets of alder, oak, vine maple, bigleaf maple, and myrtle trees. With its dense understory of rhododendron, thimbleberry, salmonberry, blackberry, and salal interspersed among the ferns and mosses that carpet the forest floor, this woodland carries up to 400 tons of plant matter per acre and sometimes more. Because of the construction industry's penchant for Douglas fir (*Pseudotsuga menziesii*), which is replanted assiduously, this tree predominates.

Oregon schoolchildren learn to distinguish between fir, spruce, and hemlock by a mnemonic device: The needles of a fir are flat, flexible, and friendly. Spruce needles are square, stiff, and will stick you. Hemlock needles have a hammock-like configuration, and the crown of the tree is curved like it's tipping its hat. *Trees to Know in Oregon,* published by the Oregon State University Extension Service in Corvallis, is an excellent aid to tree identification, as well as a compendium of useful facts.

The Oregon myrtle, *Umbellularia californica,* the only tree in its genus, is native only to the Middle East, southern Oregon, and northern California (where it's more commonly known as California laurel or California bay). The hard yellowish wood of the aromatic myrtle tree is so dense that when it's green, it sinks in water. It is prized by woodworkers and especially wood turners for its distinctive coloring and grain. The value of myrtlewood, in fact, reached a peak during the Depression, when North Bend issued myrtlewood scrip in the form of coins valued $0.50 to $10, after the only bank in town failed.

Among these coastal forests, several extraordinary individual trees have managed to survive the ax and chain saw, and the region boasts such record specimens as the 326-foot-high, 11.5-foot-diameter Doerner fir in the Coast Range near Coquille, rated the nation's largest Douglas fir by the American Forestry Association based on height, diameter, and crown size. An exceptionally large Sitka spruce grows at Cape Meares, and the state's largest Monterey cypress is found in Brookings.

Dunes, Beaches, and Bogs

Apart from the spectacular springtime fireworks of rhododendron and azalea blossoms, the Oregon coast doesn't show off its wildflowers as boldly as other parts of the state, such as Steens Mountain, the Cascades, and the Wallowas. The flowering plants of beach, dunes, and headlands tend to be subtler, but are nevertheless varied and worth seeking out. Among some of the species found only along the Oregon coast are beach bursage, yellow sand verbena, beach evening primrose, seashore bluegrass, dune tansy, and silvery phacelia. The best time for wildflowers is usually June and July.

Many coastal travelers will notice **European beachgrass** (*Ammophila arenaria*) covering the sand wherever they go. Originally planted in the 1930s to inhibit dune growth, the thick, rapidly spreading grass worked too well, solidifying into a ridge behind the shoreline, blocking the windblown sand from replenishing the rest of the beach, and suppressing native plants. Populations of formerly common natives such as beach morning glory, yellow abronia, gray beach pea, and American dune-grass are now much diminished. The endangered pink sand verbena—once abundant along the coast from British Columbia to northern California—is now restricted to a few locations along the central and southern Oregon coast. Herbicides, burning, and tilling have been employed in recent years to remove European beachgrass and restore the dune ecosystem to a more natural state, but progress against the pernicious weed is slow and difficult.

Freshwater wetlands and bogs, created where water is trapped by the sprawling sand dunes along the central coast, provide habitats for some unusual species. Best known among these is the cobra lily (*Darlingtonia californica*), which can be viewed up close at Darlingtonia State Natural Site just north of Florence. Also called *Darlingtonia* or pitcher plant, this carnivorous bog dweller survives on hapless insects lured into its specialized chamber.

Coastal salt marshes, occurring in the upper intertidal zones of coastal bays and estuaries, have been dramatically reduced because of land reclamation projects such as drainage, diking, and other human disturbances. The halophytes (salt-loving plants) that thrive in this specialized environment include pickleweed, saltgrass, fleshy jaumea, salt marsh dodder, arrowgrass, sand spurrey, and seaside plantain. For an excellent introduction to this complex ecosystem, visit the South Slough National Estuarine Research Reserve, south of Coos Bay. Bandon Marsh National Wildlife Refuge protects the largest remaining tract of salt marsh within the Coquille River estuary. Major habitats include undisturbed salt marsh, mudflat, and Sitka spruce and alder riparian communities, which provide resting and feeding areas for migratory waterfowl, shore and wading birds, and raptors.

Mushrooms

Autumn, particularly from the first rains until the onset of frosts, is the season for those who covet chanterelle, matsutake, and morel mushrooms. The Coast Range is the prime picking area September-November for chanterelles—a fluted orange or yellow mushroom in the tall second-growth Douglas fir forests. If you plan to sell what you find or gather more than a gallon of mushrooms, you need to purchase a permit from the U.S. Forest Service. Of course, you should be absolutely certain of any wild mushroom's identity before you eat it.

In recent years, fungus fever reached epidemic proportions, largely because of a matsutake mushroom shortage in Japan, where it is prized for medicinal and spiritual qualities and enjoyed as a soup garnish. Mycological harvests, along with the cutting of ferns (maidenhair ferns command an especially high price from florists), bear grass, and other ornamental greenery, helps many residents of forest communities make ends meet.

ANIMALS

The animal kingdom is well represented by a great diversity and abundance of creatures along the coast, in the air, on the land, under

Cape Kiwanda

the water, and in between. Opportunities for wildlife viewing abound all along the coast, but standout areas include the state's six coastal national wildlife refuges: Oregon Islands, Cape Meares, and Three Arch Rocks protect important habitat for seabirds, seals, and sea lions among coastal rocks, reefs, islands, and several headland areas, while Nestucca Bay, Siletz Bay, and Bandon Marsh National Wildlife Refuges preserve estuarine habitats of salt marsh, wetlands, and woods rich in waterfowl, raptors, fish, and other fauna.

Tide Pools

For most visitors, the most fascinating coastal ecosystems in Oregon are the rocky tide pools. These Technicolor windows offer an up-close look at one of the richest—and harshest—environments, the intertidal zone, where pummeling surf, unflinching sun, and the cycle of tides demand tenacity and special adaptation of its inhabitants.

Marine biologists subdivide this natural blender where surf meets bedrock into three main habitat layers, based on their position relative to tide levels. The **high intertidal zone,** inundated only during the highest tides, is home to creatures that can move, such as crabs, or are well adapted to tolerate daily desiccation, such as acorn barnacles, finger limpets, chitons, and green algae. The turbulent **mid-intertidal zone** is covered and uncovered by the tides, usually twice each day. In the upper portion of this zone, California mussels and goose barnacles may thickly blanket the rocks, while ocher sea stars and green sea anemones are common lower down, along with sea lettuce, sea palms, snails, sponges, and whelks. Below that, the **low intertidal zone** is only exposed during the lowest tides. Because it is covered by water most of the time, this zone has the greatest diversity of organisms in the tidal area. Residents include many of the organisms found in the higher zones, as well as sculpins, abalone, and purple sea urchins.

Standout destinations for exploring tide pools include Cape Arago, Cape Perpetua, the Marine Gardens at Devil's Punchbowl, and beaches south and north of Gold Beach—among many other spots. Tide pool explorers should be mindful that, although the plants and animals in the pools are well adapted to withstand the elements, they and their ecosystem are fragile, and they're sensitive to human interference. Avoid stepping on mussels, anemones, and barnacles, and take nothing from the tide pools. In the Oregon Islands National Wildlife Refuge and other specially protected areas, removal or harassment of any living organism may be treated as a misdemeanor punishable by fines.

In 2015, a viral infection caused a massive die-off of sea stars along the Oregon coast. Fortunately, juveniles seem to have survived this epidemic, and sea star populations are showing signs of a strong recovery.

Birds

One of the most immediately noticeable forms of wildlife at the coast must be the birds of sea, shore, and estuary. The abundance and variety of species you may encounter are a large part of the reason that Oregon has a reputation as one of the best bird-watching states. Seasonal variance in populations is often dramatic, so timing is important. Check out the Oregon Coast Birding Trail (www.oregoncoastbirding.com) to learn about regional hot spots and events.

The **Oregon Islands National Wildlife Refuge**—which comprises all the 1,400-plus offshore islands, reefs, and rocks from Tillamook Head to the California border—is a haven for the largest concentration of nesting seabirds along the West Coast of the United States thanks to its abundance of protected nesting habitat. During the April-August breeding season, seabirds that can be seen here include **common murres, pigeon guillemots, tufted puffins, Brandt's and pelagic cormorants,** and **black oystercatchers,** along with the ubiquitous **western gulls.** June-October you may spy **brown pelicans** skimming the waves. **Aleutian Canada geese** use Table and Haystack Rocks during March and early April.

In terms of sheer numbers and variety, the coast's mudflats at low tide and the tidal estuaries also make excellent bird-watching environments. Species to look for on the flats and shorelines include **Pacific golden plovers** as well as **pectoral and Baird's sandpipers.** The **western snowy plover,** listed as threatened under the Endangered Species Act, gets special protection at the state's nine nesting sites in Curry, Coos, Douglas, and Lane Counties. The small shorebird, which resembles a sandpiper, nests on open sandy beaches above the high-tide line and is sensitive to disturbance from human foot traffic, vehicles, and unleashed dogs. During the nesting season, mid-March–mid-September, coast visitors may encounter areas posted or roped off to protect snowy plover nests.

Resident and migratory birds commonly spotted on the estuaries and lakes of the coast include the common loon, western and horned grebes, great blue heron, American widgeon, greater scaup, common goldeneye, bufflehead, and red-breasted merganser.

Seals, Sea Lions, and Otters

Pacific harbor seals, California sea lions, and **Steller sea lions** are frequently sighted in Oregon waters. California sea lions are 1,000-pound mammals characterized by their large size and small earflaps, which seals lack. Unlike seals, they can point their rear flippers forward to give them better mobility on land. Without the dense underfur that covers seals, sea lions tend to prefer warmer waters.

Steller sea lions can be seen at the Sea Lion Caves north of Florence. They also breed on reefs off Gold Beach and Port Orford. They are the largest sea lion species, with males sometimes weighing more than a ton. Their coats tend to be grayer than the black-coated California sea lion. They also differ from their California counterparts in that they are comfortable in colder water.

Look for Pacific harbor seals in bays and estuaries up and down the coast, sometimes miles inland. They're nonmigratory, have no earflaps, and can be distinguished from sea lions because they're much smaller (150-300 pounds) and have mottled fur that ranges in color from pale cream to rusty brown.

Another marine mammal that was once common on the Oregon coast, as well as along the entire Pacific coast from Japan to Mexico, is the **sea otter.** Two centuries of ruthless hunting by Russian, European, and American fur traders nearly eradicated the species. By the time Oregon's last known sea otter was killed in 1906, the otters had disappeared from British Columbia to central California. For many years, the only sea otters living in Oregon were those in the Oregon Zoo and the Oregon Coast Aquarium, but after successful otter reintroduction in Washington, an occasional lone sea otter is sighted on the Oregon coast. Environmental groups in Oregon have investigated reintroduction in Oregon, but have encountered opposition from crab fishers, who are concerned about the otter's crab-heavy diet.

Gray Whales

Few sights along the Oregon coast (or any coast, for that matter) elicit more excitement than that of a surfacing whale. The most common large whale seen from shore along the west coast of North America is the gray whale (*Eschrichtius robustus*). These behemoths can reach 45 feet in length and weigh 35 tons. The sight of a mammal as big as a Greyhound bus breaking the water has a way of emptying the mind of mundane concerns. Wreathed in seaweed and sporting barnacles and other parasites on its back, a gray whale might look more like the hull of an old ship but for its expressive eyes.

After decades of hunting brought them to the brink of extinction, gray whales gained full protection in 1946 by the International Whaling Commission. In the ensuing years, the population has recovered dramatically. When the gray whale was delisted from the Endangered Species

List in 1994, the population was estimated at 23,000, which is thought to be close to the pre-whaling population. Gray whales continue to enjoy protection worldwide, apart from a quota of 176 whales harvested each year along the Siberian coast.

Some gray whales are found off the Oregon coast all year, including an estimated 200-400 during summer, although they're most visible and numerous when migrating populations pass through Oregon waters on their way south December-February and north early March-April. This annual journey from the rich feeding grounds of the Bering and Chukchi Seas of Alaska to the calving grounds of Mexico amounts to some 10,000 miles, the longest migration of any mammal.

Grays feed primarily on bottom-dwelling shrimp-like amphipods, scooping up huge mouthfuls from which they filter out water and sediment through the fringe of baleen inside their mouths. After fattening up in the rich waters of the arctic during the summer and fall, gray whales begin their migration south. In early December, pregnant females are the first to begin showing up along the Oregon coast, followed by mature adults of both sexes and then juveniles. Their numbers peak usually during the first week of January,

when as many as 30 per hour may pass a given point. By mid-February, most of the whales will have moved on toward their breeding and calving lagoons on the west coast of Baja California.

Early March-April, the juveniles, adult males, and females without calves begin returning northward past the Oregon coast. Mothers and their new calves are the last to leave Mexico and move more slowly, passing Oregon late April-June. During the spring migration, the whales may pass within just a few hundred yards of coastal headlands, making this a particularly exciting time for whale-watching from many vantage points along the coast. Researchers speculate that gray whales stay close to shore as a way to help them navigate.

Land Mammals

Many of the most frequently sighted animals in coastal Oregon are small scavengers, which are often encountered in woodsier campgrounds, parks, and picnic areas: **raccoons, skunks, Townsend's chipmunks, Douglas squirrels, and opossums.**

Black-tailed deer are commonly spotted in woods and meadows all along the coast, and a herd of their larger cousin, the majestic

Roosevelt elk

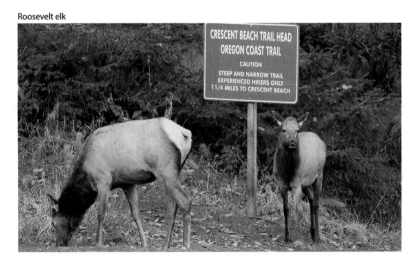

Roosevelt elk, can be seen at the Dean Creek Elk Viewing Area near Reedsport.

On streams and brooks, observant hikers may spot the handiwork of **beavers**—lodges and dams built of branches and twigs—if not the camera-shy builders themselves. The state's animal mascot is most commonly sighted in second-growth forests near marshes after sunset. Fall is a good time to spot beavers as they gather food for winter.

Although **black bears** proliferate in remote mountain forests of Oregon (the state's Department of Fish and Wildlife estimates that 14,000-19,000 black bears roam the western Cascades and the Coast Range), chances are slim that you'll sight one. Black bears shy away from people except when provoked by the scent of food, when cornered or surprised, or on human intrusion into territory near their cubs.

More to be feared are **cougars** (mountain lions), whose coastal populations have been growing in recent years. As human development encroaches on their territory, sightings of these large cats have become more common. Although they tend to shy away from big people, they've been known to attack children and small adults. For this reason, if no other, keep your kids close to the adults when hiking.

A little-known oddity of the coast, from southern British Columbia to northern California, is the **mountain beaver** (*Aplodontia rufa*), known locally as "boomers." This most primitive species of living rodents is not actually a beaver but resembles (and is roughly the size of) a grayish-brown guinea pig. Although the animal was first reported by Lewis and Clark, and it's still fairly prevalent, most people have never heard of the boomer, let alone seen one. They thrive in dense understory vegetation such as coniferous forests and coastal scrub. These herbivores eat all types of succulent vegetation, including plants that are inedible to other species such as nettle, bracken fern, and salal. Their predilection for Douglas fir seedlings has made them the scourge of the timber industry.

Another rodent common along the coast is the **nutria,** introduced to Oregon in the 1930s from South America to be farmed for its fur and meat. After numerous escapes, this furry pest established a niche in the woodlands of the Coast Range. About two feet long and similar in appearance to a true beaver (minus the flat tail), voracious nutrias damage many crop plants in Oregon. Furthermore, they may cause erosion by digging into streambeds or the levees that protect lowlands from floods. Currently, a year-round open season encourages hunting and trapping of this varmint to reduce its numbers.

Other Land Creatures

You won't have to look for long in the coast woodlands or underbrush before you encounter Oregon's best-known invertebrates—**banana slugs**—and lots of them. In few places on earth do these snails-out-of-shells grow as large and in such numbers. The reason is western Oregon's climate: moister than mist but drier than drizzle. This balance and calcium-poor soil enable the native banana slug and the more common European black slug to thrive as the bane of Oregon gardeners. When these 3-10-inch squirts of slime are not eating plants, you'll see them moving along at a snail's pace on some sidewalk or forest trail. The 16 or so species of nonnative slugs that have established themselves in the Pacific Northwest tend to prey on crops and gardens. Native species generally confine themselves to forests and eat indigenous plants.

Another distinctive but rarely sighted resident of coastal forests is the **Pacific giant salamander** (*Dicamptodon tenebrosus*), the largest terrestrial salamander found in the United States and Canada. This stout, mottled brown or blackish amphibian can reach lengths of 13-14 inches from nose to tail. They may be found around cold streams and mountain lakes in damp forests and around stagnant pools in the Kalmiopsis Wilderness. They have been known to climb in shrubs and small trees. Among the few salamanders capable of vocalizing, Pacific giants may produce a sharp, low-pitched, doglike yelp when agitated.

Their powerful jaws can inflict a painful bite and make them a formidable predator of just about anything they can catch, including insects, slugs, snails, frogs, snakes, and rodents.

Salmon and Steelhead

In recent decades, dwindling Pacific salmon and steelhead stocks have prompted restrictions on commercial and recreational fishing in order to restore threatened and endangered species throughout the Pacific Northwest. For more information about fish populations and fishing restrictions, visit the Oregon Department of Fish and Wildlife's website (www.dfw.state.or.us).

The salmon's life cycle begins and ends in a freshwater stream. After an upriver journey from the sea of sometimes hundreds of miles, the spawning female deposits 3,000-7,000 eggs in hollows (called redds) she has scooped out of the coarse sand or gravel, where the male fertilizes them. These adult salmon die soon after mating, and their bodies then deteriorate to become part of the food chain for young fish.

Within 3-4 months, the eggs hatch into alevins, tiny immature fish with their yolk sacs still attached. As the alevin exhausts the nutrients in its yolk sac, it enters the fry stage and begins to resemble a very small salmon. The length of time they remain as fry differs among various species. Chinook fry, for example, immediately start heading for saltwater, whereas coho or silver salmon will remain in their home stream for 1-3 years before moving downstream.

The salmon are in the smolt stage when they start to enter saltwater. The 5-7-inch smolt will spend some time in the estuary area of the river or stream, while it feeds and adjusts to the saltwater.

When it finally enters the ocean, the salmon is considered an adult. Each species varies in the number of years it remains away from its natal stream, foraging sometimes thousands of miles throughout the Pacific. Chinook can spend as many as 7 years away from their nesting (and ultimately their resting) place; most other species remain in the salt for 2-4 years. Theories about how the salmon's miraculous homing instinct works range from electromagnetic impulses in the earth to celestial objects, but one thing has been established with certainty—"the nose knows." When salmon's olfactory orifices were stuffed with cotton and petroleum jelly, they were unable to find their spawning streams. The current belief is that young salmon imprint the odor of their birth stream, enabling them to find their way home years later.

The salmon's traditional predators, such as the sea lion, northern pikeminnow, harbor seal, black bear, Caspian tern, and herring gull, pale in comparison to the threats posed by modern civilization. Everything from pesticides to sewage to nuclear waste has polluted Oregon waters, and until mitigation efforts were enacted, dams and hydroelectric turbines threatened to block Oregon's all-important Columbia River spawning route.

History

THE FIRST PEOPLE

No one knows when the first inhabitants took up residence on the Oregon coast, but ongoing research periodically turns up ever-older evidence. A site at Indian Sands, in Samuel H. Boardman State Park north of Brookings, has yielded artifacts dating back more than 12,000 years, making it the oldest known site of human activity yet found on the coast. Prior to that discovery, the dig site at Tahkenitch Landing, in the Oregon Dunes near Gardiner, had been the earliest known coastal habitation, dated at 9000-8630 BC. It seems likely that further digs will uncover even older human artifacts, although scientists speculate that the oldest sites lie underwater, dating to a time when sea level was significantly lower.

A study of ancient and modern genomic data has shown that the ancestors of all present-day Native Americans came over from Asia on a land bridge spanning what is now the Bering Strait. This migration, which occurred no more than 23,000 years ago, most likely spread initially down the Pacific Coast before spreading east.

Despite common ancestry, the Native Americans on the rain-soaked coast and in the Willamette Valley lived quite differently than those on the drier eastern flank of the Cascade Mountains. People west of the Cascades enjoyed abundant salmon, shellfish, berries, and game. Great broad rivers facilitated travel, and thick stands of the finest softwood timber in the world ensured that there was never a dearth of building materials. A mild climate with plentiful food and resources allowed the wet-siders the leisure time to evolve a startlingly complex culture. This was perhaps best evidenced in their artistic endeavors, theatrical pursuits, and ceremonial gatherings, such as the traditional potlatch, where the divesting of one's material wealth was seen as a status symbol. Dentalium and abalone shells, woodpecker feathers, obsidian blades, and hides were especially coveted. Later on, Hudson's Bay blankets were added to this list.

After contact with traders, Chinook—a patois of Native American tongues with some French and English thrown in—became the common language among the diverse indigenous groups that gathered in the Columbia Gorge during the summer solstice. At these powwows, the coast and valley dwellers came into contact with their poorer cousins east of the Cascades.

By the time the white explorers and settlers came, Native American culture was a patchwork of languages and cultural traits as diverse as the topography. Most indigenous coastal communities typically included a dozen or more small bands linked by a common dialect. These bands or villages consisted of an extended family in one or two houses or a larger grouping under a headman. The linguistic and lifestyle divisions between indigenous communities were reinforced by mountains, an ocean too rough for canoes, and other geographic barriers.

EARLY EXPLORERS

In 1542, the Spanish explorer Juan Rodríguez Cabrillo sailed into what are now southern Oregon waters. Although partisans in California may dispute it, there's tantalizingly compelling evidence that the English privateer Francis Drake spent the summer of 1579 at Whale Cove and named the land New Albion, claiming it in the name of Queen Elizabeth I. Other voyagers of note included Spain's Sebastián Vizcaíno and Martin de Aguilar (1603) and Bruno de Heceta (1775), and England's James Cook and John Meares during the late 1770s as well as George Vancouver (1792). Robert Gray's 1792 voyage 13 miles up the Columbia River estuary was the first American incursion into the area. A succession of Spanish, English, American, and Russian explorers followed in search of whales, sea otter and beaver pelts, and hides for the tallow trade.

A major impetus for exploring this coast was the quest for the Northwest Passage—a sea route connecting the Pacific with the Atlantic. Although the Northwest Passage turned out to be a myth, the fur trade became a basis of commerce and contention between European, Asian, and eventually American governments. The pattern was repeated inland when the British beaver brigades eventually established a western headquarters on the Columbia River near present-day Portland.

Dispatched by President Thomas Jefferson to explore the lands of the Louisiana Purchase and beyond, the first American overland excursion into Oregon was made by the Corps of Discovery, which crossed the continent 1804-1806. Led by Meriwether Lewis and William Clark, the expedition trekked to the mouth of the Columbia in the fall of 1805, spent a wet and miserable winter camped south of the river, and explored as far south as Cannon Beach. Lewis and Clark's trailblazing dramatically accelerated American interest in the Oregon Territory, and by 1811 John Jacob Astor's Pacific Fur Company had established the settlement of Astoria, just north of the Corps of Discovery's campsite.

ROGUE RIVER WARS

In the 1850s, a short-lived gold-mining boom in the Rogue River valley and south coast beaches drew settlers to southern Oregon. Another gold rush, however, had the greatest implications for development of the region. In 1849, the influx of prospectors into California's Sierra Nevada occasioned a housing boom in San Francisco, port of entry to the goldfields. The demand for Coast Range timber and foodstuffs from Oregon's inland agricultural valleys caused downriver Pacific ports such as Astoria and Newport to flourish. As a result, the coastal communities of California's friendly neighbor to the north were able to develop the necessary economic base to prosper and endure.

Like the tragic story played out all across the continent, however, the coming of white settlers to Oregon meant the usurpation of Native American homelands, exposure to European diseases such as smallpox and diphtheria, and the passing of a way of life. Violent conflicts ensued on a large scale with the influx of settlers and government land giveaways, and the mining activity in southern Oregon and on the coast incited the Rogue River Wars, when the indigenous peoples along the south coast began to fight back. The conflict lasted for six years, during which more than 2,000 Native Americans died.

The hostilities compelled the federal government to send in troops and eventually to set up treaties with Oregon's first inhabitants. In the aftermath of the Rogue River Wars in the 1850s, the Chetco, Coquille, Coos, Umpqua, Siuslaw, Alsea, Yaquina, Nestucca, and Tillamook peoples were grouped together with the Rogue River peoples and forced to live on the 1.1-million-acre Siletz Reservation, which reached from Cape Lookout in Tillamook County to near the mouth of the Umpqua River. The culture and heritage of many indigenous peoples were lost forever. More tragic than the watering down of cultural distinctiveness was the huge mortality rate resulting from people being forcibly removed to the reservation. Of the approximately 3,240 Native Americans moved to the reservation in 1857, disease, starvation, and exposure would reduce their number to 1,015 in 1880; by 1900, only 430 coastal Native Americans survived on the reservation.

Over the years, whatever wealth the Siletz peoples had left was stripped as a result of the United States not honoring a multitude of treaties. The final indignity came in 1951 with the termination of the Siletz Reservation. The divestiture of tribal status meant the loss of health services, educational support, tax exemptions, and other benefits. Predictably, this last in a long line of forced transitions brought about alcoholism and despair for many. In 1977, Senator Mark Hatfield and Representative Les AuCoin helped push a bill through Congress for restoration of the Siletz Reservation. This has resulted in the Siletz people getting the wherewithal to flourish economically in everything from logging and construction projects to gaming establishments. The casino endeavor has been accompanied by an interest in the old ways and a renewed sense of pride in Native American identity.

INDUSTRY, EXPLOITATION, AND DEVELOPMENT

The exploitation of Oregon's fishing resources has been an enduring aspect of life in the region for thousands of years. Salmon has always been the most valued species, from prehistory up to modern times. Native Americans on both sides of the Cascades depended on it, and commercial anglers have viewed it as a mainstay for more than a century. Canning technology and fishing methods first perfected in Alaska made their way to Oregon in the 1860s, in time to meet the demands of emerging domestic and foreign markets. Canneries crowded the shores of the Columbia at Astoria and all the other major rivers down the coast, exporting thousands of tons of fish yearly until the dwindling supplies finally closed them down.

Intensive logging of coastal and inland forests supplied sawmills with timber, providing jobs at nearly every port and feeding the building booms of the Pacific Northwest and beyond. A brisk coastal trade developed, as steamships plied Oregon ports on busy routes between San Francisco and Seattle. Before roads were built through the coastal ranges, transportation between coastal communities and the inland valleys was by river, and stern-wheelers moved goods and passengers up and down the Siletz, Yaquina, Umpqua, and other navigable rivers. Popular tourist areas developed in Newport, Seaside, and other towns.

In the latter half of the 19th century, rail lines began to connect the coast to the interior, but it took the development of reliable roads to bring the coast out of its isolation. In 1919, Oregon voters approved construction of a north-south coastal route, first called the Roosevelt Military Highway and later the Oregon Coast Highway. The road was completed in 1932, and the last of a dozen magnificent bridges, designed by Oregon's master bridge builder Conde McCullough, was finished in 1936, finally opening up the entire coast to auto travel.

Essentials

Transportation

AIR

Although most travelers fly into Portland's airport (PDX, www.flypdx.com), Medford and Eugene also have airports.

BUS

Greyhound has abandoned its coastal routes, some of which have been picked up by regional carriers, making for a patchwork of mass-transit providers on the western edge of the state. However, if you have time, you can easily patch together a public transit tour of much of the coast.

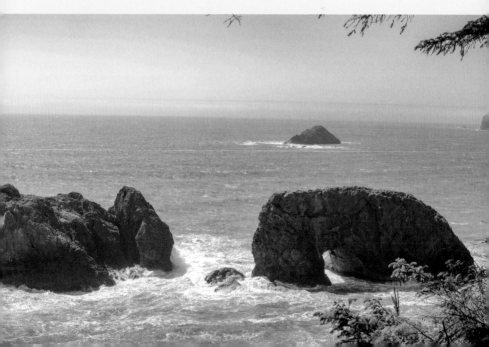

Five separate public transit agencies have created a handy website, www. nworegontransit.org, that shows long-distance bus routes around northwest Oregon. The site shows how you can take local buses to get all the way from Astoria to Yachats, and how to use public bus services to travel from Willamette Valley cities with Amtrak and Greyhound buses to the coast. Services include Portland to Cannon Beach, Seaside, and Astoria; Salem to Lincoln City; and Albany and Corvallis to Newport. Best of all, you can purchase three- and seven-day passes ($25-30) that allow a round-trip passage from the Willamette Valley to the coast and unlimited travel in Clatsop, Tillamook, and Lincoln Counties. If you just want to get to the northwest coast, **NorthWest Point** (888/846-4183, http://oregon-point.com) buses run a twice-daily coastal loop: Astoria-Warrenton-Gearhart-Seaside-Cannon Beach-Portland's Union Station and back to Astoria. You can reserve and purchase these tickets through Amtrak.

Pacific Crest Bus Lines (800/231-2222 or 800/872-7245, http://pacificcrestbuslines.com) runs along the southern Oregon coast between Coos Bay and Florence, then turns inland at Florence and goes to Eugene, then on to Bend.

On the south coast, **Coastal Express** (541/412-8806 or 800/921-2871, www.currypublictransit.org) buses run between North Bend and Brookings, Monday-Saturday.

CAR

Ever since the "Daddy Train" linking Portland to Seaside shut down in the 1930s, the automobile has been the vehicle of choice for getting to and around the coast.

Car Rentals

Car rental agencies are not unheard of on the coast, but most visitors drive their own vehicles or rent cars at a big-city airport. Renting a car is pain-free, as long as you plan ahead and have a credit card. The rental chains (Avis, Alamo, Budget, Dollar, Enterprise, National, and Thrifty) have outlets in the main population centers and airports (such as Portland, Medford, and Eugene). Astoria has the most car rental agencies on the coast, but still offers far fewer than in larger cities elsewhere.

You can try to save some bucks with an independent operator, but consider that the larger chains have more service centers set up to assist you in case you break down in a backwater. Members of AAA can call 503/222-4357 to receive tow, repair, and insurance services applicable to rental cars.

Fuel

Gas is readily available on the Coast Highway, but motorists heading to the coast via some of the 10 main routes through the coast ranges should be aware that there are long stretches without a drop, so fill up before setting out. Out-of-state visitors will soon learn that Oregon is one of the few states that does not allow motorists to pump their own gas. This, combined with the gas tax levied to help pay for Oregon's roads, helps give the state some of the highest gas prices in the country; however, the state's least expensive gas is often in Coos Bay or Reedsport.

If you're traveling in an electric vehicle, you'll find charging stations in most of the coast's larger towns (Astoria, Cannon Beach, Tillamook, Lincoln City, Newport, Yachats, Florence, Reedsport, Coos Bay, Port Orford, and Brookings), but not necessarily on the roads between I-5 and the coast. Check www.westcoastgreenhighway for maps.

Routes to the Coast

From the I-5 corridor, where most of the state's population is concentrated, 10 main routes will get you to the coast. All are two-lane highways for all or part of the journey through rural hinterlands and the coastal mountains. In addition to the routes described here, there are a number of remote back roads involving at least some travel on gravel roads. These are not necessarily open year-round; winter travelers should use great caution and check road conditions with the **Oregon Department of Transportation** (800/977-6368 in Oregon, 503/588-2941 out of state, www.tripcheck. com) or by asking in nearby towns.

From Portland, **U.S. 30** runs north through St. Helens and follows the bottomlands along the south bank of the Columbia River to Astoria, 98 miles (about two hours) to the northwest. If you're coming down from the north on I-5, cross the Columbia from Longview, Washington, to Rainier, Oregon, and continue west on U.S. 30 from there.

Busy **U.S. 26** runs west, then angles northwest, from Portland through agricultural Washington County and then into the woods of the Clatsop State Forest before joining U.S. 101 between Cannon Beach and Seaside (80 miles, 90 minutes). About 25 miles west of Portland, **Highway 6** branches off from U.S. 26 and follows a roller-coaster course alongside the Wilson River to Tillamook (73 miles, about 90 minutes).

A third route from Portland starts with **Highway 99W** and a dozen maddening stop-and-go miles through the strip development of Tigard. Past Newberg you emerge into a lovely countryside of vineyards and hazelnut orchards around Dundee. Traffic on 99W can be slow through Newberg and Dundee; if you're wanting to move more quickly, follow signs for the bypass. Pick up **Highway 18** for the second half of the trip, which runs past the popular Spirit Mountain Casino in Grand Ronde, before you hit the Coast Highway just north of Lincoln City and another Native American-owned casino, Chinook Winds. Note that the casinos attract more than three million visitors per year, which helps make Highway 18 one of the most dangerous roads to drive in the state. The 89 miles from Portland to Lincoln City usually take a little

over two hours to drive (much longer during rush hours).

From Salem, **Highway 22** runs 26 miles to the west and connects with Highway 18 about midway to the coast (about 1.25 hours).

Farther south, **U.S. 20** curves down from Albany through Corvallis and on to Philomath. From there you can continue 46 miles to Newport (1.5 hours from Albany) or veer southwest on **Highway 34** for a winding 59 miles through a remote section of the Siuslaw National Forest to Waldport (a pretty two-hour drive from Albany).

Highway 126, from Eugene to Florence, is one of the more direct routes, but after zipping through the flatlands and foothills, curves toward the coast slow this 61-mile trip through Mapleton and alongside the Siuslaw River to a nearly 90-minute drive.

Near Curtin, south of Cottage Grove, leave I-5 for a brief detour on Highway 99 before catching **Highway 38.** This scenic two-lane road—Oregon's "foremost motorcycle road," according to Harley-Davidson—follows the valley of the mighty Umpqua River to Reedsport; allow over an hour for this 57-mile trip. If you're coming from the south on I-5, cut off onto **Highway 138** at Sutherlin to save some miles on this route.

Highway 42 shadows the Coquille River through farm country for much of its course from Roseburg to Coos Bay. Although it is possible to get there in less than two hours, it's a longish 87 miles. Motorists should be aware that this thoroughfare carries more truck traffic than any other interior-to-coast road in Oregon. But weekenders will encounter fewer trucks and light traffic to impede the enjoyment of the waysides, wineries, and historic buildings. If the southern coast is your destination, branch off on **Highway 42S** at Coquille; from there it's 17 miles to Bandon.

South of Roseburg, if you're partial to pavement (which you definitely should be, except during perfect summer weather), there's no good direct route to the coast. The only option is **U.S. 199** from Grants Pass, skirting the remote eastern edge of the Kalmiopsis

Wilderness before dropping into northern California's Smith River Canyon. The highway runs through the awesome giants at Jedediah Smith Redwoods State Park before hitting the Coast Highway near Crescent City, California. From there, it's 22 miles north up to Brookings. All told, count on about two hours to travel this roundabout, albeit beautiful, 100-mile route.

Driving the Oregon Coast Highway (U.S. 101)

The Main Street of the Oregon coast, this 363-mile National Scenic Byway has been designated an "All-American Road," one of 26 in the country selected for their archaeological, cultural, historic, natural, recreational, and scenic importance.

As such, it's a route to be savored, not hurried through—and that's just as well, because sustained high-speed travel is not among the highway's many qualities. The maximum posted speed on U.S. 101 is 55 miles per hour; the actual average speed is usually 50 mph or less. Along the way, several beach loops and inland routes are often less traveled and offer some outstanding scenery in their own right.

U.S. 101 is a two-lane road most of the way, with occasional passing lanes and four lanes along the main drags of the larger coastal cities. You can count on heavy traffic during summer and holidays, and chances are you'll spend at least a little time getting to know the rear end of a slow-moving RV. Relax. Be prepared to modify your schedule to accommodate inevitable slowdowns, and enjoy the breathtaking scenery surrounding the road.

The automobile may be the first transportation choice for most visitors to the coast, but it's not the only vehicle on the road. Especially in summer, be mindful of bicyclists sharing the shoulder. Hills and dips, tight turns, and foliage can often obscure them from view until the last moment. And always beware of cars whose drivers are paying more attention to the view than to the road.

In winter, heavy rain and wind are possible dangers, and you may encounter thick fog just about any time of year. The **Oregon Department of Transportation** (800/977-6368 in Oregon, 503/588-2941 out of state) advises on road conditions by phone and via its excellent and comprehensive **TripCheck website** (www.tripcheck.com).

Recreation

The outdoor appeal of the Oregon coast is unmatched, and the beaches are only the beginning of recreational opportunities along the coast. Hikes through ancient rainforests, excellent fishing for salmon and steelhead, crabbing and clamming in bays and estuaries, white-water jet-boat rides, hiking, cycle touring, surfing, whale-watching, and birding are all on the agenda.

PARK FEES AND PASSES

Many state and federal parks, national recreation areas, trails, picnic areas, and other facilities charge day-use fees, which are separate from overnight camping fees (the exception to

this is camping at rustic campsites in national forests, which is covered by the Northwest Forest Pass). At sites that charge fees, the day-use fee is $5 per vehicle at both state parks and federal sites. Visitors can pay for day use at individual sites, though if you're planning to visit several coastal parks or hike the trails on federal lands, you can save money by purchasing one of the passes described here.

Oregon Pacific Coast Passport

The best deal if you plan to visit many state and federal sites, this pass covers entrance, day-use, and vehicle parking fees at all state and federal fee sites along the entire Oregon portion of U.S. 101. It does not cover the cost of camping at state parks, which is a separate fee. This pass was created to alleviate some of the confusion caused by having to buy different passes at the various federal (Forest Service, National Park Service, Bureau of Land Management or BLM) and state (Oregon Parks and Recreation Department) fee sites along the U.S. 101 corridor.

Sixteen coastal sites managed by the National Park Service, U.S. Forest Service, BLM, and Oregon State Parks are covered by the passport, including Fort Stevens State Park, Ecola State Park, Nehalem Bay State Park, Cape Lookout State Park, Fogarty Creek State Recreation Area, Heceta Head Lighthouse Viewpoint, Honeyman State Park, Shore Acres State Park, Fort Clatsop National Memorial, Oregon Dunes National Recreation Area, Sutton Recreation Area, Cape Perpetua Scenic Area, Sand Lake Recreation Area, Drift Creek Falls Trail, Yaquina Head Outstanding Natural Area, and Hebo Lake.

Two basic passports are available, depending on your needs and preferences. A five-day passport is $10. An annual passport, valid for the calendar year, is $35. Passports may be purchased at welcome centers, ranger stations, national forest headquarters, national memorials, and state park offices. Call 800/551-6949 to purchase an annual passport by credit card or for directions to a convenient location.

State Park Pass

Another option, valid only at Oregon state parks, is to buy a one-year ($30) or two-year ($50) **State Park Pass.** They're available from state park offices, by phone (800/551-6949), and from some sporting goods stores and other vendors. See the **Oregon State Parks website** (www.oregonstateparks.org) for more details and a complete list of vendors.

Northwest Forest Pass

In response to major reductions in timber harvests and cutbacks in federal money, revenue shortfalls have made it hard to keep up trails and campgrounds at a time when the region's population has put more demand on these facilities. The **Northwest Forest Pass** ($5/day, $30 annually) is a vehicle-parking pass for the use of many improved trailheads, picnic areas, boat launches, and interpretive sites in the national forests of Oregon and Washington. Funds generated from pass sales go directly to maintaining and improving the trails, land, and facilities. You will see "Northwest Forest Pass Required" signs posted at participating sites. Passes are available at trailhead kiosks or at many local vendors, as well as online (http://store.usgs.gov/forest-pass) or by phone (800/270-7504).

The Northwest Forest Pass is good all over the Pacific Northwest, eliminating the need to purchase a separate pass with each entrance to another national forest. This pass covers most Forest Service sites in Oregon and Washington, but is not valid for campground fees (with the exception of rustic campsites), concessionaire-operated sites, and Sno-Parks.

National Parks and Federal Recreational Lands Annual Pass

This pass is honored at all U.S. Forest Service, National Park Service, BLM, Bureau of Reclamation, U.S. Fish and Wildlife Service, and U.S. Army Corps of Engineers sites charging entrance or day-use fees. Anybody can buy one, and a pass is good for the pass holder and passengers in a noncommercial vehicle at per-vehicle fee areas, and the pass holder plus three adults at per-person fee areas. Children under 16 are admitted free. Get additional details or purchase these $80 passes from 888/ASK-USGS (888/275-8747), ext. 3, or http://store.usgs.gov/pass.

BEACHCOMBING

Among the first things a newcomer to the Oregon coast notices are the huge piles of driftwood on the beach. Closer inspection usually reveals other treasures. Beachcombers particularly value agates and Japanese glass fishing floats. The volume and variety of flotsam and jetsam here come courtesy of the region's unique geography. Much of the driftwood, for instance, originates from logging operations located upriver on the many waterways that empty into the Pacific. In addition, storms, floods, rock slides, and erosion uproot many trees that eventually wash up on shore. In addition to driftwood and floats, shells, coral, sand dollars, sea stars, and other seaborne trophies can be best culled from the intertidal zone on south coast beaches. Although you may not always come across a perfectly polished agate or a message in a bottle, you'll probably find beachcombing on the Oregon coast its own reward.

Japanese fishing floats are swept into Oregon waters when the Kuroshio current crosses the Pacific and takes a southerly turn. These balls of green and blue glass sometimes require more than a decade to reach the Oregon coast after breaking free from fishing nets thousands of miles across the sea. Although glass floats are quite rare these days, having largely been replaced by plastic and foam, March is the best time to look for them, especially after two-day storms from the northwest, west-southwest, or due west. In Lincoln City, hand-blown glass floats are planted on the beaches October-May; if you find one of these beauties, it's yours to keep. December-April is the best season to find agates, jaspers, petrified wood, and a variety of fossils. At that time, the gravel bars covered by sand in summer are exposed.

On the southern coast, the Coos Bay sand spit, Bandon's beachfront, the beaches on the western side of Humbug Mountain, and the isolated shorelines of Boardman State Park are choice treasure-hunting spots. Tenmile Creek south of Yachats and Agate Beach north of Newport are the central coast's best places to look. The more settled and accessible north coast has slimmer pickings because of the larger population of resident beachcombers and the higher visitor influx; the best beachcombing is on the Nehalem, Netarts, and Nestucca sand spits.

Even in remote locations, beachcombers may be surprised at the amount of plastic and other debris that washes up. Join with the environmental stewards at SOLV (www.solv.org) and help out with the annual springtime beach cleanup. It's a huge community effort, usually drawing well over 3,000 volunteers to beaches along the Oregon coast.

Consult a **tide chart** anytime you anticipate an extended beachcombing excursion (or any other activity on or near the sea). Every year, people perish from being washed off a beach, jetty, or outcropping. Local newspapers usually include tide predictions, and tide charts are available from visitors centers, chambers of commerce, and shops. Online, you can get free tide charts for over 40 coastal locations at www.saltwatertides.com or via their mobile app. It's also wise to anticipate weather changes, so bring layers.

BICYCLING

On Oregon's roads and highways, bicyclists have the right of way, which means that cars and trucks are not supposed to run you off the road. Most drivers will give you a wide berth and slow down if necessary in tight spots, but remember that there are also motorists whose concepts of etiquette vis-à-vis cyclists were formulated elsewhere. Play it safe: Always wear a helmet and bright or reflective clothing, keep as close to the shoulder of the road as you safely can, and use a light if you must ride at night.

Cycle Tours

Several companies offer preplanned group bicycle trips, with everything from the souvenir T-shirt to the meals and lodging included. **Escape Adventures** (702/596-2953 or 800/596-2953, http://escapeadventures.com) offers six-day trips with a choice of camping ($1,495) or hotel accommodations ($2,495). The **Adventure Cycling Association** (800/755-2453, www.adventurecycling.org, $1,449) runs a weeklong tour starting in Eugene and cutting over through Corvallis to Lincoln City, traveling down the coast to Florence, and then riding back to Eugene; accommodations are in campgrounds, but the tour is fully supported, with gear hauled in a van.

Surf Oregon

Surfing is increasingly popular in Oregon, but it can be a little confusing to know where to go, especially if you're a novice. Spend a week dropping in on the following spots, selected with a special nod to places where a beginner can show up without feeling too out of place.

Before setting out on this surf vacation, invest in or rent a good wetsuit; that, along with strong swimming skills, will go a long way toward making this a fun trip rather than an ordeal. Don't skimp on the wetsuit accessories—a hood and booties are often the key to staying comfortable. Surf shops in Seaside, Cannon Beach, Pacific City, Lincoln City, and Newport can supply rental gear. Surf with a buddy, and be aware that sharks do occasionally show up at surf spots. A good website, www.oregonsurf.com, has some tips and links to forecasting sites and webcams.

CANNON BEACH AREA

Start off with a class. Oregon Surf Adventures (run out of the Seaside Surf Shop) and Northwest Women's Surf Camps both offer friendly, supportive instructors and fun programs.

Set up camp at Nehalem Bay State Park, then head a few miles north and spend the day practicing at Oswald West State Park's Short Sands Beach. More advanced surfers may want to check out the cove at Indian Beach, at the foot of Ecola State Park; this beach is also popular with surf kayakers. Seaside can be fiercely locals-only and is not the best choice for unaccompanied beginners.

LINCOLN CITY TO NEWPORT

Another spot for surfers who know what they're doing is the Road's End State Recreation Area beach at the north end of Lincoln City. Stop here for a while, or continue south to the somewhat protected beach at Otter Rock, a few miles south of Depoe Bay. Otter Rock is quite popular, and it's a good place for beginners, although you'll need to be strong enough to schlep your board down (and back up) a long flight of steps to the beach.

In Newport, you can try Agate Beach; you'll find parking right next to the tall Best Western hotel, and be sure to read the sign on the local rip currents. Or head south of town to South Beach State Park.

FLORENCE TO CHARLESTON

Pack up and head south, perhaps with a stop at Florence's South Jetty, to Charleston, where you can check out the waves at Bastendorff Beach County Park. There's also a nice campground at Bastendorff, as well as the large Sunset Bay State Park campground a few miles away. (Sunset Beach itself is mostly a swimming beach.)

BANDON AND VICINITY

Head south of Bandon to the little town of Langlois, where you can take a break with a day of windsurfing or kiteboarding at Floras Lake. Lessons and equipment rentals are easy to come by here, and the wind is almost always ripping.

PORT ORFORD TO BROOKINGS

It may be time to head back north, dropping in on your new favorite surf spots. But if you're headed all the way down the coast, pull off the highway at Port Orford to see if the surf is up at Battle Rock Beach. Otherwise, aim for Sporthaven Beach on the Brookings jetty south of the Chetco River, a popular all-levels surf beach.

CAMPING

State park and national forest campgrounds offer low-cost overnight lodgings in attractive settings. Most of Oregon's state park campgrounds have restrooms, showers, fire rings, piped water, and electrical or full RV hookups. National forest campgrounds often cost less but offer more primitive facilities. A good source for campsite information is www.thedyrt.com, which offers crowd-sourced comments, photos, and other information for Oregon campsites.

State Parks

The coast's state parks are still the most heavily used (per state park acre) in the country—a tribute to their excellence, and a clue as to the importance of reservations during the busy summer months. Prices for camping at state parks run about $26-34 for RVs, $17-24 for tent sites, $8 for hikers and bikers, $46-56 for yurts, and $53-100 for cabins. The extra vehicle charge is $7.

Yurts are available for rent at most state park campgrounds. Yurts are canvas-walled, wood-floored, and equipped with futon-style bunk beds (no linens), heaters, and lamps but no baths; they sleep five people. Pets are permitted at some locations.

Most of Oregon's coastal state park campgrounds accept campsite reservations, but a few are first-come, first-served. The state has a central information line (800/551-6949) and a reservation line (800/452-5687). Go to www.oregonstateparks.org to look up specific rates or to get information. You can also make reservations for any of these options online with a Visa or MasterCard through **ReserveAmerica** (800/452-5687, http://oregonstateparks.reserveamerica.com, telephone hours 8am-7pm Mon.-Fri.). Reservations may be made from two days up to nine months in advance. In addition to the campsite fee, an $8 reservation fee is charged.

National Forests

The U.S. Forest Service maintains campsites, trails, and day-use areas in both the Siuslaw and Siskiyou National Forests. The Siuslaw National Forest encompasses more than 630,000 acres and is situated within the Oregon Coast Range. It's one of only two national forests in the Lower 48 that include beachfront area. The Siskiyou National Forest is located in the Klamath Mountains and the coast ranges of southwestern Oregon, with a small segment of the forest extending into northern California and the Siskiyous. It

Cyclists pull off to enjoy the view.

includes 1,163,484 acres within its boundaries, 69,234 acres of which are owned or privately managed by other agencies. Within the boundaries of these two national forests, there are hundreds of choices. Refer to the **U.S. Forest Service website** (www.fs.fed. us.gov/recreation) for listings.

Campsites generally include a table, a fire grate, and a tent or trailer space. Electric hookups are not available, although most campgrounds have water and vault or flush toilets. Most overnight sites require a user fee. You may camp in the forest a maximum of 14 days out of every 30. Fees run around $20-22 for coastal campsites. Campsites can be reserved online (www.recreation.gov) or by phone at 877/444-6777; a reservation fee and tax adds about another $10 to each booking.

It's important to note that national forest pass holders who plan to use specialized facilities (such as camping, trailhead, parking, boat launch, ramps, swimming sites, etc.) in the national forest still have to pay for an overnight campsite.

RVs

The Oregon coast is a summer haven for RVers, with activities in each coastal town designed to appeal to this perennial visitor. RV sites in private parks and state parks are abundant, but they can fill up as early as April with travelers fleeing the hot winds of the California desert for the balmy climes of the coast. Many RV grounds are open year-round, but some are seasonal, closing when visitor numbers drop.

Along the coast, many service stations, truck stops, campgrounds, and RV parks provide RV sanitary dump stations. Local chambers of commerce and visitors centers can provide information on activities for seniors, RV-friendly sites, and other services.

FISHING

Since the first people arrived on these shores 12,000 or more years ago, Oregon's rich coastal waters have provided sustenance and sport. The king of fish, in terms of economic impact as well as recreational activity, is the salmon. The once abundant fish was a self-replenishing gold mine that enriched the state and fueled the development of coastal towns like Astoria and Gold Beach.

In the modern era, Oregon salmon fisheries grew into a megabusiness until stocks dramatically declined in the 1990s. The many factors that caused the decline are complex and fraught with political tension. In the early days, fish wheels and nets depleted rivers once so choked with spawning fish that a pioneer pitchfork stuck haphazardly into the water would often yield a salmon. Dam construction and pollution joined overfishing to further reduce the catch. Watersheds have been compromised by clear-cuts, which increase erosion that clogs spawning streams with silt and mud and reduces shaded riparian environments for the cold-water-loving salmon. Cattle grazing has also affected spawning areas with collapsed stream banks and polluted water, and extra-warm water associated with climate change has caused occasional salmon die-offs in some rivers.

Despite the habitat degradation and other pressures, there have recently been several good salmon years, as well as poor ones. The numbers of returning salmon can vary greatly from year to year, and according to seasonal runs (the spring run of chinook may be healthy while the fall run is not). In addition, each coastal river has its own unique run of salmon, and due to a great many factors, different rivers often have salmon runs of varying strength.

If salmon fishing is a crucial element of your trip to the Oregon coast, it's a good idea to contact a local outfitter to find out what the salmon run will be like during your visit, and which waters will be open for sportfishing.

Runs of spring and fall chinook, coho, and steelhead draw thousands of anglers to the coast each year. Fleets of charter boats operate out of all the navigable ports on the coast, and there are countless opportunities for do-it-yourselfers from boats, banks, jetties, and piers.

Past salmon shortfalls have spawned alternative ocean fisheries. Bottom fishing for black lingcod and rockfish, together with the harvest of such long-ignored species as hake, whiting, and pollock, have increased in proportion to the decline of salmon, flounder, albacore tuna, smelt, and halibut.

Where and When to Go

Salmon are targeted offshore as well as in freshwater. For up-to-date information on exactly where, when, and how you can fish—which is subject to frequent change—get a copy of the **Oregon Department of Fish and Wildlife**'s regulations, including licensing fees (503/947-6000, www.dfw.state.or.us), available at sporting goods stores and many other outlets; better yet, check the website for the most current information.

In addition to chinook and coho salmon and steelhead in scores of coastal rivers, the Kilchis and Miami Rivers near Tillamook see Oregon's only runs of chum salmon, in the fall; this is a catch-and-release fishery only. Another catch-and-release-only species is wild sea-run cutthroat trout, which return in summer to the Alsea River and Yaquina Bay, among other waterways. Sturgeon is a popular game fish (weighing into the hundreds of pounds) in the larger rivers, particularly the Columbia and the Umpqua.

Bottom fishing for rockfish and other species is pretty much a year-round activity—depending on the weather. Warm ocean currents bring albacore tuna in August and September, and halibut are usually available in summer, although the season is variable and is set yearly by the Pacific Fishery Management Council.

Charters and Guides

Major charter-fishing centers on the coast include Astoria, Hammond, Warrenton, Garibaldi, Depoe Bay, Newport, Winchester Bay, Charleston, Gold Beach, Bandon, and Brookings. Charter rates vary a bit, but typical prices up and down the coast are $130 for a half day (5-6 hours) of bottom fishing, $225 for a full 8-hour day of salmon or bottom fishing, and $225 for 12 hours of tuna or halibut fishing. Chambers of commerce in each town can also provide extensive listings.

Crabbing and Clamming

Egalitarian ventures that require a minimum of gear, crabbing and clamming are popular ways to land a delicious meal. The Oregon Department of Fish and Wildlife's *Sport Fishing Regulations* booklet has details, or check its website (www.dfw.state.or.us) for more information. Crabbing requires a **shellfish license** ($10 residents, $28 nonresidents) that's available just about any place that rents traps or sells fishing gear.

Crabbing just requires a trap, ring, or pot and some bait (veteran crabbers recommend rotting raw poultry—chicken or turkey backs and necks). Opinions vary about the best time to crab, but many agree that an incoming tide yields the best catches. Just drop your trap in a likely spot, with a tethered float marking the spot, and haul it up 15-30 minutes later—hopefully full of legal-size male Dungeness crabs. A handy item to have is a crab caliper, a gauge that measures the minimum-size crabs you can keep. Bait shops and marinas can instruct you on how to catch dinner. Boats and crab pots are usually available to rent at these places. If boats are unavailable, many harbors have public piers. Some of the best crabbing spots are the estuaries of the Coos, Siuslaw, Yaquina, Tillamook, Netarts, and Nehalem Rivers. Bays and estuaries are open for Dungeness crab year-round; the ocean is open year-round except August 15-November 30.

A spade or small pitchfork—and a bucket to carry away your take—are all you need to dig clams on beaches and mudflats. Large gaper clams, cockles, soft-shells, and littlenecks are the most common clams found in tidewater areas, while prized razor clams are found on north coast beaches. With the exception of the summer closure for razor clams north of Tillamook Head, the season on shellfish is year-round in Oregon. Low tides, particularly morning minus tides during spring and summer, are the best times for clamming. Mussels are also available for harvest from rocky intertidal areas. Note that all oyster beds are privately owned. Check the *Sport Fishing Regulations* for catch limits, and before harvesting always inquire locally or contact the **Recreational Shellfish Hot Line** (503/986-4728 or 800/448-2474, www.oregon. gov/oda) to get current information on shellfish toxins and quarantines.

HIKING

Opportunities for hiking abound on the coast, from short loops suitable for just about anyone to the magnificent Oregon Coast Trail running the entire length of the coast, and a myriad of choices in between. Wherever you choose your outing, here are some suggestions to help keep the environment as natural as possible:

- Stay on the trails so you do not increase the rate of erosion or destroy such fragile vegetation as dune and wetland wildflowers.

- Use established campsites, and avoid digging tent trenches or cutting vegetation.

- In wilderness areas, camp several hundred feet from water sources. Bring a tool to dig a latrine, and make it at least six inches deep.

- If you pack it in, pack it out. Leave nothing but footprints.

- Avoid feeding wild animals so you don't inhibit their natural instinct to fend for themselves.

The Oregon Coast Trail

For 362 miles, from the Columbia River to the California border, the **Oregon Coast Trail** hugs the beaches and headlands, leading hikers into intimate contact with some of the most beautiful landscapes anywhere. Most of the trail runs through public lands, although some portions traverse easements on private parcels, and the trail follows the highway and city streets in several places. The only coastal long-distance treks separated from U.S. 101 are the 30 miles between Seaside and Manzanita and between Bandon and Port Orford. A free trail map and directory are available from the **Oregon Parks and Recreation Department** (800/551-6949, www.oregon.gov/oprd). This pamphlet makes it clear where the trail crosses open beaches, forested headlands, the shoulder of the Coast Highway, and even city streets in some towns. Bring water, particularly on northerly sections of the trail, because much of the trek is on beachfront away from a potable water supply.

It's easy to rent crab traps and catch your own dinner.

WHALE-WATCHING

Whale-watching charters of various kinds are offered along the coast from December into the spring. By land or by sea, early morning hours are best because winds can whip up whitecaps later in the day, obscuring the signs of surfacing whales. Remember to bring your binoculars and sunglasses. If you go by boat, dress warmly, take precautions against seasickness, and expect to get wet if you go out on deck.

You don't need to be on a boat to successfully spot whales, however. Coastal headlands and beaches provide excellent vantage points from which to spy the gray whales on their 10,000-mile round-trip between Baja and the Arctic, the longest migratory movement by land or sea of any mammal. It's possible to spot whales here year-round because several hundred have taken up permanent or semi-permanent residence in Oregon waters, but whales are far more numerous (and your chances of sighting them far better) during their twice-yearly migrations. The southward migration along the Oregon coast lasts until early February, although their numbers usually peak around the last week in December. Whales migrating northward can be sighted off Oregon March-May, with numbers usually peaking in late March. Recently, changing weather and current patterns seem to have induced a growing number of whales to remain off Oregon throughout the summer, June-October, but the peak times are August, September, and October.

By Land

Just about any coastal location with a view of the sea holds the potential for a whale sighting, but some spots are definitely better than others. Offshore reefs supporting the proliferation of amphipods, the food of the gray whale, are conducive to sightings. Combine the latter with a promontory such as Cape Perpetua or Yaquina Head and you increase your chances even more.

Whale Watching Spoken Here (www.oregonstateparks.org) is an organization of enthusiastic trained volunteers who staff 24 prime whale-watching sites in Oregon during key weeks of the gray whale migrations. In coordination with the Oregon Parks and Recreation Department, these folks provide information and assist in spotting whales 10am-1pm daily December 26-January 2 and through the week of spring break in late March. Get more information from the website.

These sites, marked by "Whale Watching Spoken Here" signs during Whale Watch Weeks, are among the best vantage points any time of year. From north to south, with their nearest town, they are:

- Ecola State Park (Cannon Beach)
- Neahkahnie Mountain Historic Marker Turnout (Manzanita)
- Cape Meares State Scenic Viewpoint (Three Capes Scenic Loop)
- Cape Lookout State Park (Three Capes Scenic Loop)
- Inn at Spanish Head (Lincoln City)
- Boiler Bay State Scenic Viewpoint (Depoe Bay)
- Depoe Bay Sea Wall (Depoe Bay)
- The Whale Watching Center (Depoe Bay)
- Rocky Creek State Scenic Viewpoint (Depoe Bay)
- Cape Foulweather (Depoe Bay)
- Devil's Punchbowl State Natural Area (Otter Rock)
- Yaquina Head Lighthouse (Newport)
- Don A. Davis City Kiosk (Nye Beach, Newport)
- Yaquina Bay State Recreation Site (Newport)
- Devil's Churn Viewpoint (Yachats)
- Cape Perpetua Overlook (Yachats)
- Cape Perpetua Interpretive Center (Yachats)
- Cook's Chasm Turnout (Yachats)

- Sea Lion Caves Turnout (north of Florence)
- Umpqua Lighthouse (Winchester Bay)
- Shore Acres State Park (Charleston)
- Face Rock Wayside State Scenic Viewpoint (Bandon)
- Cape Blanco Lighthouse (Port Orford)
- Battle Rock Wayfinding Point (Port Orford)
- Cape Sebastian (Gold Beach)
- Cape Ferrelo (Brookings)
- Harris Beach State Park (Brookings)

By Sea

Depoe Bay and Newport are the centers for whale-watching, attracting the majority of the state's whale-watching visitors. Other major ports are Charleston, Winchester Bay, and Garibaldi, but you'll find whale-watching charters operating out of just about all the ports along the coast. Rates run around $35-45 per person for a two-hour tour. See each destination for specific charter companies and details.

Food and Accommodations

FOOD AND DRINK

Visiting gourmets can tell you why many people will happily drive two hours from Portland for a meal at any number of coastal restaurants: Inventive chefs who fully exploit the freshest regional ingredients—wild chanterelles, fiddlehead ferns, marionberries, locally made cheeses, Oregon wines, and, of course, seafood—mean that limited notions of clam chowder and greasy fish-and-chips are long out of date. Not that there aren't plenty of eateries along the coast where everything but your salad—if you can get one—has been battered and deep-fried; it's just that now there are many exciting alternatives. The coast seems to attract restaurateurs who want to dispel the old myths about the region being a culinary backwater, and here they can start with unbeatable raw materials to work their craft on, especially when it comes to seafood. The fish, oysters, crab, and clams here are as fresh as they can be. At many restaurants, it's a short trip from the boat to the plate, with a short detour through the kitchen.

Tipping

Tipping for food service is customary but discretionary. As elsewhere in Oregon, the suggested rate of recompense for acceptable service is 15-20 percent. Diners in larger parties (usually six or more) may find that a restaurant enforces a mandatory tipping policy as part of the bill.

Coastal Cuisine

What will newcomers to the Oregon coast notice most on their plates? The coast boasts such delicacies as Dungeness crab, razor clams, Yaquina Bay oysters, and bay shrimp, as well as world-famous salmon.

Let's start with the bay shrimp as an appetizer. Although a hasty visual appraisal of an Oregon shrimp cocktail might prompt an unfavorable comparison to the larger gulf prawns, these savory morsels prove that good things come in small packages. Expect them to be in season during August. Another coveted crustacean is the Dungeness crab. Few West Coast chefs have mastered the succulence of Maryland-style crab cakes, but Dungeness tastes richer in a cocktail than the less meaty Atlantic blue crab. The firm texture of Dungeness in its wintertime peak season has been compared to that of Maine lobster.

Oregon's Yaquina Bay oysters are considered gourmet fare. If you want them fresh, avoid the summer months and wait until the weather is cooler. Razor clams are another indigenous shellfish—an acquired taste for some. Once you get past their rubbery

The Coast's Best Bakeries

There's nothing like a ginger scone after a morning of beachcombing . . . unless it's a still-warm cinnamon roll. The following bakeries are the real deal—no doughy white bread that ends up as gull food.

- **Blue Scorcher Bakery Cafe, Astoria:** Come for a cardamom almond roll, and then return for lunch. They make great vegetarian sandwiches, and the people-watching is first-rate. Fridays feature a range of gluten-free pastries and sandwiches.

- **Pacific Way Bakery and Cafe, Gearhart:** The café next door is locally famous; forget the struggle to get a table there and settle in with a pastry from the bakery.

- **Sea Level Bakery, Cannon Beach:** Head south of downtown for the Stumptown coffee and marionberry scones.

- **Grateful Bread Bakery, Pacific City:** French toast made from challah bread, gingerbread pancakes, and the town's best pizza make this airy café a place to spend some time.

- **Panini Bakery, Newport:** Who needs the beach when you've got a cup of coffee and a chocolate panini?

- **Green Salmon Bakery and Cafe, Yachats:** After a morning at the Green Salmon, you'll be checking the real estate ads for your own little Yachats bungalow.

- **First Rise Baking Company, Brookings:** Bagels, bread, and sandwiches fuel your exploration of the southern Oregon coast.

consistency, however, you might enjoy this local favorite. Local mussels and albacore tuna near the end of July are also worth a try.

When it comes to fresh fish, you'll notice a variance in price based on how the salmon was caught. Troll-caught salmon (usually chinook and coho in Oregon) are landed in the ocean by hook and line, one at a time. This method permits better handling than netted salmon, which are caught in large groups as they come upriver from the ocean to spawn. Thus you'll pay more for troll-caught salmon, but you can taste the difference. Currently, as efforts are undertaken to restore the species in the Pacific Northwest, most grocery-store and some restaurant salmon come from Alaska or fish farms in Canada. There are limited stocks of Oregon-caught salmon available, however, and it pays to be sensitive to nuances of how they are harvested as well as preparation.

Spring chinook salmon (Apr.-May) from the Rogue River is a can't-miss item for almost everyone. Although red snapper would normally also merit such an assessment, this is not always the situation in Oregon, largely because of a case of mistaken identity. In contrast to the red snapper found on Southern and Eastern U.S. menus, this Pacific version is a bottom fish. The brown widow rockfish and dozens of other bottom fish species that receive the "red snapper" designation out here have a similar consistency but a fishier taste than their East Coast counterpart.

Wine

As more and more wineries and wine outlets pop up throughout Oregon, it's exciting to match Oregon wines with locally grown produce and freshly caught fish and seafood. Particularly notable for coastal travelers focused on fish and seafood are Oregon wines made from pinot gris and chardonnay grapes. Pinot gris grows well in the cool valleys of western Oregon and makes a light-bodied off-dry wine that's a perfect complement to most seafood meals. Oregon's version of chardonnay is light and citrusy, without the cloying butteriness that typifies many California chardonnays. It makes a great addition to a meal of fresh oysters.

ACCOMMODATIONS

Coastal accommodations run the gamut from campgrounds and humble fishing lodges to bona fide five-star resorts. In between you will find a kaleidoscopic range that includes condominiums rented as guest rooms, bed-and-breakfasts, vacation rentals, a lighthouse keeper's quarters, yurts, a paddle wheeler, and a plethora of conventional motels.

Regardless of the lodging, you'll generally pay more for direct access to the beach or for an ocean view. If you're willing to walk a block or two, or settle for a view of mountains or forests, you'll probably save a few dollars.

In our descriptions of lodgings, the price that we quote is for a double room during high season (summer). Although there's no sales tax in Oregon, note that there are local lodging taxes—ranging 8-15.5 percent, depending on the locale—added to your bill.

Cutting Costs

Prices along the coast peak during summer, a flexible term that generally means Memorial Day in late May to Labor Day in early September. In summer, as well as during spring break, many destinations fill up, and you'll need to reserve well in advance. Many lodgings drop their rates a bit during spring and fall shoulder seasons. In winter, euphemistically called the storm-watching season, room rates can drop still further, sometimes approaching 50 percent less, with special weekend-getaway packages being quite common. This can be a wonderful time for a stay at the coast, when the crowds are long gone and the sea and sky are at their most dramatic. When making a reservation, it pays to ask (or check the lodging's website) about specials and discounts.

The cost-conscious traveler should also keep in mind that there is no shortage of large condos and vacation homes that rent out to large parties who can split costs.

Paying More

As noted, lodging prices along the coast peak in the summer, when rather unexceptional motel rooms can go for close to $200. If your budget can tolerate it, this is a good time to investigate some of the slightly more expensive B&Bs and lodges. The difference in quality between a $95 highway-side motel and a $130 B&B room can be astounding, and make for a far more memorable and enjoyable trip.

Vacation Rentals

B&Bs can add to a romantic weekend on the coast, but these establishments don't make sense all the time for everyone. This book also lists property rental agencies and real estate companies in certain locations whose properties afford more privacy. Deals are plentiful, thanks to the volume of vacation homes that often sit idle or can accommodate large-enough parties to offset a high nightly rate.

Health and Safety

EMERGENCY SERVICES

Throughout Oregon, dial **911** for medical, police, or fire emergencies. There are hospital facilities in Gold Beach, Bandon, Coos Bay, Florence, Newport, Seaside, and Astoria with 24-hour emergency rooms. Medical costs are high here, as in the rest of the United States. Emergency-room care is the most expensive.

COASTAL HAZARDS

Whether you're merely admiring its natural beauty or braving its waves, the Oregon coast holds potential dangers. Children are especially at risk because they can be easily distracted by tide pools and sand castle construction, and they may not be aware of tidal changes, shifts in weather, or other natural dangers. For both adults and children, a little common sense goes a long way.

Hypothermia

The cold temperatures of Oregon's coastal waters (as low as 40-45°F) make swimming and other water sports potentially dangerous any time of year. Even in the hottest days of summer, sea temperature doesn't exceed 62°F. Hypothermia—a condition that sets in when the core temperature of the body drops to 95°F or below—is a danger visitors should be aware of. Hikers and others engaging in outdoor activities away from the water can be at risk as well, particularly when the weather is cool and windy.

One of the first signs of hypothermia is a diminished ability to think and act rationally. Speech can become slurred, and uncontrollable shivering usually takes place. Stumbling, memory lapses, and drowsiness also tend to characterize those afflicted. Unless the body temperature can be raised several degrees by a knowledgeable helper, cardiac arrhythmia or arrest may occur. A wet human body loses heat 23 times faster than a dry one, so getting out of the water and being sheltered from the wind and rain in a dry, warm environment are essential for survival. This might mean placing the victim into a prewarmed sleeping bag, which can be prepared by having another person strip and climb into the bag with the endangered person. Ideally, a ground cloth should be used to insulate the sleeping bag from cold surface temperatures. Internal heat can be generated by feeding the victim high-carbohydrate snacks and hot liquids. Placing wrapped heated objects against the victim's body is also a good way to restore body heat. Be careful, however, not to raise body heat too quickly, which could also cause cardiac problems. If body temperature doesn't drop below 90°F, chances for complete recovery are good; with body temperatures between 80-90°F, victims are more likely to suffer lasting damage. Most victims won't survive a body temperature below 80°F.

Measures you can take to prevent hypothermia include avoiding the cold water of the Pacific, eating a nutritious diet, avoiding overexertion followed by exposure to wet and cold, and dressing warmly in layers of wool and polypropylene. Wool insulates even when wet, and because polypro wicks moisture away from your skin, it makes a good first layer. Gore-Tex and its counterparts make for more comfortable rain gear than nylon because they don't become cumbersome and hot. Finally, wear a hat to avoid heat loss through your head.

Swimming Hazards

Hypothermia aside, casual waders and swimmers alike are at risk of being swept off by riptides or undertows, which occur when one layer of water flows against the direction of the surface water. These powerful, usually localized, currents can be found just about any place along the coast and would be a challenge even to swimmers of Olympic ability. What every swimmer must know is that when caught in a riptide, one should swim with or across the current, not against it, which will only exhaust you; rather, try to swim parallel to shore, edging closer and closer to shore until it's possible to come in or call for help.

Floating debris is another concern for swimmers and waders. Storms can churn up inland riverbanks, yielding huge floating logs, which are then carried in to shore along the backs of waves. These heavy objects can slam into swimmers or pin them down, so give these potential killers a wide berth.

Sharks

"No, dude, that's a porpoise." That's what one Oregon coast surfer said a moment before the great white shark bit his foot. Although shark attacks are rare in Oregon, they do occasionally occur.

The most common areas for an attack are places where rivers enter the ocean. Some of these places, such as Florence's South Jetty, are also popular surfing spots. Anyone who goes into the ocean should seriously consider taking some precautions.

Because sharks can detect minute amounts of blood, don't go into the water if you're bleeding—this includes menstruating. Stay near other surfers, and don't go too far out from shore. Avoid areas where anglers have been using bait, or where birds are circling. Also, know that sharks are most active at twilight and after dark, and that they tend to hang out near steep dropoffs. Some experts note that shiny jewelry could resemble fish scales to a shark and that they could be attracted to brightly colored clothing (your rental wetsuit will almost certainly be black, making you resemble, above all else, a seal).

If you see a shark, or something you can't quite identify, swim quickly and calmly to shore. If you are attacked by a shark, fight. Try to punch it on the nose, eye, or gills, using your board if possible. Do not play dead! Alert other surfers if they don't hear your screams, and as soon as it lets go, swim to shore immediately.

Boating

Life jackets or vests are strongly advised for anyone aboard a watercraft. In 2003, a tragic fishing accident on Tillamook Bay yielded stark proof that life vests save lives. A 35-foot charter boat capsized while crossing the bar in rough conditions. Eleven people—none wearing life vests—were lost. In addition to keeping a person afloat and face-up, whether or not he or she can swim, the vests provide some insulation from the frigid water, decreasing the risk of hypothermia and injury.

State law requires that all children ages 12 and younger must wear a Coast Guard-approved personal flotation device (PFD), also called a life vest, while on an open deck or cockpit of sailboats or motorized and non-motorized vessels (such as canoes, kayaks, and rafts). Life vests are a smart idea for small children any time they're near the water.

Dangerous Terrain

Part of the appeal of the coast is its rugged terrain and raw natural state—two features that can also make it a dangerous place to explore. High cliffs, undesignated trails, rocky outcroppings, tide pools, and pocket beaches often lure intrepid hikers bent on getting that perfect view or photo opportunity. These are the same folks who are rescued from cliff tops, stranded by a changing tide, or worse. In other words, stay on designated paths, avoid unfenced cliff edges, check your tide tables, and follow signage. The worst damage is often done to the environment when hikers trample a native species habitat or disturb organisms living in tidal areas. Stay on paths and avoid climbing on rocks that may be home to living things.

Sneaker Waves

Many a visitor to Oregon's coast has been the victim of the potentially deadly "sneaker wave." Not as uncommon as one might imagine, these treacherous out-of-nowhere waves have a habit of cropping up when you least expect them. Most prevalent during the stormiest times of the year, sneaker waves are powerful enough to knock an angler from his or her perch or sweep an unsuspecting beachcomber out to sea. Unfortunately, small children are most vulnerable, so constant supervision is a must.

Even the unexpected large breaker can have the same effect as the rogue wave. So, be mindful of the everyday risks of strolling the beach or admiring the vista. Pocket beaches rimmed with cliffs are especially hazardous, as are rocky areas. A flat, gradually sloping sand beach is usually safer, but still not without some risk.

Tsunamis

A tsunami is not just one wave; it is a series of waves that are the direct result of seismic activity, such as earthquakes or marine quakes. A tsunami may begin in the middle of the ocean as a two-foot wave heading for shore at several hundred miles per hour—by this definition, it may sound like a great opportunity to put your surfing skills to the test—but once it reaches land or a harbor, it can strike with devastating force.

As a tsunami draws closer to the shore, driven by the force of the quake, it takes in preceding waters and builds into a series of waves traveling as fast as 500 miles per hour and reaching as high as 100 feet. Waves of this size would submerge whole towns; smaller ones would cause major property damage and threaten the lives of those in its path.

Along the coast, you will see blue-and-white tsunami evacuation signs, which warn locals and visitors of impending danger and direct them to higher, safer ground. Visitors should also be aware of the global alarm system, which sounds off when tsunami danger is high. To be fully prepared, one must be attuned to any news of seismic activity in the area or around the Pacific Rim. Also note that any dramatic change in water levels that are not part of the normal tidal activity may be nature's own early warning that a tsunami may be minutes away. In the case of a tsunami, run immediately to higher ground.

Information and Services

TRAVEL TIPS

Liquor

Note Oregon's liquor laws: Liquor is sold by the bottle in state liquor stores, which are open Monday-Saturday; some now offer limited Sunday hours as well. Beer and wine are sold in grocery stores and retail outlets any day of the week. Liquor is sold by the drink in licensed establishments 7am-2:30am. The minimum drinking age throughout the state, and nationwide, is 21.

Cannabis

Recreational marijuana (http://whatslegaloregon.com) is legal for adults age 21 and older in Oregon. Buy it in a dispensary or at a pot store. Use it only on private property (not in campgrounds), and don't drive

under the influence or take your purchases out of the state.

Festivals and Events

It seems there's some kind of festival or other event happening just about every week somewhere on the coast. Celebrations revolving around cultural or historical heritage, food and wine, crafts, kites, sand castles, windsurfing, the arts—you name it, and there's probably a festival dedicated to it—and more sprout up every year. Most are concentrated during summer, when the choices can be overwhelming.

Shopping

Visitors can revel in the shopping opportunities on the coast, which include a profusion of shops selling local art, collectibles and antiques, handmade items, as well as the requisite T-shirts and trinkets.

If it's mall-type shopping you live for, the **Seaside Factory Outlets Center** (1111 N. Roosevelt Dr., 503/717-1603, www.seasideoutlets.com) has 30 big-name manufacturers with designer labels and national brands. With products (of all quality levels) at about 20-50 percent below regular retail price, the center is also home to one of the best wine shops on the Oregon coast, the **Wine Haus** (503/738-0201), featuring more than 850 labels, plus 300 imported and domestic beers. Lincoln City is home to another outlet mall, **Tanger Outlets** (1500 SE East Devils Lake Rd., 541/996-5000), with similar offerings.

For unique arts and crafts, the coastal resort areas are overflowing with the work of local and nationally known potters, woodworkers, painters, jewelers, and glass artisans. While these arts cottage industries don't have the bottom line of timber and agriculture, they are one of the more visible and appreciated forms of economic activity on the coast.

Seasonally, farm stands, farmers markets, and you-pick options dot the routes to the coast. Oregon berries (so quick to ripen that their unparalleled sweetness is more likely to be appreciated in jams and ice cream than in the supermarket) and other local treats can be bought direct from the farmer. Oregon coast stores also purvey locally made food products, which make excellent gifts. You'll come across Oregon jams, smoked fish, hazelnuts, wines, cheeses, sweets, and similar products.

Access for Travelers with Disabilities

The **Access Pass,** which allows free entry to designated federal recreation areas such as national parks and monuments, Bureau of Land Management lands, and U.S. Fish and Wildlife sites, is available to those who are blind or otherwise permanently disabled. The pass is free to qualified applicants ($10 processing fee); get details from the **U.S. Geological Survey** (http://store.usgs.gov).

Beach wheelchairs—stable, balloon-tired chairs—allow people with mobility challenges to cruise the sands with relative ease. These are available at no charge in some towns along the northern Oregon coast; although several beach wheelchairs are available at each location, it's best to reserve at least a few days in advance:

- Bob Chisolm Community Center (503/738-7393), **Seaside**

- City Hall (163 E. Gower St., 503/440-2598), **Cannon Beach**

- Visitors center (31 Laneda Ave., 503/812-5510), **Manzanita**

- Looking Glass Inn (861 SW 51st St., 541/996-3996), **Lincoln City**

The **Oregon Department of Fish and Wildlife** (503/872-5263, www.dfw.state.or.us) puts out a really good guide called *Access Oregon,* which lists accessible recreation areas.

MONEY

Oregon has no state sales tax, which makes purchases all the more attractive, particularly to out-of-state visitors. Major credit cards are widely accepted at shops, lodgings, restaurants, and other establishments, but not everywhere. Acceptability of personal checks varies; it's best to ask beforehand. Traveler's checks in U.S. currency, issued by major firms such as American Express, are generally accepted with an officially issued photo ID.

Nearly all the towns covered in this guide have numerous banks or other businesses with an ATM, which makes getting cash easy. In addition, large grocery stores, such as Fred Meyer, Safeway, Ray's, and Clark's, all with numerous coastal locations, usually have an ATM or offer cash back with a debit-card purchase.

COMMUNICATIONS AND MEDIA

The Portland *Oregonian* (www.oregonlive.com) is available at most towns on the northern coast. Also look for the daily *Eugene Register Guard* (http://registerguard.com).

Even though regional monthlies such as *Northwest Travel* and *Sunset* magazines do not have a strictly Oregon focus, there are usually several destination pieces about the state in each edition. Sold throughout the state, *Oregon Coast* magazine is an excellent bimonthly about life on Oregon's western edge.

The alternative newspaper *Hipfish* (www.hipfishmonthly.com), published in Astoria, is one of the liveliest community-based monthlies in the state. Frequent coverage of environmental issues is interspersed with cultural listings, reviews, and commentary. It's distributed free at selected locales on the coast.

Mail

Most post offices open around 9am and close around 5pm. If it happens to be Sunday and the post office is closed, you can sometimes get stamps from grocery stores and hotels, with little or no markup. Oregon also has many FedEx, UPS, and other private shipping companies operating across the state to complement the post office.

Telephone

Coastal Oregon has two area codes: **503** for Astoria to Neskowin and **541** for the rest of the coast. Note that you must dial the area code, even for local calls. **Cell phone** users should be aware that service in some coastal areas and in the coast ranges can be spotty, particularly along the south coast.

Internet Access

Wireless internet service is widely available along the Oregon coast; it's relatively easy to find a hotel or coffee shop where you can fire up your laptop.

MAPS AND TOURIST INFORMATION

The **Oregon Coast Visitors Association** (541/574-2679 or 888/628-2101, http://visittheoregoncoast.com) is a good clearinghouse of information for the entire coast, including events listings, weather, and links to all coastal chambers of commerce. The best sources of detailed current information for the coast are the individual chambers of commerce in each town. Most do an excellent job of helping travelers with their questions, and all have websites.

The state tourist bureau, **Travel Oregon** (800/547-7842, www.traveloregon.com), is another good resource, producing several useful free maps and pamphlets about the coast and offering extensive listings of lodgings and activities throughout the state.

Other useful contacts are the **Oregon Parks and Recreation Department** (503/986-0707 or 800/551-6949, www.oregonstateparks.org), the **U.S. Bureau of Land Management** (503/808-6001, www.blm.gov/or), and the **U.S. Forest Service** (www.fs.usda.gov/r6). All offer free information and maps on the specific recreation areas and preserves under their respective auspices.

Resources

Suggested Reading

FICTION

Doyle, Brian. *Mink River*. Corvallis, OR: Oregon State University Press, 2010. Part crime novel, part magical realism fantasy, this book beautifully evokes the personalities and rhythms of the Oregon coast.

Kesey, Ken. *Sometimes a Great Notion*. New York: Viking, 1964. Set just upriver from the coast, this is one of the best novels ever about life in rural Oregon.

HISTORY

Stark, Peter. *Astoria: John Jacob Astor and Thomas Jefferson's Lost Pacific Empire: A Story of Wealth, Ambition, and Survival*. New York: Ecco Press, 2015. This page-turner turns early coastal Oregon history into an adventure story. It's all true, and will make readers want to head to the mouth of the Columbia.

NATURE

Fagan, Damian. *Wildflowers of Oregon*. Guilford, CT: Falcon, 2019. Color photos and descriptions help you identify and learn more about common wildflowers.

Irons, Dave. *American Birding Association Field Guide to the Birds of Oregon*. New York: Scott & Nix, 2018. Included in this book are beautiful photos and lots of facts (many fun) about birds and their behaviors and habitats.

Miller, Marli B. *Roadside Geology of Oregon*. Missoula, MT: Mountain Press Publishing, 2014. In this updated edition of a classic traveler's handbook, the coast chapters describe, in layman's language, the geologic forces that shaped the region.

Sibley, David. *Sibley Birds West*. New York: Knopf, 2016. This is our favorite bird guide to the entire region.

RECREATION

Henderson, Bonnie. *Day Hiking Oregon Coast*. Seattle: Mountaineers Books, 2015. Covers all the standards as well as several lesser-known but rewarding hikes, and enriched with information on flora and fauna.

Stienstra, Tom. *Moon Oregon Camping: The Complete Guide to Tent and RV Camping*. Berkeley, CA: Avalon Travel, 2018. Details more than 700 campgrounds across the state, with an excellent selection on the coast. Rich with tips on gear, safety, and other topics.

Sullivan, William L. *100 Hikes Travel Guide: Oregon Coast and Coast Range*. Eugene, OR: Navillus Press, 2016. Hikes and tips from Oregon's best chronicler of hiking trails.

TRAVEL

Nelson, Sharlene, and Ted Nelson. *Oregon Lighthouses* (Umbrella Guides). Kenmore, WA: Northwest Corner Books, 2007. Tells the stories of 11 Oregon coast lighthouses, as well as beacons on the Columbia and Willamette Rivers. A good reference for anyone curious about these romantic aids to navigation.

Oberrecht, Kenn. *Oregon Coastal Access Guide: A Mile-by-Mile Guide to Scenic and Recreational Attractions.* Corvallis, OR: Oregon State University Press, 2008. Meticulously researched and informative guide to major sights, natural features, and recreational opportunities. Contains no restaurant or lodging info, but is an eminently useful resource for travelers nonetheless.

Vaughn, Greg. *Photographing Oregon.* Rancho Cucamonga, CA: Graphie International, 2009. Advice on how, when, and where to take the best photos in Oregon, with lots of tips on capturing the best possible shots along the Oregon coast.

Internet Resources

INFORMATION AND TRAVEL

Oregon Coast Visitors Association
http://visittheoregoncoast.com
A good clearinghouse of information for the entire coast, including events listings, weather, and links to all coastal chambers of commerce.

Travel Oregon
http://traveloregon.com
A good statewide resource for useful free maps and pamphlets and extensive listings of lodgings and activities.

PARKS AND PUBLIC LANDS

Oregon State Parks
www.oregonstateparks.org
Descriptions, maps, contact information, and more details on all Oregon state parks.

Recreation.gov
www.recreation.gov
Reserve sites in U.S. Forest Service campgrounds.

ReserveAmerica
www.reserveamerica.com
The central site for reserving campsites in state park and private campgrounds.

Rogue River-Siskiyou National Forest
www.fs.usda.gov/rogue-siskiyou
Details on recreation, camping, and resources in the national forest.

Siuslaw National Forest
www.fs.usda.gov/siuslaw
Details on recreation, camping, and resources in the national forest and the Oregon Dunes National Recreation Area.

U.S. Bureau of Land Management
www.blm.gov/oregon-washington
The BLM manages numerous recreational sites along the coast and the coastal mountains, including the Dean Creek Elk Viewing Area, Yaquina Head Outstanding Natural Area, and Cape Blanco Lighthouse.

RECREATION

Oregon Department of Fish and Wildlife
www.dfw.state.or.us
Complete details on fishing and hunting seasons, licenses, regulations, and more. Includes useful species-identification charts.

Oregon State Marine Board
www.oregon.gov/OSMB
Extensive information on boating safety, ramps and other facilities, bar conditions, and more.

Surf Forecasts
http://magicseaweed.com
User-driven surf forecasting service includes forecasts, graphs, and charts designed specifically for surfers.

Surfrider Foundation
www.surfrider.org
A nonprofit organization working to preserve oceans, waves, and beaches, including beach access.

Tide Predictions
www.saltwatertides.com
Current and future tide-prediction charts for coastal Oregon locations.

Whale Watching Spoken Here
http://whalespoken.org
Volunteer organization assists visitors with spotting whales at 24 sites from southern Washington to northern California.

REGIONAL INFORMATION

Astoria-Warrenton Area Chamber
www.oldoregon.com

Bandon Chamber of Commerce
http://bandon.com

Bay Area Chamber of Commerce
http://coosbaynorthbendcharlestonchamber.com

Brookings-Harbor Chamber of Commerce
http://brookingsharborchamber.com

Cannon Beach Chamber of Commerce
www.cannonbeach.org

Depoe Bay Chamber of Commerce
www.depoebaychamber.org

Florence Area Chamber of Commerce
http://florencechamber.com

Gold Beach Visitors Center
http://visitgoldbeach.com

Lincoln City Visitors Center
www.oregoncoast.org

Newport Oregon
http://discovernewport.com

Port Orford Chamber of Commerce
www.portorfordoregon.com

Reedsport/Winchester Bay Chamber of Commerce
http://reedsportcc.org

Rockaway Beach Chamber of Commerce
www.rockawaybeach.net

Seaside Visitors Bureau
www.seasideor.com

Tillamook Coast Visitors Association
http://tillamookcoast.com

Waldport Chamber of Commerce
www.waldport-chamber.com

Yachats Area Chamber of Commerce
www.yachats.org

TRANSPORTATION

Oregon Department of Transportation Road Conditions
www.tripcheck.com
Displays current road conditions and advisories.

Ride Oregon
www.rideoregonride.com
Information on transporting your bike to and from Oregon, including downloadable maps and route-planning info.

Index

List of Maps

Photo Credits

Trips to Remember

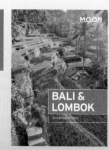

MOON
BALI & LOMBOK
CHANTAE REDEN

MOON
ECUADOR
& THE GALÁPAGOS ISLANDS
BETHANY PITTS

MOON
GREEK ISLANDS & ATHENS
SARAH SOULI

MOON
ICELAND
JENNA GOTTLIEB

MOON
TRIP OF A LIFETIME
MACHU PICCHU
Including Cusco & the Inca Trail
RYAN DUBE

MOON
MOROCCO
LUCAS PETERS

MOON
NEW ZEALAND
JAMIE CHRISTIAN DESPLACES

MOON
OAXACA
JUSTIN COPELAND

MOON
TRIP OF A LIFETIME
PATAGONIA
Including the Falkland Islands
WAYNE BERNHARDSON

MOON
PRAGUE, VIENNA & BUDAPEST
JENNIFER D. WALKER & AUBURN SCALLON

MOON
ROME, FLORENCE & VENICE
ALEXEI J. COHEN

Epic Adventure

MOON
PACIFIC COAST HIGHWAY
Road Trip
CALIFORNIA, OREGON & WASHINGTON
IAN ANDERSON

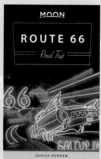

MOON
ROUTE 66
Road Trip
JESSICA DUNHAM

MOON
YELLOWSTONE TO GLACIER NATIONAL PARK
Road Trip
JACKSON HOLE, CODY, THE GRAND TETONS & THE ROCKY MOUNTAIN FRONT
CARTER G. WALKER

ARUBA

AMALFI COAST
With Capri, Naples & Pompeii
LAURA THAYER

BAHAMAS
MARIAH LAINE MOYLE

BAJA
JENNIFER KRAMER

BELIZE
LEBAWIT LILY GIRMA

BERMUDA
ROSEMARY JONES

COSTA RICA

DOMINICAN REPUBLIC
LEBAWIT LILY GIRMA

FIJI
DAVID STANLEY

FLORIDA KEYS
With Miami & the Everglades
JOSHUA LAWRENCE KINSER

FRENCH RIVIERA:
NICE, CANNES, MONACO & ST-TROPEZ
JON BRYANT

JAMAICA

MAUI
With Molokai & Lanai
GREG ARCHER

PUERTO RICO
SUZANNE VAN ATTEN

PUERTO VALLARTA
With Sayulita, the Riviera Nayarit & Costalegre
MADELINE MILNE

States & Provinces

WASHINGTON
MATTHEW LOMBARDI

OREGON
JUDY JEWELL & W.C. McRAE

BRITISH COLUMBIA
ANDREW HEMPSTEAD

Regions & Getaways

SAN JUAN ISLANDS
DON PITCHER

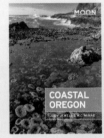

COASTAL OREGON
JUDY JEWELL & W.C. McRAE

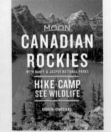

CANADIAN ROCKIES
WITH BANFF & JASPER NATIONAL PARKS
HIKE·CAMP SEE WILDLIFE
ANDREW HEMPSTEAD

Cities

SEATTLE

PORTLAND

VANCOUVER
CAROLYN B. HELLER
NEIGHBORHOOD WALKS · OUTDOOR ADVENTURES
BELOVED LOCAL SPOTS

Road Trips & Outdoors

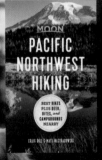

PACIFIC NORTHWEST HIKING
BEST HIKES PLUS BEER, BITES, and CAMPGROUNDS NEARBY
CRAIG HILL & MATT WASTRADOWSKI

OREGON TRAIL
Road Trip
HISTORIC SITES, SMALL TOWNS, AND SCENIC LANDSCAPES ALONG THE LEGENDARY WESTWARD ROUTE
KATRINA EMERY

VANCOUVER & CANADIAN ROCKIES
Road Trip
VICTORIA, BANFF, JASPER, CALGARY, THE OKANAGAN, WHISTLER & THE SEA-TO-SKY HIGHWAY
CAROLYN B. HELLER

We've got you covered, PNW!

MAP SYMBOLS

≡≡≡≡	Expressway	○	City/Town	✈	Airport	⌜	Golf Course
≡≡≡≡	Primary Road	◉	State Capital	✈	Airfield	▣	Parking Area
≡≡≡≡	Secondary Road	⊛	National Capital	▲	Mountain	≜	Archaeological Site
⊏⊐⊏⊐	Unpaved Road	◉	Highlight	✦	Unique Natural Feature	♦	Church
- - - -	Trail	★	Point of Interest			▮	Gas Station
·········	Ferry	•	Accommodation	🏝	Waterfall	◎	Glacier
◄-◄-◄-	Railroad	▼	Restaurant/Bar	▲	Park		Mangrove
≡≡≡≡	Pedestrian Walkway	▪	Other Location	⛏	Trailhead		Reef
⊏⊐⊏⊐⊏⊐	Stairs	Λ	Campground	✗	Skiing Area		Swamp

CONVERSION TABLES

°C = (°F - 32) / 1.8
°F = (°C x 1.8) + 32
1 inch = 2.54 centimeters (cm)
1 foot = 0.304 meters (m)
1 yard = 0.914 meters
1 mile = 1.6093 kilometers (km)
1 km = 0.6214 miles
1 fathom = 1.8288 m
1 chain = 20.1168 m
1 furlong = 201.168 m
1 acre = 0.4047 hectares
1 sq km = 100 hectares
1 sq mile = 2.59 square km
1 ounce = 28.35 grams
1 pound = 0.4536 kilograms
1 short ton = 0.90718 metric ton
1 short ton = 2,000 pounds
1 long ton = 1.016 metric tons
1 long ton = 2,240 pounds
1 metric ton = 1,000 kilograms
1 quart = 0.94635 liters
1 US gallon = 3.7854 liters
1 Imperial gallon = 4.5459 liters
1 nautical mile = 1.852 km

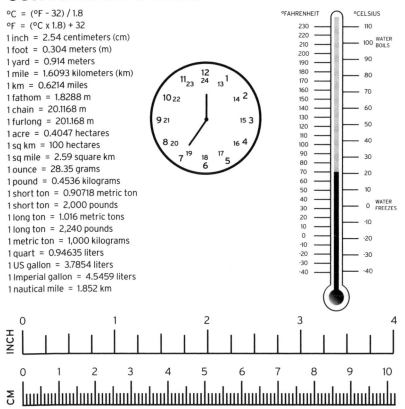

MOON COASTAL OREGON

Avalon Travel
Hachette Book Group
1700 Fourth Street
Berkeley, CA 94710, USA
www.moon.com

Editor: Kristi Mitsuda
Series Manager: Kathryn Ettinger
Copy Editor: Ann Seifert
Graphics and Production Coordinator: Scott Kimball
Cover Design: Faceout Studios, Charles Brock
Interior Design: Domini Dragoone
Moon Logo: Tim McGrath
Map Editor: Kat Bennett
Cartographers: Karin Dahl, Andrew Dolan
Indexer: Greg Jewett

ISBN-13: 9781640498945
Printing History
1st Edition — 2010
8th Edition — July 2020
5 4 3 2 1

Front cover photo: Dennis Frates, Alamy Stock Photo
Back cover photo: Glebtarro, Dreamstime.com

Printed in China by RR Donnelley.

Avalon Travel is a division of Hachette Book Group, Inc. Moon and the Moon logo are trademarks of Hachette Book Group, Inc. All other marks and logos depicted are the property of the original owners.